The Sale of the Late King's Goods

❧

JERRY BROTTON is Senior Lecturer in Renaissance Studies at Queen Mary, University of London and director of the college's MA in Renaissance Studies. He is a regular reviewer and broadcaster for both radio and television and the author of several books. He lives in London.

* * *

'Brotton has taken on a cracking good story, confidently snaking through the complicated politics of seventeenth-century European art-dealership, from Venice and the Low Countries to the Escorial and back into the side-streets of turbulent London and the thousand-odd rooms of Whitehall Palace. He beds this vast mass of convoluted activity with its great cast of characters from de Critz to Van Dyck – its rivalries, frauds, enthusiasms, bankruptcies, brinkmanship and U-turns – deeply into the political, social and artistic context of the time. This is no pillow book: that Brotton maintains his authorial grip on both the grand sweep and the elaborate detail while controlling the drive of his multi-layered narrative is a superb achievement'
KATE COLQUHOUN, *Daily Telegraph*

'Jerry Brotton, a young historian with an enviable command of the secondary literature, both historical and art-historical, and a good understanding of the way objects and works of art assume ideological significance, has told the amazing story of Charles I's collection and its subsequent sale in full'
CHARLES SAUMAREZ SMITH, *Literary Review*

JERRY BROTTON

THE SALE OF THE
LATE KING'S GOODS

Charles I and His Art Collection

PAN BOOKS

First published 2006 by Macmillan

First published in paperback 2007 by Pan Books

This edition published with a new afterword 2017 by Pan Books
an imprint of Pan Macmillan
20 New Wharf Road, London N1 9RR
Associated companies throughout the world
www.panmacmillan.com

ISBN 978-1-5098-6527-7

Visit **www.panmacmillan.com** to read more about all our books
and to buy them. You will also find features, author interviews and
news of any author events, and you can sign up for e-newsletters
so that you're always first to hear about our new releases.

For Adam Lowe, at last

Acknowledgements

I am deeply indebted to the work of curators and scholars associated with the cataloguing and interpretation of the royal art collection, and in particular Sir Oliver Millar. His inventories of Van der Doort's inventory and the subsequent Commonwealth are an exemplary feat of scholarship to which I keep returning; I wish to thank Sir Oliver for corresponding with me on various aspects of the collection. I wish to thank members of the royal household for allowing me access to their archives: at St James's Palace, the former keeper Christopher Lloyd, and Lucy Whitaker, who also shared her work on the Mantuan acquisition; and at Windsor Ms Bridget Wright. I am thankful to the Trustees of the Leverhulme Trust for awarding me a research fellowship that allowed me to complete the early stages of the research for this book and to publish the related articles listed in the bibliography.

I would like to thank all those friends and colleagues that read parts of the book. I am incredibly grateful to my colleague the late Kevin Sharpe, who read the entire manuscript and made extensive comments and suggestions based on his vast knowledge of the subject. Blair Worden offered shrewd comments on archival sources and the later material on Cromwell. Mary Hollingsworth gave insightful advice on the Mantuan acquisition. Roz Kaverney also read the whole manuscript and helped with the problem of iconoclasm. My dear friend Rob Nixon read later sections and offered incisive help on style. Matthew Dimmock also read everything, and transcribed crucial archival material for me with typical assiduousness, for which many thanks. Any errors that remain are my own.

I am indebted to those scholars who helped with queries, provided references, questioned theories and responded to various talks: Peter Barber, Karen Hearn, Glyn Redworth, Pat Parker, Felipe Fernandez-Armesto, Maurice Howard, Andrew Hadfield, Alan Sinfield, Alex Samson, Maurizio Calbi, Alan Stewart and Peter Hulme. Martin Butler and Stephen Orgel both provided crucial support for the project from the outset. Giovanna Laudiero, David McGrath, Dai Roberts and Pierre Imhoff all provided excellent translations of several key documents.

I have also been fortunate in colleagues and friends who were kind enough to offer me space to write and think. Gerald 'Mac' McLean and Donna Landry read material and provided me with refuge in Chagford just when I needed it most. Jeanette Winterson knows better than anyone the importance to a writer of a room of your own, and I will always be grateful to her for offering rural isolation with such kindness and generosity.

Other friends may not see their influence here, but I thank them for reasons often too obscure to mention: Guy Richards Smit, James Runcie, Ed Bramen, Peter Florence and Becky Shaw, Tanya Hudson and Tim Marlow. It is one of my greatest regrets that neither Thelma Lewis nor Burhan Tufail lived to see this book.

At Queen Mary, University of London, I have the privilege of working with a group of stimulating and supportive colleagues. I would like to thank Morag Shiach for her help and understanding when it was most needed, as well as Philip Ogden, Peggy Reynolds and Pat Hamilton. Queen Mary's dynamic team of Renaissance scholars also provided the ideal academic environment within which to write this book, and for that I thank Evelyn Welch, Kevin Sharpe, Warren Boutcher and Julia Boffey. I am particularly grateful to David Colclough for all his kindness and encouragement.

At Pan Macmillan, I always believed that George Morley and her assistant Kate Harvey were the ideal editors for this book, but their enthusiasm and scrupulous attention to detail at every stage of the process have been a revelation, and I want to thank them for all their hard work and attention to the finest detail, and Philippa McEwan for all she did to support the book following its publication.

Two people have been enduring influences over not just this book but also its author. Lisa Jardine was my teacher, collaborator and friend for over twenty years. Large sections of this book were completed sitting side by side with her in the south of France during some of my happiest memories as a writer. I still find it difficult to comprehend that she is no longer with us. She did not believe in debts, so rather than acknowledging what I owe her I'll register instead my profound admiration and thanks for all she did. The book is dedicated to my dear friend Adam Lowe. Nobody understands how the meaning and value of paintings change over time, in stark contrast to our friendship, which remains as immutable as ever.

Contents

List of Illustrations

Section One

1. Anthony Van Dyck, *King Charles I on Horseback*
2. Isaac Oliver, *Henry, Prince of Wales*
3. Studio of Paul Van Somer, *Queen Anna of Denmark*
4. Anon, *King James I*
5. Engraving of Charles I, when Duke of York
6. Daniel Mytens, *Thomas Howard, Earl of Arundel*
7. William Larkin, *George Villiers, Duke of Buckingham*
8. Peter Paul Rubens, *Aletheia Talbot, Countess of Arundel, and Sir Dudley Carleton*
9. Titian, *Portrait of Charles V*
10. Engraving of Balthazar Gerbier
11. Anthony Van Dyck, *Portrait of Nicholas Lanier*
12. After William Dobson, *Portrait of Abraham van der Doort*
13. Peter Paul Rubens, *Self-portrait*
14a. Anthony Van Dyck, *Charles I and Henrietta Maria*
14b. Daniel Mytens, *Charles I and Henrietta Maria*
15. Anthony Van Dyck, *The Great Piece*
16a. Anthony Van Dyck, *Triple Portrait of Charles I*
16b. Lorenzo Lotto, *Three Views of a Man's Head*

Section Two

17. Titian, *Woman in a Fur Wrap*
18. Raphael, 'The Charge to St Peter', part of the *Acts of Apostles* series
19. Titian, *Venus of El Pardo*
20. Paolo Veronese, *Mars and Venus United by Love*
21. Giambologna, *Samson Slaying a Philistine*
22a. Correggio, *Allegory of Virtue*
22b. Correggio, *Allegory of Vice*
23. Polidoro da Caravaggio, *Psyche Abandoned*
24. Giovanni Cariani, *The Lovers*
25. Giulio Romano, *Mermaid Feeding her Young*
26. Correggio, *The Education of Cupid*

Picture Acknowledgements

Archbishopric of Olomouc – 14a. The Art Archive – 4 (Palazzo Pitti, Florence), 9 (Prado, Madrid / Joseph Martin), 38 & 39 (Padro, Madrid / Dagli Orti), 41 (Prado, Madrid / Joseph Martin). Artotech / Joachim Blauel – 8. Berkeley Will Trust / D. Price – 33. Bridgeman Art Library – 3, 28, 34, 35. British Museum – 36a. Corbis – 10 (Historical Picture Archive), 37 (Angelo Hornak). The Fotomas Index – 36b. Kunsthistorisches Museum, Vienna – 11, 16b, 17. National Gallery, London – 26, 27. National Gallery of Scotland – 20. National Portrait Gallery, London – 6, 7, 12. Prado, Madrid – 32. RMN / © Hervé Lewandowski – 19, 22a & b, 29. The Royal Collection © 2006, Her Majesty Queen Elizabeth II – 1, 2, 5, 13, 14b, 15, 16a, 23, 24, 25, 30, 31, 40, 42, 43, 45. Victoria & Albert Museum – 18, 21.

NOTE ON DATES

In the seventeenth century, the English calendar (Old Style) was ten days behind the rest of Europe (New Style) and the new year began on 25 March. For the purposes of this book, all dates are given in the Old Style, but I have taken the new year to begin on 1 January.

✃

THE KING'S HEAD

THE KING'S HEAD was framed against the London sky. Storm clouds gathered in the distance, throwing into relief the figure of Charles I as he trotted back into the palace from his morning ride. As he swung his mount through the arch, light flooded the scene, illuminating his brilliantly polished armour and the forehead of his grey mare. Pierre Antoine Bourdin, Monsieur de St Antoine, Charles's life-long riding master and equerry, hurried alongside. Holding the king's helmet, he gazed at his master, ready to snatch the bridle should the horse suddenly rear up and unseat its rider. But as he rested his baton of state on the horse's withers, the king appeared in total control of his mount.[1]

Charles was the resplendent monarch, surrounded by the trappings of power and authority, mastering his horse as imperiously as he managed his kingdom. His face wore a glazed, serene expression, the eyes gazing out, meeting those of his audience. He was a king at ease with himself and his crown and at peace with the world. Bourdin held his helmet, suggesting that this was no time for war. From the blue ribbon across Charles's armour-plated breast hung a gold medallion of St George, which contained a portrait of the king's French wife, Queen Henrietta Maria. St George was the patron saint of England and the Order of the Garter, the ancient chivalric order of knights over whose ceremonies Charles presided every year in the Chapel of St George at Windsor Castle. This arrival through the arch was more than just a ritual of Charles returning from his daily ride. It was a carefully rehearsed performance of the sovereign as omnipotent imperial ruler. Here was the king as a Christian prince, a contemporary St George, defending his kingdom and his family from their foes, whoever they might be.

ANTHONY VAN DYCK completed his massive canvas of King Charles on horseback with Monsieur de St Antoine in 1633, just months after coming to London and being appointed as Principal Painter in Ordinary to the King and Queen. Urbane, sophisticated and internationally acclaimed, Van Dyck had been knighted at St James's shortly after his arrival, given an annual pension of £200 and housed in style in a Thames-side house in Blackfriars. The picture of Charles on horseback was personally commissioned by the king, who wanted a majestic and visually arresting portrait of himself to grace one end of his gallery in St James's. What Van Dyck delivered was an image that irresistibly combined Charles's private life with his public calling; here was the king as emperor, Christian knight, devoted husband, consummate horseman, generous patron and father to his peaceful kingdom.

Van Dyck's painting of the king impressed all who saw it with its vividly realistic detail and its effortless skill in attributing to Charles the various public and private personae that he always craved. It provoked an awed response from visiting dignitaries when they saw it for the first time. Sieur de la Serre was a French diplomat who accompanied the French queen mother, Marie de' Medici, on her state visit to London to see Henrietta Maria in November 1638. After admiring the architecture and decor of St James's Palace, La Serre described the fabulous collection of paintings on display:

> There is also an infinite number which cannot have been bought, according to their value, but by a great monarch. At one of the ends of the three-sided gallery, there is a portrait of the king in armour, and on horseback, by the hand of the Chevalier Vandheich; and, not to lie, his pencil, in preserving the majesty of this great monarch, has by his industry so animated him, that if the eyes alone were to be believed, they would boldly assert that he lived in this portrait.[2]

The Frenchman looked on the king at the height of his power, displaying his court and personal authority to his French mother-in-law and her diplomatic entourage. To La Serre Charles appeared happily married with a healthy male heir, finally at peace with the rest of Europe, and universally acclaimed as a discerning and astute patron of the arts.

Yet the smooth veneer and gloss of Charles's pictures masked cracks that came to define his reign. At barely five feet four inches tall, and still suffering from the stammer and weak legs that plagued his childhood, the king approved of Van Dyck's tactful decision to portray him as a towering colossus dressed in armour, astride a great horse measuring at least fifteen hands. Van Dyck borrowed the design from his master, Peter Paul Rubens, who in turn had drawn his inspiration from Titian's equestrian portrait of the sixteenth-century Habsburg emperor Charles V. The ability of both these painters to create such compelling but apparently effortless images of majesty led Charles to employ Rubens and spend most of his reign pursuing pictures by Titian.

On the sudden death of his beloved brother, Prince Henry, in 1612, Charles had been catapulted into the limelight as the new resident of St James's Palace and unexpected heir to the English throne. Where Henry began a royal English interest in the arts for their own sake, Charles followed, spending a lifetime trying to emulate his glamorous, popular brother. Henry's brief foray into collecting in the years preceding his death left a lasting impact on Charles, who, unfortunately, however hard he tried, never quite matched up. Although Henry's example inspired his younger brother to pursue ever-more impressive artworks in first the Low Countries, then Spain and finally Italy, Charles never really achieved the public affection and political authority that Henry possessed during his short life.

Instead, as both prince and king, Charles struggled with a series of increasingly disaffected parliaments that he did little to placate. Alarmed at his autocratic political style, they opposed his reckless foreign policy and questioned his religious adherence to their particular version of Protestantism. In the early years of his reign, Charles launched his kingdom on a series of expensive and pointless wars with first Spain and then France, each more disastrous than the next. In the process, despite his conscientious approach towards matters of state, Charles plunged the nation into debts of over one and a half million pounds. The shield in Van Dyck's painting that displayed the united crowns of England, Wales, Scotland and Ireland only partially obscured the religious conflicts that also dogged Charles's reign. In Scotland, Charles's insistence on imposing episcopacy and an Anglican prayer book on a predominantly Presbyterian Scottish Church led to open rebellion and the so-called Bishops' Wars of 1639–40 that saw the king's English armies humiliatingly driven out of Scotland. His uncompromising governance and colonial plantation of Ireland also caused simmering resentment among both its Catholic and settler communities which finally erupted into armed rebellion with the Ulster Uprising of 1641. Both conflicts destroyed the fragile political consensus that Charles's father, King James I, had spent his largely peaceful reign creating, and ultimately led Charles into a bloody civil war that would destroy him and many of his closest friends and family.

Nobody could have envisaged such cataclysmic events in 1638 as the French entourage gazed up at the monumental painting of the English king. Even Charles's mother-in-law was impressed by the magnificent array of pictures, sculptures and tapestries that she saw during her time at St James's and Whitehall. As well as Van Dyck's portrait, her servant La Serre approved of 'the beauty and invention' of the tapestries he encountered in the palace's state rooms. He admired pictures by Jacopo Bassano and Tintoretto, and more Van Dycks that lined the gallery in St James's, which he praised as 'ingeniously executed' and attracting 'the admiration of even the most incurious'.[3]

La Serre was not the only person to record his impressions of Charles's portrait in the winter of 1638–9. While he was admiring the king's collection, Abraham van der Doort, Keeper of the Cabinet Room at St James's, was busily inventorying it. The equestrian portrait was listed as 'A Picture of the King's Majesty in Armour upon a White Horse as big as the life in a great large carved frame by Sir Anthony Vandike'.[4] Standing at over three and a half metres in height and two and a half metres wide, the painting and its subject were quite literally larger than life and towered over onlookers so that the king gazed out as his subjects looked up. As a failed painter himself, van der Doort must have felt admiration tinged with envy for the compatriot who had painted such a perfectly executed and intimidating portrait of the man they both learned to call 'Your Majesty'.

In stark contrast to Van Dyck, van der Doort was an itinerant

Dutch craftsman born of a family of painters and engravers. He had come to the attention of Henry, Prince of Wales, who had appointed the Dutchman as the overseer of his growing collection of pictures, drawings and medals. Following Henry's unexpected death, van der Doort gradually established himself as the keeper of Prince Charles's art collection and in April 1625 Charles kept his dead brother's promise to make the Dutchman Keeper of the Cabinet Room in St James's Palace on a salary of £50 a year. His responsibilities included 'the collecting, receiving, delivering, sorting, placing & removing and causing of making by our appointing such things as we shall think fit & also to keep a Register book of them'.[5] It was a good position, but for a man who once harboured ambitions as a court painter, the time-consuming administrative job of looking after the king's pictures must have had its limitations, as a contemporary portrait of the Dutchman suggests. The worried look in the eyes and the furrowed brow hint at a life defined by frustration and disappointment.[6]

While Van Dyck spent 1639 collecting over £300 in payment 'for pictures for his Majesty's use' and preparing to marry Mary Ruthven, an aristocratic lady-in-waiting to the queen, van der Doort was combing the chilly royal palaces, scribbling down lists of the king's pictures. His role was more on a par with that of Charles's devoted equerry, Pierre Antoine Bourdin, obscured in the shadows of Van Dyck's painting, than a painter trying to emulate the Old Masters whose canvases he so lovingly repaired and catalogued in the service of his adopted sovereign.

HUNG ON EITHER SIDE of Van Dyck's towering equestrian portrait in the gallery of St James's Palace were the spectres of seven mounted Roman emperors. Dignitaries were implicitly invited to admire the greater achievement of Van Dyck, and put Charles in the same imperial league as the emperors on the wall: Julius Caesar, his adopted son Augustus Caesar, Tiberius, Claudius, Nero, Galba and Otho.[7] Yet Charles harboured another reason for proudly displaying these works. He had bought the pictures from the Gonzaga dynasty of Mantua in the late 1620s, paying over £18,000 for one of the greatest collections of Renaissance art in Italy. At the time, the purchase had seriously strained Charles's exchequer, but it finally placed him where he wanted to be – among the elite of Europe's royal collectors like the Habsburgs and the papacy. Charles craved affirmation as a powerful prince and astute collector. Unfortunately for him, the gulf between the imperial aspirations of his picture gallery and the political reality of his reign only widened as the years went by and his art collection grew. His disastrous wars with Spain and France in the 1620s strengthened domestic opposition to his rule and increasingly stretched the nation's finances. When the king actually led the English army into battle for the first time against the Scottish Presbyterians in 1639, his campaign collapsed in confusion and disarray. This was hardly the result desired by a king portrayed by Van Dyck as a conquering Roman emperor.

Van der Doort's inventory suggests that the keeper had already cast a critical eye over the artistic execution of the Roman emperors. They arrived from Mantua as a series of pairs. The Venetian master Titian painted the larger, finer portraits in the mid-sixteenth century, while the workshop of the Roman artist Giulio Romano completed the smaller figures on horseback. Titian's emperors were dramatic, imposing figures, executed with the painter's effortless grace. Giulio's response hung below each one. The entry in van der Doort's inventory was a model of diplomacy: 'A Halfe figure of Julius Caesar By Titian' was followed by its twin, 'A lesser of Julius Caesar on Horsebacke By Julio Romano'.[8] 'Lesser' usually meant smaller, but van der Doort possibly intended something a little more critical, based on close scrutiny of Giulio's panels. The wood had been badly chosen: it was full of knots and already showed signs of warping; the panels were barely primed, leaving the surface rough and uneven, hardly touched by Giulio. Instead, his apprentices had painted all seven. These were paintings finished in a hurry. Worse, van der Doort realized that the pictures were not meant to represent emperors but were in fact anonymous Roman soldiers on horseback. Such information was obviously best kept from the king.

In addition to Van Dyck's portrait and the Roman emperors, the gallery's walls were filled with some of the finest paintings of the European Renaissance. Covering the length of the room were vast, apocalyptic scenes of biblical and classical life looming out of the shadows. On one side is a scene of devastation as the biblical flood washes away a village. Terrified men and women pluck their children from the deluge and others stream towards Noah's Ark in the background. This was the Venetian painter Jacopo Bassano's dramatic painting of *The Flood*, praised for its dramatic execution, but also a prized possession for the simple fact that it was another example of Charles's Mantuan purchases. The king's acquisitions did not impress everyone. William Sanderson, an early English authority on the arts, praised the painter as 'an old and excellent Master' but complained that Bassano was 'so affected to pots and dripping-pans, to blue cotes and dogs, that his history of the deluge sometimes in the gallery at St James's by Whitehall, seems to be rather a disordered and confused kitchen than Noah's flood'.[9]

Equally striking was a painting of a beautiful, gorgeously dressed Judith waving the head of Holofernes. In her right hand she holds the sword with which she has just decapitated the general, while in her left she grasps the head by its hair. Holofernes' dismayed expression, his furrowed brow and lank beard are caught in the shocked moment of death, his head beautifully contrasted with the glowing, righteous face of his executioner. This explicit painting appears to have concerned van der Doort, not because of its violent subject matter but because he was unable to verify its painter. His inventory read 'A Judith with Holophernes head Copied after Brunzino', Bronzino being the adopted name of the Tuscan artist Cristofano Allori.[10] His picture of Judith also ended up in the hands of Charles via the Mantua purchase, but van der Doort obviously doubted that it was by the master's own hand and cautiously marked it down as a copy. He knew from personal experience that the art market was a cut-throat world where both artists and dealers possessed few scruples in selling a copy of an original masterpiece, even when they were negotiating with a king.

Van der Doort was more convinced about the artist responsible for the impressive *Rape of Helen* that hung further down the gallery. It could only be the great sixteenth-century Venetian colourist Jacopo Tintoretto. Next to it hung another dramatic painting, *Prometheus Chained to the Caucasus*, by one of Charles's favourite

Italian artists, the recently deceased Palma Giovane, and inherited by the king from his brother, Henry. Moving along the gallery, there were more pictures by Titian and Giulio Romano, as well as vividly lit paintings by the contemporary Bolognese painter Guido Reni. These were the kind of pictures that Charles particularly favoured and coveted: baroque, dramatically allegorical Italian paintings, heavy in classical allusion and religious significance. They were bought, borrowed, exchanged and appropriated by the king in their hundreds.

The gallery also contained exquisite examples of more traditional northern European pictures. Charles had difficulty luring his cherished Italian artists to London, partly because they objected to working for a heretical Protestant royal court, but also because he simply could not afford them. Instead, he used Protestant artists from the Low Countries to paint his picture, as well as portraits of his friends and family. Van der Doort could admire the handiwork of one of his other compatriots, the Dutch painter Gerrit van Honthorst, in the large group portrait that he recorded as 'The King and Queen of Bohemia and their Children'. The queen of Bohemia was Charles's elder sister, Elizabeth, who married Frederick V, the Protestant Elector Palatine of the Rhine, in 1613, just three months after the death of Henry, Prince of Wales. When Frederick and Elizabeth later accepted the crown of Bohemia, they were expelled by a Catholic army and forced into exile in the Low Countries. Family honour required that Charles support his beleaguered sister and brother-in-law, but England's politically and militarily isolated position on the edge of Europe made him reluctant to intervene. The presence of van Honthorst's painting of Elizabeth and her family was a public statement of Charles's commitment to her cause. But it was also a guilty reminder of his inability to provide tangible help for his only surviving sibling. This was a failure that would haunt both his private life and his kingship, and alienate many of his subjects, for Elizabeth was seen as a long-suffering icon of Protestantism and was viewed by some as a preferable monarch to Charles.

Finally, the gallery held another luminous portrait by Van Dyck. Van der Doort's inventory describes the picture as 'Two little figures of the young Duke of Buckingham, and his Brother the Lord Francis'. Their father, George Villiers, the Duke of Buckingham, was one of the most notorious and reviled figures in English political life up until his bloody assassination in Portsmouth in August 1628. He had established himself as the favourite and lover of King James I, wisely cultivated a close relationship with Charles and accompanied the young prince to Madrid in 1623 in his unsuccessful attempt to marry the Spanish Infanta, Maria. Buckingham's subsequent political influence allowed him to push Charles into war with first Spain and then France. His own military campaigns led to disaster and personal humiliation for his king. Nevertheless, Charles remained doggedly loyal to one of his oldest and dearest friends. As Parliament called for the duke's blood, he was stabbed to death by one of his own disaffected soldiers. Charles was inconsolable, having lost his closest confidant not only in politics but also in art.

Along with his great rival in politics and collecting, Thomas Howard, Earl of Arundel, Buckingham possessed the only art collection to rival that of the king. Van der Doort knew this, having seen the exquisite collection of over 300 paintings by Rubens, Caravaggio, Titian, Tintoretto and Bassano that hung in the duke's magnificent Thames-side residence of York House on the Strand, overseen by van der Doort's more flamboyant compatriot Balthazar Gerbier. Van Dyck's portrait of Buckingham's children was a wistful elegy to the king's dead friend in happier times. While it was a moving testament to the king's loyalty to those who remained close to him, it also revealed another side to Charles: his fatal insensitivity towards those who criticized his friends. Many politicians and diplomats looked on the portraits of the Buckinghams as an abiding image of much that went wrong during Charles's reign, and their continued presence in the royal palaces acted as a perpetual snub to those who dared to question the king.

Throughout history, people have collected objects for various reasons: self-esteem, public approval, the attainment of authority, the personal obsession to classify, and the desire for completeness. There were several deeply personal and historical factors that also motivated Charles. Today, historians of collecting tend to regard the obsessive collector as akin to the neurotic, suggesting that 'the objects in their possession are all ultimate, often unconscious assurances against despair and loneliness', intended to 'ward off existential doubt'.[11] Charles exhibited some of these characteristics. Like most monarchs, he was a deeply insecure ruler, but his particular hopes and fears uniquely predisposed him to invest his time and money in paintings. Robbed of his brother, sister and mother as a teenager, and of his father and his closest companion in his early twenties, his art collection acted as a consoling repository of the memories of those he had lost but still cherished and wished to emulate. Always unsure of his physical and personal stature, Charles came to define his royal authority through the awe and silence induced by painting, rather than the books and public disputation cherished by his father. Charles lacked the scholarly erudition of his father, James I, and the ruthless pragmatism of his son, Charles II. His close attention to detail and tendency towards prevarication made him particularly susceptible to the pleasures of collecting, with its absorption in questions of provenance, attribution, style and judgement. As a shy, awkward man with little grasp of people but a rigid belief in his royal title, he turned naturally to pictures. As his rule became increasingly autocratic, Charles collected ever more pictures and focused commissions on his royal body to provide assuring images of his power. This suggests that his collecting and patronage of the arts were not a withdrawal from the reality of political life, as is sometimes assumed, but a response to groups that increasingly questioned his authority.

Charles grew up as a ruler looking towards Europe. He was a member of the cosmopolitan Scottish Stuart dynasty, which was closely connected to the cultural influences of Italy and France at a time when the Tudor monarchy was turning its back on the rest of Europe. Like many other European monarchs and aristocrats of the early seventeenth century, Charles was caught up in the midst of the growing fashion for art that swept the Continent, which meant that to establish his royal credentials he required a collection. Rejecting the stiff, formal portraiture inherited from his Tudor predecessors, he followed his courtiers in pursuing the classically inspired works of the fifteenth- and sixteenth-century Italian masters, Mantegna, Giorgione, Raphael and, above all,

Titian. He also collected the new baroque style of contemporary painters like Peter Paul Rubens, Guido Reni and Orazio Gentileschi, with their complex classical and political allegories charged with emotion and executed in a rich, colourful and dramatic style.

As seventeenth-century political life changed, so did Charles's collecting. Across Europe's royal courts the patronage of art became less concerned with simply displaying pictures whose subjects told a story of royal power and authority. Instead, stylistic innovation and artistic achievement were sought as much if not more than explicit political content. A king's power and judgement were increasingly defined by his ability to discern and acquire great works of art by acknowledged masters. So for Charles, ownership of a Titian Madonna was as significant as a Van Dyck portrait of the royal family. His mistake was to imagine that the radical reforming Protestants among his people would understand this. Unlike Catholicism, Protestantism had little interest in the public display of visual images; nor did the very private conception of monarchy practised by the Stuarts allow for such display. Instead, Charles's interest in art was largely conducted behind closed doors, his precious pictures denied to all but a select few given access to the intimate chambers and galleries of the royal palaces. However, like most collectors, his desire to accumulate soon overtook all sense of caution, and it turned him into one of the most voracious purchasers of art that the English royal family has ever seen.

Charles was a great collector, but not the great connoisseur assumed by many. The term 'connoisseur' only began to emerge in England in the eighteenth century, to describe a wealthy collector with an instinctive taste for the fine arts, skilled in the identification of beautiful objects. Nevertheless, many art historians sympathetic to Charles's political downfall retrospectively dubbed him the first great connoisseur of the arts in England. Henry Perrinchief, writing in the 1670s, painted Charles as a sensitive, discerning connoisseur, claiming that he would pick up his painter's brush and 'supply the defects of art in the workman, and suddenly draw those lines, give those airs and lights, which experience had not taught the painter'.[12] The Victorians took such beliefs even further; the art historian Claude Philips claimed in

1896 that Charles exhibited 'the keenest and most intelligent connoisseurship'.[13] It was an appealing myth of an enlightened painter-prince, which disguised Charles's reliance on an extended network of fellow collectors, art dealers, agents and spies who were arguably more responsible for shaping the royal collection than its owner. From a young age, noblemen and courtiers close to Charles identified works he should admire and those – as a future king – he needed to buy as a way of conferring legitimacy on his rule. Charles was not born to be a collector; he was trained in its methods, techniques and rhetoric by a group of advisers and experts with vested interests in the king and his burgeoning collection.

Charles's reliance on intermediaries was understandable. At the beginning of his reign, towns and cities like Antwerp and Haarlem in the Low Countries lay at the heart of the international art market. Here artists, merchants and aristocrats bought and sold art through public sales and auctions; paintings were subject to duties, and artists' guilds provided their members with a level of social prestige and artistic autonomy unheard of in England. New artists and Old Masters came through the markets of the Low Countries, providing a bridge between Italian art and northern buyers.[14] Charles had to delegate agents and dealers in the Low Countries to buy pictures and send them back to England. The seventeenth-century art market was a complicated, cut-throat business and monarchs like Charles were required to move money and large consignments of artworks across continents with the help of a bewildering network of financiers. The profits were significant, but so were the risks. If a consignment miscarried, a bill of exchange was dishonoured or an attribution queried, it could signal humiliation for the buyer and disaster for the dealer.

Although the financing of art purchases was complex, the sums involved were not as large as is often assumed. Painting was central to the king's majesty, but that did not necessarily mean it was astronomically expensive. Estimates reveal that between 1625 and 1640 Charles spent less than £8,000 commissioning new paintings, and just over £2,000 on statues. The crown paid £18,000 for the more traditional medium of tapestry, belying the assumption that Charles remained at the cutting edge of artistic fashion. The purchase of the Mantuan collection for £18,000 was his most expensive block purchase of pictures, but this is hardly extravagant when set against the annual crown revenue of nearly £1 million. Charles and his retinue spent far larger sums on royal buildings, entertainment (including masques) and clothes. Royal courtiers could spend £500 on a fashionable suit appropriate for court appearances, but just £50 bought a full-length portrait by Van Dyck. Ideally, both were required, but these sums reveal that although art was highly valued, it was still not very *valuable* at King Charles's court.[15]

The risks inherent in buying art did not prevent Charles from accepting the practice of betrayal, fraud and theft by his agents and dealers to ensure he got what he wanted. As a result some involved in the royal collection became very rich and influential; others found themselves bankrupt and destitute. The dangers were compounded by vague and shifting notions of what constituted the value and possession of art, since there were no internationally defined criteria by which works of art could be judged and given even a provisional financial value. Furthermore, as the financial market became ever-more reliant on bills of exchange and other forms of invisible, deferred payment, it was increasingly difficult to establish who owned particular artworks at different stages in their sale and acquisition. Did a buyer own a collection at the point at which the seller accepted a bid, when a bill of exchange was honoured or when the buyer finally took physical possession of his or her acquisition? With no recourse to internationally binding laws on such matters, disputes over possession of pictures and statues could often make or break a buyer's reputation.

CHARLES I's COLLECTION was created against the backdrop of one of Europe's most bitter and internecine conflicts over religion and imperial authority, the Thirty Years War (1618–48). Like many other European sovereigns, Charles took full advantage of the conflict that engulfed the Low Countries, Italy and central Europe to acquire paintings and statues from kings, states and individuals ruined and bankrupted by war. But as he capitalized on the misfortune of his European neighbours and his collection grew under the watchful eye of van der Doort, political tensions were mounting in England that would lead other collectors to exploit his own downfall. From 1629, when Charles dismissed Parliament and embarked on over a decade of personal rule, many of the religious and political tensions that his father had skilfully managed to keep in check gradually pushed the country towards civil war. The gulf between the king's particular version of the Anglican religious faith and the varieties of reforming Protestantism practised by many of his people led some of his political opponents to question the legitimacy of monarchy itself. The religious conflicts in Scotland and Ireland only magnified the king's domestic problems, at a time when Parliament, hastily reconvened in 1640, censured him for undermining what they saw as their age-old rights to participate in the process of governance. By the time Charles left London in January 1642, intent on raising an army and declaring war on Parliament, the royal palaces at Whitehall, Greenwich, Hampton Court, Richmond and Windsor were crammed with thousands of precious treasures, many of them accumulated over the previous sixteen years of his reign – statues, drawings, medals, cameos, tapestries, rich furnishings and over 1,000 paintings.

Just seven years later Charles was dead, his wife and children were in exile or under arrest, and the precious art collection was on the verge of being sold off to the highest bidders. On 30 January 1649, after seven long, bitter years of political conflict and two periods of bloody civil war fought throughout the kingdoms of England, Scotland and Wales, Charles was taken under guard from his childhood home of St James's and led to Whitehall, where he was beheaded outside Inigo Jones's Banqueting House. Within days the new Parliament proclaimed itself a Commonwealth and drew up the Act for the Sale of the Late King's Goods, which proposed to sell off Charles's land, his property and his vast collection of art.

THE IMPLEMENTATION of the act was based on the completion of a series of inventories cataloguing the contents of the royal palaces, compiled by men of humble origin who owed their allegiance not to the king but to his parliament. If van der Doort's inventory tells one side of the story of the formation of Charles's vast collection, the Commonwealth inventories of the late king's goods tell of its sale and dispersal from a very different political perspective.[16] Parliament ordered everything to be listed and valued, not just pictures and statues but also beds and blankets, pots and pans, even the crown jewels. While van der Doort carefully inventoried painters, subjects, descriptions and dimensions of the royal art collection, the parliamentary officers briefly described the royal goods, adding in each case one crucial detail: its price. For the first time in their history, the English struggled to define a new vision of political life that judged its masters according to their financial and political worth, rather than their innate right to rule. Royalty was up for sale.

Over the next four years, merchants, drapers, glaziers, brewers, cutlers, widows and orphans across London bought or acquired objects from the royal collection. Parliament began by selling off some of the royal possessions, reserving part for their own purposes, and then gave away others in lieu of royal debts. For the first time ordinary people were able to buy, sell, admire and evaluate paintings that were never intended for their eyes, let alone their homes. Those dealers and agents involved in buying the collection for their masters acquired pictures and statues that in some cases portrayed them and their friends. Aristocratic collectors who switched political allegiance during the years of civil war bought pictures. Spanish and French diplomats acquired others for their royal masters with the connivance of Charles's servants and members of the new regime. Others simply sold their pictures to the highest bidders in search of much-needed cash profits.

Like most of the royal collection, Van Dyck's *Charles I with M. de St Antoine* was taken down from the gallery in St James's by Parliament and put on sale in Somerset House. It was bought by a member of the public for £150 and then taken abroad to be sold on the international art market. The sale of paintings like this aimed to raise revenue for a new republican regime unsure of its own political survival. Predominantly monarchical and Catholic Europe reacted with horror to Charles's execution and ostensibly supported plans by the dead king's exiled son, Charles II, to regain his father's crown. In response, Parliament sold off Charles's collection with the initial aim of raising money for the navy, which faced the threat of various projected invasions from Ireland, Scotland, France and even the Low Countries.

The political symbolism of the sale was as important as the money it proposed to raise. By repossessing the royal estate and placing a monetary value on the king's pictures, the new republican Commonwealth was deliberately devaluing the aura of monarchy, divesting it of the objects that defined its power and magnificence, and placing them in the public marketplace, to be valued, bought and sold by tradesmen and artisans. However, the monetary benefits from selling paintings and statues were pitifully small, especially when compared to the sale of land, or the levelling of fines against royalist supporters, the so-called 'delinquents'. As the logistics of selling the royal collection increasingly frustrated the new Commonwealth, the symbolism of dismantling monarchy faded. Pragmatic republican leaders saw the opportunity of buying off its creditors by virtually giving the pictures away to a public disillusioned with the promises of a more just society. Others, most famously Oliver Cromwell, saw the advantages of retaining parts of the royal collection as a way of appropriating the authority they conferred upon their owners. With no tangible symbols to define the legitimacy of the new Commonwealth, objects from the dead king's art collection were co-opted in the interests of a regime that remained ambivalent about the righteousness of its attempt to remove monarchy from the landscape of English political life.

Royalists and later historians of art were horrified at what they regarded as the sale's cultural vandalism. Christopher Wren's *Parentalia* lamented that, after the king's execution and the public sale, 'What follow'd was all darkness and obscurity.'[17] Writing in 1685, after the restoration of King Charles II, William Aglionby angrily denounced the sale, insisting that 'had not the bloody-principled zealots, who are enemies to all the innocent pleasures of life, under the pretext of a reformed sanctity, destroyed both the best of kings, and the noblest of courts, we might to this day have seen these arts flourish amongst us'. By this time Charles I was already being recast as a saint and martyr of the royalist cause, a connoisseur before his time whose death at the hands of icono-clastic philistines ended the brief flowering of aesthetic taste in England. Charles 'had once enrich'd our island with the noblest collection that any prince out of Italy could boast of; but those barbarous rebels, whose quarrel was as much to politeness and the liberal arts, as to monarchy and prelacy, dissipated and destroyed the best part of it'.[18] It was an understandably partisan perspective, but one which has been largely accepted ever since.

Aglionby failed to mention that by the time he wrote much of the royal collection was back in the royal household, the result of a remarkable process of cultural and political restitution carried out in the early years of the Restoration. Pictures like *Charles I with M. de St Antoine* were forcibly repossessed and returned to the royal galleries, which were further bolstered by gifts offered to the new king, as well as more questionable acquisitions taken from individuals unfortunate enough to suffer visits from the Restoration's repossession men. As the pictures returned, so their meanings changed. Under Charles I, Van Dyck's equestrian portrait expressed the king's absolute majesty and authority, but under Charles II it became a poignant image of the dead king's martyrdom, and the new king's filial piety.

Those who shared Aglionby's political and artistic viewpoint also ignored the fact that, as well as funding the parliamentary navy, the sale was also established to settle debts incurred by Charles I, which were paid in cash or objects including pictures. This was doomed to fail once corrupt officials and former royal servants, many involved in the original acquisition of the collec-tion, grasped how to manipulate the sale's loopholes. Nonetheless, the sale did transform public attitudes towards the value of art. Although Charles I had bought paintings from international art dealers, most had gone straight into the privacy of the royal palaces, where to speak of their monetary value was vulgar and beneath the dignity of the crown. The Commonwealth sale changed all that. In just a few weeks it transformed what were untouchable royal art objects into commodities to be traded and exchanged between public creditors, radically altering public per-ceptions of the role of art and the nature of taste in seventeenth-century English life. It would then prove impossible to go back to a situation where artistic patronage and collecting were the exclusive preserve of the king and his courtiers.

The sale created an artificial art market, a kind of tournament through which the act of exchange defined the value of particular art objects.[19] Buyers valued pictures based on a series of highly specific criteria: who the previous owner was; where it was displayed; whether there was a secondary market for a particular image. The Commonwealth sale put a price on monarchy and gave birth to the art market in England by creating the conditions for a secondary market in pictures and stimulating a broader public exposure to art. With the Restoration in 1660, auction houses began buying and selling pictures because of the lucrative possibilities of trafficking established by this. Public taste and demand began to define the public English market in art, displacing the patronage of the king's court.

WHILE KING CHARLES's death became the stuff of grand public tragedy, van der Doort's demise had its own tragic aspect. In June 1640 the Dutchman took his own life, hanging himself in his house in St Martin's Lane. His contemporaries laid the blame for his death at the door of the king's art collection. One friend claimed that he 'was jealous the king had designed some other man to keep his pictures'.[20] Others feared that a distraught van der Doort had lost one of the royal portraits in his care.[21] Whatever the truth of the keeper's death, it seems to have been closely related to his troubled stewardship.

The gallery van der Doort walked through in 1639 presented a scene of triumph and grandeur, a vivid testament to the power of King Charles I. By 1649 the same rooms were testament to the catastrophically bad judgement of a king whose fall echoed the apocalyptic scenes of biblical chaos, warfare and the death of kings that lined its walls. Many of the collection's contemporary portraits represented individuals who were dead or in exile. With Charles and van der Doort dead, and Parliament drawing up terms for the removal and sale of the royal possessions, the gallery was marked for dispersal. What followed has been called the sale of the century:

a story of the disposal of a priceless royal art collection told against the backdrop of civil war and regicide.[22] At the centre of it all, both subject and object of these extraordinary events, hung the pictures themselves. Great paintings always disclose more than their owners or even their makers wish to reveal. Nowhere is this truer than with the art collection of King Charles I.

❧

CHAPTER ONE

DEATH OF A PRINCE

It was on 1 November 1612 that the eleven-year-old Prince Charles Stuart took the short journey from Whitehall to St James's Palace to see Henry, Prince of Wales, for the last time. He knew that his elder brother, the heir to the throne, was afflicted with a terrible sickness and now lay dying. The news had come as a terrible shock to his family and the people of London. It was widely assumed that Henry would eventually accede to the English throne. His precocious intelligence and athleticism had endeared him to both the royal court and the public, leading Sir Francis Bacon to observe that 'the excellence of his disposition excited high expectations among great numbers of all ranks'.[1]

Henry's youth and promise were vital assets to his father, King James VI of Scotland, in his negotiations to assume the English crown following the death of Elizabeth I. Elizabeth died childless and, with no obvious heir, her Scottish cousin James Stuart was seen by many as the only acceptable successor. He had the advantage of being a Protestant with two male heirs: Henry and Charles. While some figures at the English court had misgivings about handing over the English throne to a Scot, their anxieties were partly assuaged by the prospect of an English-trained prince eventually assuming the crown. Henry spent the hot summer of 1612 swimming, running and riding. In mid-October he complained 'of a small kind of giddy lumpish heaviness in his forehead'[2] while playing tennis. The following Sunday he was confined to bed. The next day 'his Highness was without any fever, rose and played after dinner with [Charles] the Duke of York'. Unfortunately his symptoms soon returned. His father was informed and the doctors diagnosed 'a corrupt, putred feaver'. James sent for the eminent French physician Theodore de Mayerne to tend his son, but his treatment only hastened the prince's decline. Mayerne administered a purgative including rhubarb which 'brought away great store of putred choler, and in the end phlegm, the urine inclining somewhat towards concoction'. Rather unsurprisingly, 'his Highness after the working thereof, found not the ease that was expected'. Once Henry slipped into delirium, Mayerne summoned the king and warned him to expect the worst.

As concern grew for the young prince, people 'did almost every hour send unto St James's for News'.[3] On the afternoon of 1 November King James arrived at St James's with Henry's mother, Queen Anna, his younger sister the fifteen-year old Elizabeth, and his little brother, Charles. The family meeting was private and no record remains of what transpired. What is known is that before making the short journey from Whitehall to St James's, Prince Charles ordered courtiers to ride to Richmond Palace, Henry's residence outside London. They were instructed to remove one of Henry's most precious possessions, a collection of bronze statuettes, and bring them back to Whitehall. When the statuettes arrived, Charles chose a tiny, delicately crafted pacing horse, made of bronze and designed by the renowned sculptor Giovanni Bologna. It was part of a consignment of paintings and statuettes presented to Henry by the Duchy of Tuscany in the hope that he would look favourably upon marriage with the sister of the grand duke, Cosimo de' Medici. Oblivious to its political significance, Charles headed off with the bronze horse towards St James's Palace.

As Henry's family were ushered into his chamber that evening, the king sermonized at length while his wife and daughter wept. Finally, Charles stepped forward and pressed the statuette into his dying brother's hands. It was small enough to grasp in one hand, a sentimental toy passed from one child to another as consolation in the face of death. But Charles's gift was more than that: it was also a defining moment for the future king. Throughout his young life Charles had been in the shadow of his elder, charismatic brother. As the second-born son, he seemed destined to live the life of an eternal prince, doomed to watch from the wings as his brother assumed the title King Henry IX. The afternoon of 1 November changed all that, and as the future of England passed from the dying Henry into the hands of his younger brother, the moment was marked by the presentation of a piece of art. The gift came to personify the seductive power as well as the dangerous mortality that art represented throughout Charles's subsequent reign.

The moment stayed with Charles all his life. Years later, he recounted the story to Abraham van der Doort as he catalogued the royal art collection. Coming across the Bologna statuette, van der Doort as entered it as 'a little horse being one of the number of 18 which your Majesty did send for to Richmond in the last sickness time and there your Majesty gave it with your own hands to the Prince'.[4] The statuette was a poignant commemoration of the king's dead brother, but it also acted as an abiding testament to the fact that it was Charles and not Henry who now assumed the mantle of sovereign-in-waiting.

Within a week of this exchange, Henry was dead. The prince had rapidly declined into 'greater Alienations of Brain, Ravings and idle speeches out of purpose . . . to the great grief of all that heard him, whose hopes now began to vanish'.[5] Mayerne had resorted to ever more bizarre measures to revive him, including 'a Cock [which] was cloven by the Back, and applied unto the soles of his Feet, but in vain'.[6] This was designed to draw evil humours down Henry's body and out of his feet, but the grotesque indignity can only have added to the prince's terrible suffering. Debilitated by fever and fatally weakened by Mayerne's desperate methods, Henry finally passed away just before 8 a.m. on the morning of 6 November.

There was a spontaneous outpouring of grief at the news. One of Henry's courtiers lamented the loss of 'the Delight of Mankind, the Expectation of Nations, the Strength of his Father, and Glory of his Mother, Religion's second Hope'.[7] For the family, the anguish was deeply personal. Queen Anna would not receive condolences regarding Henry's death 'because she cannot bear to hear it mentioned'.[8] James was deeply affected: 'even in the midst of the most important discussions he will burst out with "Henry is dead, Henry is dead"'. Young Prince Charles was also dreadfully distressed, showing 'a grief beyond his years'.[9] With the death of his elder brother, the delicate young prince was suddenly thrust into the political spotlight as the heir to the English throne. He needed to grow up quickly.

His first opportunity came just one month later, on a chilly December morning, when he took his place as chief mourner at Henry's funeral. London had not seen such an overwhelming display of public grief since the interment of Elizabeth I nine years earlier. In many ways Henry's death was even more poignant. The young prince had been struck down in his prime, aged just eighteen, full of unfulfilled potential, and spared the inevitable compromise and criticism that come with high office. It took the 2,000 official mourners that followed his body to Westminster Abbey nearly four hours to clear St James's. The procession was composed of all levels of London society, from masters of the bedchamber and members of the Privy Council to priests, grooms, pages and the thirty-one artists formerly employed by Henry. At the head of the procession came Prince Charles, chief mourner in the traditional absence of his father. As the chariot made its way along Whitehall, it was followed by extraordinary scenes of 'lamentation and sorrow, some weeping, crying, swooning, sighing inwardly, others halt dead, others holding up their hands, passionately bewailing so great a loss'.[10] Once the cortège was installed in Westminster Abbey the archbishop stepped forward and preached his sermon. Amid 'an Ocean of tears',[11] members of Henry's court then stepped forward to resign by breaking their rods of office over the coffin.

Henry's funeral was the dramatic finale to a short but brilliant career characterized by a cultivation of theatre and art. Perhaps the most striking moment in the whole carefully choreographed event was the public display of a wax effigy of the prince that lay upon the funeral chariot, designed by none other than Abraham van der Doort. The effigy was 'made up as like him as possible could be',[12] dressed in the prince's coronet, cap, sword, silk tunic and breeches, flesh-coloured stockings and black shoes. Even in death, Henry struck an artful pose. The intoxicating mix of art, death, youth and royal power proved irresistible to artists and writers. The finest poets and dramatists of the Jacobean age 'rained tears of black ink' over the demise of the young prince. John

Webster, author of *The Duchess of Malfi*, penned an elegy on Henry's death, lamenting, 'The greatest of the kingly race is gone.'[13] John Donne wrote an 'Elegy upon the Untimely Death of the Incomparable Prince Henry', questioning the mysteries of divine providence in robbing the world of 'This soul of peace'.[14] As praise rained down on Henry from all sides, the grieving heir to the throne watched and listened.

Henry's death proved a turning point in the political and artistic history of the Stuart age in England. Over the following months and years the intricate world of political alliances James I had built around the assumption of the prince's eventual accession to the throne slowly but surely unravelled, and Henry's patronage of the arts came to an abrupt end. The consequences of his death would play themselves out over the next fifteen years.

KING JAMES VI of Scotland had come to the throne in 1603 faced with an English nation beset by plague, famine and international isolation. He had spent his last years as king of Scotland fending off kidnap and assassination attempts, and trying to limit the financial demands his wife, Queen Anna of Denmark, was making on his cash-strapped kingdom. It was no surprise that when the English Secretary of State, Sir Robert Cecil, opened negotiations with James to succeed Elizabeth, he jumped at the opportunity. He inherited a domestic and foreign policy from Elizabeth based on splendid but dangerous isolation from an overwhelmingly Catholic Europe, which was effectively controlled by the twin centres of Habsburg imperial power, Vienna and Madrid. James wanted to be a player in the world of European power politics and the only way to achieve this was to make peace with Spain.

In June 1604 James invited a Spanish delegation to London to establish terms and restore relations with Catholic Europe. The English wanted open trade with Spain and her colonies in the New World. The Spanish demanded an end to England's financial and military support for the Protestant states in the Low Countries, which the Spanish Habsburg Empire still claimed as its own. Religion also proved a stumbling block. The English delegation demanded freedom from the religious prescriptions of the

Spanish Inquisition, while the Spanish insisted on the right of all English Catholics to worship free of persecution. Tensions rose during negotiations held at Somerset House when the Spanish delegation insisted 'that all trade between England and the States [General of the Dutch Republic] should cease, for the Dutch drew large profits from the English market for their tapestries, cloth, tweeds and so on'.[15] Mischievously seating the Spanish delegation beneath a Flemish tapestry during their talks can not have helped matters.

By August the two sides had agreed terms. The impact on English cultural life was profound and immediate. Ever since Henry VIII's split from the Catholic Church in the 1530s, Englishmen had been forbidden to travel in Catholic Europe. Now James began appointing resident English ambassadors across Europe, while young Englishmen set out to experience the art, culture and learning of the Catholic cities of Rome, Florence, Venice and Madrid. Peace meant that these travellers no longer incurred the suspicion of the Protestant authorities back home, nor (as long as they were careful) the wrath of the Catholic Church abroad. Throughout its political and religious isolation, England had taken cultural and artistic inspiration from the Low Countries, missing out on the final flowering of the high European Renaissance and the artistic achievements of artists and architects like Michelangelo, Raphael, Titian and Palladio. It was now time to catch up.

As England settled into peace with Europe, the country also adjusted to life under a new royal dynasty. Throughout the fraught years of Queen Elizabeth's childless rule, the English had craved a 'normal' royal family, composed of kings, queens, princes, princesses and heirs. Married to a relatively young wife and blessed with two sons and one daughter, King James seemed the ideal solution to England's dynastic problems. In fact, what the English got was a royal family with a vengeance: a dysfunctional collection of physically unprepossessing individuals united through jealousy, infidelity, sibling rivalry and mutual suspicion.

James had been married for fourteen politically turbulent years to Anna, the daughter of King Frederick II of Denmark. Anna had borne James three children: Henry, the eldest, in 1594, followed two years later by his sister, Elizabeth, and in November 1600 by a second son, Charles. Unfortunately Charles was such a sickly child that he was immediately baptized for fear that he would die. In the summer of 1603, Anna followed James to take up the throne of England, bringing with her his heir, Prince Henry. Fear for his health meant that Charles remained behind in Scotland.

The little prince, not yet three years old, was left in the care of Alexander Seton, Lord Fyvie, while the rest of his family began to settle into their new royal life in London. Fyvie reported that Charles was still unable to walk or talk from 'the great weakness of his body, after so long and heavy sickness'.[16] By the summer of 1604, James dispatched an English doctor and apothecary to bring his son to London. Potential carers were put off once they saw 'how weak a child he was, and not likely to live'.[17] Charles's English guardian was also sceptical about his future, complaining, 'he was not able to go, nor scant stand alone, he was so weak in his joints, and especially his ankles, insomuch as many feared they were out of joint'.[18] Many years later, one of Charles's first biographers, Hamon L'Estrange, echoed these fears, claiming that the young prince 'was exceeding feeble in his lower parts, his legs growing not erect, but rapandous and embowed'.[19]

Contemporary miniatures of Charles capture the likeness of a sickly, withdrawn boy whose nervous gaze, delicate features and waxen pallor speak volumes of a childhood characterized by illness and loneliness. James suggested increasingly bizarre solutions to his son's physical infirmities, including iron boots to strengthen his legs and cutting the string beneath his tongue to prevent his growing stammer. Charles responded by talking with pebbles in his mouth in a fruitless attempt to control the impediment.

By the end of 1605, however, Charles's health was sufficiently improved for him to be invested as Duke of York in the old Elizabethan Banqueting House in Whitehall. After the solemnities the court was treated to a masque, a wildly fashionable new theatrical entertainment. The royal family were fortunate in having the choreographer and architect Inigo Jones and the dramatist and poet Ben Jonson at their disposal. Both set to work on a new masque to be performed on Twelfth Night, 1605, at a staggering cost of £4,000.[20] The performance was entitled *The Masque of Blackness*, and featured Anna herself, blacked up and dressed in exotic costume. The four-year-old Charles watched as his mother emerged from a scalloped shell and proceeded to sing and dance in front of the king and his court. The masque was followed by a typically lavish Jacobean banquet that ended suddenly as the ravenous guests 'furiously assaulted' the tables piled high with food, with the result 'that down went table and tresses before one bit was touched'.[21] Once again the young Charles found himself overshadowed by the flamboyant activities of his immediate family.

James was eager to place his Stuart mark on the English monarchy, and one way to do this was to commission and display portraits of his family. However, the society that the Stuarts inherited from Elizabeth was deeply ambivalent about painting and the visual arts. Since the days of Henry VIII, the Tudors had moved carefully between the use of visual iconography to display their royal power and a clear rejection of such idolatry as 'popish' and antithetical to Protestant belief. Many Protestants argued that Catholicism confused the worship of God with the worship of his image in paintings, statues and tapestries. In an attempt to reach a compromise, the Elizabethans made a clear distinction between images used for religious purposes and those created for a secular, domestic situation. The Elizabethan *Book of Homilies* stressed that 'Neither do we condemn the arts of painting and image-making, as wicked of themselves.'[22]

Nevertheless, the language associated with art and painting by Elizabethan writers was predominantly negative. Portraits were seen as 'counterfeits', women's use of cosmetics to 'paint' their faces was condemned as 'artifice', and poets including Shakespeare worried over the 'cunning', deceitful illusion of reality created by the skilful painter.[23] The importation of pictures from abroad was officially illegal, based on legislation dating back to the fifteenth century.[24] The penal laws of 1571 also forbade the importation of 'crosses, pictures . . . and other superstitious objects from Rome', although this was primarily aimed at outlawing Catholic liturgical objects like rosaries and breviaries. Neverthless, it hardly created an atmosphere conducive to the flourishing of the visual arts.[25]

If late Elizabethan London lacked a reputation for its artistic culture, it was nonetheless beginning to establish itself as an international capital after decades of diplomatic isolation. The city that

James inherited from Elizabeth was gradually asserting itself as one of the largest in Europe: around 7 per cent of the population of England lived in London, with 200,000 people crammed into settlements to the south and west of the ancient walls of the City. The City itself, stretching from Blackfriars in the west to the Tower in the east, was the commercial heartland. Its maze of streets with their timber-framed houses was home to the City's thriving domestic trades – blacksmiths, grocers, bakers, ironmongers, weavers, skinners, cloth-workers – all spilling out on to the Thames and its busy commercial traffic that connected London's port to the rest of the world. Straddling the river stood the medieval stone edifice of London Bridge, a chaotic mix of shops, houses and streams of livestock making their way into the City or south towards Southwark, where, by 1600, 10 per cent of London's population lived. Southwark was the vibrant, polluted and dangerous home to London's theatres, bear gardens, bull-baiting pits, bowling alleys and brothels, far from Westminster, back on the other side of the river, the political and aristocratic heart of London, with its imposing palace, abbey and the king's Whitehall residence.

One of the most noticeable features of James's capital was its remarkably cosmopolitan community of foreigners and immigrants. Over 7,000 economic migrants and religious refugees from the Low Countries, France, Italy and North Africa all lived and worked in Southwark and parishes in the heart of the City. From the 1560s onwards, many Protestant artists and craftsmen suffering religious persecution in the Spanish-controlled Low Countries sought refuge in England, settling in London suburbs and districts like Cripplegate, Holborn and Blackfriars, where they could work outside the City's regulations without the need to join a London guild or company.[26] By the time James's advisers realized the need for a state portrait of the new king, there were over 100 painters to choose from among the ranks of London's talented émigré community. The man chosen for this prestigious task was John de Critz, the descendant of immigrants from Antwerp.[27]

De Critz completed his portrait of James around 1606. It was an immediate success, and was quickly copied and circulated among the king's subjects and allies. But it also revealed some of the personal and political problems that would handicap the new king throughout his reign. Physically awkward and deeply insecure from years of turbulent rule in Scotland, James was a pedantic king more comfortable with the written word than the painted image, and this reticence comes across in de Critz's portrait. He wears the ostentatious attire admired by the Venetian ambassador during his first audience with the new king, who reported that James 'was dressed in grey silver satin' with 'a chain of diamonds around his neck and a great diamond in his hat'.[28] A slightly bow-legged figure warily gazes out from the picture. He wears a sullen, aloof expression, his hand casually but unconvincingly placed on his hip, his rakishly tilted hat with its enormous brooch and bejewelled St George medallion slung across his chest, striking an inappropriately flamboyant image in a portrait intended to convey a majestic authority.

James's discomfort with portraiture was thrown into even starker relief by the ability of his precocious son to adapt quickly to the medium as a way of establishing himself as heir to the throne. Henry was depicted as a vigorous, athletic prince, riding, hunting and confidently striking a military pose. The contrast between king and prince was heightened by their choice of portrait painters. James opted for a safe, cosmopolitan, established artist like de Critz, while Henry more confidently chose Robert Peake, an Englishman who had flourished during Elizabeth's reign. Henry was so impressed with the painter's work that he made him his personal portrait painter, leading to his appointment as Serjeant-Painter alongside de Critz.[29]

Young, gifted and uncompromisingly Protestant, Prince Henry represented a new generation of Englishmen eager to establish their country's political authority within the world of European imperial politics. This new generation represented a direct challenge to his father, with his more cautious, diplomatically concessive policy towards the Catholic powers of Europe, and especially Spain. Although James presided over a notoriously decadent and immoral court, he was a shrewd politician, anxious to avoid involvement in the financially ruinous religious wars of the late sixteenth century. However, he soon found himself trying to reign in the more bellicose and strongly Protestant policies advocated by his own son's household in St James's Palace. Henry's court quickly became a magnet for politically ambitious young men from aristocratic families eager for military adventure abroad. The many 'young and sprightly blossoms'[30] that flourished around Henry included Robert Devereux, 3rd Earl of Essex, William Cecil, Lord Cranbourne and Thomas Cecil, Earl of Exeter. These men represented the politically powerful Cecil clan, who remained loyal to Elizabeth during the Essex conspiracy and were instrumental in ensuring James's smooth accession in 1603. Other members of Henry's circle included Sir John Harington, Sir John Dallington, Robert Kerr (later 1st Earl of Ancram) and two men who would come to play a crucial part in the future of art collecting in England, Sir John Danvers and Thomas Howard, Earl of Arundel.[31] They were all united by their unusual experience of continental travel. Most received official licences permitting them to go abroad, pursuing an itinerary that usually included France, Germany and Italy, embarking on what later generations would see as an essential part of a wealthy Englishman's education, and which would come to be known as the Grand Tour.

An older generation of predominantly Catholic figures also exercised a significant influence over Henry's interest in the arts. The most prominent was John, Lord Lumley. The Catholic Lumley was briefly imprisoned in the Tower after his implication in plots to overthrow Elizabeth and turned his disappointment in public life into an immersion in intellectual and artistic pursuits.[32] He accumulated one of the finest art collections of his day. At his death in 1609 he owned 288 pictures, of which over half were portraits (186 in all), many of the leading figures in the violent history of Tudor England. The jewel of the collection was 'A great book of Pictures done by Hans Holbein of certain ladies, gentlemen and gentlewomen in King Henry VIII his time'. The gallery in Lumley Castle held ninety-one portraits, ranging from King Richard II to Queen Elizabeth.[33] It celebrated the prominent figures of the Elizabethan age, as well as more controversial ones, including Catholics put to death for challenging the Tudor regime – Sir Thomas More, the poet Sir Thomas Wyatt and Mary Queen of Scots. The last of these was a particularly ambiguous portrait for Lumley to possess. Having once flirted with supporting Mary's attempt to depose Queen Elizabeth, he later sat as a commissioner at her trial in a bid for political rehabilitation. Alongside figures like Mary hung more prominent Catholics, including the Habsburg emperor Charles V, his son King Philip of Spain and 'Franciscus Xavierus first of the Jesuits which brought the Christian faith unto ye Indians'. Perhaps most important of all for Lumley were the sixty-seven pictures 'of Christ, our Ladie and his Saints' listed in his inventory. Even Pope Julius II made it on to the walls of Lumley's packed gallery.

Lumley led the way in England in the relatively new fashion for displaying pictures in private galleries. Sixteenth-century collectors across Europe were only slowly beginning to make a clear separation between the display of fine art (paintings, sculptures and drawings) and other precious objects. The principles of the Italian *studiolo* and the German *Wunderkammer* stressed the arrangement of rich, diverse, exotic objects in one small room. There was little distinction between statues, paintings, manuscripts, coins, mechanical devices, natural objects and rare animals within such collections. Late sixteenth-century Europe boasted nearly 1,000 notable collections of such marvels, reflecting the curiosity of their owners and a desire to classify a rapidly expanding world that would ultimately lead to the creation of the great modern museums of the eighteenth and nineteenth centuries.[34]

To own such marvellous curiosities was to possess arcane knowledge of the natural and spiritual world, as in the case of Emperor Rudolf II and his vast collection, or the supernatural powers invested in Shakespeare's Prospero and his magical books in *The Tempest*. However, as such collections grew increasingly large and bizarre, many northern European rulers and noblemen turned to the creation of *Bilderkammern*, or picture galleries, as a more eloquent expression of their magnificence and discernment. As rich and strange curiosities became the provenance of scholars working in medicine and the natural sciences, so the collecting of paintings, sculptures and drawings became the preserve of nobles like Lumley.[35]

This shift towards displaying pictures within galleries also influenced the architecture of English Tudor homes. The early sixteenth-century 'long gallery' was originally a long hall without chambers overlooking a courtyard, and primarily designated as a place for exercise and recreation. Its design responded to a more outward-looking Tudor architectural style, as houses were no longer built according to the requirements of heavy fortification. Such galleries were usually built on first or second floors, often overlooking great halls, and acted as transitional spaces between public rooms and private apartments.[36]

With the rise of enthusiastic builders and collectors like Lord Lumley, galleries became obvious spaces in which to display portraits of friends and family. Viscount Howard of Bindon wrote in 1609 about '[t]he gallery I lately made for the pictures of sundry of my honoured friends, whose presentation thereby to behold will greatly delight me to walk often in that place where I may see so comfortable a sight'.[37] He exemplified the growing Jacobean fashion for using the gallery as a place for exercise, social dialogue and the display of collections of pictures. But as a liminal, internal place containing curious images, the gallery was also regarded as an enchanting but illicit space where political and even sexual intrigue flourished. In Ben Jonson's *The Alchemist* the venal Sir Epicure Mammon fantasizes about mirrored oval rooms filled with sexually explicit pictures, while the satirist John Marston associated the importing of Venetian pictures with the purchase of prostitutes, poisons, cosmetics and other 'strange luxuries'. In a gallery courtiers could refashion their social and political standing, even if the fantasy of grandeur displayed there was at variance with political reality.

This is exactly how Lumley used the space of the gallery. In withdrawing from public life because of his Catholicism, he fashioned a world that re-created his standing as a powerful nobleman, able to stress his links to royal power and authority, while also affirming his religion in more private, withdrawn spaces. Other figures on the margins of the Elizabethan court were more robust in using their picture collections to unite their public and private worlds. Henry Howard, Earl of Northampton, was another member of the Catholic Howard clan who experienced the vicissitudes of Tudor political life. Both his father and his brother were executed for treason, and Northampton spent most of Elizabeth's reign living his life, according to one observer, 'as a man obscured, or rather neglected',[38] subject to repeated surveillance and periods of imprisonment.

However, Northampton enthusiastically aided Cecil's plans for James's accession. For his efforts James appointed him Privy Councillor and Northampton quickly sought the cultural and artistic trappings befitting a man undergoing his sudden rise in social stature. He bought properties on the Strand and in Greenwich, where he spent £2,000 on a fashionable brick residence, insisting that his neighbour Simon Basil, Surveyor of the King's Works, demolish a wing of his own house as it obscured Northampton's view.[39]

By the time of his death in 1614, Northampton had amassed one of the finest collections in London. Stepping into his official residence of Northampton House, guests would be shown along the earl's Little Gallery, containing thirty-one portraits of family, friends and close political allies, living and dead.[40] Moving through the Long Gallery, visitors could see a range of religious paintings, including portraits of St Francis and 'Christ holding the Cross'.[41] The portraits that hung alongside these images made Northampton's religious allegiances very clear, and included three portraits of Mary Queen of Scots, and a portrait of Mary Tudor, the last Catholic queen of England.

If allowed access to Northampton's more private rooms, visitors could inspect even more religious paintings. In the Long Wardrobe he displayed a remarkable 'arched folding picture with a golden fountain in the middle and our Saviour issuing blood there into',[42] a devotional triptych of the type found in Catholic churches. But Northampton never forgot his political allies; the Wardrobe also contained more portraits of Mary Queen of Scots, and Lord Treasurer Burghley, the father of Robert Cecil, Earl of Salisbury.

As if to confirm the permeable boundaries between the public and private worlds of Northampton's life, the inventory of his household stuff lists three pictures in his bedchamber: 'one is of the Passion, another of the King [James], and the third of the Queen his mother [Mary], all three with taffeta curtains'.[43] As with Lumley, Northampton's collection combined intimate religious observance with more public statements of political allegiance. The earl clearly loved his pictures, but they also functioned as a very concrete statement of his wealth and political power right at the heart of the new Jacobean state.

Northampton's collection of 176 pictures was one of the largest in England and reflected the gradual shift in taste that took place in early seventeenth-century London. It included fourteen anonymous Venetian pictures in his Greenwich gallery, one of the earliest acquisitions of Venetian paintings by a private English collector. Unlike Lumley, Northampton prominently displayed his explicitly Catholic collection next door to the centre of power in Whitehall. This was as much a political as an aesthetic decision: Northampton was taking advantage of James I's religious tolerance, and staking his claim as a statesman as well as a collector. He was also turning his back on the Tudor regime that had turned against him. Neither Henry VIII nor Elizabeth I was to be found on Northampton's walls, which were instead lined with portraits of King James, Prince Henry and the new Jacobean elite, as well as religious pictures intended to appeal to both Catholics and fellow collectors, regardless of their religious or political persuasions.

Northampton's collection lacked one particularly prominent member of the new Stuart dynasty: the queen. The omission of a portrait of Queen Anna from his gallery highlighted the disdain with which many of James's entourage regarded the queen. Since his accession, James had transformed the Elizabethan court into an exclusively male domain. This included the king's bedchamber, which was run by young, mainly Scottish noblemen who controlled all access to James and took responsibility for every aspect of the king's life, however intimate. As a result, Anna found herself increasingly estranged from her husband. Contemporaries as well as subsequent historians, most of them men, have unfairly dismissed her as a frivolous, pleasure-seeking queen, preferring instead either the iconic authority of her predecessor Elizabeth or the sophistication of her successor, Henrietta Maria. One contemporary historian damned her with faint praise by remarking, 'Nothing could be fixed upon her that left any great impression.'[44]

Faced with the obstacle of a male-dominated court and an increasingly aloof husband, Anna responded by exerting her authority on the royal topography of London, overseeing a series of costly and ambitious architectural renovations to her various residences. This began with Oatlands Palace near Weybridge, the first home to Anna and the young Prince Henry. She also received the rights to Greenwich Palace, authorizing Inigo Jones to spend £4,000 on the creation of the Queen's House, which still stands to this day.[45] Her architectural spending spree culminated in £34,000 spent on major renovations to Somerset House on the Strand. First founded by Lord Protector Somerset in 1549, the residence passed into the crown's hands after Somerset's fall from grace and subsequent execution in 1552. Elizabeth I lived there until her royal accession. The residence was renamed Denmark House in 1617, in honour of King James's queen, and provided a location for the masquing that became a feature of the Stuart court, as well as two new galleries for the queen to display her growing collection of pictures. These architectural additions would make her residence the ideal location for the sale of her youngest son's art collection thirty years later.[46]

As Anna's relations with James and his court deteriorated, her collection expanded and her manipulation of portraiture deepened. Traditionally, queens were painted showing their left side, so that their pictures could be displayed facing their husband's portrait. In later years Anna only allowed herself to be painted with her right side facing the viewer, literally turning her back on artistic convention, as well as her husband. She commissioned large portraits stressing her personal independence, culminating in Paul Van Somer's portrait painted in 1617. Anna strikes a relaxed, confident pose, dressed for the hunt, surrounded by the trappings of the landed English gentlewoman – Arab horses, Italian grey-hounds (wearing monogrammed 'Queen Anna' collars) and a fashionable black servant. In the background stands her favourite residence of Oatlands, rebuilt by Inigo Jones. Van Somer borrowed from earlier portraits of Prince Henry hunting and on horseback to capture the queen's love of display and determined independence. If contemporary accounts of her were anything to go by, Van Somer also captured her likeness; one Venetian visitor described Anna after the portrait was completed, noting, 'Her face is somewhat long, but very majestic. She has fine eyes and a rather hooked nose, though in every respect graceful.'[47]

For Anna, collecting and commissioning pictures were attempts to reassert her diminishing royal authority, but they also commemorated the people taken away from her. Anna left her family in Denmark at the age of fifteen and one of her only ways of remembering them was through their portraits. Her collection grew significantly after the death of Prince Henry, whose pictures she inherited, and this loss was compounded by the departure of Princess Elizabeth less than two years later, following her marriage to Prince Frederick, Elector Palatinate. Anna's collection also reflected her changing attitude towards religion. It was rumoured at court that she was becoming increasingly sympathetic to Catholicism and she certainly owned a substantial number of devotional images, religious pictures and the paraphernalia of Catholic worship.[48]

Other collecting rivals, including the most powerful of all James's courtiers, Cecil, Lord Salisbury, noticed Anna's preferences for pictures over people. In November 1611 Jane Drummond, Anna's lady-in-waiting, wrote to Salisbury to inform him:

> I acquainted her Majesty with what your lordship wrote of her loving no body, but dead pictures in a paltry Gallery. Her Majesty commanded me to return this answer that she is more contented amongst those harmless pictures in the paltry Gallery than your lordship is with your employments in fair rooms all things considered.[49]

Salisbury's observation captured Anna's withdrawal into her picture galleries as a consolation against the recurrent disappointments of public life. Nevertheless, it was a devastatingly callous remark in the light of the recent death of Prince Henry. As ever, Anna's response was sharp and to the point: paintings, she implied, were as harmless and meaningless as Salisbury's own immersion in the world of Jacobean power politics, enacted inside the 'fair rooms' of Whitehall.

A consummate politician under Elizabeth, Cecil had been made Earl of Salisbury and Lord Treasurer as a reward for engineering James's accession to the throne. The diminutive Salisbury soon made himself indispensable to James, who affectionately referred to him as 'my little beagle'.[50] He was horrified at the court's profligacy and spent his later years trying to rein in the royal finances. Nowhere was this more imperative than in the case of Queen Anna's expenditure on masques, jewels and pictures – which probably explains his dig at her 'dead pictures in a paltry Gallery'.

The irony was that the financially prudent Cecil was the most lavish of all the patrons of the arts at James's court. Like Northampton and Anna, he spent a fortune developing new residences at Hatfield House in Hertfordshire and Salisbury House on the Strand. The costs were so great that he complained that architecture was a vice that 'hath almost undone me'.[51] Cecil's picture collections at Hatfield House and Salisbury House soon dwarfed those of Northampton.[52] While collectors like Lumley and Anna used their pictures to express their religion and lineage, Cecil used his collection to define and extend his influence as a pre-eminent statesman. New pictures were bought and others moved down to London from his country residence in Hatfield. As in the case of Northampton, many were portraits, although unlike Northampton's collection, Cecil's was more orthodox: King James took pride of place, as did Queen Anna and Princess Elizabeth, as well as the Tudor monarchs who originally elevated Cecil's family. But there were also religious paintings, landscapes, mythological scenes and historical paintings.[53]

Salisbury held one crucial advantage over his other collecting rivals. As Secretary of State he was responsible for recommending international diplomatic appointments, which gave him unrivalled access to information on the latest artistic developments throughout Europe. One figure he came to rely on above all others in artistic matters was his man in Venice, Sir Henry Wotton. Seventeenth-century diplomacy was a shady and often precarious profession, and Wotton was one of its more urbane and colourful practitioners. He infamously claimed 'An ambassador is an honest man sent to lie abroad for the good of his country.'[54] Despite such indiscretions, with the accession of James I Cecil saw Wotton as the perfect ambassador to England's anti-Spanish ally, Venice. Upon arriving in Venice in 1604, Wotton began a stream of diplomatic letters to Salisbury describing the colourfully ceremonial world of Venetian politics. They paint a vivid picture of Wotton's involvement in delicate matters including English pirates marauding in the Mediterranean, deteriorating relations between Venice and the papacy, ham-fisted attempts to create Anglo-Venetian alliances, and a series of bizarre plots ranging from kidnapping to assassination that Wotton flirted with throughout his embassy.[55]

Although Wotton's record as an ambassador was somewhat mixed, as an art dealer he was a revelation. By the late sixteenth century Venice was one of the great centres of Italian Renaissance art, having produced artists of the calibre of Carpaccio, Bellini, Titian, Veronese and Tintoretto. Wotton's audiences with the Doge in St Mark's palace brought him face to face with some of the greatest paintings by these masters. In his everyday activities he encountered numerous private collections, art dealers and studios, and soon grasped the opportunity to supplement his meagre diplomatic salary and retain favour back home by satisfying the growing demand for pictures among his London paymasters.

In September 1607 Wotton wrote to inform Cecil, 'I am preparing for your Lordship's own delight some things about the subject of architecture, [which] shall be within a few days sent you in picture.'[56] This was a particularly appropriate gift for Cecil, who was just beginning extensive renovations to his newly acquired estate of Hatfield House. By April Wotton was writing to Cecil to thank him for the arrival of 'your picture wherewith it hath pleased you to honour me'. This was a copy of de Critz's portrait of Cecil. Its arrival in Venice was designed to extend the sitter's political influence, but the ambassador cleverly turned the gift to his own advantage. Wotton admired the portrait, while also commissioning a new version to be sent back to Salisbury: 'I have thought that being done here in mosaic, it may afterwards be very fitly placed in the front of your buildings over the portal'[57] at Hatfield House – where it can still be seen to this day.

In the same letter Wotton also modestly offered 'two or three poor things', including several Venetian paintings and maps. The jewel of the consignment was a painting that Wotton described as 'Prometheus devoured by the eagle, done by Giacobo Palma in concurrence with Titiano, which for the emulation between two painters (both of no small name) I dare say to be worthy of a corner in one of your Lordship's galleries'.[58] Wotton's intimate knowledge of Cecil's houses, including his galleries, provided him with the ideal opportunity to present his master with the perfect gift – a mythological picture by one of Venice's finest living painters, Palma Giovane ('Giacobo Palma'). It came with the further (rather optimistic) possibility that the great Venetian master Titian also had a hand in its completion. Wotton stressed that the painter was as important as the subject matter. It was a painting by Palma, rather than an anonymous picture of Prometheus, that was meant to grace the walls of Cecil's gallery.

Wotton was not alone in putting his London masters in touch with a new world of art. Other Englishmen set out on tours of Europe, including Salisbury's relative William Cecil, future Earl of Exeter, who travelled through Italy in the summer of 1609. He wrote enthusiastic letters back home to other London collectors, suggesting that if they wanted to increase their 'magnificence' they should invest in 'the works of Benedicto Palma [Giovane] at Venice, who exceeds in doing large pictures as much as the whole side of a great chamber'. Word of Palma's fame had spread since Wotton's recommendation of his work to Salisbury. Cecil wrote home praising 'a little old man called John Bologna [Giovanni Bologna] (the Duke's servant and at Florence) who is not inferior much to Michelangelo'.[59] It was a recommendation that would have significant repercussions back in London.

Word of the reputations of artists like Palma and Giovanni di Bologna soon spread through Whitehall. The effect on the court of the fifteen-year-old Prince Henry was profound. Henry was more popular than ever and his circle increasingly defined itself as an alternative to James's court, which heightened tensions between Henry and his father. The Venetian ambassador reported that the king was not 'overpleased to see his son so popular and of such promise that his subjects place all their hopes in him; and it would almost seem, to speak quite frankly, that the king was growing jealous'.[60]

Nowhere were the differences between father and son greater than in their patronage of the arts. Henry patronized several artists and, despite his own religious views, retained connections with Catholic collectors like Lumley and Northampton. But it was Salisbury who retained closest access to the prince. He wrote to him about the paintings Wotton sent from Venice, including the Palma. The prince's adviser, Sir David Murray, wrote that Henry 'desires that you come before one of clock with your pictures . . . or if you have any business to hinder your journey, that you may send my Lord of Arundel as deputy to set forth the praise of your pictures'.[61] Arundel was another member of the Catholic Howard clan who acted as an artistic adviser to the prince. The viewing was obviously a success: shortly afterwards Palma's picture was to be found in the prince's possession, hanging in the gallery of St James. Painted in Venice, bought by Wotton for Salisbury, Palma's picture arrived in England only to be given away again – to the heir to the English throne.

The year 1610 was a defining one for Henry and his collection. He was invested as Prince of Wales, with a substantial annual income of £80,000 to match his new title as heir to the throne. He could now afford to indulge his interest in art.[62] He quickly appropriated his mother's French painter Isaac Oliver to paint his portrait before a romanticized battlefield, showing him resplendent in his armour and the Order of the Garter.[63] Henry also asked the Tuscan ambassador to London to send him an artist capable of providing his court with the magnificence associated with the Medici dynasty.

In June 1611 the Florentine painter and architect Constantino de' Servi arrived at Greenwich, where Queen Anna, a noted lover of all things Italian, immediately commissioned him to paint her portrait. As he had done with Oliver, Henry reclaimed de' Servi and put him to work at his new palace at Richmond, constructing fountains, summer houses and galleries 'according to the style of Florence'.[64] Henry tried to woo other Italian, French and Dutch artists to London, but this was never easy and he often needed to rely on more native talent. Robert Peake remained his officially appointed court painter and was paid handsomely for his grand portraits of the prince, while Inigo Jones was appointed Surveyor of the Prince's Works, and kept busy with various architectural and theatrical projects.

The ambitious court that surrounded the young prince inspired many of these initiatives. Sir Walter Cope wrote to the new English ambassador to Venice, Sir Dudley Carleton, appointed to replace

Wotton in July 1610. Cope told Carleton, 'If you meet with any ancient Master pieces of paintings at a reasonable hand, you cannot send a thing more gracious, either to the Prince, or to my Lord Treasurer [Salisbury]',[65] – politely reminding him of the need to continue the tradition of dealing in pictures established by Wotton. His letter also suggests that Henry was part of an extensive network of London collectors. Encouraged by Henry's circle, ambassadors, nobles, peers and merchants began sending pictures to Richmond and St James's. German merchants resident in London presented Henry with two paintings by Holbein, while Lady Cumberland and Sir Thomas Cecil discreetly dispatched pictures to the prince's court, although their standard was probably not up to that of the Holbeins and Palmas that arrived from Europe.[66]

Europe provided Henry with his largest donation of pictures in the last years of his life, primarily because of his growing eligibility among the European royal families of the day. King James was in the enviable position of having not one but two sons with whom to arrange politically advantageous marriages. As future heir to the English throne, Henry was particularly sought after. Following his investiture as Prince of Wales, various European powers began to petition for his favour, and the most elegant currency with which to broker political alliances was pictures. The first to enter this game of diplomatic gift-giving was the States-General of the Dutch Republic, the assembly of governors representing the seven provinces in the predominantly Protestant and anti-Spanish northern Low Countries. Following decades of war with Spain, these provinces finally concluded the Twelve Years' Truce that gave them official independence. The States-General looked to England for support as its natural Protestant ally, and in particular to its new young heir. Henry appeared to adopt a far more hawkish approach to the Spanish than his father, who had already opened discussions with Spain to marry Henry off to a Spanish princess.

Alarmed at James's growing friendship with Spain and eager to establish diplomatic and commercial relations with England, the States-General appointed an embassy to travel to London in April 1610. They allocated 16,000 guilders to buy gifts for presentation 'to some of the most important gentleman, having the most direction of affairs'.[67] The embassy chose 'a certain painting made at Haarlem by Master Vroom of the Sea Battle before Gibraltar' against the Spanish. It was deliberately chosen 'to honour the Prince of Wales with it, whose succession is certain and whose friendship is needed by this country'.[68] It was essential to establish good relations with the future king of England, and warn him against political rapprochement with Spain, and this was a particularly appropriate gift for a prince who was becoming increasingly involved in the refurbishment of England's ageing naval fleet.[69]

The Dutch ambassador noted that Henry was delighted at the idea of receiving 'some fine paintings by the best masters in this country'. Emboldened, the ambassadors bought another Vroom, portraying 'a storm at sea, to be given as a present to the Prince of Wales'.[70] The Venetian ambassador recorded that 'the Dutch Ambassadors before leaving presented to the Prince some very finished paintings on canvas. They were painted on purpose to adorn one wall of his gallery.'[71] Henry's advisers had clearly discussed the subject matter and subsequent location of the pictures at some length. Everyone was happy: Henry received a collection of handsome contemporary Dutch paintings and the States-General received key diplomatic concessions from England, including their most pressing demand – the rights to fish off the coast of England.

The gift was hardly an aesthetic coup. Henry received a collection of naval scenes appropriate for the interests of a fifteen-year-old fascinated by warships. But the gift whetted the appetite of Henry's court for Dutch art. The prince's advisers decided to source pictures directly from the art markets and studios of the Low Countries, even though their frustration at closing deals often had its more comical dimensions. Writing from Brill, one of Henry's supporters, Sir Henry Conway, complained to the prince's artistic adviser, Adam Newton, 'I have been seeking to buy some good pieces of painting but this people will as easily be bought out of their habit of drinking as out of their affections for a picture.' Despite his concern at the fondness of the Dutch for both a good painting and a good drink, Conway did concede, 'There was one piece at Rotterdam, for the master workman's sake that made it, of some reputation, and was to be sold, and I glad to hear of a price set upon a piece of work that was ancient and recommended, I bought it.'[72] It's not known what Conway purchased, but his criteria for buying were typical of those of Henry's circle – the painter had to be an acknowledged master, and it helped if the picture was reasonably old and came with a good reputation on the open market. The chances are that Conway's purchase went straight into Henry's newly designed galleries at Richmond and St James's.

Henry also set his sights on pictures and statues from even further afield. His target was Italy, but he soon discovered that the price of Italian art was calculated not in pounds or ducats but in terms of his own value as a husband. Just weeks before the arrival of the Dutch embassy of 1610, King James had opened negotiations for Henry's hand in marriage with diplomatic representatives of Cosimo II, Grand Duke of Tuscany. The complex network of international dynastic alliances provided James with a dilemma. Should he marry Henry off to a Catholic power – Spain, Savoy or Tuscany – or a less powerful Protestant state? The former was more politically and financially attractive, and would retain the delicate balance of power, but it risked domestic opposition, not least from Henry himself, who had 'resolved that two religions should never lie in his bed'.[73] However, Cosimo's Florentine court possessed money, as well as the unparalleled riches of the Medici art collection.

In September 1609 Cosimo dispatched his ambassador Vincenzo Salviati to negotiate a marriage between Henry and Cosimo's sister Princess Caterina. In the midst of discussions, Salviati asked Queen Anna and Henry to choose Florentine works of art for their collections. Henry demurred. He knew his father wanted to marry him off to a Catholic princess despite his religious objections and suspected that such gifts were, as one of his circle later claimed rather dramatically, 'means to enchain the soul of the Prince'.[74] Nothing happened until the following March, by which time the artistic curiosity of Henry and his circle got the better of their political misgivings. One of Henry's advisers approached Ottaviano Lotti with a request for books and pictures from Florence. These included painted angels by Domenico Beccafumi, the Sienese artist and follower of Michelangelo, as well as copies of the series of '*uomini illustri*', or *Famous Men* that formed the centrepiece of the duke's art collection.[75] The precision of the request suggests that someone in Henry's entourage had returned from Italy offering enthusiastic descriptions of these works. This also explains why a month later Henry let it be known that he 'would like some little stucco statues, about a braccia high, that one finds there by worthy men, such as Giovanni Bologna'.[76]

The Florentines stalled because the odds on the marriage between Henry and Caterina had suddenly shortened. Even the Queen appeared to support a Tuscan match, expressing her views through admiration of pictures. In January 1611 Lotti travelled to Greenwich to present Anna with portraits of Cosimo and his wife. The Venetian ambassador reported, 'The Queen favours this match more than any other. On the occasion when the Secretary of the Grand Duke was presenting their Highness' portraits, she even went so far as to let her wish be clearly seen, declaring that she had excellent information about the lady and asking for her portrait.'[77]

Impatient at the delay in his pictures, and determined to prove that he was not reliant upon Florence for artworks, Henry opened negotiations with Europe's other great art market, Venice. This was an astute move, as it inflamed the long-standing rivalry between Venice and Florence, and allowed Henry to extend the English artistic interests in the city begun by Wotton. Until this point Henry received pictures as gifts. He now entered the open market to buy a major consignment. Such an investment required a financier who could buy the pictures in Venice, arrange for their shipment to England and then reclaim the money loaned (at interest) at a later stage. One of the few men wealthy and cosmopolitan enough to undertake such a transaction was Filippo Burlamachi. French by birth but descended from Italian stock, Burlamachi made his money trading in goods as diverse as silk and armaments.[78] The increasing scale and complexity of international trade required financiers like Burlamachi to honour paper transactions, or bills of exchange, for large sums of money. By 1611 Burlamachi was responsible for most of the Jacobean diplomatic corps, paying their salaries overseas then reclaiming the cost through hard currency or political favours from King James and his treasury. He treated pictures in the same way as all his other investments – a profitable if rather bulky commodity to be moved from one country to another.

As a Protestant Franco-Italian, Burlamachi was the ideal Stuart financier. Sir Henry Wotton recommended him to Salisbury as an Italian Protestant, suggesting that Burlamachi, 'upon whose credit I have lived abroad, and to whom I owe upon the point of £1,000', was also capable of delivering secret correspondence, because 'he hath here [in Venice] very safe respondents'.[79] Henry was impressed with his impeccable financial reputation. In 1611 he paid Burlamachi £480 for buying and transporting an unspecified consignment of pictures from Venice. It must have been a substantial collection, because shortly after their arrival the Venetian ambassador Correr wrote that Henry 'is paying special attention to the adorning of a most beautiful gallery of very fine pictures, ancient and modern, the large part brought out of Venice'.[80] Burlamachi's money and international connections allowed Henry to extend his growing collection into Venetian art, and it would not be the last time that the financier underwrote the Stuart family's pursuit of a good picture.

Meanwhile, back in Whitehall the Tuscan match continued to gather momentum. Sensing that he now held the upper hand, Lotti pressed his Florentine superiors for the pictures and statues ordered by Henry, although it wasn't until June 1611 (twenty months after the Prince's request) that the first set of pictures finally arrived. Lotti's account of their reception at Richmond is a remarkable testament to how quickly Henry's court learned to regard and appreciate paintings:

> His Highness spent more than an hour looking at them one by one, some [portraits] he admired that seemed to be of more famous men than others, as Castruccio among the soldiers, Pico della Mirandola among men of letters, Macchiavelli among the politicians and so on with the others. Over the popes, cardinals and saints, he made neither comment or indication, except about a certain type of face, joking in a witty manner, making those around him laugh . . . And His Highness asked me several times about the decoration of their

Highnesses galleries and if there were subject pictures and what kind of statues, and he confirmed his intention of using the aforesaid pictures for his new gallery.[81]

In just over an hour Henry was introduced to some of the key figures in the Florentine Renaissance – Pico, Machiavelli, the Medici popes, as well as its leading artists. In his laughter at the religious images of popes, cardinals and saints, the Protestant prince was beginning to separate art from politics and religion. He could make jokes at such popish idolatry, but still appreciate the skill and craftsmanship of their execution. It was a defining moment in the history of the royal collection. Above all, it revealed Henry's desire to develop a gallery modelled on the Florentine ideal: perfectly positioned, interspersed with statues in a way that would magnify his own fame and magnificence as a discerning prince.

The arrival of the pictures was an artistic coup for Henry's court, but it failed to sway their views on the marriage. In fact, by late summer events beyond their control had shattered any chance of an Anglo-Florentine wedding, since the Pope refused to sanction the union. Furthermore, the prince's circle raised fresh objections to the match, claiming that Cosimo's Medici lineage was distinctly *nouveau* and mercantile, hardly the kind of dynasty into which a future king of England should be marrying. A new contender for Henry's hand had now entered the race. Duke Charles Emmanuel of Savoy was offering the hand of his daughter, the Infanta Maria.[82] Savoy was sandwiched between the imperial powers of France, Spain and the papacy, and although Catholic it was keen to retain the kind of political autonomy that King James also sought for England. Savoy offered the only realistic chance of a face-saving match for Henry, and the situation was compounded by James's decision to marry Henry's sister, Elizabeth, to Frederick V, Elector Palatine of the Rhine, the head of the League of Protestant Princes in central Europe. By the summer of 1612 the Palatine marriage treaty was agreed, and Savoy clinched agreement for a marriage with Henry by offering a dowry of 800,000 crowns.

Unfortunately, nobody told the Florentines. At the end of May

Lotti's replacement, Andrea Cioli, arrived in London with the consignment of statues requested by Henry. The Tuscan court ordered Pietro Tacca, one of Giovanni Bologna's assistants, to cast bronzes, including ten from originals made by his old master. On 28 June Cioli travelled by coach to Richmond Palace, while the statues arrived separately by barge. The Florentine was taken through a secret garden and up a spiral staircase into the prince's gallery. As the presentation was about to take place, Henry's advisers admitted that a marital agreement had been reached with Savoy. At this moment, Henry entered the gallery to admire his new acquisitions. His delight was evident. Cioli reported that he picked up one of the statues and kissed it. He then proceeded to handle each one of the statues in turn. Picking up a small bronze horse, one of Henry's advisers suggested, 'This will be good for the Duke of York', the young Prince Charles. With the superiority of the first-born, Henry instantly dismissed the suggestion, replying, 'No, no, I want everything for myself.'[83] Little did Henry realize that this gift would mark the apex of his art collection, and that the horse would be one of the last precious objects he held before his sudden death five months later. It is an even greater irony that it would be Charles who came to present the bronze statue to his dying brother.

The prince's court thanked the Florentines for the statues and then dismissed them. By the autumn of 1612 the Tuscan match was dead. James quickly moved to ratify the terms of a marriage treaty with Savoy, although Henry's court remained reluctant to accept yet another Catholic match. As James and his Privy Council met to agree terms, Henry took to his bed with the beginnings of a fever, begging the king to postpone a decision until after his recovery.

It never happened. Henry's death on 6 November put an end to all talk of marriage. The prince's many biographers have seen his death as a national tragedy, the end of a brief resurgence in English artistic and political life. However, it was probably fortunate. If Henry had lived, James would have insisted on the publicly unpopular Savoy match, whatever the prince's wishes. Henry's art collecting in the last two years of his life is rightly celebrated and the diversity of his pictures was certainly impressive. But he followed artistic fashions rather than setting them. Many of his pictures were politically motivated gifts over which he had little or no control, and most of these were studio pictures or copies. Only a handful of pictures can be incontrovertibly ascribed to Henry's collection, and his advisers and supporters owned many of the paintings traditionally believed to belong to him.

Henry was the logical beneficiary of the first wave of Jacobean travellers returning from Europe with pictures, statues, drawings and accounts of the magnificence of the Renaissance courts of France and Italy. He wanted to emulate this magnificence as a ruler first and a collector second. Today the word 'magnificence' has lost much of its original classical sense, but in the Renaissance it had a very specific meaning. Aristotle argued that 'the magnificent man is like an artist: for he can see what is fitting and spend large sums tastefully'. Aristotle's fifteenth-century Italian translators provided dynasties like the Medici with an explanation of how magnificence could represent the public good, as a sign of the authority and fine judgement of the magnificent ruler. According to Aristotle, 'the magnificent man spends not on himself but on public objects',[84] but this was certainly not a feature of Henry's collecting, or that of his brother, Charles, who kept it firmly within the private rooms of the royal palaces.

In his quest to become a leading player on the international political stage, Henry also tried (but failed) to match his art collection with that of other European monarchs, not just in cost and rarity but also in the discernment that went into it. This is why Henry's court began to value the fame and reputation of artists, and the rarity or skill with which their works were executed. What was new about Henry's collecting was its ability to distinguish between a painting's form and style and its explicit content. As a resolutely Protestant prince, Henry was nonetheless quite happy to buy and publicly admire paintings by Catholic artists representing Catholic themes. It was possible in this new atmosphere to admire a picture for its composition, execution and colouring notwithstanding the religious or ideological position of its maker, patron or subject matter.

Henry's death in November 1612 changed everything. So many plans were aborted upon the news, including an order of statues from Florence that, like Henry's prospective bride, never reached its destination. Sir Dudley Carleton recorded that Henry had placed one final order in the summer. This included a request for a copy of Michelangelo's ever-youthful David, as well as 'a royal present now prepared by the Grand Duke to be sent to the Prince, which was of the 12 labours of Hercules in statues of brass set upon so many pillars of ebony'.[85] Since Cosimo had spent years vainly labouring to secure Henry's assent to a Florentine match, his gift had seemed particularly appropriate. Poignantly, it never arrived. Instead, the weight of England's expectation shifted on to the frail shoulders of Henry's younger brother, Charles Stuart.

✧

CHAPTER TWO

DEBTS AND DISCREDITS

WITH THE DEATH OF Prince Henry, the collecting of art in England reached a crossroads. Fearing its continuing criticism of his political authority, King James quickly dissolved what remained of Henry's household. Some members of Henry's staff petitioned to retain their positions under Prince Charles, including Henry's French riding master, Pierre Antoine Bourdin, whom Charles rewarded with the position of equerry.[1] Others assumed that Charles lacked the interest or the resources to build on his brother's artistic patronage and retired to their country estates, taking their pictures with them. Some even followed the recently departed Princess Elizabeth to her new court in Heidelberg, including Henry's former Keeper of the Cabinet Room at St James's, Abraham van der Doort.[2]

The dispersal of Henry's household not only halted art collecting at St James's and Richmond but also led to the dispersal and disappearance of some of the dead prince's art collection. Without a will or detailed inventory of his household, matters quickly turned unpleasant. Members of his retinue were accused of appropriating precious plate, jewels and medals from the collection, protesting in their defence that these were royal gifts.[3] Some courtiers tried to prevent the king claiming his dead son's valuable collection by minimizing accounts of its value, in an attempt to keep the collection intact. The letter writer John Chamberlain placed a rough estimation on the prince's goods (including artworks), calculating that 'the Prince's debts are but nine thousand pound, and his moveables amount to much more, specially his horses and pictures which are many and rare'.[4] The collection was worth well over £1,000. However, when Henry's auditor, Richard Connock, submitted an inventory of Henry's goods to the king, he deliberately deleted references to Henry's 'pictures, plate, and sylven vessell, rich hangings, and furniture of his house with other things of great worth, not here valued'.[5] If this was a conscious attempt to stop James selling and dispersing the prince's collection, it worked. James sought more solutions to his financial problems than the liquidation of Henry's art collection, which stood neglected and forgotten in the galleries of St James's and Richmond palaces.

One person who did take pictures from Henry's collection was his mother, Queen Anna. The later inventories of her pictures hanging at Oatlands, Greenwich and Denmark House record the transfer of many of Henry's pictures, including some of the seascapes presented to him by the States-General in 1610.[6] Anna may have felt a strong emotional attachment to these pictures as commemorative objects of her dead son. Nevertheless, she soon appropriated them for her own collection, beginning a long history of their circulation over the subsequent decades.

The one place where the acquisition of art looked least likely to take root was at Prince Charles's newly established court at St James's. Henry was a tough act to follow and Charles hardly seemed up to the task. According to Hamon L'Estrange, 'The gallantry of Henry's heroic spirit tended somewhat to the disadvantage, and extenuation of Charles his glory.' Where Henry was 'forward, and enterprising', Charles was 'of a studious, and retired spirit'.[7] Such disparaging comparisons were painfully clear to see in newly commissioned portraits of Prince Charles. Where Henry stretched the limits of the genre, Charles's image appeared to step back into the conventions of sixteenth-century portraiture. The official 1613 engraving of the Duke of York noticeably failed to create the kind of charismatic image that Peake and Oliver successfully devised for Henry. Charles looks more like a ghostly illustration of his dead brother. Modelled on Oliver's miniature completed a year before, it repeats the pose, elaborate ruff and ribbon of his brother's portrait, but the comparison ends there. Charles stares out with wary, hollow eyes. Visibly anxious at his sudden elevation to heir to the throne, he looks sick and weary, a child at once both older and younger than his thirteen years. The background to Henry's miniature confidently predicts his future in scenes of warfare and heroic deeds; in the engraving of Charles, the future remains uncertain, a disquieting blank.

It was impossible for Charles to act like a patron of the arts when he was not even treated like an heir to the throne. His 'young and sickly'[8] disposition did nothing to inspire public confidence and many worried that he would soon follow his brother to an early death. Such fears cultivated the lack of ceremony and authority accorded to the new heir. Money was in such short supply following Elizabeth's wedding that Charles was not anointed Prince of Wales for another three years. Some probably thought the investment not worth the while until it was certain he would reach his majority. Chamberlain observed that James 'gives order that the young Prince be kept within a stricter compass than the former, and not to exceed his ordinary in diet or followers'.[9] James needed to save money but also to prevent St James's turning into another alternative court. The result was a severe reduction in finances and retinue. Charles inherited just twenty-five of Henry's original household of 250 followers.[10] James replaced many of Henry's advisers with his own appointments and slashed the household's annual budget.

Having moved into St James's, but without Henry's substantial income, Charles could neither live up to the saintly reputation of his dead brother nor meet the demands placed on him by an increasingly insecure father. His sister gone and his brother dead, Charles had only their portraits for company. His was a world of shadowy ghosts, a political twilight in which he was more concerned to correct his stammer and avoid the poisoning that rumours suggested were responsible for his brother's death than build an impressive art collection.[11]

In the hiatus caused by Henry's death, the collecting of art in England quickly spread beyond the confines of the royal courts of Whitehall. A number of advisers and political mentors had shaped Henry's interest in pictures, establishing for him a network of financiers, agents, dealers and artists across Europe. The prince's death only intensified competition for pictures among a larger group of aristocratic collectors. Many saw the political benefits of presenting Henry with pictures for his galleries. A younger generation of Jacobean gentlemen emerged who automatically assumed that the collecting and display of art were essential to their social status, regardless of what happened under the new Prince of Wales.

No one was quicker to turn the tragedy of Henry's death into an artistic opportunity than one of his closest advisers, Thomas Howard, 2nd Earl of Arundel. He was part of the art-loving Howard dynasty that included Lord Lumley and the Earl of Northampton and that supplied Henry with one of the earliest pictures to grace his new gallery in St James's. Eager to join the stream of Englishmen heading for Italy, Arundel was granted permission to travel abroad just months before Henry's death. Within weeks he was in Brussels conversing with the greatest painter of his day, Peter Paul Rubens. Arundel commissioned a portrait from Rubens (now lost), starting a relationship that would last until the painter's death in 1640, as well as making the acquaintance of Rubens's brilliant young pupil Anthony Van Dyck, before heading off to his ultimate destination – Italy.

The subsequent trip was to prove a turning point in seventeenth-century English cultural life. Arundel's entourage included his wife, Aletheia Talbot, Countess of Arundel. Ferociously independent and intelligent, Lady Arundel shared her husband's fascination with the arts and threw herself into the trip with gusto. They were accompanied by the brilliant but mercurial former Surveyor of the Prince's Works, the architect, theatre designer and draughtsman Inigo Jones. Arundel headed for the Continent with an inheritance that would allow him to compete with the finest patrons in Europe when it came to the buying and commissioning of art. Equipped with more modest means – a sack of Italian books on the Renaissance, and a sharp eye for architectural and theatrical styles that could be translated back into the English architectural vernacular – Jones set off for Italy.

In Venice Arundel toured palaces and galleries with Ambassador Carleton. In Vicenza he and Jones admired the classical proportions of the architecture of Andrea Palladio. As he walked around Palladio's elegant villas, Jones filled the margins of his copy of Palladio's *I Quattro Libri* with copious notes.[12] Travelling on to Bologna, Arundel visited its fantastic *studioli*, cabinets of curiosity stuffed with exotic flora and fauna. By Christmas 1613 he reached his ultimate destination: Rome, the Eternal City. He stayed as the guest of the city's most renowned patrons of the arts, and with Jones at his side he clambered over classical ruins, watched the spectacular rebuilding of the city and marvelled at the frescoes and altarpieces of Annibale Carracci, Paul Bril, Guido Reni and the artist whose works had decisively changed the direction of Roman art, Michelangelo Merisi da Caravaggio. While Jones took notes on the fantastic Roman masques, Arundel plunged into the labyrinthine Roman art world, commissioning sculptures to be shipped back to England.[13]

As Arundel and his wife rested in Padua, Jones travelled to the Duchy of Mantua.[14] The city housed the Gonzaga dynasty's art collection in the Palazzo Ducale and the Palazzo del Te, featuring works by the two artists most closely associated with Mantua, Andrea Mantegna and Giulio Romano. Jones saw Giulio as a kindred spirit, someone who craved the Mantuan court's approbation as painter, sculptor and architect. He knew that Giulio's reputation had even reached Shakespeare's stage. In *The Winter's Tale* (*c.* 1609–11) Hermione's 'statue' is said to be 'newly performed [completed] by that rare Italian master, Julio Romano'.[15]

Having reconnoitred Vicenza with his copy of Palladio, Jones explored Mantua with the aid of the bible of Renaissance art, Giorgio Vasari's *Lives of the Artists*. Vasari's description of Giulio led Jones down the halls and through the rooms of the Te, where he scribbled down what he saw in the margins of his book. For Jones, the building of the Te represented an architectural master-class. Each solution to a particular problem was eagerly absorbed: 'The Te a place of stables first,' noted Jones. 'Giulio saves the old walls' and builds 'columns bases and capitols of brick'.[16] Jones examined the palace's artful perspective, its elegant vistas, the stuccoed friezes and fantastic frescoes. One word is repeatedly used to define Giulio's style: the vaults are described as decorated in 'new and extravagant ornament', while rooms are 'extravagantly done'.

Jones was looking at what Vasari meant when he wrote that Giulio's innovation was to introduce a 'new and extravagant manner'[17] of artistic expression. It was the birth of this style that later art historians would claim signalled the death of the pure, classical style of the Italian Renaissance. They also gave it a name: the baroque.

What Arundel and Jones saw on their travels throughout 1613–14 was the birth of this style. Arundel glimpsed it in Antwerp in the ripe, lustrous flesh of Rubens's classical nudes. Both men saw it in Rome in the scenes of death and desire that loomed out of the shadows in Caravaggio's luminous altarpieces. And there it was in the excessive *trompe l'oeil* of Giulio Romano's Palazzo del Te, with its fantastic tableaux of bacchanalian riots and scenes of monstrous destruction. This was an exuberant, erotic, sometimes grotesque and violent artistic style from which England had been sheltered for decades. For Arundel and Jones, the shock of the new in all its vivid colour, elaborate shape and daring subject matter meant that there was no going back to the precious miniatures and stiff, naive portraits imprisoned in dark, wooden English country houses.

On his return to London in late 1614, Arundel quickly discovered that the political climate had worsened considerably in his absence. James's court was sinking into factional intrigue and relations with Parliament had broken down. Unable to extract more money from a critical Commons, James dissolved the so-called 'Addled Parliament' after just nine weeks. The king's problems were compounded by his cultivation of cronyism. And by 1614 one particular favourite had come to exercise almost complete domination over court life, if not the king himself.

The young Scottish noble Robert Carr first caught the king's eye in 1607. Within months he was knighted and appointed a gentleman of the royal bedchamber. He was showered with royal gifts of jewels, land, estates and titles.[18] By November 1613 Carr's income equalled that of Prince Henry at the time of his sudden death, and he was formally created Earl of Somerset in an elaborate ceremony held at the Banqueting House. Not surprisingly, Queen Anna and Prince Henry resented the intrusion of this upstart noble into their lives. Anna tried but failed to block his earldom, while Charles's retinue regarded his rise to power as a threat to the prince's authority. However, they were powerless to prevent the ambitious Somerset manoeuvring himself into a position of almost unassailable power. He became secretary to the king, ensuring that all diplomatic correspondence as well as requests for public employment went through him. This allowed him to accept cash in exchange for promotions and establish a network of loyal and dependent clients.

Somerset was particularly assiduous in courting an alliance with the Howard faction, and in 1613 he proposed marriage to the daughter of Thomas Howard, Earl of Suffolk, niece of Henry Howard, Earl of Northampton. Somerset appears to have genu-inely fallen for the beautiful Frances, but there was just one problem. Frances was already married to Robert Devereux, 3rd Earl of Essex. To the astonishment of the court, she submitted a petition requesting nullification of her marriage on the grounds of Essex's sexual impotence. James appointed a committee to consider the matter. The subsequent case was a sensation. The committee questioned Essex on the finer details of his alleged impotence and premature ejaculation, while Northampton taunted Essex as 'my good lord the gelding'. Essex responded by informing the com-mittee that he called several witnesses into his bedroom, 'and taking up his shirt, did show them all so able and extraordinarily sufficient matter, that they all cried out shame of his lady'.[19]

Speculation that Somerset and the Howards concocted the annulment was never fully resolved. Whatever the truth, nobody came out of the hearing with any dignity, least of all Somerset, whose decision to pursue first the marriage and then the annulment looked increasingly ill-judged. Frances Howard's personal reputa-tion was destroyed, as court gossip and scurrilous verses portrayed her as everything from a disobedient wife to a sexually voracious witch. Even the king was criticized for swaying proceedings in favour of Somerset. James pushed for a swift annulment, which was finally granted in September 1613.

The Earl of Somerset and Frances Howard were married three months later in a spectacular wedding service held at Westminster.

Somerset was now one of the most powerful men in England and was acutely aware of the need for an art collection appropriate to his status. In his rise to political prominence he had watched both Prince Henry and Northampton use their art collections as a way of drawing attention to their social status and political attitudes. He was also aware that his enemies and rivals at court were accumulating significant collections of pictures from English agents abroad. These included William Herbert, Earl of Pembroke, and Shakespeare's patron Henry Wriothesley, Earl of Southampton.

Somerset quickly made it known he was in the market for an art collection. Prince Henry's experiences showed that the acquisition of art required an extended network of artists, agents, diplomats and advisers. As a result, Somerset's secretary, Sir Thomas Overbury, opened negotiations with English diplomats abroad, copying the methods used by St James's to break into the European art world. In September 1612 Overbury wrote to William Trumbull, the English diplomatic agent at Brussels, informing him that Somerset considered it 'acceptable service' if 'upon the death of any great men in that country' Trumbull could purchase 'any good bargain of excellent hangings [tapestries] at the second hand, or pictures or any household stuff which they have there better than ours'.[20] The implication was clear. Trumbull would be richly rewarded if he could provide Somerset with dead men's tapestries or second-hand pictures bought at public auction.

Trumbull soon got the measure of Somerset's interests. Writing to ask about his preference for tapestries, Trumbull enquired 'whether you will have bespoke, or great imagery ... remember where you have seen any fair modern hangings in England; and to inquire where they were made; I will get you the like'.[21] Trumbull counselled Somerset to buy cheap off-the-peg tapestries based on what he had seen in England, as if he were buying the Stuart equivalent to rolls of wallpaper. This was delightfully circumspect advice that perfectly grasped Somerset's tastes.

Others quickly flocked to serve Somerset's interests, although not everyone was as quick at understanding what the favourite wanted. By 1615 Sir Henry Wotton was acting ambassador-extraordinary to the Dutch Republic in The Hague, after being recalled from Venice in 1610. Having lost the patronage of the recently deceased Salisbury and Prince Henry, he saw the opportunity to serve Somerset. No longer able to procure Italian pictures, he decided to send the favourite a Dutch painting. It was accompanied by a typically pompous letter discussing the relative merits of Dutch and Italian art:

> I am bold by this gentleman to entertain your Lordship with a piece of perspective which is a very busy kind of work and therefore think patient and phlegmatic hands do commonly more excel therein than Italians who rather affect draughts of spirit and action. But this piece which I now send hath a little life more than ordinary by addition of the personages which made me make a choice of it for your better delectation.[22]

It was a clever attempt to recommend the picture to Somerset, but Wotton misjudged his prospective patron's interests. Salisbury would have grasped such fine distinctions between Dutch and Italian art, but they were clearly lost on Somerset. He took the picture but did not adopt Wotton as his art agent. Wotton probably suspected that he could not provide the favourite with what he really wanted – the kind of Italian pictures from Venice that Wotton gave Salisbury, but which he could no longer procure in the Low Countries.

Instead, Somerset turned to a new supplier, Wotton's diplomatic successor in Venice, Sir Dudley Carleton. His posting to Venice in 1610 gave Carleton an opportunity to distinguish himself politically, as well as providing his patrons back home with top-quality Venetian art.[23] Upon arriving in Venice, Carleton swiftly began to accumulate a substantial consignment of pictures and statues for shipment back to England. However, the shipment wasn't originally meant for Somerset. Carleton was told to continue the tradition of finding pictures for Salisbury and Prince Henry, the intended recipient of Carleton's buying spree. When news of the deaths of first Salisbury and then Henry reached Venice in December 1612, Carleton switched his political allegiance, and with it the ultimate destination of his precious merchandise. The intended recipient was now Somerset.[24]

Carleton's diplomatic salary of around £1,200 a year plus travel expenses was hardly equal to the scale and cost of the collection. With no guarantee of financial reimbursement from London, he needed to borrow money to finance its purchase and transportation. Prince Henry had used the Italian financier Filippo Burlamachi to finance his art deals, but Carleton took a risk on Daniel Nys, a French-born entrepreneur and resident of Venice. Nys was a successful but unpredictable businessman, renowned for his flattery, fiery temper and convoluted business deals. He trafficked in anything that promised to make him a substantial profit, be it arms, intelligence, pictures or statues. Nevertheless, his wealth and connections made him a logical choice to lend money and advise Carleton on what to buy. It was a decision that the ambassador would come to regret.

By early 1615 Carleton had acquired an impressive selection of modern Venetian paintings, as well as twenty-nine crates containing nearly 100 classical statues, bought as a ready-made collection from Nys.[25] Apollo, Jupiter, Hercules, Brutus, Cicero, Julius Caesar – these were just what the aspirant Somerset required, alongside more playful and erotic pieces – Diana, Ganymede, Cupid, as well as various scenes of satyrs, youths and scenes of 'Love recumbent'. The cost to Carleton of all this classical elegance was 2,000 Venetian ducats. At the prevailing exchange rate of £1 to four ducats, this represented a potentially hazardous investment of £500 – nearly half Carleton's annual salary.[26] Carleton obviously thought it was worth the risk. He obtained nearly 100 statues without spending any money. A notional price of 2,000 ducats was placed on the collection by Nys. This presumably included the financier's cut for buying the statues, as well as interest charged against the final amount owed by Carleton once they were sold on to Somerset in London.

Nys also provided Carleton with funds and advice on the acquisition of two crates of pictures by Venetian painters. Carleton bought six paintings by Tintoretto, five by Veronese, two by Bassano and one each by Schiavone and Titian.[27] These were the kind of pictures that Jones and Arundel saw on their travels through Italy. They included scenes from biblical and classical history: the Oriental exoticism of Tintoretto's *Queen of Sheba*, his vertiginous painting of the classical *Labyrinth*, Titian's erotic *Venus*, and Bassano's dramatic scenes of *Creation* and *The Beheading of St John the Baptist*. Carleton put a figure of over £300 on the cost of these fifteen pictures. Either this was a brilliant deal or Nys was selling the inexperienced Englishman studio copies of original works. As many of the pictures have since disappeared, it is difficult to tell, but Carleton certainly seemed happy enough with the arrangement.

By April the statues and pictures were packed, insured and loaded on board the *Marigold*, bound for London. They arrived in June and were sent to Somerset's private apartments in Whitehall. For Somerset, their arrival was a triumph. Almost by default he acquired a substantial collection of classical statues and modern Italian paintings, something that even Prince Henry had failed to achieve.

Then disaster struck. Throughout 1615 interests hostile to Somerset united to mount a serious challenge to his grip on power. The atmosphere in Whitehall became increasingly febrile. 'Never,' observed one commentator, 'was the court fuller of faction.'[28] A plot was hatched to replace Somerset with another favourite. The rather surprising candidate was George Villiers, the handsome but obscure son of a Leicestershire gentleman. The scheme was to destroy Somerset by substituting Villiers in the king's affections. Remarkably, it began to work. And worse, Somerset's enemies were also circulating even more damaging rumours – that Somerset and his new wife, Frances, were implicated in murder.

Somerset's secretary, Sir Thomas Overbury, had been instrumental in establishing his master's early links with the European art market but was opposed to Somerset's marriage to Frances on the grounds that it tied his master too closely to the Howard faction. Incensed at Overbury's opposition to the marriage, James engineered his removal to the Tower, where he died in autumn 1613. In July 1615 Somerset's enemies stumbled upon evidence that Frances Howard had conspired to poison Overbury. The unfortunate man was fed poisoned jellies and cakes, and was finally dispatched with the application of a poisoned enema. James immediately launched an investigation, and in October Somerset and his wife were placed under arrest for murder.

The subsequent court case proved even more sensational than Frances's divorce proceedings. Somerset was imprisoned in the Tower and was formally charged with murder alongside his pregnant wife in early 1616. The couple were brought to trial in May 1616 and found guilty. Although James stayed their execution, they were indefinitely confined to the Tower, where they remained until 1624.

Not everyone was delighted with Somerset's fall. When news of his arrest reached Sir Dudley Carleton, he was horrified. With one patron already dead, he could only watch as another faced conviction for murder. Even worse, Carleton had not been paid for the pictures and statues now in Somerset's Whitehall apartments. He had obviously hoped for a lucrative promotion or similar payment in kind for providing such an impressive collection. As a result he had not immediately pursued a cash settlement on his personal investment. As Somerset's predicament deteriorated, the alarmed Carleton grasped the opportunity of a diplomatic recall and hurried back to London to try to salvage his investment. By the time he reached London, Somerset was doomed and all hope of payment gone. With mounting horror, Carleton learned that Somerset's belongings, including his pictures, were to be impounded, and Sir Henry Fanshawe and John Osborne were ordered to make an inventory of Somerset's Whitehall apartments.

Suddenly, Carleton's luck changed. Fanshawe and Osborne were persuaded to identify his pictures among Somerset's possessions and remove them before the king claimed them. Entering the 'Bowling ally', they marked his pictures with a cross and sent them to Carleton, who soon recovered the outstanding pictures, as well as his statues. All he had to do now was to find another buyer for them. The pictures were lodged at the residence of John Fortry, a merchant who handled Daniel Nys's accounts in London. Carleton still owed Nys the money for both the pictures and the statues, and Fortry was now holding them as security to ensure that Nys would at least get something back on the deal. Over the next few weeks Fortry's house was turned into an art gallery as Carleton directed attempts to sell the pictures. In March the hapless ambassador was promoted to the English embassy in The Hague, an acknowledgement of his diplomatic skill in Venice. But this only made attempts to dispose of his collection even harder. His solution was to appoint Edward Sherburn, former secretary to Salisbury, to act as his agent. Carleton told Sherburn to approach the only man wealthy and discerning enough to buy the collection: his old friend Arundel.

In April Sherburn excitedly wrote to Carleton, having finally enticed Arundel to a viewing. 'I have attended my Lord of Arundel to Mr. Fortry his house,' he reported, 'where his Lordship with Mr. Inigo Jones, having fully reviewed the pictures . . . is passing desirous to deal for the half of them'.[29] Just as on his trips abroad, Arundel brought Inigo Jones along to assess the quality of Carleton's pictures. Carleton and Arundel were far too experienced to close a straightforward deal for cash and elaborate negotiations began. Arundel arrived with another collector with experience of European art, Henry, Lord Danvers, a former member of Prince Henry's circle. Both men offered to buy half the collection each. Arundel also showed interest in Carleton's statues, which were also on the market. Sherburn wrote that Arundel 'hath now accepted of the Jupiter's head', which Carleton sacrificed from his consignment as bait, 'and hath placed it in his utmost garden so opposite to the Gallery doors, as being open, so soon as you enter into the first Garden, you have the head in your eye all the way'.[30] This image was so compelling that Daniel Mytens used it as the basis for his portrait of Arundel seated in front of his sculpture garden at Arundel House.

With Carleton away, Sherburn was no match for the experienced Arundel, who proceeded to run rings round the poor secretary. Arundel used Danvers as a stalking horse to split the bidding. Carleton was so anxious to keep Danvers interested in the pictures that he gave him at least one painting for free, Bassano's *Creation of the Animals*. Danvers found it 'too grave for my use', hoping instead to swap it for more exciting hunting scenes, or what he called 'toys fit to furnish a lodge'.[31] Each man agreed a price for six pictures each. Sherburn then informed Carleton that

'Arundel is content to take all the pictures (I would he were of the same mind for the statues) to himself', but sure enough Danvers had withdrawn. Sherburn awaited instructions 'when to attend his Lordship for the money, which so soon as I shall receive, I will repay to Mr. Fortry to the use of Monsieur Nys'.[32] If Arundel was responsible for Danvers's withdrawal, it was a typically ruthless manoeuvre to acquire the pictures at a knockdown price. He still refused to show interest in the statues in the hope of getting them cheaply; perhaps he knew that Carleton needed to raise money quickly to settle some of his debts with Nys.

Carleton now faced a serious crisis. Arundel had offered £200 for twelve paintings. The rest appear to have gone to Danvers. With Danvers out of the running, Carleton had no option but to accept Arundel's offer. Even worse, Sherburn now counselled him that 'Mr. Chamberlain adviseth me, if they be not fetched away' by Arundel immediately they would have to be sent to Carleton in The Hague, 'because he hears a rumour that your Lordship gave all these pictures to my Lord of Somerset'.[33] If Carleton had given the pictures to Somerset, then they were now the property of the king, who could reclaim them at any moment and Carleton would lose everything.

Unfortunately there was even worse news. Two days later Sherburn wrote, 'I omitted in my last, to tell your Lordship that my Lord Roos hath spoiled the sale of your statues.' The eccentric William Cecil, Lord Roos, a rival collector of classical sculpture, had 'now in an humour (and I may say an ill one)' given his entire sculpture collection to Arundel, 'which hath exceedingly beautified his gallery'.[34] Carleton had no choice but to ship his statues to The Hague to look for yet another buyer, and get his £200 from Arundel before the king appropriated his pictures.

A relieved Sherburn wrote to Carleton on 20 July 1616 to inform him that he had finally 'parted with the pictures' and received payment of £200.[35] The money went straight to Nys via Fortry; Carleton didn't see a penny of it. The whole episode proved to be a costly and politically embarrassing fiasco. Carleton secured just over £200 on the sale of the pictures, but he still owed over £100 for their original acquisition.[36] He fell into the trap that would ensnare many subsequent art dealers: the ambiguous ownership of international artworks in transit. Carleton paid Nys for the pictures, but this involved deferred payment made through bills of exchange. Somerset's fall allowed various interested parties to lay claim to ownership of part or all of the collection, from Nys and Carleton to the king himself. Carleton managed to salvage his reputation by reclaiming the pictures, but this was not the last time that uncertainty over financial acquisition and ownership would threaten the reputation of an English collector.

Although the whole episode seriously embarrassed Carleton, it excited even greater interest in collecting across London. Carleton proved that it was possible to obtain financial backing from abroad to fund the purchase and transportation of a significant consignment of artworks, unlike the more limited acquisitions of Arundel and Prince Henry's circle. The collapse of the deal also led to the dispersal of a distinguished collection of Italian art across London. Both Arundel and Danvers directly profited, while others appraised the pictures and statues. Some were quietly absorbed into other collections, including the royal household.

A dejected Carleton arrived in The Hague in March 1617 having sold his pictures at a loss but still in possession of his statues. Or so he thought. Their arrival brought further problems. He discovered another occupational hazard of transporting expensive art objects across land and sea: 'I find some of my heads wanting,' he told Chamberlain. Seven statues were missing from the consignment. Carleton concluded that they were 'purloined either in the custom house or the stilliard',[37] where most foreign merchants traded in London. He pointed the finger at Sherburn, responsible for their original transportation between Venice and London. Sherburn protested his innocence, pointing out that he was the first to draw attention to the discrepancy between the original inventory and what arrived in London. He concluded that the missing statues were 'either lost or left behind, unpacked at Venice, or else miscarried'. It was obvious to all concerned what had happened to the missing heads. The opportunistic Daniel Nys had taken them before they ever left Venice. Carleton had been outmanoeuvred by his own dealer.

As much as Somerset's acquisitions of expensive possessions determined his rise, so their sequestration and redistribution sealed his fall. In stripping him of his estate and possessions, James denuded him of the identity he had fashioned for himself as royal favourite. It was a harsh but fundamental feature of English aristocratic life, and in this instance its primary beneficiary was Somerset's former ally Arundel. On 1 November 1616 Sherburn wrote to Carleton:

> The chief business that now we have here, is the preparation for the Prince his creation, which doth hold on Monday next, and this day my Lord of Arundel had the honour to be made Earl Marshall during the time of this ceremony and some do say it may be longer; his Majesty hath also bestowed upon his Lordship all my Lord of Somerset's pictures, which are valued at the least worth £1,000.[38]

Arundel not only acquired Carleton's pictures cheaply and Roos's statues for nothing but also inherited what remained of Somerset's confiscated art collection, and assumed the title of Earl Marshal, making him head of the English nobility. Just three days later, Arundel led the procession through Whitehall that installed the sixteen-year-old Charles Stuart as Prince of Wales. The Earl was now one of the most powerful men in England, as well as one of its most distinguished collectors.

Somerset's fall transformed the balance of political as well as cultural power in Whitehall. Charles's investiture convinced many that he would now inherit the crown, encouraging counsellors and artists to petition for posts at St James's, which gradually regained some of its political importance. Arundel's advance was tempered by the political decline of the Howard dynasty following the Overbury scandal. Even more significant was the growing political influence of James's new favourite, George Villiers.

The anti-Howard faction had manipulated Villiers's spectacular rise to power, and watched with satisfaction as the new favourite increasingly impeded the political advancement of the Howards. Unlike Somerset, Villiers possessed a natural grace and charm, smoothly playing factions off against each other, appointing friends and family to positions at court. Despite his beauty, Villiers was no fool. He was a ruthless and skilled administrator who soon built an elaborate network of patronage that cemented his position at the heart of the royal court. In pursuit of even further advancement, Villiers also eclipsed Somerset by developing a close physical (and probably sexual) relationship with James. Courtiers noted the 'marks of extraordinary affection'[39] the king displayed towards Villiers, whom contemporaries described as 'the handsomest-bodied man of England'.[40] James even went so far as to tell his counsellors, 'just as Christ had his John, so he, James, had his George'.[41]

William Larkin's 1616 portrait shows that Villiers knew how to exploit these comments to fashion a personal iconography of power. The portrait was painted to commemorate the twenty-four-year-old's installation as Knight of the Garter. Larkin clothed Villiers in the elaborate finery appropriate to his ascent from rural gentry to Jacobean nobility, culminating in the Great George that hangs from the chain around his neck. Another Villiers-watcher could have been gazing at Larkin's portrait when he described him as 'full of delicacy and handsome features; yea, his hands and face seemed to me especially effeminate and curious'.[42] This was the effect that Villiers sought to create – as vain and shallow as the layer of paint on Larkin's canvas, a physically beautiful but intellectually innocuous poseur, sexually irresistible but politically harmless. Yet this was a deliberate manipulation and careful dissemination of his image, the first of eighty commissioned portraits of the favourite, who grasped the need to control and synchronize the personal portrait with political circumstances much better than either James or Somerset, and long before Charles.[43]

As Villiers strengthened his grip on power and the prince's court began to flex its political muscles, diplomats abroad continued to buy pictures and speculate over where to pledge their political allegiance. Sir Dudley Carleton had more to worry about than most. He returned to The Hague with twenty-nine crates of unwanted classical statues and no patron. Undeterred, he endeavoured to find a way back into the lucrative but treacherous art world. Help came in the shape of two of the most notorious English Catholic exiles in Europe, Sir Tobie Matthew and George Gage. Matthew was the son of a former archbishop of Canterbury, described by Horace Walpole as 'one of those heteroclite animals who finds his place anywhere'.[44] Gage was a more enigmatic figure, trusted by the king and employed on various diplomatic embassies to Catholic states. Having befriended Arundel in Rome in 1614, both men were ordained as priests and spent their time moving around Europe, building up a formidable knowledge of European art.[45]

After the Somerset fiasco, Carleton's main obstacle was lack of capital. Resourceful as ever, he employed Gage and Matthew to open negotiations with Rubens, who had expressed an interest in Carleton's antique statues.[46] In March 1618 Rubens wrote to Carleton that '[h]aving learned from various persons of the rare collection of antiquities which Your Excellency has gathered together', he was prepared to 'make some exchange of these marbles for pictures by my hand'.[47]

Carleton accepted with alacrity. He valued the collection at 6,000 florins, about £500[48] – the same price Nys had placed on the statues three years earlier. Rubens responded by proposing 'to offer Your Excellency of the pictures by my hand . . . to the value of 6,000 florins, at current cash prices, for all those antiquities in Your Excellency's house'.[49] He offered twelve pictures portraying classical and biblical scenes, all individually priced in florins, half identified as 'Original, by my hand', the rest studio pictures 'done by one of my pupils, but the whole retouched by my hand'.[50]

Negotiations now began in earnest. Carleton was unhappy with Rubens's attempt to include inferior studio works in the deal. He agreed to take six – 'the Prometheus, the Daniel, the Leopards, the Leda, the St Peter and the St Sebastian' – worth 3,000 florins in total, and rejected the other half, asking instead for the balance of the price of the statues in tapestries portraying the *Triumph of Scipio* and cash. It was a telling request. Just ten years earlier English agents would have evinced little interest in who painted the pictures they commissioned. Now Carleton declined Rubens's studio pieces; only the master's hand would do.

Rubens protested at Carleton's dismissal of his studio pictures. 'Your Excellency must not think that the others are mere copies,' purred Rubens, 'for they are so well retouched by my hand that they are hardly to be distinguished from originals.'[51] He was reluctant to pay cash for the statues because, as he conceded, the 'reason I would deal more willingly in pictures is clear ... they cost me, so to speak, nothing'. He therefore offered to throw in 2,000 florins' worth of tapestries, still insisting on including retouched pictures in the deal, proposing 'for the remaining 1,000 florins you may choose from the other pictures on the list'. Proving to be as adept at selling his pictures as painting them, Rubens suggested that Carleton should take three pictures, including one of the finest advertisements of his studio's achievements, the painting of *A Hunt*. This last piece would form a pair with a Rubens hunting scene that Carleton previously received in exchange for a diamond chain. 'They would match each other perfectly,' assured Rubens, 'that one showing tigers and European hunters, and this one lions and Moorish and Turkish riders, very exotic.'[52]

Seduced by Rubens, Carleton accepted the offer. He eagerly anticipated the arrival of *A Hunt* as 'a companion to the one I have at home'. Having sold Tintoretto's *Susanna* to Arundel, he was looking for a sexy replacement. He hoped rather lewdly that Rubens's 'Susanna ought to be beautiful to enamour even old men'.[53] He wrote to Chamberlain in high spirits, telling him:

> I am now saying to my Antiquities *Veteres migrate coloni* having passed a contract with Rubens the famous painter of Antwerp for a suite of tapestry and a certain number of his pictures, which is a good bargain for us both, only I am blamed by the painters of this country who made idols of these heads and statues, but all others commend the change.

Carleton was happy to see the back of his unwieldy, troublesome statues. As far as he was concerned, contemporary painting was the way forward. As a painter, Rubens enthusiastically endorsed this conclusion. Reluctant to traffic in tapestries and with 'little inclination to act as agent', he told Carleton there were few decent tapestries for sale in Antwerp. He explained that 'one evaluates pictures differently from tapestries. The latter are purchased by measure, while the former are valued according to their excellence, their subject, and their number of figures.'[54] Monarchs had previously ordered made-to-measure woven magnificence by the yard. Painting could not be treated in the same way. It required discerning judgement by men of taste as to its execution, subject matter and delineation of figures. This was good news for painters like Rubens, but bad news for the weaving studios that had supplied the courts of Europe for centuries. Carleton got the point. Both men knew they had a deal.

By June 1618 Rubens agreed to give Carleton nine pictures valued at 4,000 florins, plus 2,000 florins in cash and tapestries in exchange for more than ninety classical statues.[55] As Carleton told Chamberlain, the deal was mutually beneficial. Rubens obtained a collection of classical statues that would inspire his subsequent work; he also circulated the belief among English collectors that he was the greatest living painter in Europe. Carleton acquired a superb collection of pictures and restored his personal credit and reputation back in England. Rubens, ever the diplomat, summarized the advantages of the deal for his new patron by concluding their negotiation with the prophetic words 'in exchange for marbles to furnish one room, Your Excellency receives pictures to adorn an entire palace'.[56]

As the Protestant Carleton and the Catholic Rubens amicably haggled over pictures and statues in the Low Countries, religious conflict in central Europe was threatening to tear the continent apart. The flashpoint was Bohemia. In May 1618 its Protestant community rejected the rule of the Catholic Habsburg Archduke Ferdinand and established an autonomous government. Their staunchest supporter was James's son-in-law, Frederick the Elector Palatine. Frederick made matters worse by accepting the throne of Bohemia, much to the consternation of James and the outrage of the Catholic League, which immediately threatened military action. Frederick called on James to give his backing to the Protestant Union. It left the king in a terrible dilemma. Should he support a popular but financially ruinous religious war, or should he keep the peace he craved and turn his back on his own children?

James believed the solution to the problems in central Europe lay in his long-cherished scheme of marrying Prince Charles to the Spanish Infanta, Maria, such an alliance surely resolving the religious conflicts. He assumed that the Spanish royal family would not countenance a Habsburg army declaring war on their brother-in-law in central Europe. He also knew that an enormous Spanish dowry would solve most of his immediate financial problems. Despite popular opinion to the contrary, as far as James was concerned the Bohemian crisis of 1619 only emphasized the necessity for the Spanish match. Unlike Henry, Prince Charles appeared happy to acquiesce in his father's plans, and by the beginning of 1619 James was hopeful of a swift and successful conclusion to the marriage negotiations.

The king was soon presented with an opportunity to prepare his capital for the arrival of his son's Spanish bride. In the second week of January the Banqueting House at Whitehall burned to the ground.[57] James immediately commissioned a new one. Its proportions were intended to provide a suitably imposing backdrop to the Anglo-Spanish marriage that would dazzle the attendant Habsburg retinue. A committee was appointed to oversee the building, and all that was needed was a cosmopolitan architect sufficiently versed in the new classical architectural style. There was only one person qualified to undertake such a commission: Arundel's former travelling companion, Inigo Jones.

Jones began work immediately, in consultation with James and a committee that included Sir William Herbert, Earl of Pembroke, Sir John Digby and Arundel. The committee submitted an estimate to the Privy Council for '[t]he whole charge of the Banqueting House to be new built . . . being in length 110 foot, and in breadth 55 foot . . . the upper story 55 foot high'. The report concluded that the total cost 'will amount unto the sum of £9,850'.[58] This was a staggering amount to commit to a public building by a cash-strapped king apparently indifferent to the arts. But James understood the power of public monuments to reinforce authority, especially on the eve of a dynastic marriage destined to redraw the political and religious map of Europe.

Jones was commissioned to construct a building that could be used to entertain foreign dignitaries, ratify political agreements, hold political audiences, celebrate public ceremonies – and conduct royal marriages. His solution was to build a Palladian palace in the centre of Whitehall based on the villas and palazzi he saw in Venice, Rome, Vicenza and Mantua. The result was a dazzling conflation of classical Roman, sixteenth-century Italian and contemporary English architecture. London had never seen anything like it.[59]

As James insisted that Jones's structure should 'forthwith all expeditiously be new built',[60] the rest of the committee began to discuss what to put inside it. The political scale of the Spanish marriage required an artist of international stature to decorate the new hall. There was only one artist in Europe capable of designing something on the scale of Jones's Banqueting House: Rubens.

Rubens's purchase of Dudley Carleton's statues introduced him to the circle of English collectors who were also involved in the construction of the Banqueting House. Throughout the summer of 1619 he became entangled in a convoluted transaction with another English collector, Henry, Lord Danvers. Danvers's involvement in Arundel's acquisition of Carleton's pictures left him with Bassano's *Creation*, but he never seemed terribly happy with it. He asked Carleton to approach Rubens with a view to swapping his Bassano, having discovered to his delight that 'there hath been value enough set upon the old piece' of Bassano.[61] He even knew what kind of picture he wanted. He felt that Carleton's own Rubens, 'with those beautiful lions in the den would well satisfy my desire'.[62]

Unfortunately, the Bassano was in a terrible state, 'cracked and spoiled', and once Carleton delivered it to Rubens the painter dismissed it as 'not worth (of any man's money) above 50 or 60 gilders', although Carleton had paid 220 ducats for the painting just six years earlier.[63] A chastened Carleton turned once more to Tobie Matthew, George Gage and William Trumbull to prevent the deal collapsing.[64] Matthew visited Rubens to discuss the Danvers deal. The situation didn't look promising. Matthew confirmed that the Bassano was in a shocking condition, and that the picture Rubens was offering in its place was little better. It was of a lion hunt as Danvers requested, but with surprising frankness 'Rubens confesseth in confidence that this is not all of his own doing . . . it

scarce doth look like a thing that is finished'.[65] Rubens was up to
his old tricks, passing inferior studio pieces off as his own finished
work. Carleton was once again caught in the crossfire between a
difficult patron and a demanding supplier, but there was no
alternative but to go ahead with the deal, using his own money to
ensure that Rubens completed the *Lion Hunt*.

In January 1621 Rubens told Carleton that the picture was
ready for shipment to London. Carleton anxiously awaited news
of the painting's reception. By March he received a letter from
Danvers's servant, who delivered his master's verdict, as well as
revealing the true identity of its buyer:

> I have delivered the picture to my Lord Danvers, he made a
> motion to have me write to Rubens before he would pay the
> money to this effect. That the picture had been showed to
> men of skill, who said that it was forced and slighted, and that
> he had not showed his greatest skill in it, and for that cause
> my Lord would have him make a better if he could and he
> should have this again . . . for seeing the Prince hath none
> of Rubens' work but one piece of *Judith & Holofernes*, which
> Rubens disavoweth, therefore he would have a good one or
> none, as for this he said that he had not yet set it amongst the
> Prince's pictures, neither would until it were avowed from
> Rubens to be a masterpiece.[66]

Rubens had accidentally stumbled on to a network of English
collectors who were far more discerning than he realized. At its
centre stood the twenty-year-old Prince Charles. Danvers acted as
the intermediary in buying Rubens's pictures for the prince, who
was surrounded by a team of experts ready to assess their quality.
The 'men of skill' who rejected the picture included Arundel and
Jones, and it was these figures who encouraged Charles in his foray
into the art market.

With the encouragement of his closest advisers, Prince Charles
had somewhat surprisingly made his debut on the European art
scene. His sudden entrance came at the culmination of yet another
inheritance, this time his mother's art collection. A year earlier he
had been called to Hampton Court, where the queen lay dying.
Anna spent her last weeks sitting in her gallery admiring religious

pictures, including paintings of Christ, Mary Magdalene and the Passion.[67] As Charles sat with her on the night before her death, Anna bequeathed him her estate. It included Denmark House and her picture collection, including all the paintings taken from Prince Henry's galleries. The inventory of her possessions held at Denmark House listed an impressive 125 pictures, some already in the royal collection, but also including many religious pictures featuring Christ, the Madonna and various saints, like Northampton's pictures ritually displayed behind taffeta curtains edged with gold lace and supported by silver rods. As well as the usual dynastic portraits there were also landscapes, architectural scenes, 'pictures of Venetian women' and 'Roman Emperors', although, as with most Elizabethan inventories, painters' names remained absent.[68] Nevertheless, it was a diverse if uneven basis upon which Charles could begin to build his own collection.

By the time that Rubens's painting arrived in Whitehall the queen's body lay unburied for over a fortnight as the exchequer struggled to find enough money to pay for her funeral. James's response was to oversee the repossession of her expensive jewellery, then take to his bed. Finally on 13 May, it was left to Charles to lead the funeral procession through the streets of London, just as he had done seven years earlier at the funeral of his brother, Henry.

Charles now became the official guardian of the memory of both his brother and his mother. He inherited a collection of pictures that gave him a consoling bond with the dead and the departed. Here was an opportunity to commemorate those he had lost: Henry, Anna and Elizabeth. This was something that could finally distinguish the timid little prince, while providing him with the admiration of a group of advisers inherited from Henry's court that included Arundel, Danvers and Jones. They knew that if Charles were to survive as the next heir to the throne he had to fashion a persona in paint and marble, just as James and Henry had used learning and militarism to define their own authority. Arundel, Danvers, Jones and Carleton also realized that their continued rise to political prominence would be enhanced if they helped to establish Charles as a prince of distinction and judgement on a wider international stage. One way of doing this was through art, and the small group of advisers all agreed that the one artist who could help Charles was Rubens.

This is why the 'men of skill' surrounding Charles encouraged him to patronize Rubens in the spring of 1621. Danvers's letter to Carleton two weeks after the queen's funeral shows that Charles's circle was skilfully fashioning an image of the prince as the judicious royal collector, on a par with his late brother. The letter began sternly: 'But now for Rubens'. Danvers complained, 'In every painter's opinion he hath sent hither a piece scarce touched by his own hand, and the postures so forced, as the Prince will not admit the picture into his gallery.' He wanted Rubens to paint another picture to 'redeem his reputation in this house and to stand amongst the many excellent works which are here of all the best masters in Christendom, for from him we have yet only *Judith and Holofernes*'. Danvers declared Charles's expertise as a judicious collector, while also announcing the impressive scope of his collection. If Rubens wanted to ensure the future king as a patron, he needed to supply a masterpiece superior to those pieces currently held in the collection. Danvers looked forward to receiving a better picture than the *Hunt*, ordering its return to Antwerp, concluding drily, 'these Lions shall be safely sent him back for tamer beasts better made'.[69]

Rubens was taken aback but soon regained his composure. He assured Danvers, 'I am quite willing that the picture painted for my Lord Ambassador be returned to me and that I should paint another Hunting piece less terrible than that of the Lions', finally offering a 'new picture to be entirely of my own hand'. He went on:

> I shall be very glad that this picture be located in a place so eminent as the Gallery of H.R.H. The Prince of Wales, and I will do everything in my power to make it superior in design to that of Holofernes, which I executed in my youth. I have almost finished a large picture entirely by my own hand, and in my opinion one of my best, representing a Hunt of Lions: the figures as large as life. It is an order of My Lord Ambassador Digby to be presented, as I am given to understand to the Marquis of Hamilton. But as you truly say such subjects are more agreeable and have more vehemence in a

large than in a small picture. I should very much like the
picture for H.R.H. The Prince of Wales to be of the largest
proportions, because the size of the picture gives us painters
more courage to represent our ideas with the utmost freedom
and semblance of reality . . . As to His Majesty and H.R.H.
The Prince of Wales, I shall always be very pleased to receive
the honour of their commands, and with respect to the Hall
in the New Palace, I confess myself to be, by a natural instinct,
better fitted to execute works of the largest size rather than
little curiosities.[70]

As well as a letter of apology, this was a formal application to
secure the commission to decorate the Banqueting House for
Charles's planned marriage to the Spanish Infanta. In soothing
Danvers's anger over his poor studio piece, Rubens revealed that
his involvement with English clients was partly aimed at clinching
the Whitehall commission. He was even working on a picture for
two of the leading supporters of the Spanish match – Sir John
Digby, English ambassador to Madrid and a member of the
Banqueting House committee, and the Marquis of Hamilton.

Rubens strengthened his claim to the London commission by
exaggerating the prince's virtues as 'the greatest amateur of paintings among the princes of the world' and sending him a hastily
repurposed self-portrait requested by Danvers. 'Though it did not
seem fitting to send my portrait to a prince of such rank,' claimed
Rubens, 'he overcame my modesty', and the picture went straight
into Charles's art collection.[71] He also painted Aletheia Talbot, the
Earl of Arundel's wife, as she travelled through Antwerp in 1620.
The result was a regal portrait befitting one of England's most
important patrons. Rubens portrayed Lady Arundel surrounded
by the trappings of the wealthy English aristocrat: her coat of arms,
her fool, her elegantly dressed dwarf, Robin, her falcon and a
hunting dog. Behind her chair hovers the satisfied deal-maker,
Sir Dudley Carleton, the man responsible for uniting Rubens, the
Arundels and the collectors advocating plans for the Banqueting
House and the Spanish match.

As Rubens completed his portrait of Lady Arundel in Antwerp,
back in London Charles was sitting for his portrait by the Dutch
painter Hendrick van Steenwijk. Dressed in the robes of state of

the Prince of Wales, for the first time in his life Charles was painted to look like an heir to the throne, an aspirant collector and patron of the arts, ready to assume the title of king of England. All that was needed now was the Spanish princess.

CHAPTER THREE

MR SMITH IN MADRID

WRITING TO THE VENETIAN SENATE from London in September 1622, Girolamo Lando confirmed what many European art dealers were starting to hear from England: the heir to the English throne loved 'old paintings, especially those of our province and city'.[1] It seemed that, thanks to the activities of Arundel, Danvers and others, Prince Charles was developing an interest in acquiring fine art as well as a wife. By 1623 he had found someone else to share his passions. His father's favourite, George Villiers, was a keen collector of Italian art and an enthusiastic supporter of the prince's proposed marriage to the Spanish Infanta.

Rising to the titles of Marquis of Buckingham and Lord Admiral of England, Buckingham was the king's closest companion and political adviser, making him one of the most powerful men in England. At first, relations between Charles and Buckingham, who was eight years his senior, were unsurprisingly cool. The timid young prince resented the handsome, charismatic favourite's intimacy with his father, but Buckingham quickly launched a charm offensive to win him over. He knew he would lose his power if anything happened to the king, whose health was already poor. If Buckingham were to retain his status, he needed to extend his influence over the heir to the throne. One way of doing this was to embrace James's and Charles's support for a Spanish marriage.

James hoped the Spanish match would provide him with financial and political independence from his increasingly discontented Parliament. As well as demanding military intervention in the Palatinate to defend Princess Elizabeth and Frederick, Parliament was voicing its opposition to the royal marriage. The match also provided the opportunity for fulfilling one of his most cherished but controversial plans – the reconciliation of the divisions of the Christian Church across Europe. Despite its split from Rome under Henry VIII, the Church of England maintained a common foundation of theological beliefs with Catholicism, and James saw it as his destiny to find a way to accommodate specific points of doctrinal differences between the competing versions of Christianity. 'I do acknowledge the Roman Church to be our Mother Church,' he informed Parliament in 1604, careful to add that it was 'defiled with some infirmities and corruptions'. James's version of Anglicanism believed itself to be the true, ancient form of Christian belief, predating Rome's spiritual and temporal authority. This is what James meant when he insisted, 'My faith is the true, ancient Catholic and Apostolic faith, grounded upon the Scriptures and express word of God.'[2] He saw the possibility of the Spanish match as a significant step towards resolving the rift between Catholicism and Protestantism while retaining the political and religious integrity of the Church of England.

James's problem was in convincing the growing number of so-called Puritans among his Parliament that such initiatives were not about to deliver the English Church back into the hands of Rome. Critical debate over the definition of Puritanism continues to rage, from its precise theology to its cohesiveness as a recognizable movement in seventeenth-century England. It was, however, a term broadly applied to a particularly pious strain within English Protestantism preoccupied with their personal salvation. Many individuals who identified themselves as Puritans believed they were members of a chosen people, the Elect, governed by divine providence, and were passionately committed to further reform of the English Church. For these believers, the sixteenth-century Lutheran Reformation had not gone far enough in reforming the superstitious, idolatrous practices of Catholicism.[3] Throughout his reign, King James steered a largely successful middle way between the increasingly divergent demands of the Anglican Church and Puritanism. However, the projected Spanish match would test the limits of this middle way almost to breaking point, and identified a religious faultline that came to dominate English political life over the next thirty years.

Such delicate doctrinal matters seemed far more straightforward to the politically and religiously inexperienced Prince of

Wales. For the young Charles, this marriage represented an opportunity to restore the fortunes of his sister, Elizabeth, and indulge his romantic fantasies of dynastic union with one of Europe's most powerful imperial families. The advantages for his new friend Buckingham were not as clear-cut. The match offered the chance to consolidate his role as mentor to the future king, but would the addition of a female member to this intimate male triumvirate diminish his power? As a precaution, he continued to correspond with Princess Elizabeth in Bohemia, pledging political and financial support for her cause. He also visited the Spanish ambassador, Don Diego de Sarmiento, Count of Gondomar, to assure him of James's continued desire for a Spanish marriage.

As Buckingham was drawn further into supporting the plans for the match, he began to buy art. His collecting was as opportunistic as his politics. He watched his rival Somerset fail to advance significantly his political interests by collecting art, but once Prince Charles began to patronize artists like Rubens, he realized the advantages of establishing his own collection. As the prince struggled to obtain a painting by Rubens for his modest collection, Buckingham planned the creation of one of the finest private collections of Italian paintings in Whitehall. In the spring of 1619 he employed a personal art dealer to acquire a collection of paintings and statues from scratch. The man he chose was Balthazar Gerbier, an itinerant Dutch painter of Huguenot descent who arrived in England in 1616 as part of a Dutch diplomatic embassy.[4]

Gerbier's talents and Buckingham's interests were perfectly matched. An indifferent painter whose pictures 'had little of Art, or merit',[5] Gerbier was a confidence man, an 'intelligencer' who traded in information and flourished in the shady margins of seventeenth-century diplomatic and artistic life. He quickly established himself as part of Buckingham's household and by the summer of 1621 he was in Italy, buying what he called 'the pearls of Italian art'[6] for Buckingham's fledgling collection. Where Inigo Jones utilized the wealth and artistic discernment of Arundel on his trip to Italy in 1613–14, Gerbier employed the superior political connections and purchasing power of Buckingham. He toured the palaces and private collections of first Rome and then Venice, absorbing artistic influences and acquiring pictures as he went. Ironically, it took a Dutch Protestant to match (and in some cases surpass) the purchases of the English Catholic Arundel.

Once in Rome Gerbier began to use the £500 worth of bills of exchange provided by Buckingham for the purchase of pictures. The Dutchman was so impressed with Raphael's widely acclaimed *Banquet of the Gods* at the Villa Farnesina that he paid a Florentine artist working in Rome £42 for a copy. He also visited the workshop of the fashionable Bolognese artist Guido Reni, where he bought a painting of *The Four Seasons* for £70, one of the first examples of this artist's work to enter an English collection.[7] As he bought, Gerbier also visited the great collections and public statues of the city, recommending that subsequent travellers admire Michelangelo's *Pietà* and Raphael's paintings in St Peter's, before heading to the Capitol to see the classical statue of Marcus Aurelius on horseback.[8] He inspected the dramatic altarpieces and privately commissioned paintings of Caravaggio and Annibale Carracci. Both painters, dead by the time Gerbier visited the city, had overseen a dramatic renaissance of Italian art under the lavish sponsorship of the Roman popes. Vast in scale, their dramatic paintings captured the religious devotion and emotional intensity of an increasingly confident and militant Catholic Church. Rome felt it was finally overcoming the depredations of the Protestant Reformation and was moving forward into a golden age of spiritual authority.[9]

If Rome impressed Gerbier with the dramatic grandeur and religious fervour of its Caravaggios and Carraccis, Venice seduced his grey northern eye with the fugitive light and translucent colours of Tintoretto, Veronese and of course Titian.[10] Arriving in the high summer of 1621, Gerbier was warmly welcomed by the old Venetian hand Sir Henry Wotton, now on his second and final diplomatic tour of the city. Wotton had good reasons to assist Gerbier. A fellow connoisseur of the arts, Gerbier was also Buckingham's man, and Wotton saw the opportunity of ingratiating himself with the king's favourite in the hope of landing a lucrative post back in England once his time in Venice was up.

Wotton introduced Gerbier to the paintings of Veronese and Tintoretto in the Doge's Palace in St Mark's and the various churches and private collections across the city. The delighted Dutchman started negotiating for pictures almost immediately. Although he failed to acquire an example of the 'bold pencil' of Paolo Veronese, he bought biblical and classical paintings by Tintoretto and the Bassanos, father Jacopo and son Francesco. He paid relatively modest amounts for the Bassanos – Jacopo's *Shepherds in the Night* and *Noah's Ark* cost £30 and £15 respectively, while Francesco's more recent *History of Vulcan* cost £35. Buying works from the more fashionable Domenicho Tintoretto proved harder. Gerbier hired a go-between to assist in the acquisition of a more expensive painting of *The Woman Taken in Adultery* that cost £50.

What promised to secure Gerbier's reputation back in London was the purchase of a masterpiece by the Venetian master Titian, *Ecce Homo*, bought for an unprecedented £275.[11] It was a sign of Gerbier's confidence in his own judgement that he was prepared to offer such a substantial amount of Buckingham's money for one painting. Even Arundel never dared spend that amount of his own money on a picture, never mind someone else's. Having spent well over half his budget on one Titian, Gerbier needed to borrow more money to pay for the extra pictures, as well as frames, package and transportation required to ship everything back to England. Like Dudley Carleton before him, he turned to the art dealer and financier Daniel Nys, who arranged a loan of a further £151 10s, payable to the London merchant family of Fortry, previously involved in the sale of the Somerset collection. This time there were to be no mistakes and by the end of the year ten of the finest Italian pictures London had ever seen were delivered into Buckingham's hands, all for the considerable sum of £651 10s.[12]

Buckingham's faith in his new art agent was well placed. The collection was displayed in Buckingham's lodgings in Whitehall in view of rival courtiers like Arundel, the king and Prince Charles. Although Buckingham was not to know it, his new purchases closely reflected the aesthetic tastes and religious outlook of the

Habsburg dynasty into which the Stuart family was now proposing to marry. Throughout the sixteenth century Margaret of Austria, her nephew Emperor Charles V and his sister Mary of Hungary commissioned works from artists like Bernard van Orley, Jan Vermeyen, Leone Leoni and Titian, thus ensuring that the Habsburg Empire was deemed the most powerful and magnificent empire in Europe.[13] These Habsburg patrons also dominated the art market in paintings from Italy and the Low Countries, showing that the power to commission and purchase culture was a vital index of political and imperial power.

By the time the English began visiting the Continent in the early seventeenth century, this explicitly political dimension to painting and patronage was beginning to shift. Connoisseurs like Buckingham and Arundel showed little or no obvious interest in the religious or explicitly political content of the Titians or Veroneses they coveted. Instead, they valued questions of aesthetics – composition, colour, proportion and style – over their explicit thematic politics and ideology. For such collectors this was an exciting and novel development that opened their eyes to a whole new horizon of aesthetic possibilities, but for many Protestants back in England the influx of pictures of Madonnas and Catholic saints would prove at best baffling, at worse a sign of the dubious religious faith of Charles and his advisers.

Gerbier's return to London was overshadowed by the growing political crisis over the Palatinate. In the autumn of 1620 Frederick was defeated at the battle of the White Mountain outside Prague. Spanish troops and those loyal to the Austrian wing of the Habsburg family, the Emperor Ferdinand, then annexed the Elector's ancestral territories in the Lower Rhine Palatinate. Much to the consternation of Parliament, King James refused to offer military aid to Frederick and his own daughter, and continued marital negotiations with Spain. He claimed that this policy was aimed at a peaceful restitution of Frederick and Elizabeth, but to many radical Protestants it looked like capitulation to the old Catholic enemy.

The 1621 Parliament was particularly stormy. Buckingham and his supporters were censored for their control of grants and monopolies, and James's domestic and foreign policy came in for heavy criticism. One commentator noted that the king 'takes it not well that they should meddle with the match twixt his Son and the Infanta'.[14] Worse was to come. Parliament issued a petition demanding military defence of the Palatinate, a tightening of the anti-Catholic laws and a fulsome rejection of the Spanish match, hoping that 'our most noble Prince may be timely and happily married to one of our own religion'.[15] This was hardly a direct rebuttal of the king's authority, but parliamentary opposition to the Spanish match crystallized certain political tensions between king and Parliament that would only intensify over the next two decades of Stuart rule.

Since Tudor times, English monarchs had realized the importance of working in partnership with the two Houses of Parliament – the Lords and the Commons. Although it was widely assumed that the king held the right over the summoning and dismissal of Parliament and the enactment of law, it was also established as common practice that all statutes required the unanimous agreement of the crown, the Lords and the Commons. Throughout the sixteenth century English monarchs accepted that a partnership between crown and Parliament was of mutual benefit to the interests of both parties. The crown introduced statutes that reflected the needs of the Houses' different groups – in the Lords the peers and the clerisy, and in the Commons the landed gentry. In return Parliament assented to the crown's political and financial requirements. Since the early fifteenth century the Commons had been responsible for providing the crown with revenue from direct taxation – or subsidies – to supplement the king's income from his royal estates. Unfortunately, by the time James came to the throne inflation and the undervaluation of taxable estates among the landed gentry meant that the crown's revenue from taxes was drastically reduced in real value. Once Parliament clashed with the king over matters such as the formulation of foreign or religious policy, as in the case of the Spanish match, limiting subsidies was one of its most effective ways of registering its dissent. As the need for money grew and the political differences between crown and Parliament increased over the following years, constitutional problems would only intensify.

However, in the hands of a shrewd king like James, such problems were usually surmountable. In response to the Commons' formal protestation at their exclusion from foreign policy relating to the Spanish match, an exasperated James formally dissolved Parliament in January 1622, despite having failed to obtain the financial subsidies he required. Assuming that the Spanish dowry would solve these money problems, in May he dispatched John Digby, the future Earl of Bristol, to Madrid to advance negotiations for the marriage. Meanwhile, his hotter-headed son, Prince Charles, privately promised the Spanish ambassador, Gondomar, that he was prepared to travel to Madrid in disguise if necessary to secure his bride.[16] It was a foolhardy assurance that was to have serious political repercussions.

As negotiations continued throughout September the prince wrote to Gondomar, professing his love for the Infanta Maria: 'If you wonder how I can love before I see, the truth is I have both seen her picture and heard the report of her virtues by a number whom I trust, so as her idea is engraven in my heart where I hope to preserve it till I enjoy the principal.'[17] The prince was following his dead brother's example by ritually making love to his proposed fiancée through the medium of the formal portrait, although Gondomar's response was much more graphic and to the point. Writing to Buckingham from Madrid, where he had been recalled to discuss the match, Gondomar claimed, 'As far as we here are concerned, the decision has already been made, and with very great enthusiasm, that the Prince of Wales should mount Spain.'[18] Drawing on the practice of mixing bloodlines in horse breeding, the Spaniard grasped the dynastic implications of the marriage, while also lewdly pandering to the young prince's romantic fantasies.

More hopeful observers believed that Gondomar's support for the marriage was to be encouraged. 'The Spanish ambassador Count Gondomar doth strongly negotiate a match twixt our Prince, and the Infanta of Spain,' claimed James Howell, a member of the English embassy in Madrid, adding that Gondomar 'saith there is no other way to regain the Palatinate, but by this match, and to settle an eternal Peace in Christendom'.[19] In reality the ambassador was playing a dangerous game. His new sovereign,

King Philip IV, had ascended the throne in 1621 aged just fifteen, having promised his dying father he would oppose an Anglo-Spanish marriage unless the Prince of Wales was prepared to convert to Catholicism. Philip's senior minister, the Count-Duke of Olivares, was left in the unenviable position of trying to avert the marriage and rein in enthusiasts like Gondomar without provoking England into a costly war that neither country could afford.[20] Despite Olivares's endorsement of even tougher religious terms recommended by both the papacy in Rome and a Spanish theological *junta*, James's envoy, Endymion Porter, still returned to London in January 1623 with what he claimed was a workable draft marriage treaty.

It was at this moment that the Prince of Wales took the bold but foolish decision to go to Madrid to claim his bride. Buckingham accepted Charles's scheme to persuade his father 'how gallant and brave a thing it would be' for the two of them 'to make a journey into Spain'.[21] It was an injudicious, potentially dangerous plan that revealed the naivety and inexperience of Jacobean foreign policy. No designated Protestant heir to the English throne had ever left its shores, but the scheme risked exposing the Prince of Wales to robbery, injury and even murder along the way, notwithstanding the possibility of kidnap and incarceration as a heretic if negotiations in Spain went wrong.

James and many of his advisers were horrified at the prince's proposal. It threatened to hand the diplomatic initiative to the Spanish and create the impression that Charles was about to convert to Catholicism. Unfortunately for James, Charles could cite clear precedent for his plan. The king himself had risked storms and shipwreck to fetch Charles's mother from Denmark, while James's own father had met his future bride in France. Nevertheless, when James was confronted with his son's proposal he was inconsolable. He threw himself on his bed, crying out, 'I am undone. I shall lose Baby Charles.'[22] It is to nobody's credit that James was soon discouraged from opposing the trip.

One of Charles's last acts before his departure was to order the purchase of a series of cartoons by Raphael portraying the *Acts of the Apostles*. Cartoons were needed for the Mortlake tapestry factory, opened in south-west London in 1619 on the orders of King James. Sir Francis Crane, the head of the factory, noted that Charles ordered him 'to send to Genoa for certain drawings of Raphael of Urbino, which were designs for tapestries made for Pope Leo X and for which there is £300 to be paid, besides their charge for bringing home'.[23] This was one of the earliest and most significant attempted acquisitions in the history of Charles's collection and sheds light on his attitude towards both collecting and the imminent trip to Madrid. Leo X commissioned the cartoons from Raphael in Rome in 1515.[24] The result was a series of brilliantly illusionistic cartoons specifically designed as patterns for a huge cycle of tapestries depicting scenes from the lives of St Peter and St Paul. Technically innovative, the cartoons also provided a powerful statement of the supreme authority of the papacy by making an explicit connection between Leo and St Peter as the founder of the Catholic Church in Rome. The cartoons went to Brussels, where they were transformed into tapestries and dispatched to Catholic princes across Europe, including the Gonzaga in Mantua, the Habsburgs in Spain and King Henry VIII in London, self-styled 'Defender of the Faith', prior to his split from Rome.

What was the Protestant Charles doing trying to order Catholic cartoons on the eve of his trip to Madrid? Besides chasing sought-after art by one of Italy's greatest painters, it seems he wanted to prepare London for the arrival of his Catholic bride and cast himself, like his father, as the Anglican unifier of the Christian faith, bringing Protestants and Catholics together in the same way that St Paul preached the Gospel and converted the doubters. His intention was to use the cartoons to commission tapestries from the Mortlake factory that would adorn that other symbol of the Anglo-Spanish alliance, Inigo Jones's Banqueting House. Charles authorized Crane to buy the cartoons, then turned his attention to preparations for his Spanish adventure.

ON 18 JANUARY the prince and Buckingham left the latter's Newhall House in Essex and set off on horseback for Dover. The two men 'had false beards for disguises, to cover their smooth faces, and the names of Jack Smith and Tom Smith'.[25] Despite such brilliant disguises, a Gravesend ferryman recognized them and alerted the authorities after the bearded Smiths paid him with a gold coin. At Canterbury Buckingham was forced to whip off his false beard to reveal his identity after being detained on the orders of the town's mayor. By the next day they reached Dover and were ready to sail with two well-known Hispanophiles and Catholic sympathizers, Charles's secretary and former Spanish ambassador, Sir Francis Cottington, and Endymion Porter.

The party crossed the channel and on 21 February they reached Paris, still travelling incognito. They went to the court of King Louis XIII and watched his wife, Anne of Austria, perform in the ballet alongside her sister-in-law, Henrietta Maria. Charles evinced little interest in Henrietta, praising the queen instead in one of his first letters home to James.[26] They left Paris and headed south for the Spanish border, finally arriving in Madrid on the evening of 7 March. Ambassador Digby's servant James Howell recalled that 'to the wonderment of the world the Prince and the Marquis of Buckingham arrived at this Court a Friday last, upon the close of evening'. To Howell's astonishment 'they lighted at my Lord of Bristol's [Digby's] house, and the Marquis (Mr Thomas Smith) came in first . . . then (Mr John Smith) the Prince'.[27] Digby managed to retain his composure when confronted with the sight of the heir to the English throne on his doorstep, but the delighted Gondomar was unable to restrain himself when his spies informed him of the prince's arrival. He immediately went to see Olivares. Bemused at Gondomar's obvious excitement, the minister remarked, 'One would think that you had got the King of England in Madrid.' Gondomar replied, 'If I have not got the King, at least I have got the Prince.'[28]

Charles's unexpected arrival caused a diplomatic sensation. Madrid reacted with surprise and delight. The Spanish journalist Andrés de Almansa y Mendoza enthused, 'The coming of the illustrious Prince of Wales into these Kingdoms' was 'the strangest occurrence that in a royal Person the World hath for many Ages seen . . . it astonished whole Nations'.[29] Like most Spaniards, Gondomar, Olivares and King Philip IV assumed that Charles had come to convert to Catholicism before marrying the Infanta. Back in England, people reached the same conclusion, but with little enthusiasm. It was reported that Charles's departure 'hath left a great amazement among the people who are much perplexed',[30] while the antiquarian scholar Sir Simonds D'Ewes confessed it was a 'doleful day that made every Protestant sad'.[31] The wider international community expressed its bewilderment. French, German and Italian diplomats were concerned at how the expected marriage would alter the balance of power in Europe. The Venetian ambassador to London went so far as to dramatically condemn the trip as 'a monster among decisions, a labyrinth without head or way out'.[32]

While the international community responded with dismay, John and Thomas Smith cast off their disguises and revelled in their new-found celebrity. They were thoroughly enjoying themselves, apparently oblivious to the serious breach in Spanish royal etiquette their arrival had caused and delighted at the spectacular ceremonial entry into the city that King Philip promised his royal cousin from England.

The Madrid that Charles and Buckingham were about to enter was one of the greatest imperial cities in seventeenth-century Europe. It was also one of the newest. Philip II returned to Spain in 1559 following his father Charles V's abdication and decision to split the Habsburg Empire between its Spanish and Austrian branches. One of Philip's first initiatives was to move the imperial court from the narrow, labyrinthine confines of the medieval city of Toledo to the austere grandeur of the wide vistas of the town of Madrid, fifty miles to the north. The result was a massive programme of redecoration and rebuilding, as money flowed into the town and its population grew. To ensure a suitable appearance of imperial grandeur, Philip embarked on the renovation and creation of a network of royal palaces radiating outwards from the old royal palace, the recently refurbished Real Alcázar. To the north of Madrid he augmented the royal hunting lodge, El Pardo, with a series of imposing royal residences, while to the south he enlarged the palace of Aranjuez.

Philip's most audacious initiative was the design for the religious and imperial centrepiece of the Habsburg monarchy: San Lorenzo del Escorial. Part monastery, part palace and part mausoleum, it was designed as the final resting place of Charles V. Begun in 1563 and completed in 1584, it was one of the first baroque palaces of the Counter-Reformation, a vast, overwhelming affirmation of the Catholic faith, complete with crypts, royal apartments, monastic quarters, libraries and a dramatic central basilica, all decorated with hundreds of paintings, frescoes, tapestries and statues representing the Habsburg dynasty and the Catholic faith.[33] Philip's building programme was more than a dramatic affirmation of the wealth and unquestioned power of the Habsburg monarchy; equally it reflected a conception of monarchy as a mysterious, private institution, hidden away from the public eye through its layers of ritual and etiquette.

Prince Charles had never seen anything like it, and it had a profound effect upon him. He wrote to his father in a state of high excitement, describing how 'we had a private visit of the King, the Queen, the Infanta, Don Carlos, and the Cardinal, in the sight of all the world'. The royal entourage agreed to ride around the Prado (then a park) in full view of Charles, discreetly positioned in his private coach. He relished the attention, boasting 'there was the Pope's nuncio, the Emperor's ambassador, the French, and all the streets filled with guards and other people: before the King's coach went the best of the nobility, after followed all the ladies of the court'.[34] Charles had spent twenty-three years in the shadows of the Stuart dynasty; now he was the centre of attention in one of the great royal capitals of the world, playing the role of the romantic suitor and princely peacemaker.

It was a delightful but naive illusion that also seduced King James, already fantasizing about 'my sweet boys and dear venturous knights, worthy to be put in a new romance'.[35] The romantic theatricals intensified with Charles's carefully choreographed public entry into Madrid on Sunday 16 March. To all intents and purposes, he was treated like a Spanish sovereign, his entry 'performed with the same magnificence and splendour, as is used at the coronation of the Kings of Spain', according to one onlooker.[36] The prince processed from the monastery of San Jerónimo and rode in state with Philip under a canopy, surrounded by nobles from both the Spanish and the English courts. The thoroughfares were equipped with stages on which were performed plays, music and dancing. Convicts were released, while penitents scourged themselves along the way. Charles's triumphal entry into the Alcázar was the signal for an increasingly spectacular series of festivities organized by Olivares that included more plays, tournaments, processions, banquets, bullfights, fireworks and hunting which went on for weeks.

Amid all this ceremonial splendour, Charles and Buckingham were confronted with images and icons representing Habsburg power and the Catholic faith. According to one witness, 'all the streets were adorned, in some places with rich hangings, in others with curious pictures'.[37] The royal palaces opened their doors to reveal one of the largest and finest art collections in seventeenth-century Europe. Philip's forebears bequeathed a collection of 2,000 paintings by a mixture of Spanish and Italian artists, over half of which could be seen at the Escorial. Charles and Buckingham's agents had spent several years scouring the Continent for precious artworks. Now their masters found themselves lodging in the rooms and corridors of one of Europe's greatest imperial art collections.

The English party came to Madrid to negotiate a politically sensitive marriage. But just over a week after Charles's public entry into the city, the more experienced Buckingham began to buy pictures. Sir Francis Cottington's accounts of the trip record that on 24 March, as Buckingham began talks with Olivares, he also bought an unspecified number of pictures for 12,650 *reales*.[38] At the prevailing exchange rate, this was a hefty investment of nearly £350. Buckingham obviously felt more at ease in the midst of the Spanish art market than the less experienced prince. Thanks to Gerbier, he already owned examples of work by Bassano, Tintoretto and Titian – all artists represented in the Spanish royal collection. In stark contrast, Prince Charles's modest collection was still primarily composed of older, unfashionable northern European artists like Holbein, Hilliard, Miereveld and Van Somer.[39]

After watching Buckingham's first tentative acquisitions, Charles took the artistic initiative on 28 March, writing home to order Sir Francis Crane to secure the Raphael cartoons of the *Acts of the Apostles* from Genoa, even though their price had more than

doubled to 'near upon the point of seven hundred pounds'.[40]
It has been assumed that Rubens encouraged the purchase of
the Raphael cartoons, although a far likelier candidate has been
overlooked. The industrious Lady Arundel was in close touch with
London throughout her eventful trip to Italy. In early March she
arrived in Genoa, commissioned by King James to travel on to
Spain and escort the betrothed Infanta back to England.[41] With
her artistic interests, Lady Arundel would have been quick to relate
details of the whereabouts of Raphael's cartoons, news of which
reached Charles in late March.

It seems a peculiar moment to be thinking about buying
pictures. Yet Charles felt sure that his marriage was on the verge
of being accepted by Pope Gregory XV in Rome, petitioned by
the Spanish to issue a dispensation sanctioning the Anglo-Spanish
match. It was now vital to get the Raphael cartoons to London
as soon as possible to allow Crane to create tapestries for the
prince's return with his new wife. Charles's impatience was compounded by the display of tapestries he saw in the Spanish royal
residences. He was shown the Spanish queen's apartment, 'which
was all hung with the tapestry of Tunis, and Petrarch's *Triumphs*,
set forth in embroidery, well known both for riches, and varieties
of invention'.[42] These were tapestry cycles designed to impress and
overwhelm the visitor. The *Conquest of Tunis* tapestries were first
unveiled at another politically contentious Anglo-Spanish marriage,
between Philip II and Mary Tudor at Winchester in 1544, with
the intention of intimidating the Protestant English with their
scenes of Habsburg military might.[43] Charles was learning what an
effective tool tapestries could be in magnifying political power and
celebrating dynastic unions, and was quick to appreciate how those
based on Raphael's cartoons could provide him with the kind of
majesty and authority that they seemed to have accorded the
Spanish.

Having dealt with the Raphael cartoons, Charles turned his
attention to the Spanish art market. Not for the first or last time
when it came to matters of art, he looked to his counsellors for
advice and assistance. At the end of March the prince's entourage
was strengthened by the arrival of the Earl of Carlisle, Lord
Viscount Andover, Lord Mountjoy and others, including the

artistic advisers Balthazar Gerbier and Tobie Matthew.[44] On 10 April, just a fortnight after their arrival, 2,860 *reales* (nearly £80) were spent on 'Pictures for his Highness', but this was again overshadowed by Buckingham's purchase of over £280 worth of unspecified paintings on the same day.[45] What is striking about these transactions is not their cost but that Charles and his agents were purchasing the pictures on the open market. They were not commissioned works or diplomatic gifts; they were pictures offered for sale through picture dealers (known as *tratantes en pinturas*) or more often via estate sales (*almonedas*) that involved the liquidation of assets to settle debts and inheritances.[46] Charles and Buckingham witnessed for the first time an imperial city with a thriving public art market and a royal art collection that commissioned art in the services of both religion and politics.

The English artistic experience of Madrid was a revelation, but it was also reciprocal and mutually beneficial. The Spanish art market lacked the more secular connoisseurship of England and the Low Countries. It had never experienced the targeted pursuit of specific paintings or the direct financial approach of agents like Gerbier. This stimulated the higher end of the market and heightened the value of the painters and genres pursued by the English. Many Spanish observers were delighted. Looking back on Charles's visit in 1628, the Spanish dramatist Lope de Vega claimed, 'When he came to Spain, the Prince of Wales, now King of England, was most zealous in having brought to him all the paintings that were to be had; he valued them inordinately and paid excessive prices for them.'[47] It was a view echoed by Vicente Carducho, one of Spain's most respected court painters. He lamented the poor standing of painting as a respected profession in Spain and made serious efforts to establish a painting academy. In 1633 he published a treatise on the value of painting, entitled *Diálogos de la pintura*. In celebrating the fabulous examples of works by Titian, Velázquez, Rubens and Eugenio Cajés that could be found in the royal collection, Carducho recalled, 'Many of those we have mentioned were at great risk when the Prince of Wales (today the King of England) was here. He tried as best he could to collect any paintings and original drawings he could obtain, money being no object in their acquisition.'[48]

Despite Charles's enthusiasm for the contents of the Spanish royal art collection, King Philip was initially reluctant to offer his prospective brother-in-law pictures as gifts, and for good reason. Philip and Olivares remained sceptical about the marriage, unless Charles agreed to convert to Catholicism. Until such an announcement, it seemed pointless to offer him the pick of Philip's art collection. The Spanish court was also notoriously reluctant to participate in the elaborate exchange of gifts more familiar to the English, French and Italian courts. The Medici court struggled for decades to get the Spanish to accept diplomatic gifts. As early as 1594 the Tuscan ambassador to Madrid complained, 'There is absolutely no way to get anyone to accept anything without the King's permission,' while others would only accept gifts offered as objects of religious devotion.[49] Officially, the pious Spanish found it distasteful to traffic in religious images for political advantage. As the English were not Catholics and had no appropriate gifts to offer, their chances of getting hold of the Habsburg Titians or Correggios seemed slight.

Undaunted, Charles and his advisers pursued the more profitable avenues of the local *almonedas* and the private collections of obliging Spanish nobles. Charles visited the collection of court official and budding connoisseur Don Jerónimo Funes y Muñoz and, according to Carducho, chose eight paintings 'done by the greats', as well as a selection of swords, crossbows and harquebuses.[50] Unfortunately, when Charles attempted to buy particular pictures from individual collectors, he was not always as successful. One of the most formidable collectors associated with the Spanish court was the Roman-born Giovanni Battista Crescenzi, Marquess de la Torre, connoisseur, architect, painter, sculptor and a crucial bridge between Spain and the arts in Italy.[51] Charles tried to acquire pieces from the Roman nobleman's extensive collection that included works by Elsheimer, Carracci, Bordone and Crescenzi's Spanish protégé, Juan Fernández, El Labrador, but his requests were refused. There is no documented reason for Crescenzi's refusal to offer Charles paintings, although the papacy's reluctance to provide its blessing for the prince's proposed marriage probably contributed to his decision.

Other elite members of the Spanish court also resisted Charles's advances for a range of political and aesthetic reasons. They included the Count-Duke of Benavente and Juan de Espina, another of Madrid's leading connoisseurs. Carducho praised Espina as 'a collector of objects of the finest and most extraordinary quality', with a particular eye for the work of Leonardo. According to Carducho, Espina possessed 'two books of drawings, and manuscripts, written by the great Leonardo da Vinci, of exceptional interest and learning, which the Prince of Wales, when he was in Madrid, wished to purchase and would not leave behind for any price. But he [Espina] deemed them to be worthy of remaining in his possession alone.'[52] Subsequently labelled Codex Madrid I and II, the notebooks are still held in the Biblioteca Nacional in Madrid, the only works by Leonardo in Spain.[53] It seems that Espina knew the value of the notebooks and was determined to bequeath them to the Spanish king, not an English prince.

Charles's participation in these *almonedas* proved far more rewarding than his negotiations with living collectors. Carducho claimed that many of Charles's acquisitions came from the *almonedas* of recently deceased collectors and it was here that the English entourage made some of their finest purchases. Ever since the days of Prince Henry, Titian had represented the pinnacle of the collecting ambitions of the Stuart court. Now Charles was presented with the opportunity to buy Titians first-hand, assisted by a team of advisers with experience of appraising and, in the case of Gerbier, even buying paintings by the Venetian master.

At some stage in his visits to these estate sales the prince bought two strikingly different paintings by Titian that have puzzled critics for centuries, *Woman in a Fur Wrap* and *Allegory of the Marquis of Vasto*. What drew Charles to them? To some extent, it was simply that they were Titians, but perhaps there were other reasons. He seems to have admired the *Woman in a Fur Wrap* on the same terms that Titian created it – the erotic contrasts of soft, tactile fur and lustrous gold and pearls against pale, naked female flesh, at once hidden and revealed by the wrap and the ambiguous position of the arms. Is she about to shrug off her fur cloak or pull it protectively over her exposed breast? Her bold stare that holds our gaze looks like a rebuke – or possibly an invitation. Such explicit sexual provocation had never been seen in the private galleries of Tudor and Stuart England, never mind offered for sale in the public marketplace.

For the twenty-three-year-old prince, sexually inexperienced and full of romantic expectations about his imminent marriage, the picture must have been an erotic revelation. Olivares had joked that Charles regarded the Infanta Maria 'as a cat doth a mouse'.[55] This was the same salacious male gaze that Titian adopted to 'undress', aesthetically speaking, his anonymous lady. Here was a picture upon which Charles could project the contradictory fantasies that lay at the heart of his visit to Madrid, as both the chivalric knight come to claim his virtuous lady and the dynastic deal-maker on a mercenary mission to 'mount Spain' and bring peace to Europe.

Charles's other purchase, *Allegory of the Marquis of Vasto*, was more enigmatic, although it also focused on female breasts, this time in the hands of the soldier at the centre of the picture. Van der Doort would later catalogue the picture in his inimitable style as 'The Picture of the Marquess of Gwasto Conteyning 5 halfe figures Soe bigg as ye life which ju M bought aufit an Almonedo in Spaine'.[56] Alfonso d'Avalos, the Marquis of Vasto, was the controversial Habsburg governor of Milan, but the complex iconography of the picture suggests that it was more than just a political portrait. The two figures on the left also correspond to conventional depictions of Mars and Venus, mastering Cupid and his arrows, and blessed by the personification of Faith, crowned with myrtle. Alternatively, the woman also has close affinities with Prudence, looking into her sphere to see the future.[57] Charles had already shown an interest in the story of Venus and Mars, in 1620 commissioning a series of tapestries depicting Venus, Vulcan and Mars from the Mortlake tapestry factory.[58] Completed in the summer of 1622, prior to his departure, they lacked the complex symbolism and sexual tension that drew him to Titian's picture. Was the prince casting himself as Mars, the classical warrior abducting the beautiful Venus?

If so, the diplomatic events of late spring 1623 suggested that he was determined to return to England with his Spanish Venus whatever the cost. From the outset, Buckingham naively assumed in his letters to James that 'if the Pope would give a dispensation for a wife, they would give the Infanta to thy son's baby as a wench',[59] and the retinue could be back in London by May. Charles appreciated the obstacles that still impeded the marriage, writing to his father, 'we find them by outward shows as desirous of it as ourselves, yet they are hankering upon a conversion; for they say, there can be no friendship without union in religion.'[60] James had already responded to news of Spanish attempts to engage the prince in theological disputation by dispatching chaplains to Spain to show the Spaniards the doctrinal beliefs shared by Anglicans and Catholics.[61] The Spanish, and in particular Olivares, were quick to exploit what they interpreted as the English delegation's acceptance of their religious terms. By the time the papal dispensation arrived at the end of April, it demanded total capitulation from the English. Insisting on freedom of worship for all English Catholics and the repeal of parliamentary anti-Catholic legislation, the dispensation even claimed the Infanta's right to control the religious education of any children resulting from the union.[62] Charles was aghast; Buckingham was furious.

Alarmed at the political reception that would greet the papal demands back in London, both men wrote to James downplaying the situation and requesting plenary rights to revise the marriage treaty. James agreed, anxious to resolve the dispute and get his 'boys' back home as quickly as possible. Through a mixture of ineptitude and naivety, both men surrendered whatever slim diplomatic initiative their dramatic arrival had created and were left to spend the rest of the summer vainly trying to squeeze concessions out of Olivares and Philip. Now that it looked as if Charles might become part of the family, the Spanish finally relented and presented him with the pictures he desired.

Carducho tactfully suggested that this change of heart was inspired by Charles's enthusiastic participation in the *almonedas*, but this was a painter's response to a political situation. The rapidly changing diplomatic climate directly influenced the choice of the pictures Philip presented to Charles. One of the finest gifts was

Titian's majestic *Portrait of Charles V with Hound*. Philip could not have offered a more politically charged picture than this portrait of his revered predecessor. The Escorial was built around the dead emperor's mausoleum, a monumental tribute to the greatest of all the Habsburg rulers. Titian painted the portrait in commemoration of Charles V's coronation as champion of Christendom and Holy Roman Emperor by Pope Clement VII in February 1530.[63]

The significance of the painting's presentation to the young Prince Charles was clear to both Spanish and English representatives. He was being invited to join the Habsburg dynasty by accepting his crown from the Pope and emulating his namesake as defender of the faith. Charles's other acquisitions suggest that this was a deeply attractive message. Cottington's account of 'bookes bought for his Highness' on 15 April records that Charles bought Herrera's 'Historie of the West Indies', Cabrera's 'Historie of Phelip the Seconds life' and 'The Epitome of Carlo Quinto'.[64] The history of imperial expansion and the two great founders of the empire, Charles V and Philip II, were all compulsory reading for a prince eager and willing to marry into the family.

Charles seems to have accepted the picture and ignored its other political price tag: that he must convert to Catholicism before inheriting the mantle of Charles V. As a future king of England, he should have been alienated by the picture; but as an Anglican whose father implicitly acknowledged the spiritual (if not political) authority of the Roman Church, he seems to have found such images more appealing than many in England would have assumed. After all, this was a prince who spent the summer writing letters to the Pope, assuring him that he was 'far from plotting anything contrary to the Roman Catholic religion' and that 'we may all profess one and the self-same faith'.[65] The aspirant collector and future ruler was also seduced by the portrait's elegant combination of relaxed ease and majestic authority that would influence subsequent paintings of his own royal majesty. Charles's encounter with the Spanish Titians inspired him to try and reproduce the painter's fusion of art and power in London. It also began a lifelong passion that would lead him to acquire over thirty pictures attributed to the Venetian artist.[66]

If Titian's portrait represented the rigours of imperial and dynastic duty, Philip's other painted gifts represented the more luxurious and profane dimension of royal power. On 11 June a royal decree signed over to Charles one of the finest Titians in the Habsburg collection, his *Pardo Venus*, also known as *Jupiter and Antiope*. The *Venus* was just one of Titian's celebrated pictures known as the *Poesie*, a series of mythological scenes painted in the mid sixteenth century for Philip II. Jupiter, transformed into a satyr, bears down on the semi-clad Antiope, exposing his own nakedness as he pulls the sheet back to reveal her nudity. To the right the hunters mimic the sexual chase, complete with the breed of hound that stands to the side of Emperor Charles V in Titian's earlier portrait. Its erudite classicism barely masks the painting's prurient delight in anticipating a scene of sexual violation. Presented to an English prince invited to 'mount Spain', it was a salaciously appropriate gift.

Carducho also captured the picture's irresistible mix of profane classicism and sexual fascination in his account of its fate as one of the many pictures given to Charles:

> ... among which was one by Titian of Antiope and some shepherds and satyrs on a large canvas, which was at the Pardo, which escaped the fire that took place there in 1608, and in which so many were burned; and this one, being so profane, was able to escape from the fire. This painting was so esteemed by King Philip III for its excellence, that when news arrived of the fire, he asked if it had been burned, and upon being told that it had not, he said 'I am satisfied, for the rest will be redone'.[67]

The profanity of the picture was so overwhelming that even the flames of the Pardo fire could not destroy it. Perhaps its presentation to a heretical prince seemed appropriate, although Philip III's attachment to the picture suggests its departure was more of a loss than connoisseurs like Carducho were prepared to concede.[68]

As the summer progressed, Charles continued to exploit his position when it came to pictures. Much to the astonishment of the Spanish court, he now claimed the entire set of the *Poesie*. Carducho could hardly believe his eyes, recounting 'I then saw them packed into crates, for shipping to England, these being *Diana Bathing, Europa, Danae*, and the rest.' All that prevented their removal was what Carducho darkly referred to as 'later developments'.

These 'later developments' were the gradual but irretrievable breakdown of the match as the summer progressed and the heat rose. James predicted as much, warning Charles of 'the danger of your life by the coming on of the heats'.[69] Charles's negotiating team became increasingly worried at the concessions he was prepared to make to obtain Spanish consent to the marriage. Even worse, his threats to leave Madrid were rejected by the Spanish, making him a virtual prisoner. Charles reluctantly entertained Spanish attempts at conversion and promised parliamentary repeal of anti-Catholic legislation that made even his father despair. His behaviour grew ever more erratic. At one point he tried to confront the Infanta in her orchard. Scaling the wall, he 'sprung down a great height, and so made towards her, but she spying him first of all the rest, gave a shriek and ran back',[70] subsequently making it quite clear to her brother that she regarded the idea of marriage to the English 'heretic' with revulsion.

Suddenly, much to the Spaniards' astonishment, Charles agreed to submit to all the Spanish demands. It was a belatedly Machiavellian manoeuvre intended to force them into allowing him to leave for England with the Infanta. Back in London, James received the news with horrified resignation. The terms of the treaty demanded complete Spanish control over the marriage in Spain and its subsequent ratification in England. The Infanta was allowed a bishop, a chapel and a public church (with full access for English Catholics) and supervision over the education of the offspring, all of which required papal and parliamentary approval. More significantly, all anti-Catholic legislation was to be rescinded and perpetual toleration of private Catholic observance enshrined in parliamentary legislation.[71] The implication was that James's authority over his people was no longer absolute; Catholics could now act as they wished, given what James called 'infinite liberty'. Charles's craven and inept conduct threatened to undermine his own father's sovereignty. If Parliament ever learned of the agreement, there could be rebellion, or even worse.

Back in Madrid, Charles and Philip swore an oath binding them to the revised marriage treaty. But Charles's gamble that he would be able to leave Madrid with the Infanta failed. The Spanish refused to allow the marriage to be consummated until Christmas, for fear that Charles might return to England with the Infanta and renege on his promises to implement religious toleration. Frustrated and defeated after five months of what Gerbier described as the 'long parleys with the slow revolving Spanish Councils of State',[72] Charles announced that he would leave Madrid at the end of August. He signed an oath allowing Philip to act as his proxy in marriage to the Infanta within ten days of the arrival of the revised papal dispensation. The agreement was left in Madrid with Lord Bristol.

Even as he prepared to leave Madrid, Charles continued to buy art, including a painting of 'Our Lady' by Dürer at a cost of just £41 and antique marble heads of Marcus Aurelius, Apollo and Faustina.[73] Sadly his most discerning act of artistic patronage was one that has since been lost. Cottington's account book records that following Charles's departure the sum of 1,100 *reales* was 'Paid unto a Painter for drawing the Princes Picture. Signified by Mr Porter from the Prince'.[74] The painter was none other than the young Diego Velázquez, newly arrived in Madrid, and yet to receive his appointment as court painter to King Philip. Once again, Charles was led to a fine painter by the discernment of his advisers, in this case Endymion Porter, who proved that his connoisseurship was rather better than his diplomacy.

The English party finally left Madrid on 9 September 1623 and headed towards Santander, where the English fleet awaited. As Charles took his leave of Philip and the Spanish court, he repeated his promise to marry the Infanta via proxy and then receive her in England the following year. However, almost as soon as Philip's back was turned he wrote to Bristol, commanding him 'not to deliver my proxy to the King of Spain until I may have sufficient security both from him and the Infanta that after I am betrothed a monastery may not rob me of my wife'.[75] It was the last in a long line of inept and duplicitous decisions that finally put paid to the Spanish match.

There was one final artistic twist to Charles's visit. As the

English entourage travelled north, they stopped at Valladolid, home of La Ribera, the imposing villa built by Philip III's chief minister, the Duke of Lerma, now the royal property of Philip IV. La Ribera housed over 600 paintings and drawings collected prior to Lerma's fall from power and subsequent death in 1621.

Andrés Mendoza recorded that 'His Highness [Prince Charles] went to see the King's Garden' and 'he was much delighted with the Pictures of Raphael de Urbino, and Michael Angelo, and with the Alabaster Fountain, which the illustrious great Duke of Tuscan gave to my Lord Cardinall, the Duke of Lerma: he was served with it: it is the Portraiture of Cain and Abel'.[76] Mendoza was rather optimistic in claiming that Lerma's collections contained originals by Raphael and Michelangelo. The duke had received a carved fountain from the Tuscan representatives of the Archduke Cosimo de' Medici: it comprised a life-size marble statue of *Samson Slaying a Philistine*, one of the most accomplished pieces of the Florentine sculptor Giambologna.[77]

Those who saw the piece once it arrived in England quickly adopted Mendoza's attribution of the statue as Cain and Abel. Charles's interest in it was understandable. This was after all an example of the work of his dead brother Henry's favourite sculptor. Perhaps Charles could identify Giambologna from his own small collection of the sculptor's work, and his recollection of pressing the small bronze horse into his dying brother's hands in 1612. It is more likely that Endymion Porter or Balthazar Gerbier discreetly explained the statue's significance to Charles. The prince identified with what he saw as its graphic depiction of the ultimate act of filial betrayal. Charles and Philip had characterized each other as 'brothers' for over five months. Now Charles was performing the role of the betrayed and deceived brother, casting himself as the innocent figure of Abel, at the mercy of the figure of Cain as he raises his sword to deliver the *coup de grâce*. The even darker possibility is that Charles correctly identified the statue as depicting Samson slaying a Philistine, and saw it as a prophetic carving of the retribution the English now sought over the 'philistine' Catholics.

Balthazar Gerbier took delivery of the statue and 'a painting by Paolo Veronese of a boy fleeing from a dog'.[78] This was a wonderfully euphemistic description of Veronese's lush, erotic painting of *Mars and Venus*. Just as Mars slips off Venus's dress to reveal her breasts, Cupid interrupts the amorous liaison, toppling backwards against his mother in an attempt to escape from the little dog. Gerbier spent his Italian summer of 1621 searching in vain for a painting by Veronese. At last he was presented with the opportunity to recommend an example of the Venetian's work to Prince Charles.

Frustrated by Philip's refusal to allow the entire set of Titian's *Poesie* to leave Madrid, Charles now claimed two wonderful pieces from the Spanish royal collection in the king's absence. Veronese's painting provided a fitting conclusion to the trip. It conformed to the prince's preference for erotically charged classical scenes by sixteenth-century Italian masters. Its portrayal of the disruption of an infamous sexual union with disastrous consequences undoubtedly appealed to him as he rode ever further away from Madrid and the Infanta, finally setting sail for England on 18 September. He would never set foot on the Continent again.

FROM THE PERSPECTIVE of a disinterested collector, Prince Charles's visit to Madrid was an aesthetic success. It exposed the prince's inner circle to one of the finest collections of Italian art in Europe, while Charles discovered Titian and returned with a clutch of superb paintings that formed the basis of his expanding collection. Even more significantly, the visit marked a decisive shift in English approaches to art. Rather than seeing the religious and imperial subject matter of paintings by artists like Titian and Veronese as threatening to English Protestantism, collectors like Charles, Buckingham and their advisers were excited by what they regarded as the intrinsic artistic qualities of these works.

Once back in London, the prince was encouraged to classify his pictures on the same lines as Philip's and commissioned an inventory of his fledgling collection. The list revealed just how far Charles still had to go before he measured up to his Spanish cousin. It consisted of a meagre twenty-one portraits,[79] including Charles's parents, as well as Erasmus, Philip II, King Henry IV of France and the prince himself. Older artists like Holbein, Hilliard,

Oliver and Heemskerck painted most of the portraits. There were also signs of the impact of the Madrid visit. These included new additions – Abraham van Blyenberch, Tintoretto, Rubens and Titian. There was also a preoccupation with the identity of the artists, or what the list called 'famous masters'. This was a departure from the usual Jacobean concentration on subject matter. Several months later Charles took another step towards systematizing his collection with the appointment of Abraham van der Doort as Keeper of the Cabinet Room at St James's, charged with 'the collecting, receiving, delivering, sorting, placing & removing and causing of making by our appointing such things as we shall think fit & also to keep a Register book of them'.[80]

Charles also returned with ambitious plans to remodel Whitehall based on the Habsburg palaces in Madrid and in particular the Alcázar. The adoption of sober attire reflected a deeper assimilation of Spanish attitudes towards collecting, ceremony and privacy, all echoed in the architectural styles he saw during his visit. The trip confirmed his natural predisposition for a more private and withdrawn approach towards sovereignty than that adopted by his father. This withdrawal was reflected in the placement of art within royal apartments closed to all but the closest of friends and advisers. The effect of Charles's attempts to emulate and compete with Philip IV was felt by art dealers and painters across Europe. One eighteenth-century French commentator observed that 'the rivalry between these two sovereigns caused the price of old masters to triple throughout the whole of Europe. Art treasures became real treasures in the world of commerce.'[81] Although there is little direct evidence to substantiate this claim, it captured the perception of growing competition for paintings between London and Madrid, and Prince Charles's emergence as a serious player in the market.

However, politically the trip was a disaster. At a cost of over £30,000 it was an expensive adventure, but its diplomatic cost was even greater. Among the wiser heads of the Stuart court, it exposed the political inexperience of Charles and Buckingham, establishing their reputation for recklessness and deception. Upon their return, they were fêted as Protestant heroes, a crushing irony considering their last five months spent bargaining away England's authority over its Catholic subjects. Buoyed by their new-found popularity, both men convinced the ailing king to capitalize on the popular wave of anti-Spanish sentiment and recall Parliament in preparation for war. In attempting to diplomatically isolate Spain, Buckingham also persuaded James and Charles to open marriage negotiations for the hand of the French princess Henrietta Maria, the timid young woman Tom and John Smith had seen (and ignored) from behind their false moustaches in Paris in the spring of 1623.[82] Although Henrietta Maria's Catholicism would hardly endear her to many in England, Buckingham and Charles felt it better to negotiate from a position of relative strength with a militarily weakened French crown than with the more aggressive Spanish. Many in England comforted themselves with the thought that whereas the Spanish match looked like a capitulation to Spain's imperial designs, the French match represented a check to such designs by hopefully bringing France into an anti-Spanish axis. Nevertheless, the thought of the English heir's prospective marriage to yet another Catholic princess was greeted with little popular enthusiasm.

Before plans for either war or wedding were complete, King James I died on 27 March 1625. Having already buried his older brother and mother, Charles now led the mourners at his father's funeral in May. As soon as the ceremony was over, Buckingham set off for Paris to collect the new king's French bride, married by proxy in Notre-Dame just days before. While in Paris, he met Rubens, who was working on his series of Palais de Luxembourg paintings of the life of Marie de' Medici that prevented him from pursuing the London commission to decorate the Banqueting House. Buckingham was so impressed with the Luxembourg paintings that he commissioned the artist to paint his portrait. It drew on Titian's and Leonardo's equestrian portraits that both sitter and artist had seen in Madrid, and cost the duke the phenomenal sum of £500. At least when Buckingham returned to London the following month he brought a bride as well as paintings with him, which is more than can be said about the Madrid fiasco.

Meanwhile, as England drifted into war with Spain, Charles quietly handed the Giambologna statue over to Buckingham, who displayed it in the grounds of York House. Blissfully unaware of what had really taken place in Madrid, Henry Peacham admired the statue and its setting, rhapsodizing that 'the garden will be renowned for long as John de Bologna's Cain and Abel stand erected there, a piece of wondrous Art and Workmanship'.[83] But the statue's meaningless filial betrayal seems to have become too unpalatable, even for the new King Charles I.

❦

CHAPTER FOUR

THE ITALIAN JOB

OF ALL CHARLES I'S ART PURCHASES, none secured his reputation more than the audacious acquisition of one of Italy's greatest collections of sixteenth-century Renaissance painting. Between 1627 and 1629 the king ordered the purchase of nearly 400 pictures and classical statues from Mantua's bankrupt Gonzaga dynasty at a cost of over £18,000. This was a huge amount to spend on art in seventeenth-century terms – Buckingham spent nearly as much on a palatial mansion house in Essex – but it was a bargain considering the size and quality of the collection. Rather than cultivating the creative achievements of the Italian Renaissance among his native artists, Charles simply bought a version of the artistic phenomenon from Mantua, introducing painters never seen before in England, including Raphael, Mantegna, Correggio, Giulio Romano and Guido Reni.

For many subsequent observers, Charles's extraordinary coup established him as one of Europe's pre-eminent royal connoisseurs, a decisive and wealthy monarch exhibiting impeccable taste and discernment. It is a flattering picture, glazed with centuries of royalist *sfumato*, that obscures the mediation of art dealers, businessmen, financiers and diplomats, warfare, bankruptcy, fraud and a *coup d'état* that took the Gonzaga collection from Mantua to London. Exhibiting the diffidence and vacillation that led England into a series of militarily and financially disastrous wars, the young king nearly squandered the opportunity to purchase the collection. He was saved only by the determination of those who invested in the proposed acquisition and refused to see the deal collapse, whatever the political and financial costs.[1]

The road to Mantua began before Charles's coronation at Westminster Abbey in February 1626.[2] Hopes were high following the death of King James in the spring of the previous year that his son would bring a more consensual approach to parliamentary politics and a reformation of the decadent court of his father. After all, Charles was raised in an age of parliaments, and his initial proclamations suggested his appreciation of the need to curb the financial excesses of the Jacobean court. 'Whereas, out of our own observance in the late reign of our most dear and royal father,' announced one of Charles' proclamations, 'we saw much disorder in and about his household by reasons of the many idle persons and other unnecessary attendants following the same; which evil, we, finding to bring much dishonour to our house, have resolved the reformation thereof.'[3] Other changes were also eagerly antici-pated, including a speedy recall of Parliament and the pursuit of a more aggressive foreign policy towards the Palatinate and Spain. Unfortunately, the diplomatic consequences of Charles's visit to Madrid were already taking their toll. His marriage to Henrietta Maria was not going well. His new wife, aged just sixteen, con-fronted with a new country and already fearful of Buckingham's influence over her husband, took solace within her predominantly French-speaking Catholic entourage, much to the consternation of Charles. The shy and formal young queen, used to the splendour of the French royal court, was ordered by the Pope to uphold the Catholic religion in the 'heretical' English court. It was too much to expect from a sixteen-year-old girl more used to the arts of singing, masquing, dancing and riding than matters of state. Her clumsy attempts to assert herself soon ran into difficulties. Matters deteriorated further when Henrietta Maria refused to participate in her husband's royal coronation once she learned it would be presided over by the Protestant bishop William Laud. As a result, she was never ceremonially crowned queen of England.

Within days of Henrietta Maria's arrival in England, Charles moved quickly to recall Parliament in the hope of raising sufficient subsidies to fund war with Spain and aid for the Palatinate. However, like his father, he was voted only a fraction of the money he demanded. In an attempt to reinforce its fiscal control in the face of the crown's growing demands for money, Parliament even limited Charles's right as a new king to set 'tonnage and poundage' (duties on imported goods).

The other problem that the king faced was religion. The recognizably Anglican faith of both Charles and his father had shown itself perilously close to accepting many of the tenets of Catholic belief during the negotiations over the Spanish match, which led Parliament to renew its calls for even harsher anti-Catholic legislation. However, the secret terms of Charles's marriage to Henrietta Maria also required an end to Catholic persecution. The new king was immediately faced with a dilemma that was broadly of his own making: either limit the persecution and increase parliamentary opposition, or renege on the agreement and alienate France and his new wife. By choosing the latter, Charles put himself on the path to war with France, but he also failed to appease Parliament, which was already worried about what it saw as the growing influence of another threat to English Protestantism.

Arminianism offered a refinement of the more rigorous Calvinist approach towards predestination, which insisted that God preordained a certain elect to salvation, while others were condemned to damnation. Based on the writings of the late sixteenth-century Dutch theologian Jacob Harmenszoon (known as Arminius), Arminianism rejected the belief in absolute predestination, arguing instead that those who were prepared to repent their sins were guaranteed that Christ would intercede to save them. With this came a more ceremonial approach to worship and the role of the clergy, who conducted services using an altar railed off from the congregation. Although Arminianism explicitly defined itself in opposition to Catholicism, many English theologians influenced by Calvinism regarded such beliefs as heresy and tantamount to the Catholic doctrine of free will. When the Essex rector Richard Montagu published a pamphlet in 1624 questioning the Calvinist approach to predestination and espousing vaguely Arminian views, there was uproar in Parliament. However, Charles was sympathetic to the position, having travelled to Madrid with the Arminian chaplain Matthew Wren. He was also about to appoint another Arminian sympathizer, William Laud, to the see of Bath and Wells. Exhibiting an intransigence that would come to define his subsequent rule, Charles responded to criticism of Montagu by appointing him as one of his chaplains. This effectively ended

Parliament's attack on Montagu, but failed to defuse the broader problem of religious conflict. To make matters worse, Buckingham was showing increasing sympathies with Arminianism. Parliament was already attacking what they regarded as Buckingham's reckless counsel, and, to prevent further attacks on his friend, Charles dissolved Parliament in August 1625, less than two months after its first sitting.

Even as domestic events quickly deflated the hope and celebration of the new era of Caroline rule, the king and his advisers were making plans for a dramatic expansion of the royal art collection. Diplomats like Sir Henry Wotton and Sir Dudley Carleton achieved varying degrees of success in supplying the Jacobean court with high-quality paintings and statues, but collectors like Arundel and Buckingham realized there was potentially greater profit in employing private buyers to scour Europe. The risks were higher, but the prizes greater. Buckingham paid first William Trumbull and then Balthazar Gerbier to operate in the Low Countries as political intelligencers and art dealers. Buckingham's collecting rival Arundel dispatched his agent, William Petty, even further afield to Asia Minor, where, along with Sir Thomas Roe, he braved storms, earthquakes and imprisonment at the hands of Ottoman officials to buy, and in many cases steal, classical statuary.[4]

Such developments were partly the result of the Madrid visit, which dramatically broadened Charles and Buckingham's aesthetic horizons. Having seen the fabulous Habsburg collection, the king realized that Rome had eclipsed Venice as the greatest centre of Italian art. Within months of his return from Spain, he began trying to lure Roman artists to London. He authorized approaches to the Rome-based painters Francesco Albani and Francesco Barbieri, the latter somewhat unpromisingly nicknamed 'Il Guercino' (The Squinter). Both refused to come to England. Guercino worked in Rome under papal patronage and his achievements included an altarpiece in St Peter's. Charles promised him generous benefits if he left Rome for London, including an annual salary, but he declined the offer, claiming that he did not want to live among Protestant heretics and, besides, he had heard that the English weather was terrible.[5]

What Charles wanted, Buckingham supplied. He returned from France in June 1625 with gifts of 'rich pictures and statues' from the Parisian court,[6] and an agreement brokered by Gerbier to spend 100,000 florins (£10,000) buying Rubens's art collection, including over thirty of his pictures, the same number of classical statues, and various coins and gems. Buckingham was probably unaware that the wily Rubens was passing on statues bought from Dudley Carleton in 1618 that had already travelled to London and had originally been intended for Buckingham's rival the Earl of Somerset. Rubens copied everything before shipping it to London, then invested his capital in Antwerp real estate. Even Gerbier profited from the deal, pocketing 5 per cent of the transaction – an impressive return of about £500.[7] The deal also re-established discussions between Rubens and Whitehall on designs for the Banqueting House. Henry, Lord Danvers, wrote to William Trumbull, informing him, 'His Majesty is now upon a design of building at Whitehall which plot once resolved will give me the measure for Rubens' picture.'[8] Charles was clearly planning even more ambitious rebuilding of Whitehall on the lines of the Spanish royal palaces in Madrid.

Although Buckingham failed to lure Rubens to London, he did manage to obtain the services of a lesser talent, Marie de' Medici's Italian court painter Orazio Gentileschi. Orazio was already burned out, an itinerant painter in his sixties, but with the advantage of a Roman training in the fashionable, if still-controversial, style of Caravaggio. Unequal to the competition with Rubens, he jumped at the opportunity to work for an inexperienced but enthusiastic young king whose court painters promised little competition to his limited talents.[9]

Orazio arrived in England in October 1626, just eight months after Charles's coronation. The king was already hatching new plans to expand his collection. He employed his recently appointed master of the king's music, Nicholas Lanier, to go to Italy on a six-month expedition to buy pictures for his Whitehall palace. Lanier was the perfect candidate to act as a royal art agent. He came from a family of talented Huguenot musicians who had fled to England from the religious persecution of 1560s France, soon establishing themselves as members of the Elizabethan court's musical circle.[10] A renowned viol player, singer, composer and sometime painter, Lanier was young, handsome, cultured and fluent in French and Italian. Such talents quickly brought him to the attention of first Robert Cecil, Earl of Salisbury, then George Villiers, Duke of Buckingham. Both men valued him for his artistic accomplishments and also his suitability as a spy. Lanier made several trips to France and Italy as a court musician, circulating secret correspondence between English diplomats. On the eve of Charles's accession he was awarded the coveted title of 'Master of the King's Musick'. The new king identified Lanier as someone with a judicious eye for a fine picture, who could also move easily among the courts and cities of Catholic Europe without the burden of an official diplomatic position.

All the evidence suggests that Charles initially directed Lanier towards Rome, not Mantua. English collectors like the Arundels had spent time in Mantua, and Lady Arundel exchanged letters with the Mantuan Grand Chancellor, Count Alessandro Striggi, unsuccessfully requesting a model of Giulio Romano's Palazzo del Te. If Mantua was discussed as Lanier's destination, it remained shrouded in secrecy. Experts like Arundel, Inigo Jones and Gerbier were far more likely to recommend Rome as the obvious place to go to buy works of the Old Masters or the latest fashionable painters. However, with little diplomatic representation in Rome, it was difficult to acquire pictures without an experienced agent.

The only correspondence that survives explaining the motives behind Lanier's trip is in the form of a letter of introduction dated 2 June 1625, sent by Secretary of State Lord Conway to Sir Isaac Wake, Dudley Carleton's successor as ambassador to Venice and Savoy. Conway told Wake that the king had sent Lanier 'to provide for him some choice pictures in Italy' and that the ambassador must 'give him your best help and assistance in directing him where such pieces may be had, procuring him the view of them, and that then he may buy them at as easy rates as you can get set upon them'. With one eye on an already constrained exchequer, Conway warned Wake that Lanier 'hath bills of exchange for money, and it will be one special part of your and his care, not to make known the cause of his coming, because that would much enhance the prices'.[11] Lanier's mission was veiled in secrecy from the outset, and it seems his greatest dangers came from unscrupulous art dealers rather than religious zealots.

Wake responded by humorously calling the fashion for pictures Whitehall's new religion. He wrote back to Conway, confessing:

> ... it be a hard task for me to undertake, both because I do profess to understand nothing in that way, and because I do know that there are some in England who have taken unto themselves a monopoly of passing their verdict upon all things of this nature, so that if a man do baptise his picture or statue at the font of their censure, he cannot be admitted into the Church.[12]

It was a witty perspective on the apparent preference for art over religion among those closest to Charles in Whitehall. Wake was a tough, loyal career diplomat who appreciated that his inexperience in matters of collecting and artistic taste placed him at a distinct disadvantage in comparison with lesser diplomats but better art agents like Gerbier, Trumbull and now Lanier.

Upon arriving in Venice, Lanier was greeted by Ambassador Wake, who did as he was told and introduced the young musician to Venice's most successful and notorious art dealer, Daniel Nys. The English had good cause to regard the French-born Nys with some suspicion since his theft of statues sold to Sir Dudley Carleton in 1615. Unfortunately for them, the English collectors were stuck with the unprincipled Nys; he continued to represent Carleton's interests throughout the 1620s[13] and was one of the few dealers prepared to put aside religious and political differences to buy art for English collectors like Carleton, Arundel and now Lanier.

Lanier and Nys got on well. Nys was impressed by Lanier's musical talents and sophisticated company, not to mention his bills of exchange. Lanier paused only briefly in Venice before heading for Rome via Verona and Mantua. Indiscreet as ever, Nys wrote ahead to Count Alessandro Striggi in Mantua, warning the chancellor of Lanier's arrival. Nys recommended that Striggi introduce Lanier to Duke Ferdinando Gonzaga, 6th Duke of Mantua, because they shared 'the same exceptional taste in paintings and drawings'.[14] The implication was obvious. Through Nys's introduction, Lanier could make an offer for works from the

Gonzaga collection. Before the end of the month, Lanier was back in Venice. Nys told Striggi that Lanier 'cannot find words to express his ravishment and excitement' at Mantua's glories, concluding 'he will make an excellent messenger to the King of England's cabinet'.[15]

What excited both Nys and Lanier was the possibility that even a fraction of the legendary Gonzaga collection might be for sale. Ever since Gianfrancesco Gonzaga had been created 1st Marquis of Mantua by the Holy Roman Emperor in 1433, the tiny city had successfully manoeuvred itself into the heart of European political life through a series of shrewd dynastic marriages and lavish patronage of the arts. Under the 2nd Marquis, Ludovico Gonzaga, some of the finest artists of the Italian Renaissance were invited to work in Mantua. First Pisanello, then Leon Battista Alberti and Andrea Mantegna designed a series of pioneering churches, frescoes and paintings to adorn the city and its palaces.

The Gonzaga's aim was to compete with the aesthetic splendour and courtly magnificence of larger rival Italian city-states like Florence, Venice and Rome. This culminated in Mantegna's famous series of nine paintings depicting *The Triumphs of Caesar*: massive in scale and innovative in the realism of their depiction of the classical past, they implied that the Gonzaga were the inheritors of the imperial mantle of Julius Caesar. Such claims were wildly over-inflated, but they provided the Gonzaga dynasty with international prestige as patrons of the arts on the same scale as the Florentine Medici, the Roman popes and the Ottoman sultans.

Marquis Francesco's II marriage in 1490 to Isabella d'Este, from the powerful d'Este dynasty of Ferrara, strengthened the Gonzaga's international reputation further. Isabella possessed an 'insatiable desire' for antiquities and modern art, commissioning Mantegna, Titian and Leonardo to paint her portrait, as well as patronizing some of the finest artists of the day, including Pietro Perugino, Giulio Romano and Antonio Correggio. She oversaw the creation of a *grotta* and *studioli* where she carefully housed and ceremonially displayed her finest books, antiquities and paintings.[16]

Both Isabella and her son Federico Gonzaga, 1st Duke of Mantua, encouraged the highly mannered and explicitly erotic style developed in the mid-sixteenth century in the works of Titian, Correggio and Giulio Romano. Federico commissioned Giulio to design the Palazzo del Te, which was decorated with the artist's baroque fantasies and the sensual inventiveness that were so admired by Inigo Jones on his visit to Mantua in 1613–14 but which today might strike the sceptical visitor as rather grotesque. In the 1530s, when Isabella commissioned Correggio to paint a pair of classical allegories representing Vice and Virtue for her *studiolo*, she appears to have approved of their perverse sexuality. The *Allegory of Vice* canvas portrays a bearded figure literally torn between the pleasure and pain of various sensual desires. While one nymph peels back the flesh on his leg, a second bare-breasted figure blows a phallic flute into the anguished man's ear. The snakes that threaten to entwine him and the vine that creeps round the tree all suggest man as a prisoner of his illicit desires, a conceit reinforced by his barely concealed erection. Like the Gonzaga dynasty, Charles I's court was fascinated with this darker, erotically disturbing development of later sixteenth-century Italian art.

The 6th Duke, Ferdinando, seemed unlikely to sanction the sale of the collection because he was one of the most discerning and enthusiastic buyers of all the later Gonzaga dukes. Since his accession to the dukedom in 1612, he had spent most of his money augmenting the collection.[17] As a cardinal in Rome, he came under the influence of the new style of Caravaggio and his followers, a taste he developed in his subsequent patronage back in Mantua. He commissioned or acquired pictures by Giovanni Baglione, Domenico Fetti, Paul Bril and Guido Reni, the last of whom painted a series of dramatic canvases of episodes in the life of Hercules for Ferdinando's recently completed baroque residence, the Villa Favorita. Reni's energetic, violent paintings were in sharp contrast to the lyrical classicism of the earlier periods of the collection and reflect the changing taste of the early seventeenth century.

Throughout the early 1620s Ferdinando was buying up pictures in bulk. Perhaps Chancellor Striggi was concerned at the extravagant cost of his duke's purchases and approached buyers like Lady Arundel and Daniel Nys with a view to liquidating some of the older pictures, now regarded as unfashionable. Nys clearly faced a long and protracted round of negotiations if he was to prise pictures out of the duke. Lanier wisely left him to get on with it and headed for Rome, where he arrived in the autumn of 1625.

After the relative serenity and tranquillity of low-lying Venice and Mantua, the harsh southern light and architectural grandeur of Rome must have come as a shock to the young musician. Since 1625 was Holy Year, over a million pilgrims had crammed into the hot, bustling city, marvelling at the latest paintings, altarpieces, frescoes, chapels and tombs of Francesco Albani, Domenichino, Gianlorenzo Bernini, Guido Reni and others commissioned under the enthusiastic patronage of Maffeo Barberini, Pope Urban VIII, the creator of what one later observer called 'the golden age of painting'. As well as leading the way in the visual arts, Rome was at the forefront of innovations in choral and instrumental music, as seen in the musical subjects of Caravaggio and Artemisia Gentileschi.[18] It was a perfect environment for Lanier, but he showed few signs of being distracted by the city's sights and sounds. His mission was to buy pictures and by January of the following year he successfully applied for a licence to export over thirty paintings from Rome to London.

Lanier's acquisitions reveal that, just like Duke Ferdinando, he was heavily influenced by the baroque style in vogue in Rome at this time. He bought works by the landscape painter Paul Bril, Sebastiano del Piombo, Guercino, Perino del Vaga, Giovanni Baglione and Jacopo Palma. Most of the artists were contemporary, fashionable painters whose works were widely available in Rome – at a price. Unfortunately, they were not of the quality to which Charles and Buckingham were accustomed after their Madrid adventure. Nevertheless, Lanier spent £2,000, a substantial outlay and an impressive haul of pictures for such a short period.

Lanier's ability to move successfully through the Italian art world was confirmed by another picture listed in his consignment: his own portrait, painted by a new acquaintance, an exciting young painter and former pupil of Rubens called Anthony Van Dyck. Lanier probably met Van Dyck in Genoa, where the young painter completed his portrait in under a week. It is a vibrant, striking image of the young Lanier, who brims with confidence and youthful hauteur. Here were two young itinerant northern European artists, drawn together by their precocious talent, proudly displaying their success in the cut-throat Italian art world.

Of all the paintings that Lanier presented to his new king upon his return to London in the spring of 1626, it was Van Dyck's portrait that was most admired. In the long term, its success contributed to the decision to lure Van Dyck to England six years later. In the short term, it was a risky but clever piece of self-promotion. Not even the arrogant Balthazar Gerbier would dare commission a portrait of himself with the king's money; such grandiose image management was almost exclusively reserved for his master, the Duke of Buckingham. Lanier's tactic paid off, though. Charles hung the portrait in the Bear Gallery at Whitehall, and the courtly reputation of the King's Musician was assured.

As well as returning with paintings from Rome, Lanier brought back the sensational news that Nys was in negotiations for the Mantuan collection. It is not known how far Nys had progressed in his dealings, or how much Lanier knew about them, but by October 1626 an event took place that threatened to change the entire complexion of any possible sale. Duke Ferdinando died suddenly on 26 October and was succeeded by his younger brother, Duke Vincenzo II. For Nys, Ferdinando's sudden death threatened to complicate negotiations. He wrote to Chancellor Striggi two weeks later: 'I am extremely saddened at the death of his Serene Highness Ferdinando,' but, 'I am now consoled with the thought that the Serene Highness Duke Vincenzo has succeeded him', cheerfully promising, 'I will see to the deal in the pictures with the consent of His Serene Highness.'[19] Nys proposed to dispatch one of his servants to compile an inventory of the pictures for sale, from which he and Striggi would then negotiate a price.

Nys and Striggi were eager to finalize a deal because Duke Vincenzo's succession ignited a dangerous political crisis that threatened to engulf both the Gonzaga and Mantua. The city's militarily strategic location due south of the Brenner Pass meant that whoever ruled the city effectively controlled access to the Italian peninsula from the north. Since the late fifteenth century the Gonzaga had pledged their allegiance to the Habsburg

Empire, but Vincenzo's accession put this alliance in doubt. The problem was that Vincenzo had no direct heir to succeed to the dukedom. France saw the opportunity to expand its interests in the region by supporting the claims to succession of a branch of the dynasty represented by the pro-French Charles de Gonzague, Duc de Nevers. To complicate matters, Mantua's western neighbour, Charles Emmanuel, Duke of Savoy, also used Ferdinando's death as an opportunity to renew his claim to the contested Mantuan possession of the Duchy of Monferrato and its strategically important fortification at Casale, east of Turin.[20] Vincenzo's poor health suggested that he was unlikely to rule for very long, and Nys appreciated that he needed to complete the deal with Striggi and get his pictures out of Mantua before, as seemed likely, the political and military forces ranged against it overwhelmed the city.

Throughout the spring of 1627 Nys worked fast, regularly corresponding with Striggi in an attempt to reach an agreement. Negotiations began with the return of Nys's servant Filippo Esegren with two inventories: the first comprised pictures Striggi and Duke Vincenzo were prepared to sell; a second, more clandestine list recorded all the valuable pictures the Mantuan authorities were withholding from the sale. Nys wrote back to Striggi, smoothly informing him, 'I will now choose a few pieces from the first list, but I also wish to choose some pieces from the second list.' If Striggi was agreeable to the revised list, Nys suggested he would 'like the prices to be marked on it, and we will be able to close the deal which will be kept under strict secrecy', promising to offer 'a price so fair as to allow us to reach an agreement'.[21]

Striggi's first inventory ran to three pages of pictures valued at 19,598 *scudi*. It was a fine list of pictures, ranging from some of the collection's fifteenth-century works by Mantegna, through Isabella d'Este's commissions by Giulio Romano and Correggio, to Duke Ferdinando's more recent acquisitions of Domenico Fetti and Guido Reni. However, it conspicuously omitted the collection's finest masterpieces. But Nys was not to be cheated. He submitted his second list of an additional twenty-nine pictures, valued at just over 15,000 *scudi*.

The list's contents were enough to make any collector's mouth water. It included Correggio's two allegories, the *Allegory of Vice* and the *Allegory of Virtue*, valued at 2,000 *scudi*; a Giulio Romano *St Jerome*, valued at 1,000 *scudi*, Guido Reni's *Three Graces*, nine works by Pieter Brueghel the Elder; two Madonnas by Andrea del Sarto and one small Madonna by Raphael.[22] The most expensive item was the series of *Twelve Caesars* by Titian, valued by Nys at 5,000 *scudi*. They were commissioned by Duke Federico in the late 1530s to adorn a suite of rooms designed by Giulio Romano and, like the Mantegna *Triumphs*, they reflected the Gonzaga's desire to inflate their authority by associating themselves with the achievements of imperial Rome.

Without question the finest picture claimed by Nys and the jewel of the entire collection was one of two paintings by Raphael: *La Perla*, valued at 4,000 *scudi*. Nys knew exactly how to market the picture for its prospective buyer, the king of England. He understood that Charles appreciated paintings that magnified their owners' political authority, so he claimed that Duke Vincenzo I obtained the painting in exchange for a marquisate in Monferrato worth 50,000 *scudi*; who could resist such a picture?[23] Alongside Striggi's first list, the overall selection was truly spectacular, representing the best of the collection's approximately 2,000 paintings.

Nys was now in his element, haggling over pictures and money with unalloyed relish. He proposed to offer 35,000 Mantuan *scudi* for the pictures, but Striggi quibbled over Nys's valuations. He also demanded payment in the internationally recognized 'hard' currency of Venetian ducats. Nys came back with another cunning counter-offer. He marginally increased his valuations on some of the paintings, added a further list of six pictures, and offered to take the list of works he initially rejected for an extra 2,000 *scudi*, bringing his offer to 40,000. In his correspondence he worried that this was far too high, 'owing to my love of art', but Nys was a shrewd businessman and knew what he was doing. He was treating the pictures like any other commodity, apparently increasing his initial offer but in effect bargaining for more pictures at a significantly reduced rate. Having strategically devalued Striggi's initial list by rejecting its contents as inferior, he now effectively offered to take them off Striggi's hands at a fraction of their nominal value. It was a consummate performance.

Striggi was no match for Nys. All he could do was try and

drive up the dealer's offer as high as possible and insist on payment in ducats. Nys would have none of it. 'The currency makes a difference indeed,' he insisted in a letter to Striggi in early April. As 'compensation' he offered to raise his offer to 45,000 *scudi*.[24] Striggi still held out, so the Frenchman again requested additional pictures before raising his price to 50,000 *scudi*. Although this was an excellent deal for Nys, he suddenly pleaded financial difficulties. 'I have not replied to you promptly owing to a serious difference I had with my purse,' he wrote to Striggi in June. 'I wanted to offer more than I have done, but she [his purse] would not let me do it, saying "no more".'[25] It is unclear if Nys's sudden protestation of financial difficulties was feigned or genuine, but it galvanized London into action. Lanier was immediately dispatched to Italy to settle the deal carefully brokered by Nys.[26]

The sudden hiatus in negotiations suggests that Charles and his advisers were not as enthusiastic about Nys's progress as might have been expected. Once again, political developments were threatening to scupper the deal. The spring of 1627 was hardly the best time for Charles I to sanction the acquisition of a large collection of pictures. The previous year had seen the recall and dissolution of his second Parliament, following its attempts to impeach Buckingham for his military incompetence and domestic cronyism. Having once again failed to obtain the subsidies he required, Charles took the precipitate step of demanding what became known as the Forced Loan from corporations and wealthy individuals, some of which refused to pay and challenged the crown to justify the legality of its actions. Matters deteriorated even further as Charles, prompted by Buckingham, declared war against the French. Despite Charles's marriage to Henrietta Maria, the English court remained hostile to the French crown's persecution of the Huguenot city of La Rochelle. Having promoted one disastrous war against Spain to establish his domestic popularity, Buckingham now proposed an equally misguided war with France in a bid to reclaim the political initiative at home. He planned to take the French stronghold of St Martin on the Ile de Ré, then liberate La Rochelle.

By mid-August, as Buckingham laid siege to the French garrison on the Ile de Ré, Lanier was in Venice and Nys in Mantua, attempting to overcome the stalemate in negotiations with Striggi. The broad terms of the deal were finally agreed, with Nys offering 68,000 *scudi*, a substantial increase on his previous offer. Once again, it is unclear if Lanier sanctioned this increased offer on King Charles's authority or if the conniving Frenchman acted on his own initiative, eager to complete the deal. After over a fortnight of bargaining in Mantua, Nys proclaimed himself sufficiently satisfied to leave the fine detail to his servants, while he travelled back to Venice to await the arrival of the pictures. On 4 September he informed Striggi that the pictures had arrived. Having received his goods, Nys promised to count the money and settle his bill.[27]

So far, the negotiations between Nys and Striggi had been surprisingly straightforward. Nobody, including Lanier, really believed that after nearly twelve months of intense negotiations, Nys finally held the cream of the Gonzaga art collection in Venice, to all intents and purpose in the possession of the English crown. It was only at this stage, once payment was required, that the real trouble started.

Charles I ruled in a perpetual state of financial crisis, due to his heavy-handed attempts to persuade an increasingly reluctant Parliament to levy money in support his belligerent foreign policy. The drain on what little finances were available occasioned by Buckingham's ill-fated siege of the Ile de Ré only exacerbated the king's problems. Much of the cash for Buckingham's expedition was borrowed from one of the crown's most trusted financiers, Filippo Burlamachi. Since 1620 Burlamachi had lent the exchequer a staggering £713,264, of which over £128,000 was still owed. The siege of St Martin was reaching a critical phase and by September 1627 Buckingham requested a further £16,000 in a final desperate attempt to take the French fortress before reinforcements arrived.[28]

Just as Buckingham's increasingly importunate correspondence reached London, Lanier submitted his claim for settlement of the Mantuan account. In a letter addressed directly to Burlamachi, Lanier asked the financier to forward his notes on Nys's acquisitions to Charles, hoping that 'when the king hath perused them he will think the things are worth his money'. He also asked Burlamachi 'to solicit his Majesty's answer about the collection of statues as soon as may be'.[29] Carried away with excitement at acquiring the Mantuan pictures and apparently oblivious to developments on the Ile de Ré, Lanier required immediate settlement of Nys's bill, calculated at £15,000. Even worse as far as Burlamachi was concerned, he now asked for royal permission to go after Mantua's classical statues.

Burlamachi was horrified. He had lent Prince Henry £480 to buy Venetian paintings in 1611, but Lanier's request was on a completely different financial scale and it arrived at a particularly difficult moment. The financier forwarded the note to Endymion Porter, Charles's trusted adviser in such matters and a veteran of the Madrid visit. Burlamachi assumed that Porter had seen the letter and its financial demands, and scribbled in its margin, 'I prey let me know his Majesty's pleasure, but above all where money shall be found to pay this great sum.' Burlamachi warned Porter that '[i]f it were for 2 or £3,000 it could be borne, but for £15,000, besides the other engagements for his Majesty's service, it will utterly put me out of any possibility to do anything in those provisions which are so necessary for My Lord Duke's relief.'[30]

It was a critical moment for all concerned. In Venice the Mantuan representatives complained of Nys's reluctance to settle his bill. Back in London, the king was faced with a serious dilemma. The money required to secure the Mantuan paintings was almost exactly what Buckingham needed to continue the siege of St Martin. If Charles authorized the Mantuan acquisition it could end Buckingham's hopes of destroying the French garrison.

What happened next was a classic example of royal leger-demain. Through his advisers, Charles intimated that he wanted the pictures. It seems that the hapless Burlamachi stood the cost of the paintings by deferring payment while continuing to support Buckingham. In fact, the duke's fate was already sealed. In late September 1627 the French lifted the siege of St Martin, leaving a defeated and humiliated Buckingham to evacuate the island. Rubens rejoiced in 'the victory of the Most Christian [French] King over the English. He has driven them completely from the Ile de Ré, to their great loss and eternal disgrace.'[31] There was now little need for Burlamachi's credit. The only good news was the acquisition of the Mantuan pictures. In a striking repeat of their adventures in Madrid four years earlier, Charles and Buckingham once again salvaged aesthetic success from a military and political disaster.

Having anticipated London's ponderous financial manoeuvrings, Nys had already settled his debt for the paintings, presumably by raising money against Burlamachi's credit. Unfortunately once news of the deal started to spread, Striggi and his associates faced outraged condemnation. Representatives of the Mantuan senate pledged to 're-buy the paintings and give them back to His Highness to let him know that he was betrayed by those ministers he trusts most'.[32] But as Nys gleefully informed King Charles's advisers, it was too late: 'to the great astonishment of all Italy, and the extreme disgust of the inhabitants of the city of Mantua', the pictures were gone.[33]

As so often in the story of Charles I's collection, a dispute over art mediated broader political conflicts. Striggi was known to support the ducal accession of the pro-French Duc de Nevers. Factions opposed to Striggi now claimed that the pictures were in fact destined not for London but for another Italian collector, the rival Duke of Parma. Exporting the duke's collection to the king of England was bad enough, but selling it to a rival Italian state threatened politically calamitous dishonour. Striggi provided a robust defence of his actions, denying rumours of the Parma sale, and insisting that the English acquisition enabled him to redeem the ducal royal jewels, placed in pawn to pay the rising Gonzaga debt. Besides, he insisted, 'this household still remains so well provided with paintings that no other in Italy can compare with it'.[34] He also persuaded the politically inept Duke Vincenzo to accept that 'what is done, is done'. Fortunately for Striggi, the dissolute duke showed little interest in recovering his family's precious paintings. He was more concerned to use some of the profit to acquire the personal services of a female dwarf.[35]

Indifferent to Mantua's dented pride, Nys was impatient to proceed with his next deal: the acquisition of the Gonzaga's collection of over 100 classical marble statues, as well as pictures initially held back by Duke Vincenzo. Nys and Lanier were primarily in the market for paintings, not statues, presumably on orders from Whitehall. However, Nys sprang back into action once he realized that the Gonzaga marbles were also up for sale. Having already acquired fashionable classical statuary for both Sir Dudley Carleton and the Earl of Arundel, he believed there was sufficient demand in London from an art-loving king to justify the acquisition of even more.

To lessen the blow of the loss of his pictures, Duke Vincenzo asked that all the paintings in Nys's possession be copied. It was a telling request. For decades English collectors like Arundel and Prince Charles had commissioned prized copies of unobtainable Italian painting and statuary. Now the Gonzaga family meekly requested copies of its own collection, which was on the verge of being shipped off to London. Nys immediately agreed to the request, although the Mantuan representatives soon began to complain of the poor quality of the reproductions. The cunning art dealer's attention was already shifting to his second round of negotiations with Striggi.

Nys's eagerness to acquire more was borne of a realization that in the haste of purchasing his first consignment, he might have missed the greatest prize of all: Mantegna's *Triumphs of Caesar*. Writing to his old client Dudley Carleton some months later, Nys confessed, 'the best informed persons told me that I had left the most beautiful behind, and that, not having the *Triumph of Julius Caesar*, I had nothing at all; this touched me to the core'.[36] Nys offered 50,000 *scudi* for over 200 marble statues, a clutch of other pictures miraculously 'discovered in secret chambers' and the Mantegna *Triumphs*. This time the Mantuan representatives were more circumspect in their negotiations. They dismissed Nys's requests for various pieces of jewellery and drawings, and again demanded payment in Venetian ducats.

Protracted negotiations dragged on throughout the winter until larger political events once more intervened. In the closing weeks of December 1627 Duke Vincenzo Gonzaga fell seriously ill. Eager to ensure the smooth succession of Charles, Duc de Nevers, Striggi arranged for Princess Maria, daughter of the late Duke Francesco Gonzaga, to marry Nevers' son, the Duc de Rethel. The hastily arranged marriage service took place at the deathbed of the expiring duke, who blessed the union and the accession of Rethel's father, Charles, to the dukedom of Mantua.[37]

Within days of his marriage Rethel, assuming the title 'Prince of Mantua', wrote to King Charles in London, informing him of 'the death of my cousin the Duke Vincent, now in his glorie'. Rethel assured him, 'The Duke Charles my Lord and Father is come to the succession of these States, and both of us do succeed to the dutiful respect to your Majesty', promising to 'perform your Majesty's Commandments'.[38] It was a tacit assurance that, despite what was in effect a palace *coup d'état*, the deal to sell the Gonzaga collection was still on. The lack of any explicit reference to pictures is perfectly understandable. Princes hardly ever discussed such vulgar matters as buying and selling art: that was left to intermediaries like Nys and Lanier.

Nys was understandably delighted that Nevers intended to go through with the deal, thanks to a combination of indifference towards art and the need to raise money in the face of looming war. 'The death of Duke Vincenzo filled me with sorrow, the assumption of the Duke of Nevers filled me with joy,' chirruped the relieved art dealer in his first letter of the new year to Striggi.[39] Officially, negotiations over the collection were suspended. The pro-French Duc de Nevers had to confront Spain's political outrage at what they saw as a dangerous shift in northern Italian politics in favour of France. However, Nys knew that the collection meant little to Nevers, who would need every ducat he could raise to combat the imminent Spanish challenge to his succession.

By the spring of 1628 Spain and France stood on the brink of military intervention over Nevers' contentious succession. Spanish diplomatic pressure persuaded the Habsburg emperor, Ferdinand II, to issue an edict of sequestration pronouncing Nevers' succession illegal and backing the rival claims of Madrid's candidate for the dukedom, the Duke of Guastalla. Spain also increased the military pressure on Nevers by negotiating an anti-Nevers alliance with Charles Emmanuel I, duke of neighbouring Savoy. The alliance offered Savoy the contested region of Monferrato, while Spain took possession of the strategically important towns of Casale and Moncalvo.[40] By April 1628 Spanish and Savoyard forces were laying siege to Casale, with France powerless to intervene, due to its own preoccupation with the siege of La Rochelle. The English were delighted to see Europe's premier Catholic powers at war, as it gave their English forces much-needed respite from their Franco-Spanish campaigns, and deflected attention from Charles and Buckingham's increasingly inept foreign policy.

As the Spanish marched on Casale in April 1628, Daniel Nys wrote to Endymion Porter announcing the departure of the first consignment of Mantuan pictures and lobbying Whitehall for a second assault on the collection. Nys reported that the paintings had left the Venetian Lido bound for London on 15 April, on board the 100-ton ship the *Margaret*, manned by a crew of thirty-seven mariners. After negotiating customs waivers and carefully supervising the packing of the pictures, Lanier left Venice two weeks later, travelling by Ambassador Wake's gondola to Padua, from where he set off over the Alps to London via Brussels.[41] Most dealers and buyers preferred the safer method of overland rather than seaborne transportation of artworks and Lanier was no exception, especially considering the precious cargo he was carrying.

Nys whetted Porter's appetite by telling him that Lanier 'carries with him two pictures of Correggio, in tempera, and one of Raphael, the finest pictures in the world, and well worth the money paid for the whole, both on account of their rarity and exquisite beauty'.[42] Isaac Wake confirmed the details of Lanier's homeward journey in a subsequent letter written to Lord Conway. Despite Wake's protestations of his indifference towards collecting, he provided a knowing explanation of Lanier's conscientious travel arrangements: 'He doth carry with him the best pieces of paintings, namely those of Correggio, which were in [the] grotta at Mantua, in regard that being in water colours, they would not have brooked the sea.'[43] Wake was right. Correggio's subtle allegories of Vice and Virtue were painted in tempera, a delicate water-based medium that risked serious damage from the sea air of a month-long voyage. Lanier's actions were that of an experienced connoisseur who understood the fragility of his merchandise, right down to the composition of its raw materials.

Wake was obviously eager to ensure the safe arrival of such

precious cargo; Nys was simply after another deal. With typical bombast, he told Porter, 'I am astounded myself at the success of this negotiation.' Boasting that he had 'used every artifice to obtain them at a moderate price', he assured Porter that all his negotiations were based on his exclusive loyalty to King Charles. However, with an eye on the darkening political horizon, Nys reminded Porter that the king could not be assured of exclusive rights to the Mantua collection. He claimed that Nevers's rival the Duke of Guastalla had tried to acquire the collection for the Emperor Ferdinand, and that if King Charles wanted more from Mantua he should exploit the current political uncertainty. 'These wars against Montferrat are the cause of the Duke of Nevers pledging many of his jewels,' Nys told Porter. Nys was understandably eager to bounce the English into buying the statues before a Spanish-led invasion of Mantua put an end to any sale. If Charles wanted the Mantuan statues, Nys asked Porter to 'let me know, so that others may not carry them off, and I will then do all I can to procure them to the best advantage'.[44]

Nys reminded Porter of the significance of the pictures and statues held in Mantua and the reflected glory they conferred upon their owner – 'so wonderful and glorious a collection, that the like will never again be met with; they are truly worthy of so great a king as his Majesty of Great Britain'. Once the first consignment of paintings arrived in London, Nys believed that it would 'still be necessary to have the marbles of the Duke of Mantua', but 'as he is now involved in a war, and is pledging many of his jewels, I fear some one will carry them off'. He even concocted a bid for the statues from the Duke of Bavaria before delivering his punch-line: 'I believe they may be had (the war favouring us) for £10,000.'[45]

Having ensured Whitehall's continued interest in a further deal, Nys returned to his protracted negotiations with Striggi, which were persistently hampered by the deteriorating political and military situation throughout the summer of 1628. As Nys haggled with Striggi over the price of the statues and Mantegna's *Triumphs*, Lanier arrived back in London to supervise the presentation of the *Margaret*'s consignment of pictures to the king. But, to his shock and undoubted horror, as he unpacked the pictures he discovered that many of them were ruined. Despite his best efforts when loading them in Venice, he had not taken into account the ship's other cargo, a consignment of liquid mercury, or the furious storm that battered the *Margaret* three days out of port, upsetting the mercury and splashing the paintings. The resulting oxidization ate away at the picture's pigments and varnish, turning the canvases of Raphael, Titian, Tintoretto and Giulio Romano black.

Lanier was devastated and deeply apprehensive. The most expensive collection of pictures ever bought by an English sovereign had finally arrived in London and most of them were ruined. If the king or even Endymion Porter or Inigo Jones saw them, Lanier faced ridicule and humiliation. In desperation, he turned for help to his uncle, Jerome Lanier. Like his nephew, Jerome was an accomplished royal musician, but it was Nicholas's good fortune that he also possessed another far more recondite skill. He knew how to restore paintings.

Jerome set to work on the damaged pictures, using three tried and tested ingredients familiar to generations of picture restorers: milk, alcohol and spit. Many years later, Richard Symonds recounted how Jerome salvaged both the Mantuan pictures and his nephew's reputation: 'to cleanse them first he tried fasting spittle, then he mixed it with warm milk, and those [that] would not do, at last he cleaned upon with aqua vitae [alcohol] alone, being warmed, and that took off all the spots and blackness, and he says it will take off old varnishes'.[46] Jerome's nephew had already indulged in a spot of amateur restoration back in Venice, having 'used every care and diligence to repair and trim up the pictures procured from the young Duke of Mantua'. Quite what was involved in Nicholas's 'trimming' is unclear. Perhaps his botched 'restoration' caused as many problems as the mercury. If, as seems likely, he retouched many of the pictures, it is debatable just how much of the original brushwork of Titian, Raphael and Caravaggio was left for King Charles to admire after Nicholas and Jerome had finished their trimming and stripping in the summer of 1628.

Sadly for Lanier, all his hard work in acquiring and then restoring the pictures was overshadowed by an event that rocked the Stuart monarchy. On 23 August the Duke of Buckingham was assassinated in Portsmouth while preparing for a second expedition to the Ile de Ré. John Felton, a veteran of the first French campaign, stabbed the duke to death. The reasons were unclear, and many claimed Felton's grievance stemmed from disillusion with Buckingham's influence over England's domestic and foreign policy, although it may have been as prosaic as anger over lack of pay. The assassination was a devastating blow for the young king. Buckingham was his closest personal friend and political confidant. All interest in collecting pictures temporarily evaporated as the court paused to assess the implications of the duke's sudden death. The public rejoiced. Ever since his enthusiastic involvement in the Spanish match and his disastrous pursuit of wars against Spain and France, Buckingham had been widely hated by parliamentarians and the public at large for being vain, corrupt and politically inept. Some of these charges were unfounded, but his unpopularity was so intense that Charles was forced to bury him in Westminster Abbey at night to avoid a public disturbance. In the short term, Buckingham's death led to a shift in foreign policy and a realization of the folly of maintaining military operations against Spain and France, but in the long term it also alienated Charles from parliamentary political life. He withdrew from a political process that he believed, rightly or wrongly, had welcomed the assassination of his closest friend, whom he regarded as an integral part of the Stuart dynasty. By welcoming the death of Buckingham, Charles believed that many parliamentarians were striking at the very heart of the monarchy.

The repercussions of Buckingham's death were felt back in Venice, where they only added to Daniel Nys's difficulties in sealing a second deal for Mantuan treasures. An agreement was finally reached in September involving over 100 statues, cameos, pictures and Mantegna's *Triumphs*. Nys offered 50,000 Venetian ducats for the lot, but the Mantuan negotiators were unconvinced that he could pay promptly. Girolamo Parma, Striggi's Venetian representative, complained that Nys seemed 'keener on pledging payments than on actually paying them'.

Tempers started to fray. The Mantuans desperately needed cash to combat the impending Spanish military threat, and Nys wanted to clinch a deal before the Spanish overran the region and plundered the collection. Parma fretted over Nys's excuses for deferring final payment. He accused him of 'playing Herod or Pilate', and hoped 'that Buckingham's death does not impede his honouring the debt with us'.[47] In many ways Parma was quite right. The last thing London was prepared to authorize at this point was the payment of over £10,000 for artworks, especially after the arrival of the first consignment of damaged pictures.

Impatient with Whitehall's prevarication, Nys took a momentous risk. He settled his bill of £10,500 by drawing on the credit of Burlamachi. Large commercial transactions were often successfully completed based on deferred payment through bills of exchange drawn against the established credit of internationally respected financiers like Burlamachi. Technically speaking, Nys's behaviour was fraudulent, but in practice it was the kind of risk often taken by flamboyant entrepreneurs, soon forgotten as long as it returned a swift profit. The Mantuans happily accepted Nys's arrangements, but Burlamachi, still hugely over-extended following the Ile de Ré fiasco, was furious. He could see that Nys was exploiting the king's weakness for art to draw massive sums on his credit, knowing that Charles could not resist acquiring the paintings and allowing the financier to bear the cost.

Realizing the precariousness of his position, Nys composed a long letter to his old paymaster, Sir Dudley Carleton, now Lord Dorchester, having recently replaced Viscount Conway as Secretary of State. The letter was an attempt to justify his actions and extricate himself from a potentially ruinous situation. Carefully outlining his version of the sale, Nys emphasized the difficulty of acquiring the collection and the cut-price deal he had negotiated. He insisted that he never sought personal profit from the deal, but only ever acted in the best interests of King Charles, and stressed:

> There were no means of gaining time to advise his Majesty, but I, knowing the worth of the statues, that all the pictures were originals, and besides that, the *Triumph of Julius Caesar* of Mantegna was a thing rare and unique, and its value beyond estimation, I thought to do his Majesty a great service and to gain his gracious favour by the transaction.

His smooth words masked an anxiety that he risked financial ruin if Dorchester failed to persuade the king to settle his debt of

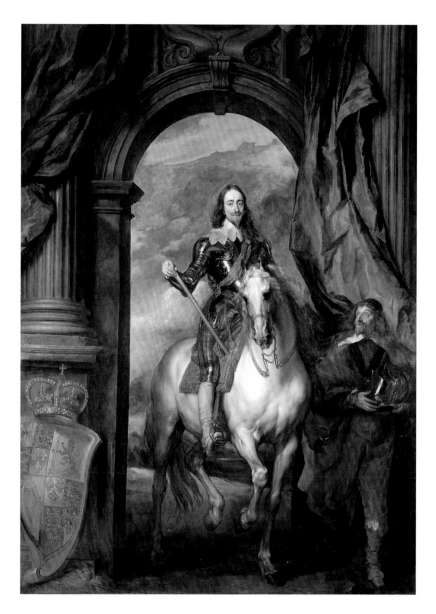

1. Anthony Van Dyck's portrait *King Charles I on Horseback with M. de St Antoine*:
a king at the height of his power.

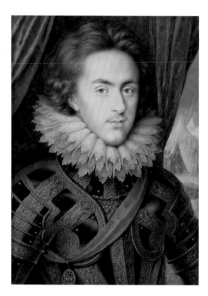

2. Isaac Oliver's romanticized miniature of Henry, Prince of Wales.

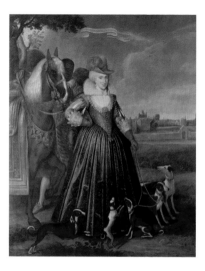

3. Paul Van Somer's studio portrait of *Queen Anna of Denmark at Leisure Before Oatlands Palace.*

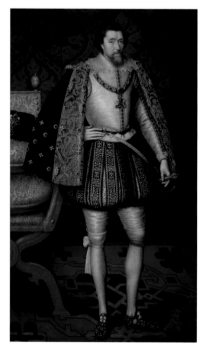

4. One of the first official portraits of King James I, a monarch clearly uncomfortable in front of the easel.

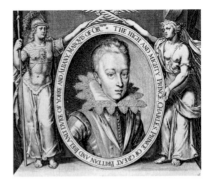

5. An engraving of the pale and sickly Charles I as Duke of York, aged about thirteen.

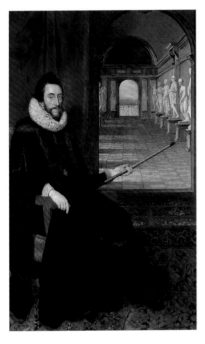

6. Daniel Mytens's portrait of Thomas Howard, Earl of Arundel, the greatest collector of his day, painted in the fashion of the time amidst his art collection.

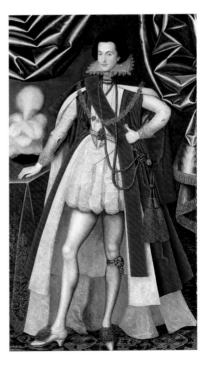

7. William Larkin's stiff but dazzling portrait of Buckingham shows off the handsome royal favourite – his legs especially – to full advantage.

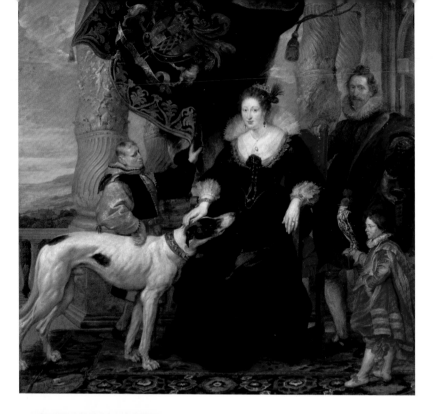

8. Rubens's portrait *Aletheia Talbot,
Countess of Arundel, and Sir Dudley Carleton*:
the English collectors abroad.

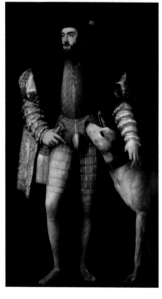

9. Titian's portrait of Charles V,
given to Prince Charles as an invitation
to marry the Infanta Maria and become
part of the Spanish royal family.

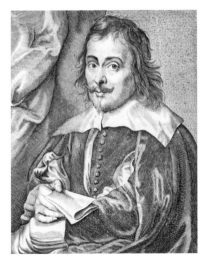

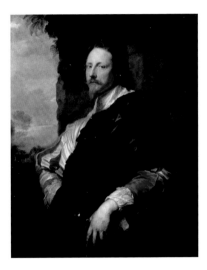

10. Balthazar Gerbier, failed painter, diplomat, spy and one of Charles's most successful art agents.

11. Nicholas Lanier, royal musician and the man responsible for the acquisition of the Mantuan collection.

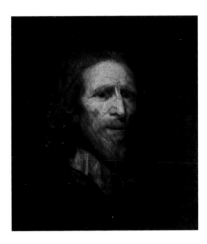

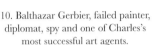

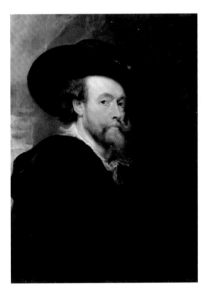

12. Abraham van der Doort, Keeper of the Cabinet Room at St James's. The strain of his position shows in his face, and even anticipates his suicide, which took place after he allegedly lost items from the collection.

13. Rubens's self-portrait hung in Whitehall following his trip to London. It shows the painter at the peak of his artistic and diplomatic career.

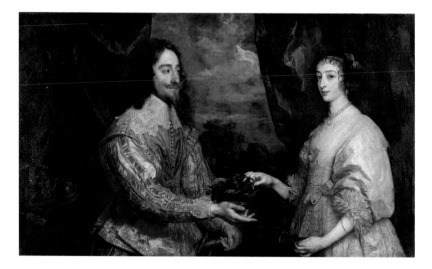

14 a & b. Van Dyck's portrait *Charles I and Henrietta Maria* (above), one of his first commissions for the king, was a deliberate reworking of his rival Daniel Mytens's lacklustre portrait of the royal couple (below). Van Dyck's superior version effectively ended Mytens's career. His portrait was taken down and he left London, never to return.

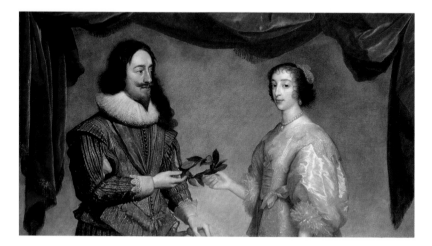

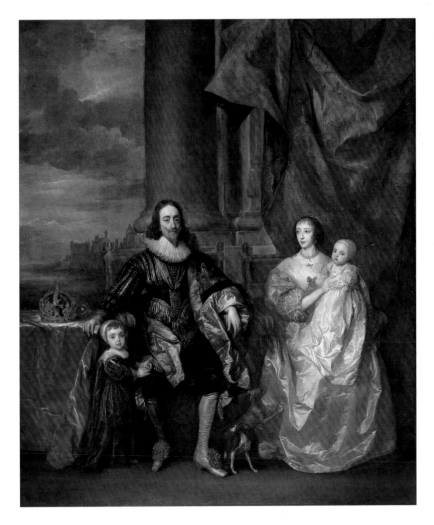

15. Van Dyck's towering portrait *The Great Piece* effortlessly renders King Charles as absolute ruler and successful family man.

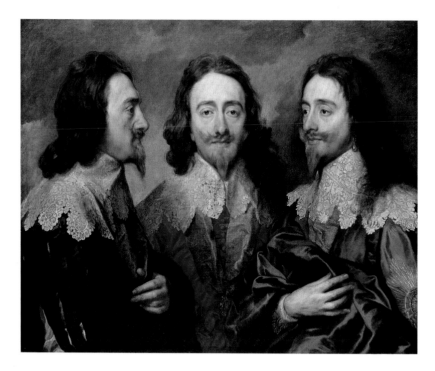

16 a & b. Van Dyck's *Triple Portrait of Charles I* drew on Lorenzo Lotto's *Three Views of a Man's Head*. It was designed to help Bernini model the king's head in marble, but now stands as an abiding, prophetic image of his doomed reign.

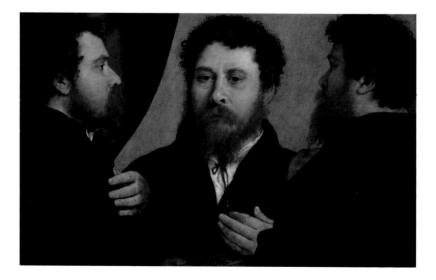

£10,500. Unable to concede charges of financial irregularity, Nys coolly noted, 'I find that the negotiation has not been received in England conformably to my own sincerity.' He explained that the problem was not his precipitate and unsanctioned spending, intimating instead that it was Burlamachi's financial inflexibility:

> ... having on a sudden disbursed the £10,500 sterling to the Duke of Mantua, and drawn on Sig. Burlamachi for the same; he not having received the King's resolution, has redrawn on me, the moneys being due, they will soon become due here, nay part are already due, and I shall then be obliged again to draw on Burlamachi to honour my drafts for that sum, otherwise I shall lose, in an instant, the credit and honour I have enjoyed through life.[48]

Nys had seriously miscalculated Burlamachi's credit in the aftermath of Buckingham's disastrous French campaign. By refusing to pay for Nys's lavish purchases, Burlamachi left the dealer to settle personally the bill for £10,500. Credit and honour were vital to any seventeenth-century businessman. Without them, they were ruined. Nys was left fighting for his commercial life, making it clear to Dorchester that, if he went down, he was prepared to take the king of England's financier with him.

Dorchester got the message. He knew from past experience just how treacherous Nys could be. Within a week the Lord Treasurer, Richard Weston, later Earl of Portland, recently appointed to resolve the king's financial difficulties, took the matter in hand and wrote to Wake in Venice in an attempt to resolve the financial dispute over the troublesome pictures and statues. 'I perceive his Majesty doth continue his resolution to buy them,' wrote Weston, 'and order is taken for the speedy making over of bills of exchange for that purpose.'[49] It seemed that Nys's plea had worked, because a week later he wrote a far more assured letter to Dorchester, enclosing prints of the Mantegna *Triumphs* and drawings of the statues and busts he proposed to send to London.[50] However, privately Nys was still anxious about his remuneration. On the same day he wrote to Dorchester, he also sent a letter to the Earl of Carlisle, another highly influential member of the Whitehall circle of collectors, currently in negotiations with Rubens (then in Madrid) for Indian perfume.[51] Nys's letter was virtually identical to his first one to Dorchester. Once again he stressed the rarity of the pictures and statues and his own refusal to profit from the deal, then reiterated his urgent need for settlement of his debts through the intervention of the king, 'whose Grace I implore to be pleased to give orders that my bargain may be paid for, I having already disbursed the money'.[52]

Once more negotiations reached an impasse. Having overcommitted himself by paying for an expensive consignment of specialized goods without securing its onward sale, Nys had lost the initiative and looked vulnerable. King Charles and his ministers could now exploit his predicament and his growing antagonism towards Burlamachi to defer payment for the pictures and statues, secure in the knowledge that there were no other buyers on the horizon. Unfortunately for Charles, in the spring of 1629 the political horizon in northern Italy shifted once again, giving Nys the opportunity to do what any businessman would do under such circumstances: he found another buyer.

Finally freed from the restraints of the siege of La Rochelle, King Louis XIII turned his attentions back to the Mantuan crisis, marching his army over the Alps and confronting the Savoyard forces at Susa in March 1629. The Duke of Savoy, Charles Emmanuel, immediately capitulated and transferred his political allegiance from Spain to France.[53] In Mantua the Duc de Nevers received the news with some relief, but the Spanish were outraged. Writing from Madrid, Rubens observed drily, 'As for the Duke of Savoy, I can only say that he always conducts himself valiantly against the Spaniards but allows himself to be beaten easily by France.'[54]

France was suddenly in the political ascendancy and Nys seized the opportunity. He offered his statues and paintings first to Cardinal Richelieu and then to the queen mother, Marie de' Medici. He also announced his sudden conversion to the pro-French Nevers camp, telling Striggi, 'I hope that his Highness' state will save itself from the hands of the Austrians', a reference to the imminent intervention of Emperor Ferdinand's imperial army. A month later Girolamo Parma observed that Nys was dispatching a servant to Paris to negotiate the sale of the pictures to Marie, 'despite his claims of having bought them for England'.[55]

It was a shrewd move on Nys's part, because by mid-May Lord Treasurer Weston was still refusing to settle the dealer's financial claim against the crown. Weston admitted, 'I wrote to you four or five months ago that I would not fail to pay and satisfy the bills that you should draw upon Philip Burlamachi for the purchase of the statues and paintings which you have made for his Majesty.' He obviously thought there was no pressure to settle the bill. Although he knew settlement was now due, he peremptorily told Nys, 'I must excuse myself, and beg that you will pay the bills of exchange which the said Burlamachi will re-draw upon you, and be assured that when you draw upon him again, they shall be paid and satisfied.' With the classic insouciance of the aristocrat dealing with the tradesman, Lord Weston told Nys to 'dispatch the said statues and paintings as soon as possible'. It was a classic manoeuvre: Weston, acting on behalf of Charles, dismissed discussion of money as vulgar, instead demanding the goods and promising payment later. Nys had little doubt that the English court was trying to obtain the pictures and statues for free. Nys had been here before with Dudley Carleton and the Earl of Somerset in 1616–17. As a result, he lost little time in opening negotiations with Richelieu through the French ambassador to Venice.

When it came to collecting, the French had far more experience than the Stuart court and drove a much harder bargain with Nys. By June the French ambassador wrote to Richelieu's advisers from Venice, recommending tough negotiations. He noted that Nys 'would like to sell everything together', including the statues and the Mantegna *Triumphs*. This was an understandable but unrealistic scheme on Nys's part. He was saddled with a large but uneven consignment of artworks specifically acquired for King Charles, a naive but enthusiastic collector who wanted ready-made collections and could easily be convinced of the value of what was in many cases inferior statuary. However, experts like Cardinal Richelieu could not be deceived so easily. They wanted original Titians and Raphaels, not dusty marbles of dubious provenance. Richelieu also wanted the satisfaction of poring over inventories and choosing what his judgement regarded as rare and valuable.

The ambassador informed Richelieu's advisers, 'I have seen to it that he will sell the statues separately, if this pleases the Cardinal, and he will even allow the said *Triumphs* to be separated from the rest of the paintings.' It was an excellent deal, but the ambassador was well aware that Nys was using the French transaction as leverage to obtain settlement of his debts from London. If the dealer received confirmation of payment from Weston, the French negotiations would collapse. He therefore advised Paris that 'we must hasten for fear that the deal with England will reach its conclusion'.[56]

Not to be outmanoeuvred, Nys also approached Marie de' Medici with the same offer of pictures and statues. However, the French ambassador was a step ahead of the wily dealer, warning Marie off buying the whole consignment. Instead he 'worked on him from all angles and did [his] best' to convince Nys to break the collection down into separate items, and 'to persuade him not to lose this opportunity to make money from a thing that has remained useless to him for eighteen months, and that in these times of war, he will find less buyers than ever'.[57] It was a compelling argument. As the ambassador wrote, Europe's courts held their breath as 30,000 of Emperor Ferdinand's imperial troops assembled along Mantua's border, poised to invade the city and depose the Duc de Nevers. Throughout negotiations the threat of war had worked in Nys's favour. Now it placed him at the mercy of a buyers' market.

His only hope was King Charles. Even as Nys negotiated the sale of pictures and statues to Richelieu and Marie de' Medici, he was making plans to ship it all to London in the hope of speeding up payment. It seems that London had got wind of the French deal, as Weston wrote to Nys again, apologizing for the delay but promising to pay all – or at least most – of the outstanding amount by October. Finally, on 23 November 1629, as imperial troops began their siege of Mantua, King Charles signed a warrant drawn up by Weston authorizing Nys's payment:

> Whereas we have contracted with Daniel Nys merchant, for certain pictures and statues which he is to deliver for our use, for which he is to have the sum of eleven thousand five

hundred pounds. We will and command you, of our treasure remaining in the receipt of our exchequer, forthwith to pay, or cause to be paid, unto our trusty and well-beloved Philip Burlamachi, or his assignees the said sum of eleven thousand five hundred pounds for the said pictures and statues.[58]

The warrant was authorized by Lord Viscount Dorchester, who once again came to the rescue of his old servant. Both the lengthy delay in payment and the language of the subsequent warrant betray the trace of a power struggle over the issue in Whitehall. Weston and Charles were obviously keen to protect the credit of their top financier, the 'trusty and well-beloved' Burlamachi, from the double-dealing Nys. However, the emergence of rival French buyers and pressure from Dorchester finally led to the reluctant payment of the £11,500 – a thousand more than Nys originally claimed for the second consignment, presumably taking into account the cost of freightage and insurance.

Nys, thinking the deal with London was finally in the bag, withdrew from negotiations with Richelieu and Marie, but not before selling the cardinal at least one exquisite Titian – *Madonna and Child with St Catherine and a Rabbit*. In the spring of 1630 he prepared to dispatch twenty-five crates of nearly 200 statues on board three ships bound for London, the *Margaret*, the *Unicorn* and the *Pearl*. Unfortunately for Nys, the king's money still had not arrived by the end of March. Once more he turned to Dorchester for assistance, writing to protest at the default in payment, but nothing happened. Finally, he made a direct appeal to the king, writing in mid-July, just a week after the fall of Mantua to the imperial Habsburg army. As Nys and Charles's advisers squabbled over Mantua's pictures and statues, the city was brutally sacked by the victorious army. Although neither Charles nor Nys acted with great honour throughout the acquisition, without Nys's duplicitous negotiations the collection would probably have been consumed by the fury of the imperial soldiers, or at best broken up and shared between the Habsburg art collections.

For Nys there was little time for such reflections. In his letter to Charles he reported further financial calamity: 'I most humbly beg leave to inform your Majesty, in consequence of a great run on the bank here, there are no means of cashing the bills for the statues.' The fall of Mantua and the worsening political situation sparked a crisis of financial confidence that threatened to ruin not just Nys but also Burlamachi. Nys went on, 'Signor Burlamachi has, on this account, quite altered his tone, and seems to have a wish to ruin me and draw me into litigation.' The only solution was for Charles 'to give Burlamachi satisfaction' by paying the outstanding £11,500, otherwise bankruptcy and politically embarrassing litigation beckoned. Nys still managed to tempt Charles with the promise that the best artworks, including the *Triumphs*, were yet to come. The recently dispatched works 'were but the refuse, from which your Majesty must not form an estimate'.[59]

Nys was so worried that two days later he dispatched his servant Giles Merrison to London, with instructions to explain his position. Revealing just how close he was to Dorchester, Nys instructed Merrison to report to the Secretary of State as soon as he arrived and take his lead in all subsequent discussions. Merrison was also instructed to tell Dorchester 'that the statues sent are far from the best; that the finest are still here', and that the French queen mother was offering £15,000 – an offer that Nys made known to Burlamachi, then in Amsterdam. The implication was clear: the French offer, if accepted, would have resolved the financial dispute between Nys and Burlamachi, but denied Charles his artworks. Prompt payment was needed from England.

Nys's final gambit was almost comically opportunistic. He instructed Merrison to tell Dorchester that, having not received payment for the pictures and statues, they had been placed on public display in Venice for all to see. Finally, he ordered Merrison to 'say that the reason I have sent the most inferior statues is, because I had directed all the finest to be exhibited, and not wishing to annul the order, or interfere with the concourse of the visitors, I despatched the worst'. It was an amazingly presumptuous and very hazardous scheme on the part of a mere art dealer to extract payment from a ruling sovereign.

For once, Nys overplayed his hand. Instead of persuading the English court to pay, it only further alienated them, particularly Dorchester, his closest ally. Even worse, Dorchester learned that Nys was spreading rumours via the inexperienced new ambassador to Venice, Thomas Rowlandson, that Burlamachi was refusing to settle the outstanding debt owing on the second consignment of pictures. Dorchester was furious. If Nys's accusations destroyed Burlamachi's credit rating, the implications for the English exchequer would be disastrous. An infuriated Dorchester drafted a letter to Rowlandson in an attempt to put the record straight.

The draft version of the letter, never before published, provides a fascinating insight into just how far relations over the sale had descended into bad-tempered deceitfulness. 'His Majesty having been informed of some ill offices done by you to the prejudice of Mr. Burlamachi hath commanded me to write unto you to the end he might understand the truth of things, and you also be better informed of all circumstances,' began Dorchester.[60] He went on to explain that 'Daniel Nys bought of his own free will and without any command or order from his Majesty certain pictures and statues of the late Duke of Mantua.' Dorchester was at pains to stress that payment would be forthcoming once all the pictures and statues reached England. He pointed out that, following the arrival of the (admittedly poor) consignment of statues, Nys received £4,000, but that no more would be forthcoming until the dispatch of the remaining art works.

In dictating the draft, Dorchester initially put aside his usual diplomatic decorum, in his next revealing comment:

> But it seems that Nys doubting (as well he might do) his Majesty did not find such satisfaction as was promised and expected by his bargain, at the receipt of the pieces sent, and therefore having ~~craftily gotten~~ drawn bills, not only the eleven thousand and five hundred pounds which sum he wrote the said statues and pictures would cost him with the expenses of the carriage, but also near the sum of eighteen thousand pound (over and above the one thousand pound already received) upon Philip Burlamachi, with this express order, in case there was no provision for it, ~~it should be had back again from him, as it~~ he should recharge it back upon him as appears by his letters of the 3 of May last.[61]

Dorchester's corrections of his initial revelations expose the crux of the financial conflict over the acquisition of the Mantuan collection. According to Dorchester, Nys drew money against Burlamachi without his agreement for both the first consignment of pictures, to the value of nearly £18,000, and the second, at a cost of £11,500. Burlamachi paid for the first consignment, but refused to countenance settlement of the second, and certainly not before the pictures were in English hands. Nys's complaint was that Burlamachi's refusal to pay the second sum brought the creditors to his door, demanding the outstanding £11,500.

Dorchester accused Nys of breaking the accepted conventions of trade and exchange. His behaviour was 'against all due course and trust of honest merchants', a line which was subsequently struck through as too confrontational. Dorchester made it clear to Rowlandson that Nys had lied. 'Mr Burlamachi is not bound unto him, as having never given order nor direction, nor his word for the said bargain or payment.' Rowlandson was instructed to put an end to the affair, which was proving to be 'very prejudicious for his Majesty's honour, and also to Mr Burlamachi's credit'. Nys could be assured settlement of his claim once the second consignment of pictures was finally released and shipped to England. Meanwhile, Rowlandson needed to urgently limit the 'prejudice or damage' done to Burlamachi's reputation and credit by disseminating 'the true state of this business' among the Venetian financial community.

In a postscript Dorchester shifted tone from minister to collector, regretting the acrimony directed at Nys after all his hard work in securing the Mantuan collection. He asked Rowlandson to warn the dealer that he was playing a very dangerous game with the king. '[T]ell him from me,' wrote Dorchester, 'that if the statues and heads which are to follow are not better than these which are already arrived it will prove as well in the opinion of his Majesty as all others of good judgement who have seen that but a very bad bargain.'

Unfortunately Nys was unappeased. Seeing the opportunity to exploit Rowlandson's inexperience, he protested his innocence to Dorchester. 'I beg leave to inform your Excellency that Sig. Rowlandson has never spoken to me ill or well of Burlamachi,' he wrote, adding slyly that Rowlandson 'told me that Sig. [Thomas] Carey had written to him saying his Majesty had given orders that

I should receive payment'.[62] By dragging in the word of a go-between, Nys was deliberately muddying the waters, capitalizing on London's failure to specify clearly the financial terms of the acquisition of the pictures. 'As to what your Excellency says, touching the contract for the statues and paintings, that payment was not to be made until they reached London,' concluded Nys, 'nothing was ever said about it.' To back up his claim, he attached copies of correspondence with Weston. Turning to Dorchester's assertion that 'my proceedings have tended towards the dishonour of the King', Nys adopted an offended tone: 'Surely not; the ill is only between Burlamachi and me, and his Majesty may very easily set us right. If he directs payment to be made, all will be well.'[63]

The problem for the English was that both Nys and Burlamachi were now beyond their effective control. Burlamachi was furious, writing to Dorchester in early August, imploring the crown to help him recover the substantial amounts involved in settling Nys's acquisitions. He claimed no interest in the acquisition, except a desire to fulfil the king's wishes to own the collection,[64] and followed this with another letter worryingly confirming Nys's version of events. According to Burlamachi, the king had written letters sanctioning the purchase, and if the matter went to litigation, Nys could indeed produce Carey's letters confirming the transaction. He warned Dorchester of the effects this might have on the king's reputation, concluding rather impotently that Nys was a wicked man who deserved a stroke of the poignard. Later the same month he confirmed the substantial losses incurred in paying Nys's bills for the first Mantuan transaction, assuring Dorchester that he was now prepared to do everything in his power to ruin Nys.[65]

Back in Venice, Ambassador Rowlandson informed Dorchester that he feared the king could be embroiled in a scandal unless the dispute between Nys and Burlamachi was resolved quickly. Mediation failed, and although the ambassador used all his financial resources to settle some of Burlamachi's debts, he dreaded what might happen if Nys released his damaging correspondence: 'I pray God the total business betwixt them be accommodated without going to law, for I know not who to appear in it according unto his Majesty's commandments, in respect of those letters that

Mr Nys may produce against my reasons which would reflect much upon the reputation of His Majesty's service.'[66] Rowlandson was convinced that Nys possessed enough damaging letters to expose everyone involved in the deal, from himself to King Charles, for reneging on an agreement to settle payment for the pictures before their arrival. It was an extraordinary allegation, made even more astonishing because the English obviously knew it to be true.

By the autumn of 1630 both sides finally reached a deal. Rowlandson wrote to Lord Weston on 15 October confirming the departure of what he believed to be the final items held by Nys. Thirty chests of statues and two chests of pictures, including Mantegna's *Triumphs*, were loaded on board three ships bound for London. 'I must confess,' Rowlandson wrote, 'I do long to see them aboard',[67] not only because of the nerve-racking dispute which had seriously damaged his reputation but because the plague was raging throughout Venice. This outbreak was probably related to the epidemic still sweeping Mantua following the death and destruction of the city's sack earlier that summer.

By this stage not even the plague could prevent the shipment of the collection. Confirmation of the consignment's departure from Venice elicited the issue of a warrant in London for £3,000 to be paid to Nys in late November. A further £4,325 was issued in January 1631, probably about the time the consignment arrived in England. By March Nys finally obtained full settlement of the £11,500 first promised by the king fourteen months earlier.[68] However, the contested payment for the first consignment, already installed in St James's and Whitehall, remained unresolved. It was at this point that Nys played his final crooked card.

In June 1631 the bailiffs came knocking at Nys's door. He confessed to Thomas Carey that he 'opened my coffers and my house to them', dramatically challenging his creditors to '[p]ay yourselves all, even to the last farthing, which they did'. And then, in the midst of 'this general removal and turn out, my people, in a back place, came upon paintings and statues belonging to the King my most gracious Master, at which I was greatly astonished and also rejoiced'. The scheming Nys deliberately held these items back from the final shipment as an insurance policy against London defaulting over payment. He claimed they represented some of the finest pieces from the Mantuan collection – three Titian portraits, one Raphael, statues attributed to Praxiteles, Sansovino and Michelangelo, and the antique marble statue of Venus.[69] He even managed to pass Bronzino's *Portrait of a Lady in a Green Dress* off as a Raphael, an attribution that would cause confusion throughout its subsequent life in the English royal collection. Nys's stunt was incredibly devious, reminiscent of his 'repossession' of Dorchester's statues in 1617, but no more so than the deceitful behaviour of King Charles and his advisers in trying to avoid paying for what they had initially agreed to buy.

As Nys and Whitehall completed one final round of bad-tempered negotiations over contested claims to pictures and statues, France and Spain reached a fraught peace settlement over politically disputed claims to northern Italy. In June 1631 the Treaty of Cherasco restored the Duc de Nevers to his Mantuan dukedom. It was a hollow victory. The duchy lay shattered by war and shrunken by the territorial demands of neighbouring Savoy and the Habsburg-backed Duke of Guastalla. However, Spain hardly fared much better. Having spent ten million ducats on the war, it still lacked a corridor through which to send its troops from the north. Besides, it was partly pressurized into an agreement because of the need to confront the invasion of Germany in June by the new champion of European Protestantism, King Gustavus Adolphus of Sweden.[70]

In comparison, King Charles must have regarded his own involvement in the Mantuan crisis as relatively successful. It was certainly far cheaper than Spain's profligate military expenditure. Van der Doort listed 124 'Mantua pieces' in his 1639 inventory, and this did not include acquisitions like Mantegna's *Triumphs*, which were hung in Hampton Court. Over ninety statues and 190 busts were installed in the gardens at St James's, Somerset House and Greenwich. At a stroke the royal art collection was transformed.[71] Titian and Giulio Romano's Roman emperors went to St James's Palace, while many of the statues were placed in the gardens of Henrietta Maria's Somerset House residence. By far the largest proportion of the newly acquired pictures went to Whitehall. The prized Titians, Raphaels, Correggios and Giulio

Romanos were hung in Charles's privy lodgings in the heart of the palace. The irony was that very few people apart from the king and his closest advisers ever saw them. They were hardly an example of power on display, because few were allowed to admire them. In addition, '[T]he remnant of the utterly ruined and spoiled pieces by quicksilver which came from Mantua' were abandoned on a back staircase of Whitehall, victims of poor transportation and Lanier's disastrous attempts at restoration.[72]

Charles's first seven years in power led the crown into two disastrous wars and singularly failed to establish him as one of the most powerful monarchs in Europe. At least he was now one of its most prominent art collectors. However, despite several opportunities, he never repeated this most audacious acquisition, which suggests one other reason for the Mantua purchase. Luxury commodities like jewels or pictures were increasingly useful securities – especially in times of war and economic uncertainty. The Mantua collection was a shrewd investment and the possibility that Charles's interest in it was as much financial as aesthetic cannot be overlooked.

The cost to the exchequer of the king's Mantuan adventure was considerably less than the expense to his international diplomatic reputation. Between 1630 and 1633 he authorized payments to Nys totalling of £18,280 12s 8d. It was a large but hardly scandalous amount of money, representing as it did more than Charles received annually from his land rents.[73] However, the combined price of the two consignments totalled nearer £26–28,000: approximately £15,000 for the first load of pictures and at least £11,500 for the second of pictures and statues, notwithstanding the cost of freightage and insurance.

We may never conclusively know who stood the cost of the outstanding figure of £8–10,000. However, the torturous and frustratingly incomplete paper trail of double-dealing, lies and fraud that remains provides some compelling clues. Daniel Nys protested louder than anyone about King Charles's financial skulduggery, petitioning the king for £3,000 as late as 1634 and claiming that the whole affair forced him into bankruptcy and that 'he was compelled to give up his business'. By this stage it is doubtful that anyone believed a word Nys said, although he was forced to sell off his own collection of rarities in 1636–7. It is also possible that many of the bills of exchange were simply never honoured as the Mantuans were plunged into the chaos of siege, sack and plague.

It is more likely that Charles's financier, Burlamachi, was forced to absorb the shortfall in payments thanks to Nys and the king's underhand behaviour. If this was the case, Burlamachi must have added the outstanding amount to the growing loan owed by Charles and his exchequer. Ambassador Wake once commented that 'great merchants, as Burlamachi, forget sometimes sums which are not in the thousands'.[74] Unfortunately for Burlamachi, by the spring of 1633 the sums failed to add up and he was declared bankrupt. Although the financier confessed that he often disbursed £15,000 – the cost of the first Mantuan shipment – based on verbal requests from Treasurer Portland, the crown refused to come to his aid.[75] By 1641 he found himself in prison, destitute and penniless.

Rubens, a former painter and buyer for the Gonzaga, captured the widespread distaste felt by many European Catholic artists and connoisseurs, claiming '[t]his sale has upset me so much' that he wanted nothing to do with it.[76] The collection's arrival polarized public opinion. As the pictures were hung in the palaces and the statues placed in their gardens, the Puritan lawyer William Prynne launched a vituperative attack upon the growing number of 'Catholic' paintings entering the country. He claimed that parliamentary statutes 'do absolutely condemn, as sinful, idolatrous, and abominable the making of any image or picture of God the Father, Son and holy Ghost, or of the sacred Trinity, and the erecting of them, of crucifixes, or such like pictures in churches, which . . . should be without all images, or saint's pictures'.[77] Nevertheless, as far as most of Whitehall's courtiers were concerned, Mantua's loss was England's gain. The circle of connoisseurs around Arundel and the king were all delighted. Painters and sculptures ranging from Daniel Mytens and Hubert Le Sueur to Van Dyck pursued new directions in their portraits, landscapes and sculpture because of their access to the recently imported collection – even though many of its finest pieces were 'restored' by the Laniers or damaged on board ship.

Writing on the subject 'Of Antiquities' in the 1634 edition of his guidebook to connoisseurship, the *Compleat Gentleman*, the courtier Henry Peacham captured Whitehall's excitement at the recent arrival of the Mantuan statuary, observing that, 'King Charles also ever since his coming to the crown, hath amply testified a royal liking for ancient statues, by causing a whole army of old foreign emperors, captains and senators all at once to land on his coasts, to come and do him homage, and attend him in his palaces of St James, and Somerset House.'[78]

Peacham's book provides the first appearance in English of the term 'virtuoso' – someone with a taste for the fine arts, a collector in pursuit of beautiful objects. The word derives from the Italian, meaning 'learned' or 'skilful'.[79] The ships carrying the crates of pictures and statues from Mantua brought a new word into the language by establishing what it meant to be a *virtuoso*, in seventeenth-century Caroline England. The king took the credit, but his behaviour throughout the affair did not bode well for the future.

CHAPTER FIVE

❧

LASTING MONUMENTS TO POSTERITY

On 10 March 1629 King Charles marched into the House of Lords and announced the dissolution of Parliament. This was the third dissolution in the king's four year-old reign and by far the most divisive. Whereas the previous two Parliaments had both hoped for religious and financial accommodation with the crown, Charles's third Parliament had assembled in March 1628 with constitutional government itself in question. Hitherto, legislative government was based on the assumption of a common religious position between the crown and the two Houses of Parliament. However, by the time that Bishop William Laud rose to preach the first sermon of the new Parliament, it was clear to most of its members that this was no longer the case. Thanks to Charles's enthusiastic promotion of their supporters, Arminians of Laud's persuasion effectively controlled the Church of England. Parliament was broadly opposed, on religious grounds, to this shift within the Church's hierarchy. For many Puritan members of the Commons, the refusal to grant Charles the financial subsidies he required presented one of their few ways of opposing what they saw as the king's erosion of parliamentary rights and liberties through his centralization of royal authority and concentration of power among a small clique of unelected supporters.

Parliament quickly took the advantage, demanding that Charles agree to a Petition of Right. This made it unlawful to levy taxes without Parliament's agreement, imprison subjects without trial (both consequences of Charles's heavy-handed Forced Loan of 1626) and billet soldiers on unwilling citizens (a result of the recent overseas wars). In return, Charles sought parliamentary acceptance of his right to collect tonnage and poundage. As agreement seemed imminent, Parliament accused the king of reneging on his agreement to the Petition of Right. On 2 March, the day the Commons agreed to meet to discuss a series of religious resolutions, Charles ordered that the Speaker announce a five-day adjournment, an obvious prelude to dissolution. Chaos ensued. Several members of the House leapt on the Speaker and held him down in protest. 'The house thereupon was much troubled,' noted one onlooker, 'many pressing violently and tumultuously.'[1] Charles condemned the 'vipers' responsible for the fracas, officially brought Parliament to a close and vowed never to recall one again in his lifetime.

So began the era of personal rule which was to transform English political life over the next decade. It would also change the tenor of collecting and artistic patronage, as Charles and his closest advisers sought to fashion a royal image appropriate to the new political climate. The parliamentary tumult that dominated politics throughout the spring of 1629 also partly explains the prevarications over the completion of the Mantuan acquisition, as Charles turned his attention away from direct artistic acquisitions and towards the commissioning of art intended to celebrate both his family and his own personal majesty.

However, his first act of artistic patronage as personal ruler was more fortuitous than deliberate. In May 1629 Peter Paul Rubens, widely regarded as Europe's greatest living painter, arrived in England, although not to paint pictures. His patron, the Spanish ruler of the Low Countries, the Archduchess Isabella, had appointed him to act as a diplomatic intermediary. Rubens was rich, successful and hugely ambitious. His career as a court painter able to move with charm and discretion between the rival courts of Catholic Europe equipped him with all the qualifications required of a successful diplomat. Such a position also allowed him to widen his network of politically influential clients and patrons.

He had begun in 1628 with King Philip IV of Spain, leaving Antwerp for Madrid with an official commission to paint Philip's portrait. However, he also travelled under orders from Isabella to liaise with Charles I's Madrid-based representatives – and well-known connoisseurs – Endymion Porter and Balthazar Gerbier in reconciling Spain and England and negotiating a peace treaty between the two countries. Upon his arrival in Madrid, Rubens set to work painting the king and opening discussions with the English. To assist Rubens and 'give the greater reputation to his negotiation', Philip appointed him Secretary to the Privy Council. The king complained about the wisdom of entrusting a mere painter with such delicate diplomatic responsibilities, but Isabella realized it was a shrewd move. Rubens was widely admired at the English court, as much for his artistic ability as his diplomatic tact.[2]

Both sides desperately needed peace. Spain was financially and militarily over-extended in northern Italy and the Low Countries, and possessed no appetite for the escalation of a costly war with England. Since Buckingham's assassination, those who rallied round Charles and his decision to embark upon an era of personal rule were noticeably anti-parliamentarian and pro-Spanish. Charles's fiscally cautious Lord Treasurer, Richard Weston, along with Arundel and the Chancellor of the Exchequer, Francis Cottington, strongly supported peace with Spain. Charles had little choice. Having accumulated war debts of over £270,000 and dissolved Parliament, thus losing the tax-raising revenues it traditionally voted the crown, the king was in no position to sustain one let alone two overseas wars. The queen had already successfully lobbied for peace with her brother, Louis XIII. News of the Anglo-French peace settlement reached Madrid in April, just as Rubens and Porter opened negotiations. Worried at the implications of an alliance between London and Paris, the Spanish dispatched Rubens to England to conclude terms as quickly as possible.[3]

Rubens travelled via Paris and Dunkirk, where he set sail in late May. Following his landing at Dover, he was whisked off to London, where he lodged with his fellow negotiator and art dealer Balthazar Gerbier.[4] The pro-French Venetian ambassador Contarini regarded the painter's arrival with suspicion. 'Rubens is an ambitious and covetous man, so he probably aims at being talked about and at some good present,'[5] he complained in his diplomatic dispatches; but he acknowledged how connoisseurship could oil the wheels of diplomacy: 'I do not know whether the king will see him, but he may under the pretence of pictures, in which he delights greatly.'

The king was indeed willing to see Rubens. His portrait still hung in the room adjacent to Charles's bedchamber, and it was hoped that Rubens would finalize plans for the decoration of the Banqueting House. On 25 June 1629 the two men met for the first time at Greenwich Palace. They immediately withdrew to discuss peace negotiations. Charles wanted a formal peace treaty on terms similar to those established by his father in 1604, plus the evacuation of Habsburg garrisons in the contested Palatinate territories. Rubens told the king that he came to negotiate a truce between Spain and England, but that as secretary to the Privy Council of the Spanish-controlled Low Countries he lacked the authority of an ambassador to agree to such terms. Having reached a deadlock, the meeting ended.[6]

If Rubens discussed pictures with the king, he was unlikely to mention it in his regular dispatches to Madrid. He was anxious, having recently completed several portraits of Philip of Spain, to quash any suggestion that he might now transfer his artistic allegiance to the English connoisseur-king. However, Charles was delighted at the arrival of such a famous painter, even if the reasons for his presence were primarily political. For Rubens, London provided yet another opportunity to extend his growing international network of royal patronage. He had worked in Mantua, Paris and Madrid and had tried and failed to secure a major commission in London in the early 1620s, following the fiasco over the exchange of pictures involving Carleton and Danvers. London now offered even greater political and artistic opportunities, which he quickly set about exploiting to the maximum during his ten-month stay.

Within weeks of his arrival Rubens wrote to his old friend Pierre Dupuy describing his new surroundings. He praised England as 'a spectacle worthy of the interest of every gentleman, not only for the beauty of the countryside' but also for 'the incredible quantity of excellent pictures, statues, and ancient inscriptions which are to be found in this court'. To his own surprise, he admitted, 'I find none of the crudeness which one might expect from a place so remote from Italian elegance.'⁷ As English connoisseurship had developed, so attitudes towards wealth and consumption were changing. Rubens noted that 'all the leading nobles live on a sumptuous scale and spend money lavishly, so that the majority of them are hopelessly in debt . . . since splendour and liberality are of primary consideration at this court'.⁸

Rubens singled out specific English collections for particular praise. 'I must admit,' he told Nicolas de Peiresc, 'that when it comes to fine pictures by the hands of first-class masters, I have never seen such a large number in one place as in the royal palace and in the gallery of the late Duke of Buckingham.'⁹ Even allowing for the impact of the arrival of the first pictures from Mantua, this was a surprising exaggeration, especially considering Rubens's recent inspection of the Habsburg's much larger collection. Nevertheless, there was a certain element of self-promotion in his claims. The royal collection held several of his paintings, while Buckingham's collection contained thirty statues that he had sold to the duke just two years earlier, as well as thirty of his own works. It was all part of Rubens's extremely successful attempt to inveigle his way into the Caroline court, and assure his continental supporters that London was a worthy place in which to showcase his talents.

Poor Orazio Gentileschi. Having left Paris following Rubens's arrival to paint for his patron Marie de' Medici, the hapless Italian could only watch in despair as his old rival reappeared, seemingly out of nowhere, and proceeded to dominate the one court that the ageing Orazio had believed was safe from the superior talents of his old adversary. Gentileschi simply could not compete. Rubens possessed a consummate technique, the experience of working on an epic scale and an unparalleled repertoire of classical references. What he also brought to Charles's court was an understanding of European dynastic politics. This more than anything allowed him to create pictures that fused art and power in ways which the courts of Mantua, Paris, Madrid and now London found irresistible.

With Gerbier's help, Rubens started work on a canvas that provided King Charles with the image of majesty he longed for, while also promoting the benefits of the Anglo-Spanish political peace he was busily proposing. *Landscape with St George and the Dragon* was the first masterpiece of this new age of personal rule. Months before the picture's completion, and within weeks of the dissolution of Parliament, Charles had resurrected the tradition of a royal procession to St George's Chapel at Windsor Castle on the eve of 23 April, the saint's day. It was a provocatively feudal gesture, aimed at reinforcing the power of his personal rule by investing those closest to him with the Order of the Garter and parading them at all official ceremonies.[10] First formed in the early fourteenth century under King Edward III, the order was conceived as a brotherhood of knights appointed by the ruling monarch and dedicated to royal service and chivalry. It was the perfect medium for Charles: an elite, highly ritualized, all-male club pledging allegiance to their leader, a self-styled latter-day St George – just how Rubens portrayed the king in his painting.

If, as seems likely, Rubens watched Charles's St George's Day ceremony in April 1630, it profoundly affected his subsequent painting. It portrayed a romanticized Charles as St George, slaying the dragon and rescuing the Virgin, represented as Henrietta Maria. In the background Whitehall can be seen on the banks of the Thames, the kind of idealized English landscape admired by Rubens in his letter to Dupuy. While Renaissance Italy was familiar with the grafting of classical scenes on to contemporary settings, England had never experienced anything of the sort before. Rubens knew the Catholic iconography in Madrid's Habsburg collection by the likes of Titian, which portrayed emperors as St George, crushing the dragon as a personification of heresy, be it Protestantism or Islam. The genius in his own painting was to modify the religious bite of the dragon and represent it as the Devil sowing religious discord across Catholic *and* Protestant Europe, still ravaged by the Thirty Years War. Rubens also shrewdly used Henrietta Maria as a religious intermediary between the warring factions, a Catholic princess whose union with a Protestant prince promised to banish religious and military conflict from Europe for ever.[11]

It was a consummate response to the political situation in which Rubens found himself. Charles was delighted, Rubens fêted: they made an excellent combination. Charles appreciated Rubens's ability to provide the effortless political iconography he required and Rubens regarded his diplomacy as a perfect foil to his increasingly ambitious artistic objectives. Emphasizing the painting's political import, Joseph Mead praised the artist, 'who in honour of England & of our nation from whom he hath received so many courtesies, hath drawn with his pencil the History of St George; wherein, if it be possible, he hath excelled himself'.[12] Although the painting was inspired by his visit to England, Rubens took it to Antwerp when he left London, but its impact was so profound that just five years later Endymion Porter bought it back and sold it to the king, who hung it in the breakfast chamber in Whitehall.

Rubens painted one more picture during his time in London that left Charles in no doubt as to the dangers of turning his back on peace with Spain: *Allegory of Peace and War.* In the foreground Rubens portrayed another idyllic prospect of peace and abundance. The luxuriant figure of Pax (Peace) presides over the scene, gazing indulgently at her children, three of which were modelled on Gerbier's daughters. Pax sits suckling the infant Plutus, god of wealth, vulnerable and oblivious to the menacing spectre of Mars, god of war, rising up over her left shoulder, about to lift his sword and unleash the Fury Alecto and the violent spirits that loom out of the murky landscape. Only the formidably armed Minerva, goddess of wisdom and the arts, is able to stay Mars's hand and prevent the onset of chaos and destruction.

By early 1630 Rubens had successfully negotiated the exchange of ambassadors between Spain and England and was preparing to leave, his mission completed. Sir Francis Cottington, that old Hispanophile and trusted veteran of the 1623 royal visit to Madrid, was dispatched once again to the Spanish capital, while Whitehall prepared for the arrival of Carlos Coloma, the new Spanish ambassador. Coloma was received with spectacular ceremony at the Banqueting House in the second week of January. Dorchester re-created the scene for Cottington's benefit, describing the lines of elegantly attired ladies at court as so tightly packed that there were 'many fallings out for spoiling one another's ruffs'.[13]

As Rubens took his place amid the throng of courtiers, he knew that the commission to decorate the blank ceiling above his head was finally his. Having first applied over eight years earlier, he had spent his time in London lobbying the king and his advisers to secure the coveted commission. Lack of money and political inertia had frustrated the original plan to employ him, but Charles now required a ceiling that reflected the majesty of his personal rule and confirmed his status as Europe's leading Protestant connoisseur. Rubens's qualifications for the job were unequalled. Having completed the dynastic masterpiece of the life of Marie de' Medici in Paris, he was conversant with the baroque designs Charles had admired during his time in Madrid. He also drew on the Flemish tradition exemplified in the great painted civic halls of Antwerp and Brussels. His portrait of Charles as St George had confirmed that he possessed the ability to fashion a series of pictures showing the king as he wished to be seen. Most scholars agree that Rubens discussed the subject matter with the ceiling's architect, Inigo Jones, before leaving London in the late spring of 1630.

Diplomatically and artistically the trip was a huge success. Rubens paved the way for the subsequent Anglo-Spanish Peace of Madrid of November 1630, while securing the lucrative patronage of England's finest collectors, including the Earl of Arundel and the king himself. The new ambassador to Spain, Sir Francis Cottington, who partly owed his new posting to Rubens, was particularly impressed. Rubens, he wrote, 'is not only very clever and adroit in negotiating matters but also knows how to win the esteem of everyone and especially the king'.[14] Before Rubens left for home to begin work on the Banqueting House commission, the king summoned him for one last audience at Whitehall where he presented him with a diamond-studded hat-band worth £500, a ring from his own finger and a jewelled sword with which he knighted the painter Sir Peter Paul Rubens.

Rubens had fashioned a royal image for Charles, but even before his departure the king's advisers were negotiating to secure the services of another painter to build on what he had begun. The candidate supported by connoisseurs like Arundel, Carleton and Porter was Rubens's most famous pupil, Anthony Van Dyck. As a promising twenty-one-year-old artist, Van Dyck had visited England in 1620, but despite the patronage of both Arundel and

Buckingham, he did not settle and left for Italy after just four months. Nevertheless, English admiration for the painter remained. Porter commissioned a mythological picture from him, the erotic, Titianesque *Rinaldo and Armida*, at a cost of £78, to stand alongside the *Portrait of Nicholas Lanier* and convince Charles of Van Dyck's ability. Its arrival in London within days of Rubens's departure only increased the court's interest in the painter.

Nevertheless, Van Dyck remained reluctant to commit himself to London. As court painter to the Archduchess Isabella, a move to the English Protestant court without the kind of diplomatic brief given to Rubens might limit his prospects and appear imprudent on religious grounds. So the king hit on the dubious idea of luring Van Dyck into making a brief visit to London, then exercising his royal prerogative to coerce the poor painter into staying.[15] But Charles made the mistake of choosing his ambassador in Brussels and old travelling companion from Madrid in 1623, Balthazar Gerbier, to execute his plan.

Things went wrong almost immediately. Gerbier excluded Van Dyck from negotiations with Isabella over his release; then, assuming the deal was a foregone conclusion, he bought a *Virgin and Child*, attributed to Van Dyck, and smugly dispatched it to Charles as a gift for Christmas. Unfortunately for Gerbier, Van Dyck heard what was happening from a friend in London, George Geldorp. Unlike Rubens Van Dyck never warmed to the pompous, scheming Gerbier and now saw the opportunity to humiliate him. He wrote to Gerbier, suspending any plans for his London trip. Even worse, he announced that the *Virgin and Child* was not by his hand; it was merely a studio copy. He promptly left town, leaving a chagrined Gerbier muttering, 'Since Van Dyck wrote me this letter he has not suffered himself to be seen.'[16]

Gerbier was furious. Not only was Van Dyck threatening to wreck his negotiations with the archduchess, he was also impugning his reputation as a judicious art dealer and connoisseur. Gerbier launched an indignant counter-attack, dispatching letters to Lord Weston protesting his innocence. 'All this misunderstanding emanates from the malice of Van Dyck,' he insisted, and 'a sudden caprice has come into his head that he will not enter on the voyage'. The insults flew: Gerbier claimed Van Dyck's 'fickleness' offended the archduchess and that his 'maliciousness' in denying the provenance of the *Virgin and Child* was a deliberate attempt to discredit Gerbier in King Charles's eyes.[17] The Lord Treasurer, still embroiled with the troublesome Daniel Nys and the Mantuan acquisition, was no doubt heartily sick of art dealers by this stage.

Worse was still to come. The disputatious Gerbier tried to rescue the situation by blaming others. On 12 March 1632 he drew up an affidavit swearing that he had bought the picture in good faith from a local art dealer, even dragging his old friend Rubens into the dispute to verify it as an original. Gerbier claimed that Rubens knew that 'this Van Dyck by some malicious underhand dealing has sought to disavow his work'. For a resident ambassador, it was all very undiplomatic.

The following day all sides reached an uneasy truce. Gerbier wrote to Charles, informing him that Van Dyck had reappeared and was now resolved to travel to England. 'He pretends to be very ill pleased with me,' continued Gerbier, 'because that babbler Geldorp has written that I had orders to speak to the said Van Dyck on the part of your Majesty, and that I concealed it from him. Your Majesty so commanded me, consequently I was not called on to give an explanation to anyone.'[18] It was another revealing example of King Charles's inexperience (or worse) when it came to acquiring pictures and painters. Even if he did not instruct Gerbier to exclude Van Dyck from the negotiations, the choice of the volatile and divisive ambassador to manage the affair showed extremely poor judgement.

The irony of the whole bad-tempered business was that the painting *was* regarded by many as an original Van Dyck. What was the painter up to? It is likely that his reluctance to commit himself to King Charles, once combined with his encounter with Gerbier, led the petulant Van Dyck to make life as hard as possible for the English. Finally, in late March 1632 he arrived and was lodged at the king's expense in St-Martins-in-the-Fields in the house of his old friend Nicholas Lanier's brother-in-law, the miniaturist and royal illuminator Edward Norgate.

The London Van Dyck saw in the spring of 1632 had changed from the city he had first encountered in 1620. Despite the parliamentary turbulence that had led to the dissolution of 1629 and strengthened religious opposition to the king, the City itself, at peace with Spain and France, was growing in stature as a capital of finance and trade. The development of international joint-stock companies and the influx of spices, ceramics, silks, tobacco and other luxuries from America and the Far East transformed Londoners' domestic lives. Manufacturing and new crafts boomed, as glass-makers, gun-makers, distillers and spectacle-makers all formed new companies. The shape of the city also changed as the population rose from 120,000 in 1550 to nearly 300,000 by the 1630s. North-east of the City walls the population grew to over 90,000, creating a definable 'east end', characterized by crowded tenements, heavy industry and endemic plague in districts like Whitechapel, Stepney and Shadwell. At the other extreme, the demand for desirable property from the influx of country gentry led to the development of a 'west end' around the Strand, Covent Garden, Soho and Westminster. In 1631 Francis, 4th Earl of Bedford, paid £2,000 for a licence to develop expensive property and the city's first 'square' in Covent Garden. By the late 1630s, there were over 1,300 new houses in the area, bringing the population of the western suburbs to nearly 40,000.[19]

The city's skyline was also changing. In Westminster, the Banqueting House was complete and Inigo Jones's new classical portico dominated the gothic aspect of St Paul's. Renovations to Somerset House (the queen's residence), York House (former home of the Duke of Buckingham) and Arundel House (residence of the connoisseur earl) all dominated the area around the Strand. Recently bought and commissioned artworks adorned the interiors of these grand residences and this demand meant that the city's suburbs were increasingly populated with artists jostling for royal and aristocratic patronage. The painting families of de Critz, Gheeraerts and Oliver were already well established in the populous parishes of Holborn and St-Martin-in-the-Fields. Recent additions to the Blackfriars district included the sculptors Isaac Besnier, Hubert Le Sueur and the brothers John and Maximilian Colt, and the court painters Daniel Mytens and Cornelius Johnson. Van Dyck's arrival sparked further artistic immigration from the Continent. The painters Jan Lievens and Hendrick Pot arrived the same year, followed by Cornelis van Poelenburgh and Alexander Kierincx, as well as the silversmith Christiaen van Vianen, who all took up residence in Westminster's Orchard Street.[20]

Many of these artists worked directly for the king and were granted an annuity, subsidized accommodation and additional fees by the crown. Portrait painters earned most. King James had paid the prolific court painter Daniel Mytens an annuity of £50, but under Charles's reign artists could expect double that figure. Both Orazio Gentileschi and his rival Gerrit van Honthorst earned £100 per annum, plus payments for specific commissions. Sculptors and silversmiths were paid slightly less, between £65 and £40 a year. In all, Charles employed eleven foreign artists, not to mention a host of other limners and miniaturists, including Peter Oliver.[21] However, the work was irregular and in many cases rather mundane. The court did employ specific artists for particular artworks, but also paid for a monopoly on both their talent and their time. Sculptors like Le Sueur were required to make various public statues of Charles throughout the 1630s, while portrait painters and miniaturists like Oliver and Pot found employment on a more intermittent basis, commemorating royal births and anniversaries. Craftsmen like van Vianen were required to beautify Whitehall's interior, while others took their royal annuities and sought what other work they could find. Many, like the sculptor Besnier, traded on their royal appointments to obtain commissions from those close to the king, but the proscription on reproducing the king's image without prior consent left many artists feeling frustrated and neglected.

Comparability with other professions is notoriously difficult due to the complex system of additional fees, pensions, board wages and other benefits common to most seventeenth-century trades. Within the royal court painters certainly earned substantially more than most working Londoners, as well as courtiers such as grooms, pages and ushers. But they realized less than senior court officials like the royal surveyor, who collected a fee of £145 a year, plus £35 expenses, and far less than a resident ambassador, who could expect to earn anything from £2,000 a year.[22] Court painters also faced a further difficulty in that Charles was notoriously bad at paying them promptly. This was primarily due to the perennially chronic state of the exchequer, but it was also because the fees provided still restricted artists to the social status of skilled crafts- men rather than gentlemen – with notable exceptions like Van Dyck. In 1630 Orazio Gentileschi was forced to petition the king for three years' arrears of his annuity, a debt again settled by the long-suffering Richard Weston.[23] By 1638 Charles owed the French sculptor Hubert Le Sueur nearly £500 for unpaid statues, and Van Dyck a further £1,603 for five years' unpaid pension and outstanding payments on twenty-five commissioned portraits.[24]

As well as the non-payment of royal commissions, London's international artistic community faced professional rivalry from local artists. London's Company of Painter-Stainers had regarded foreign artists as unwelcome competition since the days of Holbein and, in 1627, as Charles and his courtiers brought increasingly talented artists to London, the Company issued a petition against Mytens, Gentileschi, van der Doort and Steenwijk, claiming they threatened its members' livelihood.[25] The dispute festered through- out the 1630s. Like the religious reformers, native artists sought to establish an association in the public mind between 'popery' and the baroque art of Gentileschi and Van Dyck.[26]

Such antagonism explained why most foreign artists lived in districts beyond the City walls, officially outside the legal reach of the Company's wrath. However, this rarely prevented internecine quarrels and feuds between London's various French, Italian, Dutch and Flemish artistic communities. In January 1629 the Gentileschi clan came to blows with Balthazar Gerbier after Orazio criticized his acquisitions for the Duke of Buckingham's collection. Gerbier responded by accusing Gentileschi of embezzling money from the duke, including £400 that the painter 'squeezed out of his purse'. Gentileschi revealed just how deep the national and religious tensions ran when he complained to Charles that 'all the Dutchmen had combined together to weary me, and make me leave the kingdom'.[27]

This was the kind of volatile, competitive artistic world which confronted Van Dyck upon his arrival in the spring of 1632. His response was to embark on a monumental series of portraits of the king and his family. Measured simply in terms of material rewards, the results were extraordinary. By May he was given an elegant

Thames-side house in Blackfriars, conveniently outside the jurisdiction of the Company of Painter-Stainers, a large country residence in Eltham and an annuity of £200 – double that of his nearest rivals, Gentileschi and Mytens. By July he was not only appointed 'Principal Painter in Ordinary to his Majesties' but also knighted by Charles at St James's Palace. In a matter of weeks he had managed to outstrip the achievements of his great mentor, Rubens.

The reason for Van Dyck's spectacular success was that he provided Charles with an image of a ruling king of England that no painter had ever previously achieved, or since surpassed. He started by demolishing the opposition. Commissioned to paint a portrait of Queen Henrietta Maria, Van Dyck drew on a double portrait of the king and queen painted by the competent but uninspired Daniel Mytens. Mytens had produced a florid, podgy king and his pallid, weak-chinned wife, juggling an olive branch, set against a flat, drably lit backdrop. Van Dyck responded by injecting the scene with glamour, beauty, drama and, it seemed, genuine affection. His queen is pale and delicate, with cheekbones, an elegant jawline and tapering fingers grasping her olive branch. The king is divested of his unfortunate ruff and is dressed in a beautiful slashed red doublet, prominently displaying his precious Order of the Garter. Slim and handsome, he gazes at his wife attentively. His hand reaches towards her rather than the olive branch. The body language is completely transformed. It anticipates an embrace rather than the conclusion of a tiresome public relations exercise. Even the rich, turbulent backdrop serves to foreground the serenity and beauty of the couple.

The unfortunate Mytens could not compete. His double portrait was taken down from the king's bedchamber and his royal commissions dried up. Two years later he left England, never to return. For Van Dyck, it was just the beginning of a series of glittering portraits of the king's family and his courtiers. His task was made somewhat easier because, against all initial expectations, Charles and Henrietta Maria had fallen in love with each other. After the assassination of Buckingham, Charles had turned to his wife for solace and she quickly responded. The birth of their first son, Charles, in May 1630, followed by the arrival of Princess Mary the following year, confirmed what many courtiers were saying: that Henrietta Maria had taken the place of all others as Charles's 'favourite'. Van Dyck quickly capitalized on this most unlikely of royal romances and followed his double portrait with an even grander family portrait, *King Charles and Queen Henrietta Maria with their Children*, also known – due to its height of over three metres – quite simply as *The Great Piece*.

The painting's sheer physical presence is overwhelming. The king sits in his chair of state wearing his Order of the Garter, resting his hand on a crimson tablecloth on which sits the imperial crown, orb and sceptre. At his knee stands the heir apparent, Charles, Prince of Wales, the future King Charles II. To the king's left sits Henrietta Maria, who holds the ten-month-old Princess Mary. In the background appears the material embodiment of Charles's kingdom – the Thames at Westminster, Parliament House and Westminster Hall. The painting's success lay in Van Dyck's ability to represent the group as a 'normal' family rather than a dynastic alliance created out of the pragmatic need to provide male heirs. Neither James I nor Elizabeth I before him could convincingly portray the kind of royal family that Charles put on show for Van Dyck. *The Great Piece* combined the meticulous realism of Holbein's royal Tudor portraits with the lustre and grandeur of the dynastic portraits Van Dyck had seen on his travels in Italy. It was a taut synthesis that Charles found irresistible.

In his royal portraits Van Dyck also achieved what Rubens was unable to do: he created a domestic intimacy free of the ponderous allegory that defined Rubens's London pictures. In *St George and the Dragon* Charles and Henrietta Maria are literally and figuratively distant personifications of mythological figures, weighed down with religious and political allegory, in keeping with Rubens's diplomatic brief. Van Dyck was under no such pressures and consequently was able to produce a series of sympathetic and authoritative royal portraits that confirmed what Charles's supporters wanted people to believe: the king and his wife were in love, and their offspring were a guarantee that the Stuart line would rule unbroken for the foreseeable future.

The Great Piece was so successful that Charles paid its painter £100 and ordered it to be hung in pride of place at the end of the Long Gallery in Whitehall. Such renown and royal patronage allowed Van Dyck to nearly double his rates by the end of the decade. Half-length portraits rose from £20 to £30, while a full-length portrait doubled from £25 to anything from £50 upwards. This was more than Rubens had been charging twenty years earlier for a small history painting. However, Van Dyck did not always get his way. When he submitted an invoice for £685 for eighteen pictures, Charles or his treasurer slashed the amounts they were prepared to pay. The large equestrian portrait of the king and a family portrait of the three royal children, both valued at £200, were reduced to £100 each. Royal patronage brought fame and prosperity, but there were limits and Van Dyck wisely refrained from contesting the reductions.[28]

More was still to come from the painter's productive brush. In May 1633 Charles left Whitehall for Scotland, intent on a royal coronation that would finally fulfil his father's desire to unite the two kingdoms. The move represented an extension of his personal rule, with its intention of drawing the Scots closer to English control. The coronation took place on 18 June, but the Scottish Church, or Kirk, continued to have reservations about what they saw as the increasingly Catholic dimensions of the king's Anglicanism.

The possibility of a serious threat to Charles's personal rule seemed highly unlikely. When Van Dyck unveiled what remains one of the abiding images of the king, *Charles I with M. de St Antoine*, at the end of 1633, the painting's meaning was unmistakably aggressive. Unlike the more domestic scene of harmony represented in *The Great Piece*, the symbolism of the equestrian portrait was public and political. Charles was portrayed riding in triumph, as if returning from Scotland, with the royal crown and unified national coat of arms the closest objects to the viewer, as brilliantly illuminated as the king. The portrait captured him in his prime, aged just thirty-three, obviously relishing his authority. Like Rubens, Van Dyck layered his painting to ensure it would endure beyond its immediate, highly political moment of creation. It drew on a repertoire of classically inspired images of military leaders on horseback, from Marcus Aurelius down to Charles V and Rubens's own portrait of the Spanish Duke of Lerma, but unlike Rubens's earlier pacific image of Charles as a riderless

St George, Van Dyck's image threatened war to those who, in Charles's eyes, endangered his kingdom's peace. The picture was also indebted to the recently arrived portraits of Titian's Roman emperors from Mantua, some of which Van Dyck was asked to repaint due to their ruinous condition. It must have given him enormous satisfaction to see the Mantuan emperors paying homage to his equestrian portrait as it took pride of place at the end of Charles's gallery in St James's Palace.

One of Van Dyck's more neglected achievements during his time in England was to raise the artistic and political profile of Charles's Catholic queen. Henrietta Maria was often unfairly characterized as frivolous and a political innocent, but her love of plays, masques and music were also subtle ways of establishing her own (admittedly limited) influence at the royal court. Papal envoys despaired of her apparent disregard for her co-religionists, complaining that she 'thinks little of the future, trusting entirely to the king'.[29] Despite her increasing reluctance to challenge her husband in matters of politics and religion, Henrietta Maria established an alternative court at her lavishly redecorated residence in Somerset House that welcomed a diverse group of Catholic sympathizers and developed a pro-French cabal among some of Charles's closest political advisers. It was a sign of the queen's abilities that she drew two of the most powerful statesmen of their day into her influence – the previously Hispanophile Secretary of State Sir Francis Windebank and Chancellor of the Exchequer Francis Cottington. However, when she became embroiled in attempts to discredit Charles's pro-Spanish Treasurer, Sir Richard Weston, in 1633, her husband roundly chastised her.

The queen's adherence to Catholicism went unchallenged by the king and the court and she pursued it with fervent sincerity. Unfortunately, the increasingly bold assertion of her faith throughout the 1630s did little to enhance her popularity among the public. Although her propensity for providing Charles with a string of heirs only increased his love for the woman he called his 'jewel' and 'my heart', others feared her religious influence over future monarchs. Charles even gave his wife the leverage to commission Inigo Jones to build a Catholic chapel at Somerset House just six months after Van Dyck's arrival in London. Erected on the site of

the palace's former tennis courts, the queen's chapel was a beautiful but provocative statement of her religion. Jones's baroque
design, with its Doric fluted columns and niches with statues of
St Peter and St Paul, complemented the high altar designed by the
Roman-trained sculptor François Dieussart. When the chapel was
officially opened in December 1636 it 'excited admiration, joy, and
adoration in Her Majesty and in all the Catholics', and Charles
himself praised Dieussart's altar, saying 'he had never seen anything more beautiful'.[30]

It was here that the queen's official painter, Orazio Gentileschi,
was laid to rest following his death in 1639, and where Van Dyck
practised his Catholic faith, despite growing public opposition to
what was regarded as the incipient spread of popery throughout
the court. Henrietta Maria remained unconcerned, clearly approv-
ing of Van Dyck's portrayal of her family, as she invited his brother
Theodor to act as her chaplain just months before sitting for her
portrait with her pet dwarf, Jeffrey Hudson.[31]

At only eighteen inches tall, Jeffrey had burst into the queen's
life in 1627, when he popped out of a cold pie presented to the
royal couple by the Duke of Buckingham. He took his place among
her exotic menagerie of black servants, hounds and monkeys, like
the one perched on his shoulder in Van Dyck's painting. Adopting
the sobriquet 'Lord Minimus', Jeffrey quickly established himself
as a firm, if somewhat infamous, court favourite. During the Civil
War he followed the queen to France, scandalized the court and
severely embarrassed the family of the much taller Captain Crofts
when he shot him dead in a duel. In 1630 Jeffrey was dispatched
to France to collect a midwife for his pregnant queen. On his
return he was abducted by pirates. He managed to escape, wiser
but inexplicably taller, returning to London in glory to the delight
of his queen and the admiration of the poet William Davenant,
who penned a mock heroic poem, *Jeffereidos*, in honour of the little
courtier's tall tales of captivity.[32]

Henrietta Maria's involvement in court life extended beyond
the commissioning of a Catholic chapel and an exotic retinue. She
was also instrumental in re-establishing the first direct diplomatic
relations between London and the papacy since the days of Henry
VIII, and in the process she paved the way for another iconic Van

Dyck portrait of her husband. Towards the end of 1633 she corresponded with Pope Urban VIII with a view to receiving a papal representative in Whitehall. Such a move was fraught with difficulties and soon met with criticism. Religious disquiet at the queen's openly Catholic court in Somerset House was growing and, as she opened dialogue with Rome, William Prynne published his assault on the theatre, *Histrio-mastix*. As well as attacking a litany of offences that included playgoing, dancing, music, laughter, bonfires and effeminacy, Prynne condemned 'the very art of making pictures and images as the occasion of Idolatory',[33] a position that many regarded as a thinly veiled attack on the queen's Catholic court and its activities at Somerset House.

Prynne's position revealed the growing religious gulf between the Anglican king and many of his Puritan subjects, who equated the influx of Italian pictures, Henrietta Maria's chapel and the growth of Anglo-Roman diplomacy as a sign of creeping popery. The intellectual distinctions between idolatry and aesthetic admiration were very subtle, as Henry Peacham pointed out in his conduct manual *The Gentleman's Exercise*, published in 1634, just months after Prynne's *Histrio-mastix*. Peacham appeared initially to support Prynne in his belief that 'Neither by any means may the picture of our Saviour, the Apostles and Martyrs of the Church be drawn to an idolatrous use, or be set up in Churches to be worshipped'. However, he went on to criticize Prynne and his followers, adding that for the purposes of display, religious images were 'very lawful and tolerable in the windows of Churches and private houses, and deserving not to be beaten down with that violence and fury as they have been by our Puritans in many places'.[34]

Peacham's position was much closer to that of Richard Montagu, who had established a similar distinction between the admiration and idolatry of religious images in his earlier book *A Gag for the New Gospel?*, published in 1624. Montagu insisted, 'No Protestant ever said that it was unlawful to make or have images. No Protestant but hath or hath had in his house, closet, study or the like, Pictures and Images, many or few. That which Protestants mislike and condemn in Papists, is not the having, but adoring and worshipping of images, the giving them honour due unto God.'[35]

His conclusion that images 'are not unlawful, for civil uses: nor utterly in all manner of religious employment' held sympathies with Arminian religious doctrine, and it increasingly defined King Charles's own religious and aesthetic values.[36] As far as Charles was concerned, these arguments justified his wife's Catholic chapel and his own display of Titian and Raphael Madonnas and saints in Whitehall's galleries. Such display was in keeping with his Anglican beliefs. For Prynne, however, it was further evidence of the spiritual decay and bankruptcy at the heart of the English Church. Having established an explicit connection between 'the very art of making pictures' and Catholicism, Prynne showed that collecting art was now a more politically contested activity than ever. It was a sign of how nervous such accusations made the Caroline authorities that the lawyer was tried for his libellous attacks, found guilty and condemned to suffer the brutal humiliation of having his ears cut off by the hangman.

The unfortunate Prynne was closer to the truth than he realized. As in so many cases involving Charles's art collection, the diplomatic negotiations with Rome were carried out under the thinly veiled guise of artistic exchanges. Henrietta Maria and Charles commissioned Van Dyck to paint the king's portrait in order to help the Pope's greatest sculptor, Gianlorenzo Bernini, to carve a lifelike marble bust of Charles. For the king it was an artistically vain and politically dangerous project; for Van Dyck it was the opportunity to rise above an apparently menial commission ultimately designed to glorify Bernini.

Van Dyck returned from Antwerp in the spring of 1635 to discover both the details of his new commission and that one of its brokers, the papal nuncio Gregorio Panzani, was now officially settled in London. The brief posed a classic conundrum: how to represent the three-dimensional facets of the king's head on a flat canvas. For inspiration, Van Dyck turned to the recently installed Mantuan collection, hanging in the galleries of Whitehall and St James's. In the privy lodging rooms hung a painting attributed to Titian, entitled *Three Views of a Man's Head*, dated around 1530. It was in fact the work of another Venetian and a contemporary of Titian's, Lorenzo Lotto.[37] The picture portrays a goldsmith holding a case of rings, thought to be Bartolomeo Carpan, a craftsman from Treviso. It provided a witty pun on the sitter's home town – tre-viso – as well as the subject matter, three visions, or tre-viso of the same person. It also drew on the long-standing *paragone* debate regarding the relative merits of painting and sculpture, seized on by Van Dyck 100 years after the picture's composition.

Lotto's portrait of a humble Italian goldsmith provided Van Dyck with the perfect model for his portrait of the English king, painted in three positions – full frontal, profile and half-profile. It also gave Bernini everything he needed to complete his bust. It was a perfect portrait of royal power: the image of a king from every angle, prominently displaying his garter medal. The sheer level of physical and psychological detail of every facet of the king's countenance, or what Edmund Waller in his poem 'To Vandyck' called 'Not the form alone, and grace, / But act and power of a face', meant that subsequent events would see it lifted out of context and hailed as a timeless image of doomed majesty.[38]

In the summer of 1635 Charles financed the construction of a wooden causeway and flight of stairs adjoining Van Dyck's Thames-side residence, allowing him to pay discreet visits to the painter, possibly sitting for the triple portrait and certainly admiring Van Dyck's collection of Titians. Charles left no record of these meetings and their discussions, but they established a relationship of intimacy never before seen between an English king and his painter. Van Dyck's status reached new heights when Bernini's finished bust arrived at Oatlands Palace two years later, in July 1637. Thomas Chambers, the man entrusted to transport the statue from Rome to London, spent three anxious months travelling on papal galleys, boats, horses and mules, via Genoa, Marseilles, Lyons, Paris, Rouen and Dover to bring the bust to England. He braved pirates, robbers and avaricious customs officers before finally reaching the royal court at Oatlands on 27 July. His journey was worth the trouble. Chambers left a vivid recollection of the statue's royal reception: 'we had to open the case that very night, so great was the eagerness of the King and Queen. I cannot write sufficiently of the great contentment of the King and Queen and of the astonishment of the whole court and in particular the superintendent of the statues, who exclaimed with an oath as the first plank of the case was raised that the bust is a miracle'.[39]

Henrietta Maria confirmed that she commissioned the bust by promising to send the pope's nephew, Cardinal Francesco Barberini a diamond set in a ring worth £1,000.[40]

One rumour that rapidly grew up around the statue was that the marble's minute stains, or flaws, would only disappear once Charles converted to Catholicism.[41] Opponents like Prynne suspected that the papacy believed that increasing diplomatic and artistic exchanges between London and Rome might lead to the king's conversion. Cardinal Barberini admitted as much, conceding that he was prepared to 'rob Rome of her most valuable ornaments, if in exchange we might be so happy as to have the King of England's name among those princes who submit to the Apostolic See'.[42] He had not accounted for Charles's increasingly sophisticated attitude towards art and collecting. The king's strongly held Anglicanism valorized the pomp and ritual of the established Church, but this in no way made him susceptible to Catholic conversion, whatever critics like Prynne claimed. The paradox of such criticism was that Charles was well aware of the boundaries between religion, politics and art. Although he might admire a painting for its skill in representing the Virgin Mary, throughout the 1630s his marked preference was for art that focused on his royal person.

For Charles, assisted by his advisers, Van Dyck's art fulfilled the highly specific political function of ratifying his personal rule. The acquisition of the Mantuan collection brought something slightly different: international cultural capital, confirmation that he was a great *virtuoso* as well as a powerful king. The presentation of the Bernini bust conferred international prestige but also possession of an artwork from one of Europe's finest sculptors who, as the Pope's favoured artist, would otherwise remain forever out of Charles's reach. Charles could move from admiring the statue as a beautiful piece of art to commissioning a series of politically prescriptive imitations from his sculptor Hubert Le Sueur to stand in town halls and squares throughout England.

A remark by the Earl of Arundel from 1636 captures Charles's growing confidence as a collector during this period. Negotiating the purchase of Titians for Charles that year, he announced, 'The king knows best what he hath *gusto* in.'[43] Gregorio Panzani glimpsed a similar side to Charles when presenting him with another gift of pictures from Rome earlier the same year. The king was with Inigo Jones, who, as soon as he saw the works attributed to Leonardo, Andrea del Sarto and Giulio Romano, 'greatly approved of them, and in order to be able to study them better threw off his coat, put on his eye-glasses, took a candle and, together with the King, began to study them very closely'. Panzani found Jones 'conceited and boastful', because 'as the king had removed the names of the painters, which I had to each picture, he also boasts of having attributed almost all the pictures correctly'.[44] It is a striking scene. The energetic, self-important Jones briskly pushing his way forward, showing off his knowledge before the awkward, reserved king. Charles in turn is gradually drawn into the excitement shared by most collectors, of examining their newly acquired possessions, carefully scrutinizing the surface of the canvases by candlelight, then playfully removing the labels and teasing his conceited surveyor to indulge in a game of artistic attribution (in which Jones failed to impress, wrongly attributing at least one picture to Leonardo).

Charles issued few written pronouncements on art – like most kings, he regarded it beneath his dignity to commit his views on such matters to paper. This was at best the preserve of gentlemen like Peacham, but it was certainly not for kings to discourse on objects handled by common artisans, merchants and guilds. However, in one of his rare comments on pictures, Charles comes across as a hard-headed sovereign with an eye to the political preservation of his royal image. Royal paintings were, he told the Lord Keeper in 1638, 'lasting monuments remaining to posterity',[45] which was how he viewed the work of artists like Mytens, Gentileschi, Le Sueur and Van Dyck. It was only his poor political judgement, and single-minded desire to pursue the art he wanted, regardless of the financial or political cost, that allowed his opponents to make a connection between collecting and Catholicism that was never there in Charles's mind.

One of the most abiding of all the lasting monuments to posterity arrived in England in late 1635. Nearly six years after his departure from London, Rubens's paintings for the ceiling of the Banqueting House were finally completed and on their way to

Whitehall. Unfortunately, Charles was entangled again in accusations of delaying payment, this time the £3,000 promised to Rubens. The problem was compounded by the fact that yet again the go-between in the deal was Balthazar Gerbier. Despite severe criticism of Gerbier's ability as both a diplomat and a connoisseur, Charles chose to keep faith with him, presumably because of his relationship with Rubens.

Gerbier wrote to the king in August 1634 to 'relate what malicious tongues or ignorant spirits utter seeing the great work Sir Peter Rubens hath made for your Majesty's Banqueting House, lie here, as if for want of money'.[46] This was surprisingly direct even for the garrulous Gerbier and suggests that his allegiances were becoming perilously divided. Rubens does not appear to have finished the pictures, which might imply that Gerbier was working in the financial interests of the painter, not the king. Like Daniel Nys, Gerbier was trying to exploit the ambiguous gap between a picture's acquisition and its delivery. After working for so long on such large and oddly shaped canvases, Rubens obviously felt he deserved at least some payment and let Gerbier do his bidding.

Gerbier responded to Whitehall's annoyance at his financial demands by protesting that he was 'a royal sentinel' looking out for the king's best interest, but slyly reminding London, 'I have my stake in the game.' Once again, his reputation and his percentage were on the line if such an important and long-standing deal collapsed.[47] Writing to Charles in September 1635, Gerbier assured him that the pictures would be dispatched any day. He also took the opportunity to interest the king in another purchase following the Archduchess Isabella's death, offering to buy 'the late Infanta's movables and jewels' for £5,000.[48] Charles wisely stuck with Rubens's pictures. By the end of the month these were en route to London, where they arrived in mid-December. Rubens had to wait nearly three years for full settlement of his bill.

In the winter of 1635, £880 was spent painting and gilding the Banqueting Hall, and the masques regularly performed before the court were banished to a temporary hall outside, for fear that the smoke from the candlelight would damage the paintings.[49] The final installation of all nine canvases represented one of the finest

and most enduring moments of King Charles's career as a collector; it also provided London with what Sir Roy Strong has called
'the greatest baroque ceiling north of the Alps'.[50] Yet Charles
himself was almost completely absent from the nine huge canvases
that towered above his head as he sat in state beneath the royal
dais. Rubens's paintings were a glorification of the founder of the
Stuart dynasty, Charles's father, King James I.

Evidence suggests that the designs for the ceiling stretched
back to the early 1620s, when Rubens was first linked to the
Banqueting House and its projected commemoration of the Spanish match. Following King James's death, Charles's advisers
persuaded him to raise a fitting monument to his father. Instead
of a statue, it was agreed to rework Rubens's and Jones's initial
plans for the Banqueting House. The ceiling would be subtly
transformed into a living mausoleum to the dead king, beneath
whose reflected glory his son would sit, enthroned under the
canopy of state.[51]

Like the masques they replaced, the paintings were designed
by Rubens and Inigo Jones to interact with the political drama of
state played out on the ceremonial space below.[52] Seen from the
centre of the Banqueting House, the ceiling is a symmetrical but
forbiddingly complicated series of nine canvases composed of three
central panels with three more either side running the length of
the hall. In King Charles's carefully segregated court, the place in
which courtiers stood defined their relationship to what was
depicted on the ceiling and affected how they interpreted it – and
how it framed them. What the courtiers saw was invariably partial
and fragmented, unlike the king, who was able to see everything.
The first image that the king saw from his throne as he looked up
was the central square panel directly above the entranceway,
known as *The Union of the Two Crowns*. It shows King James seated
on a throne in a circular temple, blessing the political union of
England and Scotland, symbolized by the two naked women
gazing up at him. The infant standing between the two women
and trampling the paraphernalia of warfare and discord personifies
the union of the two crowns and the birth of James's most
cherished political institution: Great Britain.

The founding symbolism of the painting was Jacobean, but for Charles, only recently crowned king of Scotland, its effect was resoundingly pro-Caroline. As he gazed up at the panel, Rubens and Jones were obviously inviting the king to see himself as the infant monarch, the natural heir to his father and, even more importantly, the unified throne of Great Britain. Nobody thought to interpret the infant as Charles's long-dead brother, Henry, the first-born prince. While Rubens's ceiling celebrated Charles's father, it also quietly erased the legacy of Prince Henry, now finally eclipsed by his younger brother.

These complicated family relations were displayed for public consumption in the panel immediately visible to visiting dignitaries when they first entered the hall and which hung directly over Charles's throne. Entitled *The Benefits of the Reign of James I*, it shows James in another highly theatrical and architectural scene. He sits in a richly carved niche decorated with rusticated columns, dramatically dispatching the damned to Hell, while shielding the female personifications of Plenty and Peace. Minerva appears again, this time alongside Mercury, God of Eloquence, beating down the forces of discord, as winged figures circle overhead, crowning James with the victor's laurel. As in the first panel, James is portrayed as King Solomon, a comparison he favoured during his lifetime, the wise patriarch dispensing judgement and justice from a particularly Protestant perspective. Hanging above Charles's throne and in the direct gaze of visiting dignitaries, the picture was intended to emphasize royal and religious inheritance; like his father, Charles was the unquestioned priest-king, the personal ruler over both Church and state on the kind of absolute terms that James tried but failed to achieve during his reign.

In the middle of the ceiling, positioned between these two panels, hangs the climactic central oval painting, *The Apotheosis of James I*. The most technically ambitious of all the paintings, Rubens used dizzying foreshortening to create the effect of James's heavenly ascension. Deities swirl around him in a spiral that draws the eye upwards, past his guides, Fortune and Religion, the putti that trumpet his arrival and Minerva again, preparing a garland of laurel to crown the king. As James ascended heavenwards, Charles remained below, his father's earthly representative, dispensing Solomonic judgement in the pursuit of unity, peace and prosperity.

The ceiling's side panels act as striking contrasts to the scenes of judgement, union and harmony displayed in the three central panels. The four oval panels in each corner portray allegorical scenes of the virtues triumphing over the vices that threaten Stuart rule. To one side of *The Union of the Two Crowns* Hercules clubs a serpentine Envy into submission, while to the other Minerva vanquishes Ignorance; to the left and right of *The Benefits of the Reign of James I* Temperance subdues Intemperance, and Liberality prevails over Avarice. Flanking the central *Apotheosis* are classical scenes of a Stuart-inspired golden age of temperance and plenty, as putti rein in wild beasts and enjoy the fruit of the earth. All six panels act as visual counterparts to the masques they replaced. The classic masque began with a scene of confusion and disorder – the antimasque – that threw into relief the second half of the performance that restored harmony and order. In this way the ceiling offered a visual substitute for the masque, and no wonder: Inigo Jones devised both.

Although the king was ostensibly absent from the paintings, every panel above was designed to magnify his authority below. Without his presence they become as they appear to some today – contrived, overblown allegories. But with the king enthroned and his court in attendance, the ceiling represented a brilliant fusion of Catholic Counter-Reformation style with the Protestant symbolism and political imagery of Caroline personal rule. The paintings were filled with references to a range of styles and motifs, most of them Catholic. From his own paintings in English collections, Rubens adopted Minerva and the exotic wildlife of his *Lion Hunt*, as well as quoting from other works in the royal collection: Raphael's *Acts of the Apostles* for the Roman architecture, Guido Reni's *Hercules* and Giulio Romano's putti. His *Apotheosis* was a familiar style developed by Catholic Counter-Reformation painters from Michelangelo to Caravaggio that fused the Assumption of the Virgin with a Roman imperial triumph.[53] Memories of the proposed Spanish match and Charles's visit to Madrid also remained in the ceiling's architectural references to the Temple of Solomon. Most Caroline courtiers might have understood the flattering comparison between King James and Solomon, but few realized that Rubens's and Jones's model was heavily influenced by the Spanish architect Juan de Herrera's designs for the Escorial in Madrid, which were based on the reconstruction of the Temple of Solomon.[54] This was international baroque in the service of Caroline royal power.

Jones cleverly tempered Rubens's Catholic designs with the kind of Protestant symbolism more familiar to a Caroline audience – the reference to Scripture, the Order of the Garter and the damnation of the many-headed Catholic hydra. Rubens showed few qualms when confronted with such obvious manipulation of his work. As a pragmatist he followed prestigious commissions, not religious ideology. 'As for me,' he wrote to a friend around this time, 'I assure you that in public affairs I am the most dispassionate man in the world, except where my property and person are concerned.'[55] However, he tempered some aspects of his earlier designs, erasing references to rival Catholic kings and portraying Religion looking on as James's ascends to heaven, rather than leading him by the hand.[56]

This remarkable fusion of Rubens's technique, Jones's design and Charles's dynastic requirements created the first piece of truly baroque English art. The European baroque is often defined by its style – sensual, dramatic, heavily allegorical, rich in tone, colour and modelling – but it also responded to the religious and political demands of the time. It provided clients in Rome, Madrid, Vienna and even London with a vision of grandeur, triumph and persuasion that emperors, popes and kings like Charles I found captivating.[57]

CHAPTER SIX

WHATEVER THE COST

THE INSTALLATION OF RUBENS'S Banqueting House ceiling marked a new phase in the development of the king's personal rule, as well as his interest in art. By the mid-1630s painting had become integral to Charles's concept of himself and his royal authority. The ideal of peace offered by Rubens in both his *Allegory of Peace and War* and the Whitehall ceiling appeared to have come true. Domestically the turbulent years of negotiating with troublesome Parliaments appeared to be over. Charles ruled supreme, and seemed happier and more secure than ever. As one historian put it, 'The King was in the prime of life, in excellent health, devoted to active exercise in the open air, happy in his domestic relations, attentive to business' and deeply committed to the 'principles of government' established under personal royal rule.[1] Charles's stature abroad also looked increasingly secure: while central Europe continued to tear itself apart in a series of bloody wars over territory and religion, England was at peace with both Spain and France.

Such unaccustomed harmony and the artistic response to the era of personal rule significantly expanded the king's aesthetic horizons. The influx of new artists, as well as the arrival of objects from Mantua, boosted the size of his collection and broadened its scope. Charles was now confident in his artistic tastes after nearly two decades of watching and learning from Arundel, Jones, his old friend Buckingham and his long-dead brother, Prince Henry. International peace allowed him to look abroad in pursuit of new works, as well as those of established favourites. The political rapprochement with the papacy allowed him to accept the work of contemporary Italian painters based in Rome, and between 1635 and 1636 he received gifts of pictures by Giovanni Baglione,

Francesco Albani, Alessandro Turchi and Jacques Stella. The ruling Roman Barberini dynasty dispatched earlier works attributed to Leonardo, Giorgione, Giulio Romano and Andrea del Sarto, in keeping with Charles's growing enthusiasm for sixteenth-century painting.[2]

Despite his admiration for Italian art, Charles also sought work by other artists in a range of styles from across Europe. Peace with Spain brought a resumption of the artistic exchanges that had ended abruptly with Charles's departure from Madrid in 1623. Throughout the 1630s Sir Arthur Hopton, resident English agent in Madrid to Ambassador Cottington, brokered various art deals on the king's behalf. In 1631 he acquired a still life by Juan Labrador, the Spanish artist greatly admired by Charles during his time in Madrid, in exchange for a copy of the Titian given to the king by Philip IV, the *Pardo Venus*. Hopton reported on Orazio Gentileschi's attempt to secure Habsburg patronage by sending his pictures from London to Madrid, and when King Charles sent Michael Cross to Madrid to copy the Spanish Titians that the English had failed to obtain in 1623, Hopton financed the painter's visit. He helped Cross to send his copies back to London, where they went straight into the king's rapidly expanding collection.[3]

Hopton also helped the king and queen to proclaim their international reputation as patrons and collectors by presenting portraits of the English family to the Spanish court. At last the English court possessed a painter fit to rival Philip IV's court painter, Velázquez, and Henrietta Maria was also able show off a vigorous male heir to her sister, Queen Isabel of Spain. In 1638 Henrietta Maria dispatched pictures of herself, her husband and their eldest son, the seven-year-old Prince Charles, painted in Van Dyck's studio. The implication was unmistakable: the Stuarts possessed an heir and a painter who were the equals of any European royal family. While Van Dyck struggled to come up with a suitably majestic painted persona for the king, his son provided no such problems. Large, muscular and handsome, the young heir to the English throne grasps his pistol with an air of confident virility. The contrast with the pale, sickly miniatures of his father at the same age could not be greater.

Unfortunately, Charles and Henrietta Maria slightly misjudged their gift, underestimating the connoisseurship of the Spanish court. The prince's portrait was a studio copy of Henrietta Maria's original hanging in Somerset House. The unfortunate Hopton was forced to write to Cottington in July 1638 with the news, 'I delivered those her Majesty sent, which were discovered to be no originals.' He explained that the Spanish 'are now become more judicious in & more affectioned unto the art of painting than they have been, or than the world imagines'.[4] Van Dyck might rival Velázquez, but King Philip's experts were way ahead of Inigo Jones when it came to spotting a studio copy. Nevertheless, Philip bolstered King Charles's collection by matching the gift with the dispatch of Velázquez studio portraits of himself, his wife and their son, Prince Baltasar Carlos.[5]

Ever since his departure from Madrid in 1623, Charles had harboured ambitious plans to transform Whitehall into an imperial palace on the same scale as the Habsburg royal palaces. Money and political circumstances continued to delay the project, but he made his intentions clear by creating a new cabinet room in Whitehall to house some of the most precious objects in his collection. In 1633 the joiner Peter Penson was paid for fitting 'the king's rich cabinet' with cupboards, cases, shelves and window shutters.[6] The finest pieces were transferred from St James's Palace, not only consolidating Whitehall as the nucleus of Charles's collection, but also providing the king with the kind of luxurious cabinet originally envisaged by his brother. Eighty-eight classical and modern statues stood on plinths, including recent acquisitions of Fanelli, Duquesnoy and Le Sueur. There were seventy-three paintings and drawings, including Mantua pieces and gifts from Wotton, Carleton, Porter, Cottington, Hopton and Hamilton, ranging from Raphael's painting of *St George* and Leonardo's *St John* to Rubens's designs for the Banqueting House ceiling. The cabinets also contained fifty-four books and numerous drawers of coins, medals and gems.[7] It was an impressive testimony to the collection's rapid growth and encompassed its finest small-scale objects. The cabinet room's position adjacent to his bedchamber also indicated its private as well as public value to the king.

Improving diplomatic relations with the rest of Europe were central to the augmentation of the collection. Since the early days of the embassy of Sir Dudley Carleton, The Hague had been a crucial posting for ambassadors keen to monitor political events in central Europe while also keeping an eye on the burgeoning art market across the Low Countries. Once the exiled Elizabeth and Frederick of Bohemia established themselves in the 1620s at the court of Frederick Hendrick, Prince of Orange, stadtholder of the United Province of the Dutch Republic, a steady stream of royal portraitists moved back and forth between The Hague and London, including Mytens, van Honthorst, Lievens and Pot.

It was under these conditions that Charles came into possession of the first paintings sold outside the Low Countries by the rising star of the new Dutch School of painting, Rembrandt van Rijn. In 1629 King Charles sent Sir Robert Kerr, a veteran of the Madrid trip and future Earl of Ancram, to console Elizabeth and Frederick over the accidental drowning of their eldest son. Kerr met Frederick Hendrick of Orange and his secretary, Constantijn Huygens, both patrons of the arts. Huygens also championed Rembrandt's work, which probably influenced Kerr's decision to purchase three small pictures, including a self-portrait of the artist and the sombre *Old Woman*, all of which he presented as gifts to the king.[8] With his muted palette and portraits of ordinary people going about their everyday lives, Rembrandt hardly appealed to the tastes Charles had learned from his mentors – grand, allegorical scenes of classical and biblical stories full of movement and action. It was Kerr, not Charles, who was ahead of his time in appreciating the Rembrandts, which were hung in the Long Gallery at Whitehall, unremarked and largely forgotten among the larger Van Dycks, Tintorettos and Giulio Romanos.

The ongoing international dispute over the Palatinate also brought other northern artists into the royal collection. In April 1636 Charles dispatched the Earl of Arundel on a diplomatic embassy to Germany in the forlorn hope of resuscitating Elizabeth's claims to the Palatinate. Following the death of her husband, Frederick, Elizabeth placed her political hopes in her son Prince Charles Louis. Unfortunately Emperor Ferdinand appointed the Catholic duke of Bavaria as Elector Palatine, effectively ending Charles Louis's claims to the Palatinate territories. Unlike the bellicose Buckingham, neither Charles nor his advisers (including

Arundel) had any appetite for military intervention, instead coun-
selling diplomatic negotiation with Ferdinand in what Arundel
conceded was a 'desperate' business.[9]

Travelling through the war-torn cities of Düsseldorf, Cologne
and Nuremberg, Arundel split his time between negotiating with
the emperor's advisers and corresponding with his art agents,
who were scattered across Europe. Writing to William Petty from
Nuremberg, he painted a graphic picture of the effect of nearly
twenty years of warfare on Europe and its art market. Nuremberg,
he reported, offered 'nothing by the way to be bought of any
moment, here in this town being not one scratch of Albrecht
Dürer's painting in oil to be sold, though it were his country, nor
of Holbein, nor any other great master'. The reason for the scarcity
was the pillage and plunder of art carried out by both Catholic
and Protestant armies throughout the Thirty Years War; 'within
these three or four years,' continued Arundel, 'great store of
good things have been carried out at easy rates', including works
by Dürer. What he failed to tell Petty was that for 350 *Reichstaler*
he bought the library of the renowned humanist Willibald Pirck-
heimer, as well as an etching by Dürer.[10] He also took on a new
servant, the Prague-born artist Wenceslaus Hollar, recruited en
route. The admiring Arundel observed that he 'draws and etches
prints in strong water quickly, and with a pretty spirit'.[11]

The war was providing the avid collectors with some new
opportunities. As Arundel began protracted negotiations with the
emperor at Linz, he dispatched servants to Italy in pursuit of art
and antiquities for himself and King Charles. From the early 1630s
Arundel had been so keen to dominate the Italian art market
that he had installed his faithful agent William Petty in Venice to
provide him with weekly updates on potential purchases. Other
London collectors were unable to compete with Arundel's industrious servant, who was instructed to place exorbitant reserves
on particular pictures, pricing visiting English dealers out of the
market, because 'no Englishmen stayeth long in Italy'.[12] With the
competition out of the way, Petty reduced his initial offer, which
was invariably accepted by the hapless seller. By 1636 Arundel was
keen to bid for one of Venice's finest collections of sixteenth-
century art, owned by the merchant Bartolommeo della Nave. He

dispatched a team to Italy that included Dr William Harvey, the physician whose treatise *Exercitatio Anatomica de Motu Cordis et Sanguinis* would revolutionize medicine with its theory of the continuous circulation of the blood. Arundel even poked fun at Harvey's medical innovations, referring to him as 'the little perpetual movement called Dr. Harvey', but despite the jokes he made it quite clear that he was not the only person interested in the della Nave collection, because Harvey was instructed to travel to Italy in pursuit of 'pictures for his Majesty'.[13]

As Arundel returned through Germany in the winter of 1636, his embassy a failure, he wrote to Petty with exciting news. The Protestant city authorities had presented him with two Dürer portraits, including a magnificent self-portrait, as a gift for King Charles. Even better, travelling through Würzburg Arundel was presented with a Dürer Madonna by the town's bishop. He told Petty with delight that 'though it were painted at first upon an uneven board, and is varnished, yet it is more worth than all the toys I have gotten in Germany, and for such I esteem it, having ever carried it in my own coach since I had it; and how then do you think I should value things of Leonardo, Raphael, Correggio and such like!'[14] Arundel's reaction was typical of obsessive collectors: unalloyed excitement at taking possession, the dismissal of all earlier acquisitions as mere 'toys', or 'trash', followed by the careful examination of the object itself. What is significant about Arundel's reaction is that, unlike most English collectors, he obviously regarded the portraits as highly as those of Dürer's Italian contemporaries.

The London to which Arundel returned in early January 1637 boasted a growing faction of connoisseurs who gathered themselves around the king, creating even greater demand for the kind of art available at a price across war-torn Europe. Other rising stars of the Caroline court also combined their political careers with an interest in collecting. By the 1630s the two activities were so tightly enmeshed it was hard to disentangle them. The increasingly tolerant religious attitude in Whitehall, combined with economic momentum encouraging increasingly elaborate displays of conspicuous consumption, made possession of an art collection a prerequisite for involvement in the royal circle. A large, modern collection featuring portraits of its owner and his family proclaimed wealth and discernment, and brought royal attention and (hopefully) political preferment. Algernon Percy, 10th Earl of Northumberland, combined his reputation as one of Van Dyck's foremost English patrons and a discerning collector with a high-flying political career as Knight of the Garter and Lord High Admiral. He amassed a diverse collection of over 100 paintings, including over twenty works by Van Dyck, who often received more in a year from Northumberland's commissions than he did from the king.[15]

Van Dyck's other great patrons included Philip Herbert, Earl of Pembroke, the king's Lord Chamberlain of the Royal House-hold, with responsibilities for the redecoration of the royal palaces and the staging of court masques. A patron of poets and dramatists with Puritan sympathies, Pembroke's name was closely associated with the 1623 publication of the first folio of the works of Shakespeare. He also used Inigo Jones and Van Dyck as designer and painter for his ancestral home of Wilton, still adorned to this day with a series of Van Dycks portraying the earl and his family.

Another important patron lay even closer to the heart of Caroline political power. Thomas Wentworth, 1st Earl of Strafford, Lord Lieutenant of Ireland and the king's chief minister, sat for Van Dyck on four separate occasions, accumulating a relatively small but discerning collection of nearly sixty portraits distinguished by Van Dyck and including works by Mytens and van Honthorst. His imposing portrait with an Irish wolfhound is a direct reworking of the king's Titian portrait of Charles V, a suitably aggressive and confrontational portrayal of Strafford, whose recent appointment to subdue political and religious opposition to the king's rule in Ireland was implied in his controlling gesture towards the docile wolfhound.[16]

Among these collectors, Arundel remained the greatest English connoisseur with the finest collection apart from the king's. By the end of his life he owned approximately 650 paintings reflect-ing his wide-ranging tastes. Italian artists represented over a third of his collection, including thirty-seven pictures attributed to Titian (far more than in the king's collection), thirteen ascribed to Raph-ael and twenty Veroneses. Arundel also embraced early northern

European artists as well. He owned forty-four works by Holbein, sixteen by Dürer and over fifty sketches and portraits by Van Dyck.[17]

The impact of such a marked escalation of English connoisseurship on the royal collection was profound. Art attained the status of political currency, as the collectors surrounding Charles practised an elaborate series of presentations and gift-exchanges involving the trade of art in exchange for continued royal preferment and political elevation. As soon as Arundel returned from Germany in 1637 the papal envoy George Con reported that 'the king went privately to the house of the Earl of Arundel, to see the pictures he has brought from Germany'.[18] A month later, as the king and queen entertained Con and the Arundels at Somerset House, Henrietta Maria showed off her recent gifts from Rome before the party then went along the Strand to Arundel House to admire officially Arundel's latest acquisitions. Con's report captures the humorous rivalry of English royal collecting at its height:

> His Majesty said that he would narrate to me a miracle of the Earl; which was that he had sent a picture by Holbein as a present to the Grand Duke [Cosimo II of Tuscany]. I replied that the Earl could perform twenty similar miracles, because he had in one room more than thirty pieces by that same painter. The Earl thereupon vehemently denied having this power, while I besought him to remember the true doctrine of free will. He protested that he was most ready to support that doctrine in everything except in the matter of giving away pictures.[19]

That the king, queen, earl and papal envoy could humorously compare the pressure to relinquish pictures to the Catholic doctrine of free will shows the sophistication of Stuart connoisseurship at the height of Charles's reign. To share the joke, everyone had to understand that by the mid-seventeenth century secular, aesthetic admiration of art in a gallery looked and probably felt very close to the religious adoration of icons in a church. Charles and Arundel obviously believed they could distinguish between religious and aesthetic aspirations; their only mistake was to assume that everyone else understood such a distinction.

Con's visit to Arundel House also revealed the tensions and rivalries that surrounded London's elite collectors. Looking at her husband's paintings, Lady Arundel expressed her desire to present Henrietta Maria with 'a most beautiful altarpiece by the hand of Dürer'. Offering her husband's finest acquisition from an otherwise miserable tour of Germany was a typically mischievous offer on the Catholic countess's part, inciting the queen to install the altarpiece in her Somerset House chapel, already the site of growing public concern. Con joined in the fun, revelling in the domestic tiff. 'A controversy followed between her and her husband,' he reported. 'The Queen at first made difficulties, saying it would be a pity to deprive people of what they seemed so much to delight in; but I assured her Majesty that it would be a work of charity to remove any occasion of dissension between husband and wife.'[20] As ever, Charles remained silent, but his presence suffuses the anecdote; listening with detached amusement, fully aware of what Con and the countess were up to, and delighting in the haughty earl's embarrassment.

It is unclear if the queen got her Dürer altarpiece, but the king certainly received the two portraits presented to Arundel in Nuremberg, as well as a host of other pictures as gifts or in exchange for items in the royal collection considered superfluous to requirements. Arundel gave Charles a *Tarquin and Lucretia* by Titian, but also profited from items no longer in royal favour. Van der Doort records a triangulated exchange between Arundel, Charles and the 3rd Earl of Pembroke involving works by Raphael and Holbein. The surveyor listed Raphael's 'St George, which your Majesty had in exchange of my Lord Chamberlain [Pembroke] for the book of Holbein's drawings wherein many heads were done with crayons which my Lord Chamberlain immediately so soon as he received it of your Majesty gave it to my Lord Marshall [Arundel]'.[21] Pembroke's stock rose by providing the king with the first known Raphael to reach England. In exchange he acquired a book of Holbein drawings that ended up in the hands of his brother-in-law, whose love of Holbein was in inverse proportion to the king's.

Charles's indifference towards Holbein also enabled him to acquire one of the finest pictures in the entire collection, Leo-

nardo's *St John the Baptist*. King Louis XIII's courtier the Duc de
Liancourt presented Charles with the painting in exchange for a
Holbein portrait of Erasmus, plus a Titian Madonna which had
come to the king via the Earl of Carlisle, who in his turn obtained
the painting from the poet John Donne.[22] Such convoluted transactions were often the only way for the king to obtain the
exceptional pieces he now coveted. Since the chaotic and acrimo-
nious purchases of the Mantuan collection, he preferred to conceal
his interest in particular acquisitions, acting instead through old,
trusted intermediaries like Porter and Arundel.

By the late 1630s Charles and his advisers had transformed the
palace's main galleries out of all recognition from their original
Tudor designs. One of the grandest changes had taken place in
the Bear Gallery, one of the palace's semi-public spaces abutting
on to the Great Hall in the north-east corner of the palace. Here
the Elizabethan conception of a long gallery was updated to
include full-length pictures along its walls, but it was the nature of
the pictures and the way they were hung that were new. As well
as Tudor and Jacobean full-length portraits of Charles's parents,
James and Anna, his grandmother Mary Queen of Scots, the
Prince of Orange and the Elector Palatinate, were pictures of his
closest allies: the earls of Pembroke and Nottingham, Buckingham
and even little Jeffrey Hudson. Of all these portraits, none was
more imposing than Titian's *Charles V with Hound*, brought back
from Madrid in 1623. Around the doorways, acting as a contrast
to the sombre portraits, hung smaller Italian landscapes and
religious paintings set in gilded, carved frames. Interspersed among
the traditional dynastic portraits were more modern and intimate
paintings – Rubens's *Daniel in the Lions' Den* and the dramatic
Allegory of Peace and War, and five new portraits by Van Dyck, the
most beautiful the portrait of Nicholas Lanier. The gallery, with
its thirty-five paintings, provided its audience with a glimpse
of King Charles's dynastic lineage, but it also displayed his
friends, his dealers and his collecting abilities – an intimate,
personal relationship to paintings never seen before in an English
monarch.

One of the Bear Gallery's portraits depicted the Marquis of
Hamilton, a distinguished collector in his own right and father to

one of Charles's closest political advisers, James, 3rd Marquis of Hamilton. The young marquis saw himself as the natural successor to Buckingham's position as the king's favourite, marrying the duke's niece Mary Feilding and taking up arms against the Habsburgs in Germany in 1631–2. Charles admired the young Scot, but unfortunately he lacked Buckingham's charm and dynamic flair in matters of state, and many regarded him as arrogant and politically inept. Distrusted by many of his fellow Scots as the king's lackey, others in England regarded his pretensions to take absolute control over Scottish affairs with profound suspicion. However, Hamilton realized that one way to cement his royal favour was to collect art. He inherited a small but judicious art collection from his father, from which he immediately started to offer Charles the finest pieces, as well as presenting him with pictures acquired on his military campaigns in Germany.

Charles even forced undesirable pictures on Hamilton, including two fifteenth-century Dutch altarpiece panels presented to him by the States-General in 1636. The Dutch were eager to curry political favour with Charles, whom they saw as pursuing an increasingly pro-Spanish foreign policy. Unfortunately the gift of five old-fashioned Dutch paintings, along with horses, needlework and 'some fine and big cows' intended for Queen Henrietta Maria, catastrophically misjudged the sophisticated Italianate atmosphere of the English court. Hamilton agreed to take the two panels in exchange for two paintings by Cranach purchased in Germany. The swap did little for Hamilton's collection but wonders for his political standing.[23]

Alive to the rewards of collecting, Hamilton sought to rival Arundel and cement his place at the king's side by representing Charles's collecting interests abroad. In just two years between 1636 and 1638, he amassed an astonishing 600 paintings, nearly half the size of the entire royal collection. It was an impressive achievement in terms of its number of post-sixteenth-century Italian artists, many of which were, unsurprisingly, admired by the king. Hamilton held one crucial advantage over other London collectors in that his brother-in-law, Basil, Viscount Feilding, was appointed English ambassador to Venice in September 1634. This gave Hamilton excellent access to the Venetian art market, although it also placed him on a direct collision course with the other great collector employing a resident art agent in Italy, the Earl of Arundel.

As a collector, Arundel had good grounds for worrying about the ruthlessly self-interested alliance of Hamilton and Feilding. Hamilton was moody and aloof, acutely aware of his failings as a military leader, and unpopular in Whitehall as much for his personal shortcomings as his enigmatic political ambitions. Feilding moved in less rarefied circles, but had also experienced military failure, fighting alongside Buckingham in his ill-fated expedition to the Ile de Ré in 1628. In pursuit of political preferment Feilding had married Lord Treasurer Weston's daughter and, despite his limited diplomatic abilities, saw the opportunity of exploiting his posting to Venice by supplying Hamilton with pictures. What both men lacked in connoisseurship and political acumen they soon made up for in the pursuit of paintings.

By January 1636 Hamilton was already buying heavily from Feilding, claiming 'I am much in love with pictures and will bestow £1000 or £1500 on them.' However, at this stage his real reason for collecting lay in his desire to act as royal intermediary. Hamilton told his brother-in-law, 'I have told the king what you wrote to me of any rare picture that was at Venice, he is desirous to know the story, and what bigness it is of and the price.'[24] As Hamilton's first consignment of paintings by Titian, Tintoretto and Bellini started to arrive in London, Charles began to appreciate the rich potential of the Hamilton–Feilding partnership, while Hamilton was genuinely caught up in the excitement of the artistic chase. Dismissing Feilding's warning that he was becoming 'too much intoxicated with those enticing things',[25] he instructed Feilding to pursue a group of pictures initially targeted by Arundel: the celebrated della Nave collection.

Hamilton's interest in the della Nave collection represented a serious threat to Arundel, because the king was beginning to favour Hamilton in the acquisition of Venetian paintings. In early July Charles signified his intentions in a remarkable letter, one of his few explicit statements on art, which is worth quoting in full as it captures his highly competitive approach towards collecting:

Whereas we understand that an excellent collection of paintings is to be sold in Venice, which are known by the name of
Bartolomeo della Nave's collection; we are desirous that our
beloved servant, Mr. William Petty, should go thither to make
the bargain for them; we ourselves being resolved to go a
fourth share in the buying of them, so it exceed not the sum
of eight hundred pounds sterling; but that our name be
concealed in it. And, if it please God that the same collection
be bought and come safely hither, then we do promise, in the
word of a King, that they shall be divided with all equality in
this manner, *videlicet* – that they shall be equally divided into
four parts by some men skilful in paintings, and then everyone
interested in the shares, or some of them, shall throw dice
severally; and, whosoever throws most, shall choose his share
first, and so in order, every one shall choose after first, as he
casts most, and shall take their shares freely to their own uses,
as they shall fall to them.[26]

To reduce such a logistically complex sale to the roll of a dice
was an extraordinary and rather disingenuous scheme from a king
already responsible for pressurizing members of his court into
surrendering pictures in the guise of 'gifts' or 'swaps'. There were
obviously reasons for Charles's bizarre plan, namely financial
pressures – £800 was a surprisingly modest investment in such an
ambitious consortium – but was there also a growing anxiety at
the response of the likes of Prynne to the acquisition of yet more
'popish' images? Charles was obviously eager to avoid drawing
the attention of international art dealers, but this was still a new
approach to the acquisition of pictures.

Hamilton and Arundel were obviously members of the consortium, although the identity of the fourth investor remains unclear.
At this stage, Arundel was the favourite to acquire the collection,
as the king had recommended that his agent, William Petty,
complete the sale. But then, as Arundel trailed around Germany
and Hamilton's impressive collection grew, Charles peremptorily
withdrew his investment and transferred all his backing to the
Scottish noble. This was not the first of Charles's broken promises
when it came to buying art.

Excitement mounted throughout the summer as Feilding

tempted Hamilton with inventories of the della Nave collection. Their correspondence reveals how far the English court had travelled in its artistic discernment of and hunger for Italian art. Feilding declined to buy paintings by Veronese because he knew the painter was 'not very acceptable to the king'. He pored over the inventory of the della Nave collection, worrying over the number of studio works by Titian, rejecting copies out of hand, and expressing concern at the number of 'Rittratos', or portraits, 'which lessens much the value' of the collection. Notwithstanding Hamilton's concerns, it was an extraordinary collection of 224 Italian paintings, predominantly sixteenth-century and heavily Venetian – ideal for Charles. As well as original Titians, the collection included works by Raphael, Correggio and, to Hamilton's delight, 'one of old Palma, the best of his hand both for story and Ritratto'. Those 'of old Bassano are very excellent, two of Bordenone of great esteem, most of those of Paris Bordone very perfect', but according to Hamilton 'those of Giorgione are of his first way, and not comparable to some which I have seen of his hand'.[27] It was an exacting assessment, but exposure to Charles's royal collection allowed buyers like Hamilton to make such careful judgements, ruling out copies, studio works and juvenilia, and convincing the marquis that 'if they could be had for £1500 I think they would prove richly worth that'.

However, once Charles examined the inventory, the whole tenor of the purchase changed. Hamilton wrote to Feilding with a mixture of excitement and trepidation to inform him:

> . . . his Majesty who having seen the note of della Nave's collection is so extremely taken therewith as he has persuaded me to buy them all, and for that end he has furnished me with moneys, so brother, I have undertaken that they shall all come into England, both pictures and statues, out of which he is to make choice of what he likes, and to repay me what they cost if I have a mind to turn merchant.[28]

Charles realized that the della Nave collection promised to eclipse the Mantuan collection in its quality and price. Even better, Hamilton could settle financial matters without the need for troublesome foreign dealers and financiers like Nys and Burlamachi. The king signalled his intent with a series of instructions passed on to Hamilton that reveals how much he had learned from the mistakes involving the Mantuan sale. His language was that of the virtuoso, honed over many years as a patron and collector. First, Charles insisted, 'the rarest pieces be not cancelled', or withdrawn from the sale. Secondly, 'that the originals be not retained and copies given in their place'. Thirdly, 'extraordinary care be taken in packing them up', and that ornate frames be removed and the canvases carefully packed in cases. Finally, with the memory of the arrival of damaged pictures and broken statues from Mantua still fresh in everyone's mind, he solemnly ordered that 'the ship wherein they come may have no quicksilver nor currants in her'.[29]

Hamilton immediately issued Feilding with new instructions. He was now duty-bound to purchase the collection, telling his brother-in-law 'I shall buy them what sum ever they cost.' He explained that Charles's desire for the collection was that of the hopelessly obsessed collector: 'there are some masters of whose hands he has none that he doth more esteem and will give more for them than for others though the greater masters of whose hand he has already'. For Charles, the acquisition of della Nave's pictures represented the fantasy of the complete collection featuring all the great Italian masters. It was an impossible wish, but one that Hamilton now had the unenviable task of delivering to his king.

Matters intensified in August 1637, when Charles completed the purchase of yet another group of twenty-three Italian paintings from his postmaster of foreign affairs and a protégé of Arundel's working in Italy, William Frizell. Compared to the della Nave collection it was a relatively undistinguished selection of works attributed to Tintoretto, Guido Reni and the unpopular Veronese. It also included nine panels portraying Cupid and Psyche by the early sixteenth-century Milanese painter Polidoro da Caravaggio. They were frivolous bedroom furniture, but Charles adored them, hanging all nine in the Long Gallery at Whitehall and asking Hamilton if Feilding could get hold of any other examples of Polidoro's work. He was careful to distinguish Polidoro from his namesake Michelangelo Merisi da Caravaggio, whose superior

Death of the Virgin Charles also acquired from Mantua.[30] The history of connoisseurship would not judge King Charles kindly for his enthusiastic preference for Polidoro over the likes of Caravaggio, Veronese and Rembrandt, but there was no time for Hamilton to dispute the king's taste with his rival Arundel back in the frame.

Feilding assuaged Hamilton's concerns with welcome news. His great rival William Petty had just bought the collection of Daniel Nys for Arundel 'at an excessive rate' of £3,000. Having fallen on hard times, partly due to the scandal surrounding the Mantuan sale, Nys was forced to sell his remaining collection of medals, coins and other 'rarities'. Feilding was also in the market for Nys's collection, this time in the interests of King Charles, but once the possibility of the acquisition of the della Nave collection emerged, Charles lost interest in buying the collection of the dealer whose reputation he was primarily responsible for destroying. It was a sign of the rapaciousness of the international art market, and Feilding believed that 'this news I am sure will not displease the King'. Arundel was prepared to pay more for Nys's trinkets than the price of over 220 priceless della Nave pictures, exhausting his financial interest in the collection and leaving the way open for Hamilton and the king. Hamilton was delighted, fearing that if he lost the pictures to Arundel his 'jesting will trouble me more than losing double their value'.

Feilding provided even better news. He was now in a position to buy yet another fabulous collection of Venetian paintings owned by one of Venice's most distinguished elder statesmen, the Procurator Michiel Priuli. It included the 'Santa Margarita of Raphael with one of Giorgione's, two of Bordone's and one of Titian's for 3500 ducats and perchance for less money'. Hamilton was almost beside himself, telling Feilding, 'My heart is set on those pieces', as he scrambled to raise bills of exchange to provide his brother-in-law with sufficient credit to secure the pictures. Although he claimed, 'I love cheap bargains', Hamilton also stressed that he was now 'addicted' to pictures and was prepared to pay 5,000 ducats even 'if those ducats were turned into pounds'.

To Hamilton's consternation, Feilding haggled over the price even as the representatives of Charles's old rival King Philip IV made a late bid and Arundel prepared to re-enter the fray. Finally, in late November 1637, Feilding announced the completion of both the della Nave and Priuli deals. His main concern was to inform Hamilton of his victory over the luckless William Petty, who 'found no other reward but an extraordinary mirth I took at his choler expressed at the news of the conclusion of the bargain'.[31] Feilding's glee was compounded just months later when he reported that 'the good old Procurator Priuli, who lately sold your lordship the St Margaret of Raphael, entangling his foot in his gown, fell down a pair of stairs, and is since dead'. Informed opinion believed 'it was impossible he should live, after he had parted with his saint'.[32]

Feilding's parting shot was an appropriately callous conclusion to a deal defined by aggressive double-dealing and concerted deceit on all sides. This also ensured it was one of the most successful transactions ever concluded by a seventeenth-century English connoisseur, and it did not even involve the king. Charles monitored events from London, his only concern being to take his pick of the pictures once they arrived in London. Hamilton paid £2,000 for the della Nave collection and approximately 3,500 ducats for the Priuli pictures – a total of £3,000 for nearly 250 superb pictures that were superior in quality and value to the Mantuan collection. It was a great coup for Hamilton, but once the pictures arrived in London in October 1638 King Charles threatened to impose crippling duties on the consignment unless given the freedom to pillage it as he wished. Yet again the king had reneged on his word. In the undignified stand-off that followed, Hamilton's servants tried to remove the pictures but were blocked by his brother-in-law's entourage, who were eager to retain the king's favour in Hamilton's absence.[33]

As Charles and Hamilton struggled over possession of the consignment of pictures, Abraham van der Doort was at work compiling his inventory of the royal collection. It was a daunting task. He was faced with listing hundreds of pictures, statues, drawings, coins, medals and gems, most acquired over fourteen turbulent years of Charles's rule. What van der Doort produced was more than just an inventory of royal possessions. It was a capsule history of the formation of one of the greatest collections of art in seventeenth-century Europe, chronicling all its various

acquisitions, inheritances, gifts, exchanges and dubious appropriations. At its centre stood the king himself, addressed throughout
the inventory as 'your Majesty'. When the inventory was complete
Charles even annotated the finished copy. He only got as far
as page 11, but his corrections are revealing. He merely deigned
to confirm the attributions and spellings of those artists he knew
were important – Raphael, Titian and Mantegna. On one page
he corrected van der Doort's German 'Rafell Urbin' to 'Rafael
d'Urbino', and 'Montanio' to the Anglicized 'Mantenia' (Andrea
Mantegna), although neither he nor van der Doort realized that
both pictures were copies, not originals.[34]

In other places Charles revealed his mischievous attitude
towards the royal collection briefly glimpsed by Con and Panzani.
Listing medals held in the Chair Room, van der Doort recalled:

> The king going alone into the chair room with his servant Ab
> Vanderdoort showed him 27 golden medals in black turned
> hoops lying upon the table and said look Abraham how comes
> these here. I answered I see by this that there is more keys
> than the one which your Majesty hath given me and he said
> yes I have one.[35]

It was a poor, almost cruel joke on Charles's part, particularly
considering van der Doort's difficulty in keeping a check on the
collection. While the king slipped into the Chair Room to deliver
recent additions, other courtiers also took the liberty of 'borrowing'
coins and medals, much to van der Doort's anguish. But for all his
troubles, the Dutchman finally reached the end of his labours with
the completion of the inventory in 1639.

Neither Charles nor Hamilton had much time to enjoy their
new acquisitions. The period of Charles's personal rule, represented by the glittering pictures of Rubens, Van Dyck and others
that lined the royal palaces, could not conceal the political and
religious conflicts that had only intensified since the dissolution of
Parliament back in 1629. Puritan opponents like Prynne increased
their attacks on Charles's sympathy for the Arminians and Henrietta Maria's Catholicism. Charles assumed, not incorrectly, that
if he could continue to raise revenues without recourse to Parliament, opposition to his rule would remain relatively ineffective.

However, such complacency led him to make one of the greatest miscalculations of his reign.

For all the parliamentary opposition to Charles's rule throughout the late 1620s, the origins of his ultimate political downfall lay not in England but in his birthplace, Scotland. Ever since James I's accession to the English crown in 1603, one of the Stuart dynasty's most cherished political projects was the unification of the kingdoms of England and Scotland. The theme dominated Rubens's Banqueting House ceiling and reappeared more obliquely in Van Dyck's 1633 equestrian portrait of the king. Prior to 1633 Charles had ruled Scotland as an absentee monarch, his authority exercised by a Privy Council based in Edinburgh. His coronation as King of Scotland in 1633 was intended as a further step in strengthening his personal rule over the three kingdoms of England, Scotland and Ireland. Charles now wanted to bring the Scottish Church into line with Anglicanism. On returning to England after his coronation, he ordered the creation of a Book of Common Prayer and canons intended to reform the Presbyterian Scottish Church.

A new prayer book created by Anglican bishops was always going to cause controversy in Scotland. While the Anglican Church embraced a more formal approach to service, railing off the altar, acknowledging saints' days and performing consecration with a surpliced celebrant, Presbyterianism celebrated praying extempore among a congregation presided over by lay elders and ministers who paid little attention to the rituals of service. Instead of overall rule by bishops, or episcopacy, Scottish parishes elected members to a synod that in turn reported to the national Kirk, a mixed body containing Episcopal and Presbyterian elements. This balance was maintained until Charles's imperious attempt to reform what he saw as the 'disorderly' and disrespectful elements of Presbyterianism with the introduction of the new prayer book. The imposition of the English service was a radical departure from Scottish practice, and the first reading of the prayer book at St Giles's in Edinburgh on 23 July 1637 led to a riot among the congregation, with shouts of 'the Mass is entered among us!'[36]

Having already alienated many Scots because of his refusal to consult them on the introduction of the prayer book, Charles now refused to back down, seeing the riot as a direct challenge to his political authority. The Scottish protesters responded by composing a Covenant that not only defended the Presbyterian foundations of the Kirk and condemned Arminianism, but also asserted the right of the Scottish Parliament to rule over and above the king's authority. Charles was outraged. In June 1638 he dispatched Hamilton to Scotland to continue negotiations, but his mind was made up. 'Flatter them with what hopes you please,' he instructed Hamilton, 'until I be ready to suppress them.'[37] By spring 1639 Charles stood at the head of an army of 28,000 men poised to invade Scotland. His choice of general fell on the fifty-four-year-old Arundel, the greatest collector of his day but a man with absolutely no military experience. It was a sign of how far collecting had permeated Charles's court that two of its greatest practitioners, Arundel and Hamilton, lay at the heart of the king's diplomatic and military response to the Scottish. Unfortunately, neither man proved equal to his allotted role.

By the time Charles's army arrived outside Berwick the initiative was already lost. Most of Scotland was in the hands of the Covenanters, who had also mobilized a substantial army to repulse any invasion. By mid-June both sides agreed to the Pacification of Berwick, a series of vague compromises involving military disengagement and a political settlement to be ratified in Parliament. The agreement made little impact on the intractable problem of religion, and Charles left Scotland intent on raising sufficient revenue to crush the unrepentant Scots once and for all. However, for that he needed Parliament.

In February 1640 Charles issued writs for Parliament to assemble in April. When it took its place, he asked for massive and unconditional subsidies to prosecute a second war against the Scottish Presbyterians. Unfortunately, many of the new members were sympathetic to the Scots, while veterans of the previous Parliament still harboured grievances over its abrupt dissolution. Opposition to the king's demands focused on John Pym, an official in the exchequer, a brilliant orator and skilled parliamentarian deeply opposed to the rise of Arminianism. On the second day of the new session Pym rose to deliver an excoriating attack on what he regarded as Charles's abuse of government and infringement of

Parliament's liberties. He cited the king's encouragement of Catholicism, the threat posed by the rise of Arminianism and the imprisonment of members of the House who had dared to challenge his financial levies during the previous Parliament. The speech set the tone for the Commons' future debates, and when they demanded that the king give up his right to ship money in return for war subsidies, Charles dissolved the so-called Short Parliament after just three weeks.

In retrospect, Charles's dissolution was yet another political miscalculation. Parliament had offered him larger subsidies than ever before – over £800,000 of an estimated £1 million required to prosecute the war against the Scots. Instead, the king decided to try to find the revenue independently. Although he raised enough to send a second army north in the summer of 1640, their first engagement in August ended in disaster and the Scottish army occupied Newcastle. The humiliating peace terms demanded that a delegation would accompany Charles back to London to receive parliamentary ratification of the Scots' political demands. Having lost a second campaign in Scotland, Charles was also rapidly losing the political initiative. When he recalled Parliament once again in November 1640, it was virtually his only hope of salvaging a vestige of his seriously compromised authority.

All was still not lost for Charles. Although the new Parliament was more vociferous than ever in addressing its long-standing grievances over religion, finance and what members regarded as the king's erosion of parliamentary privileges, their sympathy with the Scottish Presbyterians was politically delicate. Many parliamentarians sympathized with the Scots' anger at Charles's imperious attitude towards their liberties while remaining hostile to Presbyterianism. If Charles had been able to reach an accommodation with the Scots, he would have had a real chance of using their religious and military influence to turn the tables on Parliament. With John Pym as their unofficial leader, the Commons pressed their advantage, demanding the banishment of key Catholics, many of them distinguished collectors, including Sir Kenelm Digby and Tobie Matthew. Their main target was Charles's ablest adviser and former patron of Van Dyck, Thomas Wentworth, Earl of Strafford. Pym realized that Strafford's skilful political counsel and substantial army held in check in Ireland could still swing the political initiative back towards the king. Throughout the winter of 1640–41, fuelled more by fear and mistrust of Strafford than legal right, Pym used all his considerable political resources to engineer a charge of treason against the earl. When the Lords finally passed a bill of attainder in May 1641, circumventing a trial and declaring the accused guilty as charged, Charles was faced with the terrible dilemma of rejecting the bill and accepting political turmoil, or ratifying it in the unlikely hope of reaching a political compromise with Parliament. However, in ratifying the bill he effectively signed the death warrant of his closest and most powerful political adviser since Buckingham. On 12 May 1641 Strafford was executed on Tower Hill in front of a jubilant crowd of 100,000 people.

With Strafford removed, Pym and his followers began to systematically dismantle Charles's political authority, forcing the king to surrender his prerogative to dissolve Parliament, outlawing his right to ship money, dissolving his Courts of Star Chamber and High Commission, and limiting his rights to tonnage and poundage levies. William Laud, Archbishop of Canterbury since 1633, was also impeached and many of the founding principles of Arminian-ism outlawed, leading to a brief outburst of iconoclasm, marked by the destruction of stained glass and religious carvings in some churches. Desperate and increasingly isolated, Charles took the decision to head north to Scotland again, not to make war but to accept the Presbyterian demands he had rejected just two years earlier and to request Scottish military support against Parliament. His departure in September 1641 was a dangerous moment for Pym and his supporters. Although eager to wrest executive power from the king, the Commons were not prepared to take the momentous step of questioning the basic principles of monarchical rule. Unfortunately for Charles, he failed to reach agreement with the Scots and returned to London two months later to discover that Pym was constructing a Grand Remonstrance, a damning list of the royal abuses of power that – during the fifteen years of Charles's reign – had subverted 'the fundamental laws and prin-ciples of government'.[38]

The regime was dying and so were its artists. Orazio Gentil-eschi died in February 1639, having completed the *Allegory of*

Peace and the Arts under the English Crown for the Queen's House at
Greenwich. Even with the help of his daughter Artemisia, it was a
pale imitation of Rubens's Banqueting House ceiling; within the
context of the rapidly deteriorating political situation, it looked
hollow and unconvincing. Artemisia abandoned London the following spring. Her departure was followed by news of Rubens's
death at Antwerp in May 1640. With typical callousness, Balthazar
Gerbier offered to obtain items for the king from Rubens's estate,
but by this stage Charles had neither the political will nor the
money to take up such a tawdry offer.[39] Just days later van der
Doort was found hanged at his house in St Martin's Lane, the
result of a real or imagined slur on his reputation as the Keeper of
the royal collection. When, the following December, Van Dyck
died in Blackfriars, his burial in Old St Paul's Cathedral was
conducted against a backdrop of London's descent into political
chaos.

These events had no impact on the bitter political struggle
between the king and Parliament in the winter of 1641. News of
an Irish rebellion fuelled by Catholic and settler communities
angered by Charles's neglect of their political and religious grievances compounded his increasingly hopeless situation. As protesters
gathered outside Parliament with chants of 'No bishops!' Pym
pressed on with his Grand Remonstrance and its specific demand
for the exclusion of all bishops from Parliament. Charles's futile
attempts to forestall such demands led to one final injudicious act.
On 4 January 1642 he marched into the Commons to arrest five
of its members, including Pym, and charge them with treason.
Apprised of his arrival, the five fled. When Charles demanded to
know their whereabouts, the Speaker responded in terms that
crystallized the absolute breakdown of relations between king and
Parliament. 'May it please your Majesty,' he said, 'I have neither
eyes to see, nor tongue to speak in this place, but as this House is
pleased to direct me, whose servant I am here.'[40] Charles stormed
out of the House, never to return.[41]

Six days later, on the night of 10 January 1642, King Charles
fled the capital he no longer controlled and headed for Hampton
Court with his family and his faithful servant Endymion Porter.
Fearful for his wife's safety, Charles dispatched Arundel to conduct

Henrietta Maria into exile in the Low Countries, while he headed north to gather an army. On 22 August he raised his standard at Nottingham. The country was at war and the royal collection left hanging in the deserted royal palaces, its future as uncertain as its absent owner.

❧

CHAPTER SEVEN

CLOUDED MAJESTY

EDGEHILL, NORTH OF OXFORD, 23 October 1642: the scene of the first military confrontation between the armies of King Charles and Parliament. During a day of fierce combat watched by the king and the Prince of Wales, both sides fought their way to a bloody stalemate. Legend has it that the twelve-year-old Prince Charles was nearly killed by a cannonball as he withdrew on the morning of the battle to follow events with his tutor, Arundel's former art dealer William Harvey, and that later he narrowly escaped capture by parliamentary cavalry. The next day the king marched on Oxford, where he established his court for the duration of the war. William Dobson, a court painter who rose to prominence by portraying Charles's retinue during their time in Oxford, commemorated the Prince of Wales's first experience of battle with a portrait depicting him resplendent in his armoured breastplate, clutching the baton of command and resting his hand on his helmet held by his page. In the distance the battle rages, while just behind the prince lies the Fury Envy, or possibly Medusa, covered in battle standards and armaments.

Lacking immediate access to the royal collection in Whitehall, Dobson provided the court at Oxford with a comfortingly familiar image that drew heavily on Van Dyck, Rubens and the Mantua collection. With his vigorous good looks, dressed in armour and adorned with the Order of the Garter, Prince Charles's portrait evoked memories of the martial miniatures of his dead uncle, Prince Henry. The pose is that of a Roman emperor, modelled on Titian's emperors from Mantua, and the setting and architecture are almost identical to those in Van Dyck's *Charles I with M. de St Antoine*: the same pillar and draped hanging, the same overcast skyline and the same expression of concerned devotion from the royal attendant. However, in Dobson's portrait the baton of command is raised in anger, fighting fills the horizon and a heap of standards and weapons replaces the unified coat of arms. The Fury is straight out of Rubens's Banqueting House ceiling, partly obscured by the armaments and about to be crushed by the young prince.[1]

Dobson's portrait was more than just a reminder of what the court had left behind in Whitehall; it was intended as a memento to be admired in future years by King Charles II, portraying him crushing rebellion while drawing on the triumphant imperial iconography of his father and grandfather. The court was impressed by Dobson's ability to conflate the finest elements of the royal collection in his rich, baroque portraits. After over twenty years of collecting and commissioning art, they understood the importance of circulating images of the court at Oxford showing its leaders as glamorous cavaliers, patriots fighting what they believed to be a 'just war'.

By the time Dobson completed his portrait of the young prince, King Charles and his military commanders did indeed have good grounds to assume that they would soon be victorious in the war with Parliament. Although the battle of Edgehill proved inconclusive, throughout the first half of 1643 Charles's forces won a series of battles giving the king control of most of the north and west of the country, partly due to the superior discipline and organization of his men. Seriously shaken by this success and under pressure from the provincial gentry to reach accommodation with the crown, Parliament turned its attentions back to Scotland in an attempt to secure military support for the war against Charles. In August 1643 a parliamentary commission agreed to Scottish demands for a Solemn League and Covenant pledging all Englishmen to the preservation of the Scottish Church and the reformation of the English and Irish Churches 'according to the word of God'.[2] This ambiguous wording was the only concession the commissioners could obtain from the Scots, but at least they came away with assurances of military support.

The conflict widened further once Charles completed a truce with the Irish that released a substantial contingent of troops to fight under his banner in England. The result was the largest military engagement of the war, at Marston Moor outside York on 2 July 1644. Parliamentary forces totalling 28,000 men faced 18,000 royalists led by the king's nephew, the dashing Prince Rupert, brother of the Elector Palatinate. The parliamentary forces carried the day, thanks to the bravery and discipline of the Scottish cavalry and the Eastern Association cavalry of one of the army's rising heroes: Oliver Cromwell. At the end of the fighting over 4,000 royalist troops lay dead and the balance of power in the north had swung back in favour of Parliament.

Nonetheless, the victory at Marston Moor proved inconclusive. Charles's supporters won a series of engagements in Scotland towards the end of 1644, splitting the Scottish forces committed to Parliament. It was increasingly clear to Parliament in London that it needed to finance a professional, national army with discipline and resources if Charles was to be defeated. Throughout the winter of 1644–5 the Commons pushed on with plans for the creation of a New Model Army, despite the misgivings of the Lords, whose members were excluded from serving in the new force. One of the most energetic supporters of the creation of the new army was Oliver Cromwell, fresh from his impressive military achievements and now emerging as a shrewd and skilful politician. Cromwell supported the appointment of Sir Thomas Fairfax, a brilliant but relatively inexperienced campaigner, as commander-in-chief of the new army. Militarily, the results were decisive. In a series of victories throughout 1645, first at Naseby near Leicester in June, then at Langport in Somerset the following month and finally at Philiphaugh just north of the Scottish border, Charles's army was all but destroyed. The king rode north to Scotland, where he gave himself up to the Scottish forces in the spring of 1646, effectively ending the Civil War after more than three years of bitter and bloody fighting.

The parliamentary victory had come at a heavy price. It is estimated that over 60,000 people were killed in this first phase of fighting and that all told the death toll as a proportion of the population was higher than the losses incurred during either the First or the Second World War. This is not to mention the destruction of property, and the imposition of unprecedented taxation and conscription, and the commandeering of goods and property by both sides in a desperate attempt to keep their armies operational.[3] The ravages of war had also taken their toll on Parliament's popularity. Many of the 'middling sort' – gentry and prosperous yeoman in the provinces – continued to look for a rapprochement between the two sides, regardless of their instinctive support for king or Parliament. This hope for a partial restoration of the king and the institutions of monarchy was echoed by the majority in a Parliament which, after all, had been called by Charles himself back in 1640.

There was also profound distrust in Parliament of the power of the New Model Army, which was pressing for even greater religious and political changes than many in Westminster were prepared to accept. A split began to emerge between those who supported the army's demands and those who favoured the restoration of the king but with radically diminished powers. The English army took King Charles into their custody in 1647 but this only compounded their divisions. The decision was taken within the main body of the army to open negotiations with a view to offering the king limited political restoration.

Charles finally came face to face with Oliver Cromwell, his senior by a matter of months, at a meeting held in the town of Childerley near Cambridge on 7 June 1647. Cromwell's powerful physique and ruddy, fiery countenance contrasted sharply with the king's hauteur and physical weakness after over three ultimately unsuccessful years of military campaigning. In many ways, Cromwell possessed what Charles lacked. In a later assessment of Cromwell's abilities, the Venetian ambassador wrote that 'he has a deep and profound expression, wears a large sword at his side, is both soldier and orator and is skilled in both persuasion and action'.[4] Such comments only served to magnify the king's shortcomings. However, the meeting at Childerley revealed one crucial point on which both men agreed: the sanctity of the monarchy. Cromwell still clung to the possibility of restoring the king, albeit with considerable curbs on his authority, despite the misgivings of many in his own army.

Quick to exploit his opponents' divisions, Charles refused to agree terms and instead opened negotiations with the Scots, who were making political and religious demands in return for military backing. These proved unsuccessful and in November 1647 Charles escaped his captors and fled to the Isle of Wight. His flight provoked sporadic rebellions through Wales and Scotland, and Cromwell was called on to face the invading Scottish army, which was led by none other than the Duke of Hamilton. In August 1648 Cromwell engaged and destroyed Hamilton's army outside Preston, taking over 10,000 prisoners and losing just 100 men in one of his most brilliant and ruthless campaigns of the war.

Following the royalist defeat, Parliament opened negotiations with Charles with the intention of offering him limited monarchical restitution. By this stage the more conservative parliamentary members feared the political and religious demands of the army more than the restoration of the king. As ever, Charles negotiated with his thoughts elsewhere. Agreeing to all of Parliament's demands over his proposed military and religious authority, he wrote in October, 'The great concession I made this day – the Church, militia, and Ireland – was made merely in order to [help] my escape ... for my only hope is that now they believe I dare deny them nothing.'[5] Alarmed at what they saw as Parliament's capitulation, the army, led by Fairfax, marched on London, intent on preventing any political settlement that involved the restoration of the king. On 5 December with thousands of Fairfax's troops garrisoned throughout the city, the Commons voted to accept Charles's concessions, paving the way for his return. The following day Colonel Thomas Pride stood in the lobby of the House, identifying those members sympathetic to negotiations with the king. Out of a House of 471 members, Pride arrested forty-five MPs and barred entry to another 186. It was in effect a military *coup d'etat*. The following day Oliver Cromwell returned from laying siege to the royalist garrison at Pontefract and pronounced his support for what became known as Pride's Purge.[6] What remained of the purged legislature became known as the Rump – a polite but derisory reference to an animal's fleshy hindquarters or backside.

Up to this point Cromwell's position had been opaque and contradictory. Having attempted to negotiate a partial royal restoration with the king in the summer of 1647, by the end of 1648 Cromwell gradually came to accept the need to put the king on trial for his life. His decision was based as much on his religious faith as on his political beliefs. He profoundly believed that he was a member of God's Elect, chosen to pursue the 'godly reformation' of the English Church. Charles's increasingly pronounced Arminianism led Cromwell to ever more vociferous opposition to him, first in Parliament and finally on the battlefield. The defeat of the king's forces in the summer of 1648 convinced Cromwell that God had spoken and that royalist attempts to prolong the conflict were pointless and causing unnecessary bloodshed. 'Their fault who have appeared in this summer's business is certainly double to theirs who were in the first [war],' thundered Cromwell, 'because it is the repetition of the same offence against all the witnesses that God has borne, by making and abetting to a second war.'[7] He finally came to the belief that the king should stand trial for his 'sins' and that a negotiated political settlement involving even partial restoration was unacceptable. The second period of civil war was over and with it Charles's hope of dictating the terms of his return to political power.

THE EFFECT OF the Civil War on London had been to deeply divide the City aldermen and merchants. As early as 1642 parliamentary leaders like Pym realized the financial and political importance of ensuring that the municipality remained loyal to the reformed cause, and, with the appointment of the Puritan sympathizer Isaac Pennington as Lord Mayor, Parliament felt assured enough of the City's support.[8] Pennington had already encouraged the Commons to pursue a more active reformation of religion in exchange for loans of City money in the last months of the king's reign, as crowds demonstrated outside the queen's Catholic chapel at Somerset House, demanding the destruction of its 'superstitious monuments'. In the volatile, charged atmosphere that had followed Charles's departure for Edgehill, Parliament and the City had actively encouraged the iconoclastic 'reformation' of churches and chapels, unleashing in the process some of the godly Parliament's more colourful characters.

Attention immediately fell once more on the queen's Somerset House chapel. In March 1643 a parliamentary deputation led by

John Clotworthy was ordered to destroy the chapel's religious images. Clotworthy was a committed Presbyterian, a wealthy member of the New English settlers in Ulster who fiercely opposed the autocratic rule of Lord Deputy Wentworth. Sitting as an MP, he mediated between the Scottish Presbyterians and Parliament and led the attack on Wentworth and Archbishop Laud, who called him 'a firebrand brought from Ireland to inflame this kingdom'.[9] According to eyewitness accounts, it seems that Clotworthy took his Presbyterian beliefs with him when he entered the queen's chapel. Breaking down the doors, he 'climbed on top of the altar table and looked at the very valuable painting in its gilt frame by the hand of the late Rubens, which earlier, due to its rare quality, had been presented by the Duke of Buckingham to the king, who then bestowed it on the queen'. Next, 'calling for a halberd, he struck Christ's face in contempt with such offensive words it would be shocking to repeat them. His second blow was at the Virgin's face, with more hateful blasphemies, and then, thrusting the hook of his halberd under the feet of the crucified Christ, he ripped the painting to pieces'.[10] The wrecked picture was then tossed into the Thames.

This lurid description of iconoclasm, written by a French Catholic chronicling the expulsion of the Capuchins from London, should be treated with some caution, although Rubens's picture was indeed destroyed during Clotworthy's visit. What the account does show is that such zealotry made a clear distinction between acceptable pictures held in private galleries and unacceptable icons located in places of worship. If the Rubens had remained in Buckingham's gallery at York House, it would have avoided such violent retribution. There were certainly equally explicit religious images in the collections of Buckingham, Arundel, Hamilton and the king, but very few suffered a similar fate. Only when the picture entered the chapel to be used for religious purposes did its status change, leaving it exposed to Clotworthy's wrath.

This careful distinction between pictures as either secular objects of admiration or religious icons of devotion shaped subsequent iconoclastic activities sanctioned by Parliament. On 24 April 1643 the Commons appointed Sir Robert Harley to chair the Committee for the Demolition of Monuments of Superstition and Idolatry.[11] Harley was another passionate Presbyterian who had spent much of the 1630s opposing episcopacy, ship money and the Scottish wars. A dedicated parliamentarian, from 1642 he chaired various committees on Irish affairs, elections and Church reformation. His appointment to the committee coincided with his wife Lady Brilliana's stout defence of the Harley family estates in Herefordshire against besieging royalist forces.[12] In London, her husband's committee began its work in churches, removing religious statues, images and painted-glass designs. These actions undoubtedly proved popular with London's Puritans, but there was also a political dimension to Harley's work. At a time when Parliament was attempting to ally itself with the Scottish Presbyterians, this public reformation of churches also helped the English cause north of the border.

THE ROYALIST PRESS quickly responded to the committee's activities. It painted a lurid picture of Harley marching through Whitehall into:

> . . . his Majesty's gallery, which he reformed of all such pictures as displeased his eye, under pretence that they did favour too much of superstitious vanities (for Kings and Queens, as well as apostles, fathers, martyrs, confessors, are counted monuments of vanity and superstition) and so went on, according to the principles of reformation, till there was nothing left which was rich or glorious.[13]

The reality was much more prosaic. There is no evidence of Harley destroying or even defacing a single picture in his inspection of Whitehall. The committee's interests lay primarily in churches and chapels, not royal galleries, as they made clear in the bill passed by both Houses in August 1643 'for the utter demolishing, removing and taking away of all Monuments of Superstition or Idolatry'. The legislation ordered:

> . . . that all crucifixes, crosses, and all images of and pictures of any one or more persons of the Trinity, or of the Virgin Mary, and all other images and pictures of saints or super-

stitious inscriptions in or upon all and every one of the said churches or chapels, or other places of public prayer . . . shall before the said first day of November [1643] be taken away and defaced.

However, the ordinance ended with a striking caveat that its remit 'shall not extend to any image, picture or coat of arms in glass, stone, or otherwise, in any church, chapel, church-yard, or place of public prayer as aforesaid, set up or graven only for a monument of any king, prince, or nobleman'.[14] This final qualification effectively placed the royal estate, as well as the collections of royalists like Arundel, Buckingham and Hamilton, beyond the committee's reach. Harley and his supporters were more interested in dismantling the Arminian paraphernalia of communion rails and raised chancels than in attacking the royal art collection. Even though they regarded King Charles as a tyrant, many reformers like Harley still believed in the ideal of monarchy and had no desire to dismantle the Stuart dynasty's pictures and monuments.

By making such a clear separation between religious icons and royal monuments, Harley paved the way for later legislation that would judge the king's pictures and statues as commodities to be sold for cash on the open market, rather than superstitious icons to be defaced or destroyed. Throughout 1644 Harley's committee focused its attention on London's churches and chapels. St Paul's Cathedral and Westminster Abbey were both 'reformed'. Pietro Torregiano's Renaissance high altar in Henry VII's Westminster Abbey chapel was dismantled and its copper screen broken down and sold off as scrap to tinkers. Harley's committee dispatched the MP Cornelius Holland to 'reform' the chapel in St James's Palace, built in 1623 for the proposed marriage of Charles and the Spanish Infanta.[15] As he supervised the removal of rails and whitewashing of religious images, Van Dyck's *Charles I with M. de St Antoine* looked on from its privileged vantage point at the end of the palace's gallery, untouched by Holland's men.

When Harley's committee gradually started turning its attention to Whitehall's aristocratic residences, royalist collectors like Arundel and Hamilton feared for their own collections and began making plans to smuggle them out of the country. Arundel travelled to Cologne to sell off some of his artworks, raising an impressive £54,000 for the king's war effort.[16] Parliament responded by trying to seize his property and possessions in an attempt to prevent the flight of money and resources from the capital. When, in 1644, Colonel Robert Morley, soon to be appointed one of Cromwell's major-generals, intercepted a consignment of Arundel's paintings, he was outraged to discover what he believed was a portrait of King Charles, Henrietta Maria and Pope Urban VIII. Morley sent the painting to Parliament in London, describing it as 'an hieroglyphic of the causes and intents of our present troubles', recommending that it be publicly burned.[17]

However, in most cases financial expediency overwhelmed religious extremism. In 1644 Parliament ordered the seizure of the property and possessions of the 2nd Duke of Buckingham, including his substantial art collection held at York House and Suffolk House, which was valued at £20,000. MPs conceded that under the prevailing conditions of war and international isolation, 'the pictures are not like to yield so great a value as they are worth'. This led Sir Robert Harley to go to York House to adjudicate over which pictures were 'superstitious', which 'lascivious', which should be burned, but also which could be sold to pay for the war effort.[18] Fortunately for Buckingham, Harley came up against York House's tenant, the renowned collector and patron of Van Dyck, Algernon Percy, the Earl of Northumberland. The former Lord Admiral had switched political sides and was now a valuable and influential supporter of Parliament. However, he protested at plans to requisition Buckingham's pictures. He claimed their loss would adversely affect his rented property, but his undoubted aim was to secure for himself some of the superb paintings assembled by the 1st Duke of Buckingham. He arranged with Parliament to take the pick of the pictures in lieu of £360 still owed to him for losses incurred in the early stages of the war.

It was an excellent deal. Northumberland walked away with twelve paintings by artists all admired by Buckingham and King Charles, including distinctly 'superstitious' and 'lascivious' paintings by Palma Vecchio, Andrea del Sarto and Adam Elsheimer. By far his best choice was Titian's highly influential *Cardinal Georges d'Armagnac and his Secretary*. Bought in Italy by Gerbier in 1624, its arrival at York House had caused Inigo Jones to fall to his knees in admiration and inspired several of Van Dyck's finest English portraits. Subsequent valuations placed on the pictures suggest that Northumberland's deft act of embezzlement was well worth the annulment of his parliamentary debt.[19]

With a substantial debt still owed to him by Buckingham, Northumberland successfully petitioned against the sequestration of the estate, allowing the duke to smuggle the rest of the collection out of England. By 1650 over 200 pictures were sold for £7,000 to the Governor-General of the Spanish-controlled Low Countries, the Habsburg archduke Leopold-Wilhelm of Austria. The archduke had recently acquired nearly 200 paintings from the Duke of Hamilton's collection, also smuggled to Europe, and the Buckingham collection gave him the opportunity to double his haul.[20] Unfortunately for the profligate Buckingham, the profits from the sale hardly covered his substantial debts and financial support of his boyhood friend Charles while in exile.

Following the purchase of the Buckingham and Hamilton collections, some of the pictures were transported to the imperial collections in Prague, but most went to Vienna, where they still form the heart of the Old Master collection in the Kunsthistorisches Museum. Leopold-Wilhelm's reasons for acquiring the artworks were both aesthetic and political. Many of Buckingham's pictures had formerly belonged to Leopold-Wilhelm's ancestor, the Emperor Rudolf II, and had come to Buckingham via the Dutch art market.[21] Since the dispersal of a royal art collection invariably signalled the political weakness of its owner, the Habsurgs were eager to avoid such implications – even if it meant profiting from the political downfall of their Stuart relatives.

In London, dynastic considerations were eclipsed by an undignified scramble for paintings, now regarded as valuable commodities. Even the dead failed to escape. Van Dyck's death in 1641 had left behind a tangled estate, including a precious collection of Titians. The painter's wife, his sister and his creditors all claimed the pictures as Parliament closed in on what they saw as the property of 'delinquents', or royalists. Once again Van Dyck's former patron Northumberland intervened, allowing the Titians to slip out of the country, but not before buying two of the finest pieces, *Perseus and Andromeda* and *The Vendramin Family*, for the bargain price of £200.[22] Northumberland was talking like an anti-monarchist but acting like a connoisseur. Over the next few years of republican rule in England, the behaviour of many like him would prove that the two positions were much closer than many historians of the period have assumed.

In contributing to the downfall of King Charles and the royalist art collections, Northumberland was responsible for one final act of artistic patronage that showed his understanding of how painting could serve both king and Parliament. In 1647, as Charles and the army opened what proved to be fruitless negotiations for a political settlement, Northumberland took custody of Charles's three children, who were held at Syon House. He paid the German-born painter Peter Lely to paint *The Three Children of Charles I* and *Charles I with James, Duke of York*.[23] The impact of these portraits, showing the gaunt, beleaguered king and his captive children after the wearying campaigns of the first Civil War, was so shocking to royalist supporters that Richard Lovelace wrote an elegiac poem characterizing the portrait of Charles and James as an image of 'clouded majesty'.[24] Throughout the 1630s Van Dyck had repeatedly portrayed the monarch and his heirs in dazzling postures of power and authority. In these pictures Northumberland turned the tables on the royal family, displaying ownership of not just the portraits but also the immediate fate of the king's children.

By the late 1640s, with the war moving in Parliament's favour and the initial Presbyterian enthusiasm for religious reform subsiding, Parliament began to consider the unthinkable: the requisition and sale for cash of the royal estate, including Charles's art collection. The lucrative sale of portions of the collections of Arundel, Hamilton and Buckingham had convinced many in the Commons of the financial and political benefits of selling off the king's goods. Other interested onlookers started to reach similar conclusions. In 1645, as he watched the proceedings of the sale of Buckingham's collection, the Spanish ambassador to London predicted that, 'the same would be done with those of the king'.[25] If put up for sale at home and possibly even abroad, Charles's art collection could prove a vital financial asset in funding the ongoing war and any subsequent political settlement. Stripped of the aura of majesty, its royal owner absent, the collection could be gradually transformed from a visible emblem of Stuart wealth and power to a commodity like any other: to be valued, bought and sold for profit. It was a significant shift in the way in which its parliamentary guardians understood the collection, and one that mirrored the rapidly declining fortunes of the king himself.

AN ARMED GUARD arrived on the Isle of Wight just days before Pride's Purge to escort the king to Windsor. It was there that he awaited the outcome of the purged Parliament's deliberations. On 4 January 1649 Parliament agreed to put the king on trial for making war upon his own people. Just over two weeks later, Charles was placed on trial for his life in Westminster Hall. His refusal to enter a plea or accept the authority of the court made little difference to the proceedings. With typical passionate conviction, Cromwell intervened to convince the court's commissioners of the righteousness of enforcing the death penalty and on 27 January fifty-nine commissioners put their signature on the death warrant of the king of England.

Three days later, on the afternoon of 30 January 1649, King Charles I stepped out of a window of the Banqueting House to meet his executioner. As he was led through the palace, he could look up for the last time to see Rubens's ceiling and the image of his dead father rising up to heaven. Just after 2 p.m. he was beheaded in front of a silent crowd.

❧

CHAPTER EIGHT

WHO BIDS MOST?

WITHIN JUST DAYS OF the execution of King Charles I, the Rump Parliament began debating the terms of the sale of his goods and personal estate. For many in the army who, like Cromwell, had backed the creation of the Rump, simply executing the king was not enough. The trappings of royal power and authority must also be broken up and sold off in an attempt to rid the country of the institution of the monarchy for ever. Behind this reforming ideal-ism lay more pragmatic motives. Having confiscated art collections like Buckingham's, valued at £20,000, during the Civil War, Parliament appreciated the financial possibilities of liquidating the royal collection to raise badly needed revenue to keep the new regime afloat.

Two days after Charles's execution, the Commons turned their attention to the fate of the deceased king's goods. Debating the ownership of his jewellery, they denied the Prince of Wales his father's St George brooch, his diamond of state and his royal garter. Even the sceptre and the crown jewels passed into the hands of Parliament.[1] It was an understandable decision. Prince Charles, living in exile in the Low Countries, was still a threat to the new regime and, upon hearing the news of his father's execution, had immediately assumed the title King Charles II. Parliament was anxious to deny him any of the paraphernalia associated with the Stuart monarchy and particularly those objects intimately connected to the royal body of his dead father. How-ever, during the same parliamentary session it was also reported that 'the present necessities of the navy are so pressing, that the same requires a speedy supply of monies, without which those affairs cannot be carried on'.[2] The urgency of this request was particularly pressing in the early months of 1649. Within weeks of the king's death Prince Rupert, the new commander of the royal navy, landed at Kinsale on the south coast of Ireland with a fleet of ten warships intent on resuming hostilities. The Rump's response was to propose doubling the size of Parliament's navy in just three years by building twenty new warships and reforming its composition to ensure its political loyalty.[3] The projected expropriation and sale of the royal goods was therefore one way of funding this initiative while, at the same time, signalling an attack on the aura of monarchy.

Having executed the king, the Commons swiftly moved to abolish the institutions that had underpinned his authority. On 6 February it was proposed that 'the House of Peers in Parliament is useless and dangerous and ought to be abolished'. Even Cromwell objected, but the vote was passed by forty-four votes to twenty-nine to dissolve the 400-year-old House of Lords. The following day the Commons went even further, proposing that the office of king 'is unnecessary, burdensome, and dangerous to the liberty, safety and public interests of the people of this nation, and therefore ought to be abolished'.[4] The proposal was passed without a division. England was now a Commonwealth, with the Commons exercising the force of law on behalf of the people and through the creation of a new executive body, the Council of State. Composed of forty-one MPs, peers and judges, it included army veterans like Oliver Cromwell and Thomas Fairfax, but also peers who had changed allegiance during the war against the king, including Philip Herbert, Earl of Pembroke, and Basil Feilding, Earl of Denbigh and Hamilton's former art agent in Venice.[5]

On 17 February the Council of State met for the first time. As the meeting progressed Cromwell made a statement that would decisively influence the fate of the royal possessions. Convinced more than ever of the righteousness of the king's execution, Cromwell was in no mood to compromise over the fate of his estate. He issued a dark warning that 'divers goods belonging to the state are in danger to be embezzled'. The council immediately ordered 'that the care of the public library at St James, and of the statues and pictures there, be committed to the Council of State, to be preserved by them'.[6]

It became clear that Cromwell was using the threat of theft

and embezzlement to secure as many of the king's goods as possible with a view to selling them before – as had been the case with the collections of Arundel and Buckingham – they were smuggled out of the country by royalists. Most of the royal palaces were under parliamentary control anyway, looked after by caretakers or used as army billets, so there was little chance of large-scale theft. Nevertheless, it was an effective way to push the issue up the political agenda. By late March the Commons took matters a stage further, resolving that 'the personal Estate of the late King, Queen, and Prince, shall be inventoried, appraised, and sold; except such Parcels of them as shall be thought fit to be reserved for the use of the State'. An important caveat ensured that the new ruling elite would be able to take its pick from the king's possessions, insisting that 'it be referred to the Council of State to consider and direct, what parcels of the goods and personal estates aforesaid are to be reserved for the use of the State'.[7]

London's diplomatic community watched the unfolding of events with a mixture of shock and concern. On 25 March the Venetian ambassador observed that 'the Commons are unrelenting towards the memory of the late king. Thus they have recently ordered all his jewels and valuables to be sold, to use the money for the fleet.'[8] The king's execution sent shockwaves through the royal households of Europe; it was a blow against monarchical absolutism, but it also threatened to transform the European balance of power. In exile in Breda, Charles II tried to capitalize on the general uncertainty, seeking military alliances with both the Scots and the Irish to spearhead a new war against Parliament to regain his father's crown. He also took heart from the bitterly divided public response to the late king's execution. Several towns across England now pronounced him king, London's mayor refused to proclaim the abolition of the monarchy and the City governors repeatedly defied the new Rump's authority.

Purged of its more conservative members sympathetic to the return of the king, the Commons paid little attention to such opposition and pushed on with plans to sell off the royal estate. Mindful of Cromwell's warnings of theft and embezzlement, a decision was taken to catalogue the contents before framing legislation to sell it off. As a result, the Commons appointed politically sympathetic 'commissioners', who, 'being no members of this House, shall be elected and chosen to inventory, secure, and appraise the said goods, and personal estate, of the said late King, Queen, and Prince: and that other commissioners, being no members of this House, be appointed to make sale of the said personal estate, to the best value'. It was a highly effective way of retaining absolute control over the estate and the terms of its eventual sale. Throughout March the House also agreed that any legislation should ensure that revenue from such a sale was to assist the new state in two ways. First, to settle the 'debts of the said late King, Queen, and Prince, for household expenses, as were contracted before this War, and to persons not Delinquents; and for public uses of this Commonwealth'. This was a new development, partly in response to demands from the more radical sections of the army for the settlement of debts incurred throughout the war; however, it also answered the needs of those royalists indebted to the dead king whose political support the Rump was eager to enlist. Secondly, the Commons recommended that the first £30,000 from the sale 'shall be paid to the Treasurer of the Navy, to the use of the Navy'.[9] As the Venetian ambassador noted, here was an opportunity to equip the fleet from royal revenue and confront Prince Rupert's naval force in Kinsale.

Having established the broad terms of the redistribution of the king's goods, it was 'Ordered, that it be referred to the Committee for the Act for inventorying and preserving the Goods of the said late King, or any three of them, to bring in an Act to the Purpose of these Resolutions'.[10] The committee appointed to draw up the act for the sale of the king's goods was composed of Cromwellian loyalists, many with progressive business interests in the City, and most openly hostile to radical Presbyterianism. They included Gilbert Pickering, MP for Northamptonshire, a regicide judge regarded by many as 'a most fiery, furious, implacable man', as well as parliamentary commissioner John Ireton, brother of the parliamentarian army officer and regicide Henry Ireton, husband to Cromwell's daughter Bridget. Another 'fiery spirit' was Cornelius Holland, MP for New Windsor, responsible for the 'reformation' of religious monuments in Westminster Abbey, and with a reputation as a fund-raiser for the war effort and enthusiastic

prosecutor of royalist 'delinquents'. Francis Allen, MP for Cocker-
mouth, was another wealthy financier who had been angered by
Charles I's fiscal policies during the period of personal rule and
actively embraced the new regime, sitting in judgement on the
king and subsequently working for the Rump's council of trade.

The complex logistics of selling off the royal estate meant that
the committee required the expertise of former members of the
royal household to assess the scale of their task. Such consultation
represented an excellent opportunity for former royal servants to
come to a pragmatic accommodation with the new regime. One
of the more enterprising was Clement Kinnersley, who acted as
the Yeoman of the King's Wardrobe from 1635 until the Charles's
departure from London in 1642. He was part of a circle of
courtiers appointed by the king to positions of surprising intimacy.
Like his father before him, Charles had concentrated his political
rule upon his Privy Chamber. Kinnersley's position as Yeoman of
the King's Wardrobe involved advising the king on what to wear,
keeping an inventory of the royal garments and coordinating the
general sartorial elegance of the court. This was not the mundane
job it might seem: Charles's expenditure on his wardrobe averaged
over £5,000 a year and a suit for performing in one of Inigo
Jones's masques could cost the exchequer up to £500.[11] Kinnersley's control over the supply and consumption of silk, velvet and
furs, as well as the elaborate collection of jewels that adorned the
royal garments, gave him unique access to the king's most expensive goods. From the early 1640s he offered his services to the new
regime. He furnished the House of Commons with tapestries and
cloth of state, shrewdly positioning himself as the gatekeeper to the
absent king's wardrobe. He was an obvious appointment as one of
the key contractors to the sale and was soon busy submitting
inventories of the goods held in the Whitehall wardrobe.[12]

Anthony Mildmay was another former royalist who embraced
the new cause with apparent enthusiasm. As a young man he had
attended James I and had risen to the rank of Gentleman of the
Privy Chamber under King Charles, but he came to despise the
king's decisions as the country slipped towards war. By the time
Charles was put on the block at the end of January 1649, Mildmay
had already transferred his allegiance to the new regime and he

was given the grisly task of removing Charles's body after the execution and taking it to St George's Chapel in Windsor. It is a gauge of his unrepentant bitterness towards his former master that Mildmay forbade any words to be spoken over the casket as it was lowered into one of the chapel's vaults. Having buried his king, Mildmay then rode back to London to act as a trustee in the forthcoming sale.

By early summer the committee had framed a bill for passage through the Commons, who spent several weeks debating its terms. The relative political cohesiveness of the Rump ensured there was little dissent. On 26 June the bill was read for the third time and on 4 July, after several amendments, 'An Act for sale of the goods and personal estate of the late King, Queen and Prince' was finally passed. As befitting the zeal of those members who pushed the act through the Commons, it was uncompromising in its terms. It insisted that 'the Goods and Personal Estate heretofore belonging to the late King Charles, and to his Wife and eldest Son, have been, and are justly forfeited by them for their several Delinquencies'. It concluded that the Commons had decided that the goods 'shall be inventoried and apprized, and shall also be sold, except such parcels thereof as shall be found necessary to be reserved for the uses of state'.[13] This reservation of goods 'for the uses of state' would prove one of the bitterest principles of the sale and reflected the tensions between the progressive minority in the Rump, eager for radical economic redistribution of wealth, and the conservative majority, who wanted to use the sale as a way of raising cultural and financial capital for the new regime. The act reiterated the Commons' wish that the first £30,000 from the proceeds of the sale should go to the navy, but that this should be regarded as a loan, repayable within the year.[14] With Cromwell en route to Ireland to put down a royalist uprising there, this was no time to question the wisdom of funding the navy through the sale of the dead king's art collection.

The specific details of the act called for the appointment of eleven trustees for 'the enquiring out, inventorying, apprizing, and securing of the said Goods and Personal Estate'. As the Commons had already approached these so-called 'commissioners' earlier in the year, the act was able to name its trustees with overall responsibility for inventorying the royal collection. They were 'John Humphreys and George Wither of Westminster, Esqs; Anthony Mildmay, Ralph Grafton of Cornhill, Michael Lampier, John Belcamp, Philip Cartwright [Carteret] of the Isle of Jersey, Gent. Henry Creech, John Foach, David Powel, and Edward Winslow, Gentlemen'.[15] Their remit and the terms of the recovery and subsequent sale of the king's goods represented a classic example of republican bureaucracy. They were given sweeping powers, including the right to search out royal goods already purloined by opportunists or hidden by royalist sympathizers. As trustees they were also required to get their paperwork in order and make 'a true and perfect Inventory' of the goods, along with an account of 'the true value thereof, as they in their judgements and consciences shall think the same may reasonably and probably be sold for'. However, such qualifications hinted at the difficulties that the sale represented. Most of the trustees were prosperous merchants and tradesmen, capable of putting a price on pots and pans, even tapestries and carpets, but not on the royal art collection. What was the 'true value' of Titians or Raphaels? What criteria could the trustees use in valuing such paintings, beyond their 'judgements and consciences'? This sounded more like a religious than a financial assessment of worth, which provided few checks or balances to assess the validity of any subsequent valuations, or prevent the abuse of such power and the possibility of corruption.

However, the act established the terms of a tortuous paper trail that would prove invaluable in following the twists and turns that defined the subsequent sale. Inventories were to be made in triplicate and a clerk-register was appointed to hold all the originals. A team of contractors was appointed to oversee the practical arrangements for the sale and collection of payment owed on sold goods. These men were in turn answerable to a group of treasurers, who arranged the sale of the goods and were responsible for collecting the revenue. It was an optimistic but naive attempt to place checks and counterbalances upon the forthcoming sale, but the byzantine complexities of its administration only created more loopholes for fraud and corruption, which were quickly exploited by the more opportunistic members of the new regime.

In attempting to maximize the profitability of the sale, the act also created the conditions for potentially controversial dealings by widening the remit to involve buyers from outside the country:

> ... whereas divers of the said goods and premises are of such nature, as that though by reason of their rarity or antiquity, they may yield very great prices in foreign parts, where such things are much valued, yet for particular men's use in England, they would be accounted little worth ... It is therefore further Enacted and Provided, that for such particulars of the premises as the said Contractors shall finde to be of that nature, they or any three or more of them may treat and agree with any Merchant-Adventurer or foreign Merchant, about transporting such of the said goods into any foreign parts where they may be sold at the best rates.[16]

In one piece of legislation the status of the king's pictures was suddenly transformed from royal ornaments to commodities ascribed a cash value just like all the other inventoried goods. Surely God's Elect Protestant Nation had no interest in idolatrous pictures and naked classical statues – or did it? The sale of the royal collection represented a conscious act of political iconoclasm as much as a brutal piece of financial asset stripping. The clause allowing royal goods to be sold to 'foreign parts' was a significant concession of the need for revenue, even at the expense of selling the king's goods to potential enemies of the state (no proviso was made forbidding the sale to politically hostile Catholic regimes). Better to sell the paintings back to the Catholic idolaters than keep them and so taint the new era of godly republicanism. The clause was to prove one of the most lucrative but also most controversial dimensions of the subsequent sale.

The sale was both an attempt to raise much-needed capital for the new state and a remarkable act of symbolic revenge. Parliament saw itself as having purged the body politic of the king, and now it was expunging the nation of the material and artistic manifestations of what it saw as decadent and idolatrous royal power.

If the act was to some extent aimed at settling scores with the dead king, its final clauses also revealed an appreciation of the need to resolve his outstanding debts to creditors who had proved loyal to the new republic. However, the closing paragraphs of the

legislation were to become one of the bitterest legacies of the plan
to sell off the king's goods:

> . . . considering the many debts owing from the persons of the
> said King and Queen, and from their said Son, contracted
> before the late Wars, and due unto divers persons that are not
> Delinquents, but have constantly adhered to the Parliament,
> and suffered for the same . . . The Parliament hath thought
> fit, and do hereby ordain, that the moneys to be raised by sale
> of the said goods and premises, shall be imployed and disposed
> for and towards the satisfaction of the debts aforementioned,
> and of such of them especially as were contracted for neces-
> sary household expences; which debts shall be paid out of
> the moneys to be raised aforesaid, as far as the same will go,
> in such manner, and by such proportion, as by authority of
> Parliament shall be hereafter directed.[17]

This was a generous, idealistic plan, presumably a legacy of the
more radical members of the committee tasked with drawing up
the legislation. It also contained a neat piece of poetic justice: the
debts incurred by Charles's lavish court and household, left unpaid
since the king's flight from London, were to be paid for with the
very objects that had cost his exchequer so dear.

The act concluded by instructing the trustees 'to receive such
Information and Accounts concerning the debts aforementioned'
and to establish a list of creditors. However, the legislation attached
rather vague conditions to those defined as most deserving financial
compensation. Decisions about who to include on the lists were
ultimately based on 'whether their conditions be necessitous, so as
they cannot bear the want of their said debts', but were also taken
on grounds of political allegiance. The trustees were authorized to
establish whether the creditors 'appear to be delinquents or friends
to the Parliament; and whether they have lent or advanced any
money, plate, horse, arms or furniture upon the Parliaments
propositions . . . and whether they have constantly adhered to the
Parliament, or suffered for the same'.[18]

That the act was an opportunity to repay old political debts
was clear to all, but the scale of compensation for those poorer
individuals who had lost loved ones, property or possessions, regard-

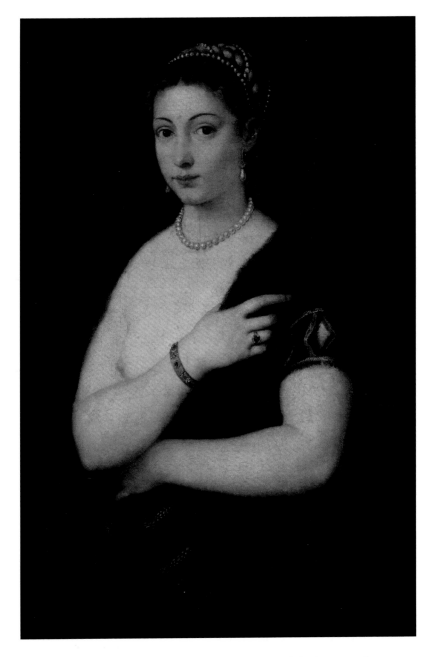

17. Titian's sexually titillating *Woman in a Fur Wrap*, bought by the young prince while in Madrid.

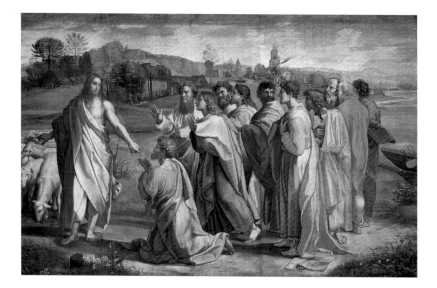

18. Raphael's cartoon 'The Charge to St Peter', part of the *Acts of the Apostles* series, bought by Charles for £700 during his time in Madrid. As part of the Whitehall collection, the cartoons were used as tapestry designs before being reserved for Cromwell's use under the Protectorate. They remain in the possession of the royal family, on loan to the Victoria and Albert Museum.

19. Titian's *Venus of El Pardo*, another erotic painting acquired in Madrid. It hung in Whitehall before being sold for £600 in the sale. The French ambassador paid over £1,000 to ensure it ended up in Paris.

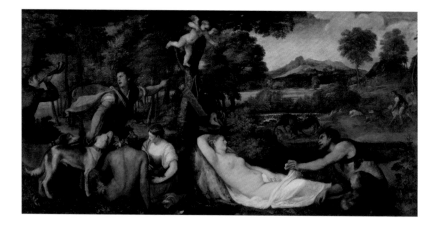

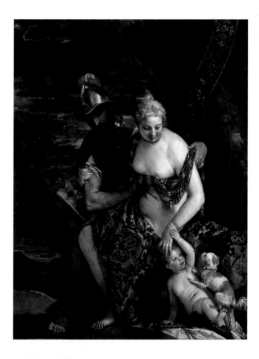

20. Paolo Veronese's *Mars and Venus United by Love*. Veronese was not one of Charles's favourite artists, but the painting was another sexually and politically charged trophy from the Madrid visit.

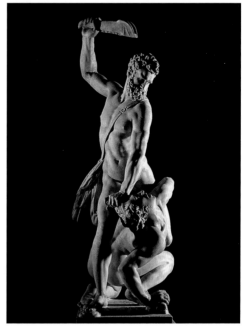

21. Giambologna's marble statue of *Samson Slaying a Philistine*, brought back from Madrid, and mistakenly believed to represent Cain and Abel.

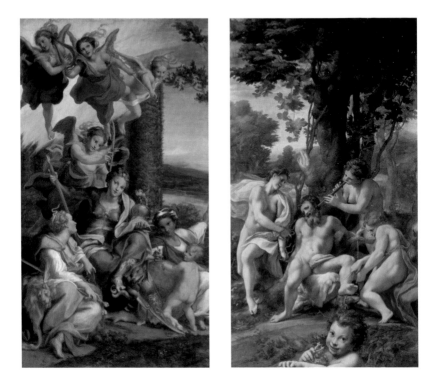

22 a & b. Correggio's two allegories, the left showing Virtue, the right Vice.
Commissioned by Isabella d'Este and bought from Mantua by Nicholas Lanier,
during the sale they lived in Emmanuel de Critz's house before being sold to
international buyers, including the French ambassador.

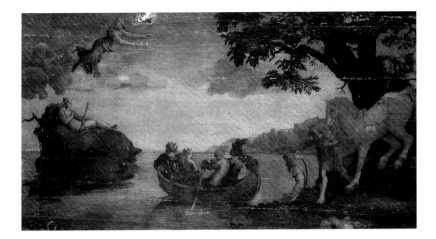

23. Polidoro da Caravaggio's frivolous *Psyche Abandoned* was part of a nine-piece set that appealed to King Charles's taste for mythic, erotic painting, and hung in Whitehall's Long Gallery. Sold to Jerome Lanier at the sale for £42, it returned to the collection after 1660.

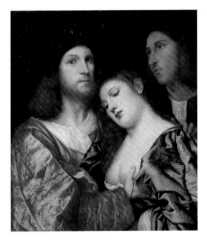

24. Giovanni Cariani's sensual painting *The Lovers* was mistakenly attributed to Titian, which probably explains why a consortium of two of the sale's biggest buyers spent £100 on it in 1653.

25. Giulio Romano's peculiar *Mermaid Feeding her Young* came from Mantua and was one of King Charles's favourites, hanging in his breakfast chamber. Viscount Lisle bought it from dealers for just £8, but was forced to return it to Charles II in 1660.

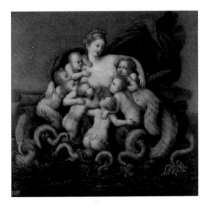

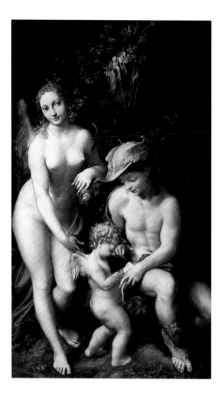

26. Correggio's luminous *The Education of Cupid*, bought from Mantua, was valued at a staggering £800. It passed between various creditors and dividend holders before the Spanish ambassador bought it for £400 and shipped it out of England.

27. Peter Paul Rubens's *Allegory of Peace and War* was painted during his diplomatic embassy to London in 1629–30. Eerily prophetic of subsequent international events, it went during the sale for £100. The Spanish ambassador bought it from the dividends for just £77.

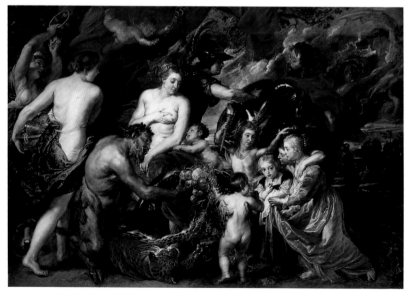

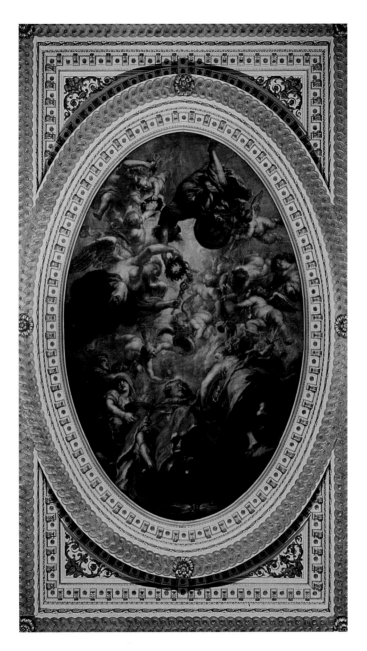

28. The central panel of Rubens's Banqueting House ceiling, showing
Charles's father James ascending to heaven. The culmination of years of planning,
it remains to this day one of the abiding images of Stuart royalty.

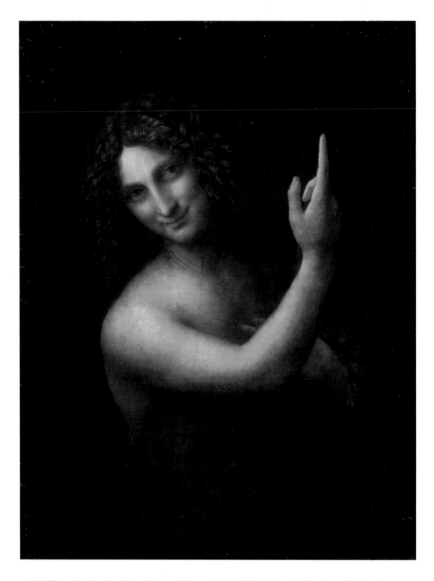

29. The collection's only undisputed Leonardo, *St John the Baptist*. Charles traded a Holbein for the Leonardo, which was sold at the sale for £140 to settle the debts of another painter, Jan van Belcamp. His executors sold the picture back to the French.

less of their political allegiance, remained worryingly vague. Even more ominously, just two weeks after the passage of the act, a committee was appointed to decide which goods it wished to reserve for the state's use to the value of £10,000. The committee prevaricated, causing tension among the trustees and delaying the beginning of the sale for nearly three months.[19] It was an inauspicious start.

ON THE MORNING OF 30 July 1649, three weeks after the passage of the act and six months to the day after the king's execution, a convoy of horse-drawn carriages moved up King Street, travelling north from Westminster. Riding through Holbein Gate, the procession passed between the walls of the palace and the Banqueting House before sweeping into the arched Great Court of Whitehall. As the entourage drew up in the palace courtyard, four men alighted from one of the carriages. Their modest appearance and sober dress were at odds with their regal surroundings and belied their new-found authority. George Wither, Ralph Grafton, Henry Creech and Philip Carteret were four of London's most prominent citizens, part of the team of trustees appointed by the new Parliament to catalogue, evaluate and remove the treasures accumulated by the Stuart monarchy over the previous half-century.

For the first time in English history, common people began to take possession of their king's goods, moving through palaces specifically designed to exclude them and to reinforce the awe and wonder central to the power and mystique of monarchy. Skinners, drapers and itinerant poets were now wandering through Whitehall, handling and assessing the most intimate and cherished possessions of their dead monarch. It was a remarkable moment of liberation – or violation, depending on your political persuasion – and it was to resonate for generations.

Carteret was originally from Jersey, where he had been an enthusiastic supporter of the parliamentary cause, and his reward was a respectable if minor position within the new regime. Henry Creech was a skinner by trade, one of the solid, respectable citizens of London whose endorsement was invaluable to the new regime in ensuring the collapse of support for the royalist faction. Like Creech, Ralph Grafton was a prosperous tradesman, a draper and upholsterer, and another vociferous government benefactor. The unofficial leader of the team was also its most colourful and controversial member, George Wither. A poet, satirist, pamphleteer and soldier, his bombastic, opportunistic nature meant that he never excelled at any of his self-appointed professions. After a chequered career as a pastoral poet, he fought for Charles I in Scotland in 1639, but in 1642 switched sides and declared his support for Parliament. Later that year a party of royalists led by another poet, Sir John Denham, captured him. The delightful anecdote began to circulate that his life was spared by Denham, who claimed 'so long as Wither lived he [Denham] would not be accounted the worst poet in England'.[20]

Having failed as a military figure and smarting from Denham's acid comment, Wither turned his attention to capitalizing on the vulnerable royal assets as war rent the country. In June 1643 he was part of the team instructed by Harley's committee to recover royal regalia from Westminster Abbey. Forcing their way into the Abbey, his colleagues proceeded to crown 'George Wither (an old Puritan satirist) in the royal habilments. Who being thus crown'd, and royally array'd, (as right well became him) first marched about the Room with a stately garb, and afterwards with a thousand apish and ridiculous actions exposed those sacred ornaments to contempt and laughter'.[21] Wither was clearly enjoying himself and soon earned a reputation in Parliament for confiscating the estates of royalist sympathizers, including, to his undoubted delight, the assets of Sir John Denham. As an expert in the repossession and expropriation of goods and property, Wither was an obvious choice to lead the trustees into the royal households.

The palace they confronted was, by the mid-seventeenth century, a sprawling collection of buildings, some of which had been built as early as the thirteenth century. It was a maze of 1,161 rooms, which included fifty-five closets, seventy-five garrets and thirteen kitchens. It stretched west from the wharves of the Thames, across present-day Whitehall, into St James's Park, and north from Westminster up towards Charing Cross. Ever since Charles's hasty departure in 1642 a small group of royal servants had remained in situ, but the king's apartments were empty. One pamphleteer characterized the deserted palace as a grieving court-ier surrounded by the abandoned trappings of royal power. A 'palace without a presence! A White-Hall clad in sable vestments! A Court without a Court!'[22] he cried. Mourning the impact of war upon the palace's decor, he warned the reader that 'if you be minded to survey the lodgings and withdrawing rooms, you shall find those rich and costly hangings of Persian Arras and Turkey-work (like the Bishops) thrown into the Tower, and the rest clapt close prisoners in the wardrobe'. The removal of the paraphernalia of royal power was such a shock that 'the very walls as if they were sensible of this calamity, doe weep down their plaster in grief that their ornaments should suffer so hard a fortune'.[23] If some of the palace's goods had, as Cromwell suspected, already been removed, it was nothing compared to what was about to happen.

The trustees' job was to make a record of the royal palace's possessions with a view to selling them off to the public. Unlike those involved in the reformation of churches, Wither and his team were required to put a price on everything they found. The first room that they entered was the Great Hall, the outermost room in the palace. At over seventy feet in length and with a dramatic pitched roof, it was one of the most impressive buildings in Whitehall. Its inlaid wooden walls were hung with vivid, imposing tapestries of classical and biblical scenes. In the early years of Charles's reign it was used as a theatre, but for skinners and drapers like Creech and Grafton it represented so much wood and fabric, measured and priced by weight and length. As the trustees moved westwards into the domestic quarters of the palace, they were confronted with an assortment of goods that ranged from the regal and luxurious to the domestic and mundane. Tapestries, carpets, jewels, silver and gold plate, curtains, swords, chairs, cushions, clocks, globes and royal regalia lined with silk and sable were discovered alongside basins, ewers, spoons, fruit dishes, trencher plates, candlesticks, snuffers and chamber pots.[24]

The impact of all this on the four members of London's merchant class can be gauged from the inventories they compiled as they moved from room to room. The mixture of awe and wonder mingled with shock at the sheer scale of possessions they discovered. Moving through the court and into the domestic rooms, servants' lodgings and kitchens, the trustees inventoried everything they encountered. In one sweep of the palace's kitchens they listed six brass pots valued at £18, ten brass pans at £14, three dripping pans at 6s, eighteen spits at £2 10s, one large frying pan at 8s, one pair of scales and weights at 10s, three copper pans at £45 and one pair of iron racks at £1 10s.[25]

As the trustees moved into the palace's minor domestic rooms, the lavishness of everyday court life was recorded in the minutiae of the goods. The contents of one modest room were valued at £147 15s and 6d.[26] Other rooms revealed countless beds, tapestries, carpets and curtains, as well as blankets, cushions, chairs, stools, musical organs, gowns, furs, swords, scimitars, candlesticks, riding saddles and stranger objects, which included 'One clock with 12 bells' valued at £100, 'Three hundred tons of stone' at £150 and '95 pair of stag's horns' at £23 15s.[27] No distinction was made in the inventory between domestic goods, furniture and luxury goods like pictures and statues. Everything was carefully recorded and valued according to the trustees' respective expertise.

Tapestries were everywhere, both vast and imposing series extolling the power and authority of the Stuart line and more intimate, decorative designs filling the private apartments. They were priced according to cost per 'ell' – one ell equalled forty-five inches. Tapestries with figures were the most expensive art objects in the entire Whitehall inventory but also aroused the trustees' greatest concern. The tapestry in one room was listed as 'rich hangings but Popish', a brief glimpse of the ideology that motivated their work.[28] Many of the goods were also listed complete with their royal monogram: Carolus Rex – 'CR'. Charles placed this royal imprint upon everything he owned, from beds and blankets to paintings by Titian.

Charles's imprimatur was felt even more strongly as the trustees ventured deeper into the palace towards its Privy Lodgings, the royal apartments reserved for the use of the king and his intimates. Here, the four men were confronted with one of Whitehall's most spectacular sights – the Long Gallery. It was lavishly decorated, 'the ceiling being marvellously wrought in stone with gold, and the wainscot of carved wood representing a thousand beautiful figures'.[29] At over 200 feet in length, this was the gallery where Charles chose to display some of the grandest paintings in his collection. As the trustees walked its length, they looked on walls crammed with 103 of the finest examples of sixteenth-century Italian painting to be found anywhere in Europe, hung vertically one on top of the other, overwhelming in their sheer profusion.

The trustees were now faced with a further problem: how to evaluate the paintings. Their trades were little use when it came to inventorying such ephemeral objects as pictures, which, unlike tapestries, could not be valued based simply on their size and raw materials. It seems that van der Doort's inventory was consulted and courtiers like Kinnersley and Mildmay provided advice, but their ambiguous political allegiances hardly recommended them as objective assessors. Even retrospectively it is difficult to assess the accuracy or the soundness of the trustees' valuations, because in many instances they put a price on pictures never before ascribed a monetary value.

Gradually, as the trustees examined the artworks in the gallery, they began to identify a cross-section of styles and painters that typified the king's taste. The majority were biblical and classical scenes, but the gallery also boasted magnificent portraits. As the pale English tradesmen looked up at the canvases, their gaze was returned by a series of handsome, olive-skinned Italians: for instance, the poet Giovanni Della Casa, whose portrait was painted by a follower of Francesco Salviati. The trustees marked it down at just £20.[30] On one side of the gallery hung the erotic paintings brought by the king from William Frizell, Polidoro da Caravaggio's *Psyche Abandoned* and *Psyche Discovers Cupid*.[31] Next to the bedroom scene of Psyche hung a pair of pictures that at first glance appeared to emphasize Charles's piety and religious devotion. Known as *The Good Thief* and *The Bad Thief*, they had been painted by the Florentine artist Perino del Vaga in the 1520s. Fragments from a larger Deposition scene, the panels show the good and bad thieves crucified next to Christ. Both panels had been brought from Rome by Nicholas Lanier in 1626[32] – cultural trophies wrenched from their original location and placed in Charles's gallery as a sign of his discernment and purchasing power, but not necessarily his religious fervour.

A large number of the paintings in the Long Gallery were also testimony to Charles's greatest artistic coup, the purchase of the Mantuan collection. As the trustees checked their inventories with van der Doort's, they repeatedly found the phrase 'A Mantua peece' preceding descriptions of the paintings. These included Giulio Romano's paintings on panel, *The Omen of Claudius's Imperial Power* and *Nero Playing While Rome Burns*.[33] The irony of *Nero Playing While Rome Burns* could not have been lost on the trustees as they valued the picture at £24. Here was an image of a complacent ruler, sitting in a beautiful classical building and watching his city burn as a stream of distressed refugees files across the foreground, while in the middle ground a group of five women laments.

Of even greater poignancy was a smaller work that hung towards the end of the gallery and which also came from the Mantua collection: the northern Italian painter Girolamo Romanino's *Salome with the Head of the Baptist*. Just six months after Charles's death, the trustees stood before the pitted and darkened canvas that seemed to foreshadow the beheading of the king only yards away in the palace courtyard. Salome holds a dish on which sits the severed, bearded head of John. Her eyes are downcast and she looks away from the viewer, reflecting on the enormity of her violent act. The trustees referred to van der Doort's description of the picture as 'A Mantua Peece, don bij romanino . . . the Picture of Herodia wth St Johns head in a platter lookeing towards her right Shoulder to another old woeman standing by with One hand at her breast',[34] valued it at £25 and once more moved on.

As Wither and his team walked back down the gallery and turned westwards, they finally entered the most intimate apartments in the entire palace – the Privy Lodgings. Charles had fitted triple locks to ensure absolute privacy, and, as the trustees turned the keys, they found themselves face to face with the king's own bedchamber and Cabinet Room. All the rooms faced on to the Privy Gallery, his private gallery that connected the apartments with the Long Gallery. Whereas the previous display of grandiose pictures had been designed more for consideration by the few, the trustees were now confronted with a deeply personal row of paintings, a family album of European royal power.

The gallery was hung with gloomy, sombre portraits of European kings, queens, princes, princesses and dukes, all of whom were related to the Stuart dynasty through blood or marriage. Glaring down at the trustees were the Duke of Savoy, the King of Hungary, the Duke of Alba and the Holy Roman Emperor Charles V. Altogether, 102 pictures lined the walls of the corridor. This was one of the inner sanctums of Stuart royal power, where only the most intimate friends and family were invited. The likes of Wither and his men would certainly never have been given access to the gallery, and yet here they were, calmly inventorying royal portraits that seemed to embody the political system against which they had fought for nearly a decade.

At the end of the gallery the trustees entered the Bear Gallery, which overlooked the tiltyard. Here they discovered another thirty-five paintings, including Titian's portrait of Charles V, acquired in Madrid, and Rubens's *Daniel in the Lions' Den*. Moving on to the staircase connecting the Bear Gallery with the Privy Gallery, the trustees came upon another twenty-four pictures, as well as eight sculptures.[35] This was the gallery created by Charles and his courtiers throughout the 1630s, uniting the Caroline court with its Elizabethan forebears.

If dynastic politics ruled the Privy Gallery, it was matters of the flesh that defined the pictures in the spacious rooms that ran off it. Retracing their footsteps, the trustees entered the first Privy Lodging Room, where they were assailed by scenes of flirtation, seduction and nakedness. This was the king's Titian salon, influenced by his trip to Madrid in 1623. The room contained no fewer than eleven pictures attributed to Titian, ranging from the rather daring *Venus Disrobing*, purchased by Charles from the Duchess of Buckingham and valued by the trustees at £25,[36] to the Correggio studio painting of *St John the Baptist*, bought in Madrid (valued at £40),[37] and the more prosaic portrait study *Titian and his Friends*, valued at £100.[38] Four of the Titians came from Mantua, three from Madrid and one from Arundel. These were some of Charles's finest and most expensive paintings; they were also predominantly erotic, as befitting their intimate location in a room that few ever saw.

The second Privy Lodging Room would have seemed even stranger to the trustees. It continued the playfully erotic theme of the first, but with a more definably pagan atmosphere. The

centrepiece was the erotic mythological Titian from Madrid, the
Pardo Venus, but the picture which drew the trustees' particular
attention was the sexy, enigmatic painting, variously attributed to
Titian, Giorgione and Giovanni Cariani, entitled *The Lovers*. This
was a boudoir picture, with its explicitly erotic portrayal of a classic
love triangle. In the centre a beautiful young woman in a green
dress sinks into the arms of her lover, who caresses her left breast,
while confidently returning our gaze. On the far right a melancholy
young man, possibly a discarded lover or husband, gazes sadly at
his rival. Many believed it to be a painting by Giorgione of his
mistress, while others claimed it was Titian's portrayal of a husband
betrayed. When the painting was inventoried at Kensington Palace
in 1818 it was innocently and rather comically listed as 'A sick
Lady, her Husband and a physician'. Although Wither was not so
easily deceived, his team was obviously struck by the painting,
valuing it at £100.[39]

In the third Privy Room the tone shifted once more, this time
to Italianate preoccupations. Its fifteen paintings included yet
more of Polidoro Caravaggio's flirtatious cupids, alongside works
by Raphael, del Sarto and Correggio. The two erotic Correggios
from Mantua, *Mercury Teaching Cupid to Read* and *Venus with Satyr
and Cupid*, were prominently displayed, but the room was dominated by the other great Mantuan acquisition, Raphael's *La Perla*.
The room was a virtual shrine to the Italian Renaissance and
Charles's love of its artists.

The contrast with the next room the trustees examined could
not have been greater. They were now at the heart of the king's
collection, his prized Cabinet Room or 'rich closet', refurbished
in the mid-1630s. Here were some of the finest pictures, statues,
drawings, medals, gems and books in the entire collection. Finally,
the trustees came to the most private room of all: the king's
bedchamber. If the Privy Rooms revealed the more salacious side
of the Stuart court, Charles's bedroom was hung with ten deeply
personal and poignant pictures of his politically turbulent reign.
The first picture the trustees encountered was a virginal painting
of Henrietta Maria, described as 'the Queen's picture in a white
habit to the knees'.[40] The queen's religious tastes appeared to
account for the presence of a picture of 'Our Lady', followed by a

more intimate painting of Princess Elizabeth, Queen of Bohemia. Despite the public celebration of his filial piety in commissioning Rubens's Banqueting House ceiling, Charles chose not to hang a picture of James I. Instead, the trustees were confronted with the other two men who had loomed so large in the king's life: his long-dead elder brother, 'Prince Henry in armour', painted by Van Dyck, and George Villiers, Duke of Buckingham.[41]

As Wither and his team closed the door to the king's bedroom, their circuit of the palace was at an end. How long it took them is unclear, but van der Doort's inventory had proved particularly useful in appraising pictures, statues and drawings, despite its lack of monetary valuations. King Charles and his courtiers never deigned to discuss or record the monetary value of their collections, but the trustees now took the momentous step of putting a price on every single item in the royal household, from tablecloths to Titians. Over 1,200 entries were listed in the inventory of Whitehall alone, and this fails to account for those that covered multiple examples of the same object. It was a massive bureaucratic undertaking, but it represented an even more profound innovation. The trustees were doing something never attempted before in English history: they were putting a price tag on the monarchy.

As the inventories were slowly completed, Whitehall's silence was broken by the noise of removal and dispersal. Pictures were taken down from the walls, tapestries and curtains were unhooked, carpets rolled up and furniture dismantled. The workmen, many unfamiliar with and probably scornful of the objects they removed, dropped and broke statues, cracked picture frames, ripped carpets and tore tapestries. In moving smaller items, there can be little doubt that a great sum of the late king's goods ended up in the pockets of the removal men.

All over the country, similar teams were entering Charles's palatial residences and carefully listing their contents. The royal residences of St James's Palace, Hampton Court Palace, Greenwich Palace, Richmond Palace, Nonsuch Palace, Windsor Castle, Wimbledon, Oatlands, Kenilworth Castle, Syon House, Bewdley House, Ludlow Castle, even the Tower of London and Carisbrooke Castle on the Isle of Wight were all unlocked, occupied and slowly inventoried by the new regime's hand-picked repossession men. The king's gorgeous palaces had finally fallen, but not to the parliamentary armies wielding muskets and pikes. Instead it was the ledgers, inkpots and inventories of the bureaucrats appointed by the new Council of State to dismantle and sell off what remained of his legacy that truly defeated Charles I.

In Whitehall, carriages drew up in the cobbled courtyard and were packed with whatever they could carry. Laden down with their royal cargo, they made their way back up Whitehall towards Charing Cross, passing the hawkers and curious onlookers. From here, they clattered north-east in the direction of Old St Paul's, picking their way along the Strand, a virtually derelict street whose miserable shops stood empty and condemned, another victim of the war. They soon reached their final destination, swinging right into the archway of Somerset House, where, as the new government had decreed, the late king's goods would be finally disposed of in the greatest public sale that England had ever seen.

> *Enter Cryer with a crown and sceptre, a carcanet of jewels, two or three*
> *suits, with some robes of state.*
> CRYER: O yes, O yes, O yes, here is a golden crown, worth
>   many a hundred pound: 'twill fit the head of a fool,
>   knave or clown: 'twas lately tane from the royal head, of
>   a king martyred: who bids most? Here is a sceptre, for to
>   sway a kingdom in a new reformed way; 'twas usurped
>   from one we did lately betray; pray customers come
>   away: here be jewels of wondrous price, they will dazzle
>   your eyes; come, come, who buys.[42]

JUST THREE WEEKS before the passage of the act for the sale of the late king's goods in July 1649, John Crouch published his savage satire lampooning the planned sale, *A Tragi-Comedy, called New Market Fayre or a Parliament Out-Cry of State-Commodities Set to Sale*. Mocking the trustees' detailed inventories, Crouch condemned the sale for putting every sacred vestige of monarchy up for sale at 'New Market Fayre'. Announcing the sale, the Cryer offers his 'customers' (the audience) the king's crown and jewels, followed by the more intimate paraphernalia of Charles's rule:

Here be his libraries and books, and pictures that contain his
looks; here you may all things buy that belongs to monarchy;
here's a bowl his blood to carouse, and all the goods
belonging to his house; here be rich hangings, chairs and
stools, belonging to the house of lordly fools; here be seats of
wool packs, and many pretty knacks. Come customers buy,
for the state wants *money*.

Cromwell, Ireton and other leading members of the new
government enter and are greeted by Fairfax: 'Gentlemen, welcome to New-market-fayre; here are commodities worth your
purchasing.' He and Cromwell then squabble over the royal crown.
Sir Anthony Mildmay's brother Henry then intervenes, suggesting,
'We will equally divide the houses and goods of the late King,
Queen and Prince amongst us; you two shall cast lots, which shall
be king of England, and which of Ireland.' In return he requests
the title of 'Jewel-keeper to your Majesty'.[43] Messengers arrive to
announce that Prince Charles has landed to reclaim his crown and
everyone falls on their swords in despair.

Notwithstanding its dubious literary merit, *New Market Fayre*
reflected public unease at the impending sale on both sides of the
political divide. Now that the king was dead, was the value of
everything at the mercy of anonymous market forces? Was nothing
sacred? It was a fear that would afflict the sale and its subsequent
critics for generations to come. Crouch even predicted the corrupt
practices he expected from individual trustees once the sale of
land began: 'Here is Grafton and Belcalf [Belcamp], that intend
to steal half; Tony Mildmay and Lampier are entrusted to sell
deer.'[44] Although undoubtedly hostile to the Rump, the author was
clearly worried about the lack of transparency involved in the sale
and its participants. Such concerns would prove extremely prescient, although deer were one of the last items that Lampier and
Mildmay ended up selling.

Somerset House, site of the queen's controversial Catholic
chapel, was a particularly resonant location for the sale of the
king's art. Once Charles and Henrietta Maria fled the capital in
1642, the perfume and silk of the courtiers that filled the palace
gave way to the sweat and leather of the politicians and soldiers.

During the Civil War, Somerset House was used as a barracks, and after Charles's execution it became the residence of Lord General Fairfax, as well as members of the Rump Parliament, many of whom protested at the disruption caused by the sale. Fairfax was rather more considerate about the need to give the trustees space, and the Commons gratefully acknowledged that 'the Lord General and his officers forebear coming to Somerset House until the goods are sold, there being need to use them for showing the goods'.[45]

Fairfax's decision meant that he could avoid the chaos, confusion and sheer number of goods that began to arrive at Somerset House in the autumn of 1649. Carriages came from various London palaces weighed down with precious cargo. Crate after crate of objects were offloaded and broken open in the house's courtyard, checked against inventories, and carried into the rooms and galleries of the palace. As the contractors hastily labelled and priced objects, workmen trudged by carrying statues and hanging pictures on the walls. Somerset House was gradually transformed from a queen's palace into a cavernous shop. Altogether just over 1,300 pictures were offered for sale, alongside hundreds of statues, tapestries, carpets and other assorted royal paraphernalia that came flooding into the capital from Charles's outlying palaces. Finally the contractors were ready and in October 1649 the doors of Somerset House opened to the public for the sale of the century.

Initially the trustees had envisaged a completely open sale, where anyone could come in off the street and lodge a bid for whatever caught their eye. The public were able to ascertain the price of whatever they wanted to buy, based on the recently completed inventories, and if they made an offer close enough to the asking price it was invariably accepted. Throughout the long winter months, business was slow to say the least. Perhaps Parliament should have realized, but trade in the dead king's goods was hardly likely to be brisk. Royalist sympathizers were reluctant to purchase goods formerly belonging to their king for fear of exposure, while religious radicals and republicans were not enthusiastic about trading in objects tainted with Charles's autocratic reign. Many of the finest collectors of art were either dead or in exile, and by releasing such a large number of pictures so quickly, the trustees saturated the market, allowing what few prospective buyers existed to sit back and wait for prices to fall before making their offers.

The economic climate was unpropitious too. The effect of two periods of civil war on London had been catastrophic. From the early 1640s, the royalist naval blockade and prohibition of trade with London had badly affected the city's international finance and manufacturing industries. The departure of the royal court had also damaged the economy. Crown revenues of over £1 million had once found their way into the pockets of the capital's artisans and tradesmen, but no longer, and the exodus of royalist supporters from the wealthy and fashionable districts of Westminster and Covent Garden hit landlords and shopkeepers already struggling under the weight of taxation required to fight the war. As the Committee for the Militia complained in 1643, 'Our rich men are gone, because the City is the place of taxes and burdens; trade is decayed, and shops shut up in a great measure; our poor do much increase.'[46] Such was the sale's symbolic power to Parliament that it went ahead regardless of the economic reality faced by most Londoners in the autumn of 1649.

In addition to all this, the sale was badly organized. Pictures were hung and stacked in obscure corners of the palace, statues were broken and tapestries torn. Rather than a glittering curiosity cabinet, the palace looked more like a gloomy warehouse. The Dutch diplomat Lodewijck Huygens visited Somerset House on an official visit to London several months after the sale began. A keen art collector himself, Huygens went to the sale on several occasions. Towards the end of his trip he wrote in his journal:

> We went to Somerset House again and saw a number of beautiful things, among them the most costly tapestries I ever saw. One room was valued at £300. In that same room were many antique and modern statues, although nearly all damaged. There was also a unicorn cane as thick as an arm, with a large crystal knob. In the gallery above, we saw a very large number of beautiful paintings, but all so badly cared for and so dusty that it was a pitiable sight. There was an admirable

portrait by Van Dyck of King Charles sitting on a white horse, which could be obtained for £150. Five or six Titians, however, surpassed everything there, and yet these also could be purchased at a very reasonable price.[47]

Through Huygens's eyes, everything had a price, most of which he seems to have thought quite reasonable, but this was clearly weighed against the destruction and neglect caused by the hurried removal of so many fragile and precious objects. In focusing on the objects that came to represent the power and splendour of the Stuart court – the imposing tapestries, the rare statues and the collection of Titians and Van Dycks – Huygens anticipated the buying patterns of subsequent customers.

The first buyers through the door were insider traders, politicians and military men who knew just enough about art and money to realize that if they chose their purchases carefully, they could make a fortune. One of the most enthusiastic early customers was Colonel William Webb, a parliamentary officer who saw active service throughout the Civil War and was rewarded with the post of Surveyor-General of crown and church lands confiscated by the new state. Using his political position to get first pick of the paintings, Webb immediately went on an extraordinary buying spree. On October 20 he went to the sale and bought his first piece, 'A naked Venus asleep' by Isaac Oliver.[48] This was a reasonably modest copy of Correggio's *Venus with Satyr and Cupid* that Webb snapped up for £6, although its rather salacious subject matter might appear a surprising choice for such a Protestant military officer.

Five days later he went back to the sale and spent nearly £200 on paintings, a staggering amount of money for an army colonel. His first purchases were cautious – a fragment of a portrait attributed to Titian which he bought for 10s[49] and a small anonymous painting of the tower of Babylon for £2.[50] Emboldened, he went on to bigger things. In one afternoon he bought 'John Baptist putting a garland to a lamb by Cavalier [Giovanni] Ballione'[51] for £25, 'Lucretia and Tarquin figures by Titian'[52] for £70 and, perhaps most surprisingly, two paintings by Van Dyck, listed as 'Prince Charles at length in Armour' for £25 and the even more poignant painting of *The Three Eldest Children of Charles I*, portraying the young princes Charles and James with their sister Mary and two spaniels, for which he paid £60.[53]

Webb's early acquisitions seem to have been based on individual taste: small, anonymous pictures that catch the eye. However, purchasing the Titian fragments and Van Dycks demonstrates his growing financial acumen. In buying the work of both painters at a moment at which they had fallen so far from political favour, Webb was indulging in a clever piece of aesthetic speculation, gambling on the future rise of both painters' stock. Just two days later, he was back for more, and this time he was prepared to pay even greater sums. On 27 October he arrived at the sale to make successful bids for three Van Dycks, including his most expensive purchase so far, the *Rinaldo and Armida* that Porter had acquired for Charles in 1630 at a cost of £78.[54] Nineteen years later it cost Webb £80, suggesting that where information was available the sale valuations often corresponded with earlier prices. Webb extended his rapidly growing collection of royal portraiture with the purchase of a picture that spanned the entire late Tudor dynasty, portraying 'King Henry VIII, Prince Edward, Princess Mary & Princes Elizabeth together in one piece', unfashionable subject matter but a bargain at just £15.[55]

By now Webb's confidence was up and he began to attend the sale every day, secure in his artistic taste and purchasing power. On 29 October he returned to buy more Van Dycks, including portraits of King Charles and Queen Henrietta Maria, both of which had hung in Somerset House since the 1630s and which were sold to the colonel as a pair for £60.[56] The following day he returned to spend even more heavily on politically sensitive paintings. This time, as well as buying Titians and royal portraits, he purchased one of Charles's prized Mantuan pictures, Giulio Romano's rather grotesque painting *A Mermaid Feeding her Young*, for just £8. This painting had hung in Charles's Breakfast Chamber in Whitehall, alongside Van Dyck's portrait of his five children, and had clearly been one of the king's personal favourites.[57]

Webb moved quickly to secure most of his paintings in the first few days of the sale, but his purchases show that he also took his time in weighing up the acquisition of a small selection of the more expensive pictures. He waited until 22 November before successfully bidding £135 for Palma Vecchio's 'Mary & ye Child & St Sebastian'.[58] This was the largest amount that he had paid for a single picture. Within just a few weeks of the beginning of the sale, he bought fifty-six pictures at a staggering cost of £1,302. As the basic average wage for a military officer was just £15 per year, Webb was obviously acting on behalf of consortia and private buyers who, for various reasons, had no wish to be identified publicly with the sale.

One such buyer, and Webb's primary client, was Philip, Viscount Lisle.[59] He had served under Charles as a diplomat and soldier in France and then Ireland, before switching sides during the Civil War and ultimately sitting as a commissioner at the king's trial. Lisle was subsequently appointed a member of the Council of State and the Committee for the Reservation of Royal Goods. A keen collector and close relative of Van Dyck's patron the Earl of Northumberland, Lisle was eager to buy from the sale while retaining his political integrity. His solution was to pay various agents and middlemen like Webb to buy pictures and statues from Somerset House. Among the pictures Webb bought for Lisle and which went into the viscount's Sheen House collection were Giulio's *Mermaid Feeding her Young* and the pair of allegorical paintings sent to England by Cardinal Barberini. Lisle spent nearly £700 on thirty pictures, most of which came from generous pay and allowances provided by Parliament.[60]

Other buyers, whose relationships with the royal collection were more politically ambiguous, also bought shrewdly. In April 1650 the painter Peter Lely, briefly associated with Charles I's artistic circle and future court painter to King Charles II, visited the sale twice, buying a Dutch portrait and landscape, as well as a Tintoretto and *The Finding of Moses* attributed to Veronese. All four cost him £92.[61] Lely's assistant, the Flemish portrait painter Jan Baptist Gaspars, also profited from the sale, buying fifty-five paintings at the lower end of the market for a total of £1,073. Another Flemish visitor to the sale was Remigius Van Leemput, assistant to Van Dyck and a skilful copyist in his own right. Van Leemput had worked for Charles I in the 1630s, and – over a period of six months – used his knowledge of the royal collection to buy nearly thirty paintings and sculptures. On 3 November he spent £75 on Titian's *Lucretia* and £55 on a painting of Mary Magdalene.[62] In the spring of 1651 he also spent heavily, buying a picture of Mary, Christ and Joseph by Andrea del Sarto for £174, and a Christ carrying the Cross attributed to Giorgione for £45.[63]

Other more surprising buyers shared Colonel Webb's ideological outlook. Colonel John Hutchinson was another veteran of the Civil War who took advantage of the sale. By the time he arrived in London as a Member of Parliament in 1646, his career was well established. Appointed governor of Nottingham Castle, he defended it for two years against repeated royalist assaults. He joined the Long Parliament in 1646 and supported the creation of the Rump. Like Lisle, he acted as one of the commissioners who oversaw the king's trial and signed the death warrant. A confidant of Cromwell, Hutchinson was a member of the Council of State, and, even more significantly, also sat on the committee involved in reserving royal goods for the state's use.[64]

By the end of October Hutchinson was buying pictures at the sale. However, unlike Webb, he appears to have bought primarily for his own pleasure. In the *Memoirs of the Life of Colonel Hutchinson*, his wife, Lucy, recalled that:

> The only recreation he had during his residence in London was in seeking out all the rare artists he could heare of, and in considering their workes in payntings, sculptures, gravings and all other such curiosities, insomuch that he became a greate virtuoso and patrone of ingenuity. Being loath that the land should be disfurnisht of all the rarities that were in it, whereof many were set to sale in the king's and divers noblemen's collections, he lay'd out about two thousand in the choycest pieces of painting, most of which were bought out of the king's goods, which were given to his servants to pay their wages; to them the collonell gave ready money, and bought so good pennieworths, that they were valued much more worth then they cost. These he brought down into the country, intending a very neat cabinet for them.[65]

This is the voice of a proud wife; but it also reveals how people like Hutchinson were suddenly being allowed access to the kinds of paintings, drawings and sculptures previously reserved exclusively for the eyes of the royal elite. Lucy could not help boasting that her husband's £2,000 was money well spent on an investment that was, as she put it rather clumsily, 'valued much more worth than they cost'. Like Webb, Hutchinson saw the opportunity to capitalize in a buyers' market, purchasing pictures for 'pennieworths' but helping the king's destitute creditors by giving them 'ready money' in exchange for their pictures.

Hutchinson bought some bargains, but they cost him more than just a few pennies. He first bought from the sale on 30 October, when he picked up two still lifes and two landscapes for a few pounds, a picture of 'A man with one hand' for £30, two portraits of 'Monsieur duc d'Orleans' and his wife, both painted by Van Dyck (£80 for the pair), and, perhaps most surprisingly for a man of his Puritan convictions, 'A Naked Venus' at a cost of £15.[66] Hutchinson was a far more methodical and expansive buyer than Webb. He attended the sale every few weeks, choosing his purchases carefully and exhibiting a much more varied and sophisticated taste than his fellow officer. As well as buying the usual favourites – the grand historical and classical paintings of the Italian masters – he also chose unusual portraits, landscapes and the unfashionable genre of the still life.

On 8 November he returned to the sale and bought two ebony cabinets for £70, but this was just a prelude to one of the most expensive purchases of the entire sale. In one day he paid the staggering sum of £930 for three outstanding Titians. The first was a devotional picture of Mary, Christ and St Mark, valued at £150 and bought for £165. He paid the same again for *Venus and Cupid with an Organist*, but this was a very different picture. It portrayed a voluptuous Venus sprawled on her bed as a musician plays his organ, gazing intently at the goddess's nakedness. It was as unmistakably erotic as Hutchinson's third and most expensive acquisition, Charles's prized Titian brought back from Madrid, the *Pardo Venus*. Hutchinson was confronted with a sale tag of £500 for the painting. He faced opposition in his attempt to buy it (possibly from Colonel Webb), finally paying a massive £600 to secure it.[67]

For decades the painting graced the palatial walls of the Escorial and the Second Privy Room in Whitehall; by the end of November 1649 it found itself, along with its two companion pieces, in the humbler surroundings of Colonel Hutchinson's estate at Owthorpe in Nottinghamshire.

By the time Hutchinson stopped purchasing in June 1650, he was the largest cash buyer of paintings from the dead king's collection, having spent £1,349 on twenty-three pictures. That nearly half this amount went on Titian's *Pardo Venus* gives some idea of how much the colonel wanted it. Other visitors to the Somerset House sale did not share his enthusiasm for Charles's pictures. Of the few people who did buy, many held some previous association with the royal collection, or were themselves artists eager to capitalize on the sale for aesthetic or financial reasons, like Lely, generally regardless of religious or political ideology. Others, however, were ordinary men and women who visited the sale and bought an assortment of different objects – from works of art to mundane household goods – although their motives remain unclear. Nonetheless, these purchases formed part of a slow but noticeable transfer of royal possessions from the palace to the people.

What made staunch Protestants like Webb and Hutchinson buy erotic pictures of naked classical goddesses and 'idolatrous' scenes of religious devotion? Hutchinson's wife, Lucy, hints at some of the explicit reasons. Buyers regarded their acquisitions as part of a national effort to keep the royal treasures in the country at a time of widespread fears about the flight of capital from London. To buy one of the king's pictures was also a way of buying a little piece of royalty, a means of dismantling the very fabric of monarchy by paying a fixed – and almost certainly advantageous – price for a literally priceless object. To buy was also a way of making a symbolic investment in the new regime, of putting money back into the parliamentary coffers and contributing to the larger settlement of national debts incurred during the late king's reign.

Art historians still tend to assume a certain religious and moral hypocrisy in these acquisitions, labelling buyers like Hutchinson as 'Puritans'. However, the term 'Puritan' describes a diverse spectrum of religious and political beliefs held by people from a range of social backgrounds and regions, encompassing those who demanded the persecution of Catholics and the abolition of Charles's Book of Common Prayer and those who supported the reformation of episcopacy and a limited return of the monarchy. The traditional perception of Puritans as humourless prosecutors of drunkenness, fornication, revelry and Sabbath-breaking is true of only a small strand, and although many who regarded themselves as part of the godly Elect would have responded with horror at some of the pictures in the royal collection, others, like Webb and Hutchinson, held more sophisticated and pragmatic views.

Sir Robert Harley's 1643 legislation on 'monuments of superstition or idolatry' had excluded secular art collections from the threat of mutilation or destruction, suggesting that many Puritan sympathizers regarded paintings as commodities to be bought and sold notwithstanding their subject matter, which was perceived as harmless outside church or chapel. This was a subtle but important distinction, which allowed buyers like Hutchinson and Webb to purchase pictures without fear of official religious censure. The risks were financial, not religious.

The astronomical amounts spent by Webb, Hutchinson, Gaspars and Van Leemput were way beyond their financial means and, unlike in the 1630s, when art dealers had been prepared to accept letters of credit as security against art purchases, the trustees required prompt settlement of all sales in cash. Many purchasers were obviously acting as frontmen for a series of international buyers with sufficient capital to make good their offers. Yet there is one other tantalizing possibility: that trustees, contractors and buyers were all conspiring to keep prices down in anticipation of making lucrative profits by selling them on.

Virtually everyone involved in the sale – trustees, contractors, treasurers, secretaries and clerks – made their own purchases, many for sums far in excess of a lifetime's salary. This suggests that as well as buying for international collectors, most of them were pooling financial resources to acquire goods in bulk and then sell them on for a profit. As the trustees and their team were also responsible for putting a value on everything they inventoried, it is possible that they were deliberately undervaluing certain items, buying them through the sale and then selling them on to a third party at a profit. If the sale was prey to insider trading, then this suggests that rather than undervaluing pictures because of their royal associations, buyers were actively pursuing pictures by deflating their sale value, then selling them for higher prices on the open market.[68] At this stage in the sale, Parliament hardly cared where the money came from, as long as the trustees were able to report a steady stream of income.

Unfortunately, however, the trustees were unable to alleviate the exchequer's problems. By May 1650 the combination of economic recession, religious anxieties, bureaucratic mismanagement and insider dealing left the sum total from the sale of the king's goods at a mere £35,000. This included £7,770 on the sale of just 375 pictures sold to thirty-eight individuals. Even worse, the trustees were also slow in drawing up a list of the most urgent of the king's creditors, who were becoming increasingly vocal in their dissatisfaction with the ways in which the new regime was trying (and failing) to redistribute the dead king's wealth.

As a means of distracting the public's growing disquiet at the lack of any tangible relief for those most affected by the war, the Council of State sponsored a fresh wave of iconoclasm. This included the decapitation and destruction of statues of the king still standing in the Royal Exchange, in a macabre re-enactment of Charles's execution. John Gibson recorded the event in his commonplace book, writing:

> On August the 10 1650 the king's statue in the Royal Exchange in London was broken and defaced, these words written over the head, *Exit Tyrannus Regum ultimus, anno primo restitutae libertatis Angliae 1649*. That is, The Last Tyrant King (or Ruler) goes out, on the 30th day of January, 1649, in the first year of liberty restored to England.[69]

The attack on the statue was a calculated political gesture, but it could not mask the failings of the sale of the broken and decapitated king's goods. A new approach was required. The sale was about to enter its second phase.

CHAPTER NINE

THE FIRST LIST

By the start of 1650 it was clear that the sale of the late king's goods was not going as well as expected. When it began, in the autumn of the previous year, it attracted a relatively small group of buyers, due to poor management and public reluctance to purchase the dead king's goods. The limited financial returns were not sufficient to provide significant capital for the navy or the financial remuneration of the king's creditors. Even worse, radical elements outside Parliament, including voices from within the army, were questioning the conservatism and apparent apathy of the Rump. In an attempt to regain the political momentum, the trustees took the decision to submit a list of 120 of the neediest royal creditors to the House of Commons, with the recommendation that their claims be settled immediately.

As a result 'An additional Act for the Discovery and Selling of the personal estate' of the royal family was passed in the Commons on 14 March 1650. Yet another committee was established, 'to take consideration of the list of the necessitous servants and creditors to the late king, and the monies due to them'. The committee made recommendations to the trustees, who were 'authorised to cause payment to be made unto such persons of such sums as the said committee shall approve of, out of the monies to be raised by the sale of the said goods'.[1] The committee agreed to release £12,800 already raised by the sale to settle the claims of the list of the 'necessitous servants and creditors to the late king'. What subsequently became known as the First List was primarily composed of the king's servants and those widowed and orphaned by the recent wars. This was an astute public relations exercise, but the Commons were reluctant to dispense immediately the much-needed cash raised in the first months of the sale.

Instead, they decided to settle larger debts chiefly in goods – a decision that was to profoundly affect the way the sale developed over the next four years.

The release of royal goods to those on the First List, and in particular artworks, had an immediate effect. Some creditors attempted to liquidate their new-found capital straight away, on the assumption that, according to the royalist antiquarian Richard Symonds, 'pictures would pay debts'.[2] Others took the opportunity to discuss pictures, matters of perspective, even take up painting themselves. Sir Thomas Nott, Symonds noted, 'begins to colour and design at 45 years old'. Another recipient of the king's pictures even indulged in a spot of amateur restoration. The parliamentary officer Captain Robert Mallory bought several paintings from the royal sale, including 'a little piece from Mantova' that, Symonds observed, 'he has caused to be daubed over but endeavoured to make me believe 'twas so fresh always'.[3] Mallory was out to make money on his paintings, while retaining an interest in their composition and execution. Overall there was no consistent response to this phase of the public redistribution of the royal collection.

It seems unlikely that the more desperate cases had any say in the items they received. Unfortunate victims of the Civil War like Mrs Elizabeth Hunt, who had lost her husband in the conflict, received a pair of andirons from Whitehall on 7 June 1650 valued at 15s. She also collected six pictures worth a total of just over £87. Most were anonymous religious scenes, including two Madonnas, one St John, one St Peter and a circumcision by Dosso Dossi, but pictures of the *Head of St John* and *Three Baboons* can have done little to assuage the grief of the widow of a soldier who died for the parliamentary cause.[4]

Other creditors with better political connections within the new regime fared much better than poor Mrs Hunt in influencing what they received. The Rump was inevitably bowing to the claims of the powerful City creditors from whom it drew political and financial support, neglecting the claims for settlement coming from its popular base among London's citizens. It was a dangerous move that would fuel subsequent accusations of cronyism. It was hardly surprising that the royalist draper and silk merchant William Geere was one of the king's largest creditors, claiming £2,300 in the First

List. He was also a royalist delinquent, fined £400 in 1644 and swindled out of his property by John Ireton, brother of General Henry Ireton. Geere obviously needed the money from the list, but he was hardly the most deserving republican.[5] Appropriately enough, he received valuable hangings among his reparations. He signed for six pieces of tapestry from the queen's collection in Somerset House, valued at £276 15s,[6] followed by 'Seven pieces of fine tapestry hangings with large figures upon a white ground given to the Queen by Sir Henry Vane',[7] worth £495, and five further pieces of *The Five Senses*, valued at £270.[8]

Geere took possession of cloth of silver and gold, mirrors, carpets and expensive hangings worth hundreds of pounds, most of which were considered to be worth more than pictures. Tapestries, carpets and cloth of gold were priced objectively according to size and weight, but pictures represented a much less quantifiable investment. Their monetary value was subject to the idiosyncratic and often fickle assessment of collectors based on their previous owner(s), their location, their maker and the quality of their execution. Nevertheless, Geere appears to have influenced the trustees to ensure that, unlike Mrs Hunt, he received a selection of fourteen pictures by acknowledged masters. They were valued at a total of £230. He took possession of paintings attributed to Titian, Holbein and Perugino, as well as Van Dyck's *The Five Eldest Children of Charles I*, valued at £120. This same painting appeared in de Critz's house just over a year later, suggesting that Geere either sold the picture on to the Dutch painter or asked him to sell it on his behalf. By the time the picture reached de Critz's house, its value had dropped to just £80 – an example of the volatility of the emerging art market under the Commonwealth.

Another substantial creditor who made sure that his debts were repaid in pictures as well as goods was the king's plumber, John Embree. He claimed £903 on the First List. On 21 May 1650 he acknowledged receipt of Persian and Turkish carpets, green velvet canopies, pewter dishes, stools and beds, as well as pictures by Tintoretto, Palma, del Sarto and Clouet. His most valuable acquisitions were two Titians – a *St Margaret* and an *Egyptian Madonna*, valued at £100 and £50 respectively, as well as one of Van Dyck's earliest English portraits of Queen Henrietta Maria. Its value, a meagre £30, highlighted the unpopularity of the exiled queen. Embree also received Jacopo Bassano's *The Flood*, valued at just £60. Bought from Mantua by Lanier, hung in St James's, derided by William Sanderson as looking more like a messy kitchen than a biblical deluge, there was a certain wit in the trustees' decision to present *The Flood* to one of London's finest plumbers.

Subsequent events suggest that many creditors were unconvinced by the nominal valuation placed on their pictures, although there is no record of anyone refusing or even attempting to return canvases to the trustees. But others on the First List with more of an investment in the art world encouraged and welcomed the receipt of paintings. Six months earlier, in November 1649, Nicholas Lanier paid just £10 to buy his own portrait by Van Dyck, a nostalgic investment in a picture of the royal musician and art broker in his prime. On 3 May he received seven pictures in settlement of his claim as one of the king's most 'necessitous servants'. These included two Giulio Romanos that he had helped acquire from Mantua (each valued at £50) and 'A Picture of Music' attributed to Giorgione.[9] The presentation of such a picture to the former master of the king's music was fitting, although it is unclear whether the trustees decided that this was an appropriate picture to give to Lanier or if he used his old powers of persuasion to petition for it.

The irascible Balthazar Gerbier was one creditor who unsurprisingly manipulated the list for his own benefit. Following the king's downfall, he fled to France but he returned after Charles's execution, seeing the opportunity to capitalize on the new regime. By March 1650 he had reinvented himself as a staunch republican and boldly inveigled his way on to the First List of royal debtors. With characteristic impudence, he claimed £350 owing from his tenure as a roving royal diplomat. In June he took possession of two pictures in lieu of his debts: an unidentifiable equestrian portrait of King Charles by Van Dyck, worth £200, and Titian's *Charles V with a Hound*, valued at £150.[10]

If anyone knew the value of Charles's collection it was Gerbier. Twenty-five years earlier, under the benevolent patronage of the Duke of Buckingham, he had boasted, 'Our pictures, if they were to be sold a century after our death, would sell for good cash, and for three times more than they cost,' adding, 'I wish I could only live a century, if they were sold, to be able to laugh at these facetious folk who say it is money cast away for baubles and shadows. I know they will be pictures still, when those ignorants will be lesser than shadows.'[11] It seems unlikely that even the crafty Gerbier could ever have envisaged the sale of the collections of Buckingham, Arundel and even the king in his lifetime. Nevertheless, once they came on the market, he made sure he placed himself right at the front of the queue.

Like Lanier, Gerbier enjoyed a sustained and intimate relationship with the pictures he bought. Both men picked up works that would probably never have reached England without their efforts. While others in the sale shied away from the royal portraits of the suddenly unfashionable Catholic Van Dyck, Gerbier gambled on his long-term artistic value. He had also played a role in the artistic negotiations in Madrid that brought Titian's magnificent portrait of Charles V to London in 1623. He took possession of the portrait and hung it in his lodgings in Bethnal Green, but it soon transpired that he had other plans for it.

As the dispersal of goods continued throughout the summer of 1650, Gerbier realized that the pictures relinquished on the First List represented only a fraction of the collection that remained under the jurisdiction of the trustees. He knew that more pictures, tapestries and statues would be released. For an entrepreneur like Gerbier, the temptation to get involved with the sale of a collection he had helped to create proved irresistible and he set about convincing the trustees of his ideologically sound credentials. He embarked on a campaign of political reinvention that was breathtaking in its opportunism. By January 1651 the Council of State recommended him to the trustees as a loyal servant of the Commonwealth.[12]

His first task was to rewrite his own relationship with King Charles. He launched his political makeover with the publication of _The None-Such Charles his Character_. Setting out to justify his own diplomatic involvement in the Stuart dynasty, he promised to acquaint the public 'with the crying sins which have brought down so signal a wrath from God upon that Family'.[13] His condemnation of Charles was savage. Attacked as a 'pernicious, horrid, depraved' 'hypocrite', the dead king was accused of 'domestic extravagancies' and condemned for 'his perjury, by his introducing of idolatry.'[14] Gerbier even invented fictional portents of the king's downfall, claiming that while Charles was at Greenwich palace in the late 1630s:

> ... there happened an ominous sign which fell from the Firmament, on a time were as his own Statue graved in Marble which was newly brought from Rome, where it had been made, was at the late Earle of Arundel's request, brought out of the House into the open air, that it might be the better viewed: The said Statue being set forth (as aforesaid) three drops of blood fell on the face of it, which the Earle himself with his own Handkerchief did wipe away, though the stains of the same could never be gotten off since; wherefore it will not seem to be an impertinent question, whether or no those three drops of blood did not signify the blood that had been since spilt amidst these three Nations? And whether also they fell not on his said Statue by a Divine Providence, as a significant token of his disastrous end?[15]

It was a suitably baroque tale of Bernini's bust of Charles, designed to pander to Puritan suspicion of Charles's dealings with Rome and strengthen the popular belief that he was a murdering tyrant.

Gerbier reminded his readers that Charles sacrificed his political responsibilities in the extravagant acquisition of art, although omitting to mention that he was himself the enthusiastic broker in many of these purchases. Condemning the king's refusal to intervene in the Palatinate, Gerbier thundered, 'Yet nevertheless in those exigent times, when moneys, the soul and sinews of War were so scarce, yet great sums were squandered away on braveries and vanities; On old rotten pictures, on broken nosed Marble.'[16] With characteristic hyperbole, he went on, 'Is not this a rare project to squander away millions of pounds?'[17] Referring to the acquisition of the Mantua collection, Gerbier concluded his diatribe with self-confessed amazement 'that this money should be employed to buy Images, and dumb Statues which cannot call for Justice'.[18]

It was an astonishing performance, made all the more remark-able because, even as Gerbier was writing his tract criticizing Charles's aesthetic investments, he was negotiating the sale of his Titian portrait. His double-dealing was compounded by the fact that the purchaser was neither an Englishman nor a republican but an aristocratic Spanish Catholic. The mystery buyer was King Philip IV's ambassador to England. His name was Don Alonso de Cárdenas and he was already in the process of transforming the nature of the Commonwealth's sale of the king's art collection.

ALONSO DE CÁRDENAS arrived in England as a diplomatic agent in 1635.[19] King Philip regarded him as one of the Spanish crown's most experienced and skilful diplomats. His distinguished politi-cal career hardly suggested an interest in art, but events conspired to turn him into one of the biggest buyers at the king's sale. His diplomatic brief was to prevent any political alliance between England and France that would isolate Spain. Unfortunately, Cárdenas's initial experience of English public life was hardly auspicious. He spoke little or no English and had to negotiate with a pro-French King Charles, who regarded him as a 'silly, ignorant, odd fellow'.[20] In response, Cárdenas was appalled at Charles's mismanagement of his foreign and domestic affairs, and could only watch as the country drifted towards war. As it became clear that both Parliament and the Spanish crown shared a mutual interest in limiting French and Dutch naval and commercial power, Cárdenas moved closer to an accommodation with Parliament. In the spring of 1643, he encountered Gerbier for the first time, paying him £52 for information on parliamentary discussions.[21] Typically, Gerbier took the money but failed to deliver, and Cárdenas had to look elsewhere for his political information as he moved towards tacit recognition of parliamentary authority in the spring of 1644.

In May 1645 Cárdenas was one of the first diplomatic observ-ers to report that Parliament was seriously considering selling off the king's goods. In response to this startling information, King Philip was brutally pragmatic. He instructed Cárdenas to buy paintings 'which might be originals by Titian, Paolo Veronese, or other old paintings of distinction', but to avoid letting 'it be known that you are acquiring them for me'.[22] If he was to stand a chance of buying the calibre of pictures that Philip wanted, the first thing that Cárdenas required was a guaranteed supply of money. The king pledged money through the Spanish administration in Naples, but insurrection in Italy and bankruptcy in Spain left Cárdenas needing a private backer.

With the passage of the act for the sale of the king's goods in July 1649, Cárdenas finally obtained the financial backing he required to participate in the forthcoming sale. His financier was Luis de Haro, Marquis del Carpio, principal minister to Philip IV, as well as nephew and successor to the Count-Duke of Olivares. Like his uncle, Haro appreciated the political as well as cultural capital involved in acquiring such a fantastic collection of pictures for his king and guaranteed to channel money through the low Countries to cover the cost of Cárdenas's acquisitions. As the sale began in October 1649, Cárdenas wrote to Geronimo de la Torre, secretary of the Spanish Council of State, telling him, 'I am keeping my lord don Luis de Haro informed about this ... after his excellency wrote to me that he wanted to acquire some tapestries and paintings and offered to have funds sent to me to buy them.'[23] In fact, assured of Haro's financial support, he was already buying pictures from the sale.

Cárdenas faced several difficulties that prevented him publicly walking straight into the sale and buying what he liked. Anti-Spanish feeling was still running high, and Madrid refused to recognize the new Commonwealth, leaving the ambassador in diplomatic limbo. King Philip was also understandably reluctant to sanction the public acquisition of the pictures of his recently executed relative. Cárdenas responded to the problem by making it clear to members of Parliament that he was prepared to pay cash for the dead king's pictures.

On 22 November Colonel William Wetton, who raised a parliamentary regiment during the war, made his one and only visit to the sale and bought three pictures. He paid £165 for a painting of *Solomon* attributed to Giorgione, £175 for a *Madonna* by Titian and £230 for a *Madonna and Child with St Matthew and an Angel* by del Sarto. This was a staggering investment of £570 in one day by someone unlikely to earn such an amount in a year.[24] Yet on the same day Cárdenas recorded buying all three pious images from Wetton, paying £300 for the del Sarto, £225 for the Titian and a colossal £350 for the Giorgione.[25]

In just one day Colonel Wetton invested £570 and turned an immediate profit of £305. It is hard to escape the conclusion that he went into the sale with the explicit intention of buying pictures for Cárdenas. His decision to acquire paintings by three of the most famous artists in the collection (exactly the kind Philip IV requested of Cárdenas) suggests that the ambassador may have even provided Wetton with a shopping list. What is not clear is who funded Wetton – either Cárdenas or another larger consortium of buyers using the colonel as the middleman to supply pictures to the Spanish diplomat.

Wetton was not the only veteran of the war to make a profitable visit to the sale on the Spaniard's behalf. Colonel William Webb and Sergeant-Major Robert Gravener both sold paintings and statues to Cárdenas in the early months of the sale for substantial profits.[26] Cárdenas bankrolled speculators like Wetton, Webb and Gravener, who then inflated the purchase price of the paintings they acquired from the sale to maximize their profit. The Spaniard knew what was on sale because he was paying London-based artists to act as advisers as well as buyers in compiling a series of memoranda to send to Haro and keep him informed of the merchandise and its prices. In December 1649 Cárdenas drew up the first memorandum for Haro with a detailed account of the quality, size and cost of the finest pictures entered in the sale. Compiled with the help of a team of advisers, including artists who visited the sale and took notes on its finest pieces, these memoranda provided lists 'of the King's original pictures, the most notable examples held in the greatest regard, which are being sold' at Somerset House, Hampton Court and St James's Palace. These provided detailed descriptions of over forty of the finest pictures in the royal collection, in three of the Stuart dynasty's grandest residences. They included paintings by Caravaggio, Giulio Romano, Van Dyck, Mantegna, Veronese, Giorgione and Palma Vecchio. There were four Correggios, three Raphaels, three del

Sartos and no fewer than sixteen Titians. This was the cream of Charles's collection, amassed over thirty years. Pictures from Madrid, Mantua and Rome were on the list, as well as paintings commissioned by the king in London, including Van Dyck's equestrian portrait of King Charles, listed at 1,200 ducats (£300) and described by Cárdenas as 'among the finest ever done by Van Dyck'.[27]

The lists reveal how pictures were evaluated and appreciated by seventeenth-century dealers and agents like Cárdenas. They also provide an insight into the artistic values of a representative of the Spanish Habsburg emperor, and how his tastes varied from those of King Charles. What is immediately striking is that, with the exception of two pictures by Van Dyck, Cárdenas chose sixteenth-century Italian artists. This was in line with the collecting history of the Habsburg dynasty. Philip IV and his predecessors admired and collected artists like Titian, Raphael and Correggio for their orthodox religious piety, as well as their titillating scenes of eroticism, wrapped in the respectable mantle of the classical past. This mixture of piety and prurience runs throughout Cárdenas's list. He applauded Titian's *Mary Magdalene*, priced at £100, as 'a devout picture and very lifelike', while observing that Correggio's erotic rendering of the pagan scene of *Venus with Satyr and Cupid* was 'in good condition, and although its subject is very profane, it is much admired'.

Modern painters like Reni and Caravaggio were regarded with more circumspection. Cárdenas was particularly unconvinced by Caravaggio's dramatic *Death of the Virgin*, an acquisition from Mantua. 'This is held to be a good picture,' he conceded, 'but it does not seem to be well finished, seeming to have been done to be viewed from a distance.' These remarks betrayed his conservatism and inexperience. What he regarded as criticism of Caravaggio was precisely what established the painter's reputation as a master of the boldly executed and visually striking altarpiece. For both Cárdenas and King Charles, Caravaggio seemed a dangerously modern and experimental artist.

Cárdenas reserved his greatest admiration for the two painters with the finest reputations in the entire collection: Titian and Raphael. He praised Titian's pictures as 'excellent' and 'much admired'. But the jewel of the collection was unquestionably Raphael's *The Holy Family*. Listed as the most expensive picture in the entire sale, it was described by Cárdenas as 'measuring one and a half *varas* [or yards] high by one wide, more or less, on panel, with the figures of Our Lady, St Anne, St Joseph, the Infant Jesus and St John, by Raphael'. He valued it at '12,000 ducats, which has been reduced to 9,000'. In the margin, he added, 'This picture has been well looked after, but at such a high price, no one is showing any interest in it.'[28] In 1627 Daniel Nys had valued it at 4,000 *scudi*. By 1649 its reputation ensured that this amount had doubled. Valued by the trustees at £2,000, the luminous canvas, just over one metre square, was estimated to be worth nearly as much as the seven-piece tapestry set of *The Seven Deadly Sins*. While Cárdenas protested at its exorbitant cost, he also noted its earlier reduction in price, indicating to Haro that there might be room for future negotiation.

Cárdenas learned fast. As his English counterparts like Carleton and Lanier knew, success in the art world required the diplomat's skills of secrecy, timing and arcane knowledge, and Cárdenas was quick to exploit these accomplishments. The fine detail of the memoranda reveals a man trying to learn all he could about the intricacies of a new art market and its products. He took advice from a team of experts in concluding that one Raphael painting 'is pleasing to few', while another Titian canvas 'is dreary and dark and not a pleasing painting'. He expressed concern that Correggio's pair of paintings *Allegories of Vice and Virtue*, 'although of great esteem, seem to be at a very high price for works done in tempera'. Mantegna's imposing *Triumphs of Julius Caesar* were considered too risky to acquire because, in Cárdenas's opinion, 'If these pictures are removed from their present location, and are prepared for transportation, it is said by all that they would suffer as a consequence.' Cárdenas also expressed his reservations with a painting by Veronese, thanks to a common problem that bedevilled the royal collection: 'There are doubts as to whether this picture is a copy, although it is on sale as an original.'

In the space of just a few weeks Cárdenas quickly learned the language and behaviour of the connoisseur. He understood how to assess the quality of a painting in terms of its artist, size, subject matter and medium. He appraised its condition, its history and if it was a copy or genuine. But he needed a team of specialists to provide him with the expertise he lacked. Throughout the list, Cárdenas suggests that he paid artists and dealers to visit the sale and report back to him, but in certain revealing descriptions of the pictures, he disclosed that he too visited the sale. 'I have not been able to view this picture properly because it has been taken out of the sale to be copied,' he writes in describing a Titian, and on another occasion he reports that pictures by Tintoretto 'have not yet been viewed'. Despite King Philip's admonitions to keep a low profile, Cárdenas was getting sucked into the sale, employing advisers to provide an outline of what was on the market, then visiting the sale to see the pictures for himself.

One of his buyers, who also acted as his paid artistic adviser, was the Flemish-born painter Remigius Van Leemput.[29] He was the perfect agent for Cárdenas – an expert in pictures, indifferent to the political situation and in need of money. By early December, Van Leemput was already spending huge sums at the sale, way in excess of the kind of money he could expect to earn as a copyist. He bought pictures by del Sarto and Correggio, as well as statues by Giambologna and Fanelli. The Giambologna statues had once represented the pride of Prince Henry's art collection at St James's, back in 1612. Van Leemput now acquired them for as little as £3 each.[30] As he bought pictures from the sale that went straight to Cárdenas, Van Leemput presumably also acquainted the Spaniard with accounts of what else was on offer.

By the beginning of the New Year, Cárdenas had spent nearly £1,000 on pictures, and by spring 1650 he had bought twenty-six paintings and statues from Van Leemput. Over the next few months he significantly curbed his profligate expenditure. He started to appreciate the need to gauge the timing of his purchases if he was to acquire the best pictures at the cheapest prices. He was also awaiting further instructions, as well as cash, from Haro, who in February finally provided him with £3,000 to cover his initial purchases. The complex financial transaction involved Haro sending a bill of exchange to a Spanish merchant based in Antwerp, who then cashed the bill in local currency. This in turn was converted into sterling and shipped to Cárdenas in London.

After taking into account exchange rates and commission, Cárdenas received £2,965 10s and 10d.[31] It only just covered his expenditure.

Interest in the sale also waned throughout the spring as rumours spread of parliamentary plans for the creation of the First List. Potential buyers like Cárdenas waited to see which pictures would be taken out of the sale, in the hope of negotiating better deals with private owners hard up for ready currency. Cash buyers were reduced to a trickle. Some continued to make shrewd purchases at the lower end of the market, like the Flemish painter and dealer Jan Baptiste Gaspars. On 28 January 1650 he paid just £11 for the Veronese *Mars and Venus* that Prince Charles had acquired on his trip to Madrid in 1623. He returned in March to pick up two of the finest bargains of the sale – Van Dyck's seductive portrait of his mistress, Margaret Lemon, for just £23 and Mantegna's magisterial *Death of the Virgin*. Painted in Mantua, what van Doort described as 'a little piece of Andrea Mantegna being the dying of our Lady' was moved between St James's and the Privy Gallery in Whitehall before being sold to Gaspars for just £17 10s.[32]

Gaspars cheerfully capitalized on the sinking market, but most people felt that a time of growing dissatisfaction with the Rump Parliament, with the prospect of renewed political unrest, was not the moment to be purchasing works of art. The return of many of the Rump's original 'purged' members had diluted much of its initial reforming zeal, and a disillusioned populace, many of whom were still owed money from the royal debt, was increasingly calling for a limited restoration of the monarchy.[33] Throughout the spring of 1650, as Charles II moved towards a religious and political alliance with the Scots, such sentiments began to look increasingly serious. Worried by the threat of another Scottish invasion, Parliament once again turned to the indefatigable Cromwell, who was still in Ireland, successfully putting down rebellion. Appointed Lord General and commander-in-chief of Parliament's army, Cromwell headed for Scotland in June 1650, and by September he found himself outnumbered by nearly two to one before a Scottish army of over 20,000 at Dunbar, east of Edinburgh. On the morning of 3 September he launched his attack. When the battle concluded the Scots had lost over 3,000 men with 10,000 taken prisoner. It was possibly Cromwell's greatest victory, and it prevented any immediate hopes for the restoration of the Stuart monarchy. The Rump was saved, and with it plans to revise the terms of the sale.

The publication of the First List of creditors in the spring of 1650 had not stemmed the growing tide of public criticism at the failure to address public debt. Creditors omitted from the list were quick to air their grievances against Parliament. As the pictures were distributed over the following weeks and months, the recipients faced another problem: who would buy their paintings? The public sale proved slow enough, but if the creditors now wished to sell, they would have to go in search of private buyers. Apart from Cárdenas, who still dominated the market, London's resident French envoys seemed likely customers. Sieur de Croullé, the secretary to the French embassy, was busy compiling a list of pictures with which to tempt his master back in Paris, Cardinal Mazarin. He also kept a wary eye on Cárdenas as he visited the sale at Somerset House, where 'he asked to be shown all the tapestries and then spent a long time viewing the paintings about which he had some notes taken down, and he has already purchased many'.[34] Cárdenas finally faced some competition, but as he awaited the arrival of more money from Haro, larger political events suddenly threatened to terminate not only his participation in the sale but also his residence in London.

Since the king's execution, both Parliament and the exiled Charles II were eager to court political links with Madrid. In mid-1649 Charles sent an embassy to Madrid led by Edward Hyde and his father's veteran ambassador, Lord Cottington. Alarmed at news of Cottington's arrival in Spain, Parliament dispatched their representative, Anthony Ascham. However, within a day of arriving Ascham was stabbed to death by a group of English royalist soldiers. The murder caused a diplomatic storm. Cárdenas faced immediate expulsion. King Philip had little choice but to recognize the republican regime by providing the diplomat with formal credentials as Spain's ambassador to England. His decision was undoubtedly influenced by news of Cromwell's victory over the Scots at Dunbar. The battle convinced Philip that he should be doing business with Parliament. Having faced an ignominious return to Spain, Cárdenas's political position was suddenly secure. His French opposite number was expelled by Parliament, exasperated at Louis XIV's refusal to acknowledge the new regime, and Haro sent a further £2,000 in September 1650 to bolster Cárdenas's finances. With no competition, he was now in an unrivalled position to take full advantage of the changing complexion of the sale. Even more fortuitously, the glut of pictures and lack of purchasers presented him with an unprecedented buyers' market.

Nobody was more relieved to see Cárdenas restored than Balthazar Gerbier. In the light of Cárdenas's difficulties throughout the summer, Gerbier's acquisition of two pictures for £350 started to look rather reckless. By October 1650 he was happy to bargain with the rehabilitated ambassador. Despite attempts to convince him that he had other potential buyers, Gerbier could only persuade the hawkish Cárdenas to pay £200 for his Titian, giving him a profit of £50. Unfortunately for Gerbier, Cárdenas was more interested in closing one of the biggest deals of the entire sale.

The ambassador was a great admirer of the nine-piece tapestry set the *Acts of the Apostles*, based on the cartoons by Raphael that Charles had acquired in 1623. Royal collections across Europe contained tapestries based on Raphael's designs. As a gift for a pious Catholic sovereign, delivered from the clutches of an ungodly republican regime, the acquisition of a set would represent a huge coup for Cárdenas. His original memorandum gave a detailed account of the tapestries, but a price tag of £4,429 5s discouraged any initial bids. By early October 1650 Cárdenas felt politically and financially secure enough to make his move. On 11 October the trustees sold the tapestries to Robert Houghton, one of the king's more influential creditors, former royal brewer and now a staunch parliamentarian. Cárdenas's accounts reveal that Houghton was buying royal tapestries on his behalf. The ambassador submitted an account of £3,559 4s 4d, which represented 'the price of nine panels of tapestry in gold and silk of *The Acts of the Apostles* designed by Raphael ... bought in the said sale by an agent named Robert Houghton'. To disguise his involvement in the sale, Cárdenas paid one William Atkins £75 to act 'as a consultant to the person who bought the tapestry from the sale [Houghton], and having negotiated the price with him, and having assisted him until it was obtained'.[35] With Atkins's help, Cárdenas bargained Houghton down by £870, nearly a fifth of the original asking price.[36]

The acquisition of the tapestries was a major success for Cárdenas, but it also presented him with a new set of logistical problems. Moving small canvases around London was one thing, but nine large, heavy tapestries was quite another. To add to his difficulties, he also needed to dispose of the three crates of pictures acquired since the beginning of the sale. Haro wanted a return on his investment. Cárdenas needed to get the tapestries and pictures out of England and to Madrid quickly and quietly, having guaranteed Haro that he would 'give no account of these purchases to anyone in this Court', ensuring 'that news of all dealings reaches the hands of Your Worship in secrecy'.[37] Fearful of marauding Dutch and royalist frigates, he arranged for the eight crates of tapestries 'to be taken as cargo on a warship of Parliament, along with three other crates, which contain the paintings'.[38] It was a neat irony, as payment for the tapestries and pictures should in theory have gone straight into the coffers of the navy. Although Cárdenas was at pains to keep his acquisitions a secret from the general public, he showed little compunction in sharing his activities with Parliament.

However, even as the tapestries made their way to Madrid, Cárdenas was confronted with yet another problem. The publication of the First List of creditors had not assuaged public demand for a greater redistribution of the king's goods. In the winter of 1650–51, as political discontent with the Rump Parliament increased still further, the sale's trustees responded to the criticism by proposing the dispersal of even more former royal possessions among a second list of creditors. The sale was about to take yet another convoluted turn.

CHAPTER TEN

REAPING DIVIDENDS:
THE SECOND LIST

AUSTIN FRIARS in the Broad Street ward of London was not one of the capital's more glamorous districts. Situated to the east of Whitehall, it was an overcrowded, noisy neighbourhood, populated by Dutch immigrants, musicians, actors and painters like Emmanuel de Critz, son of King James's Serjeant-Painter John de Critz. By the autumn of 1651, however, it had become home to some of the finest paintings and sculptures in Europe. When Richard Symonds visited de Critz's house in early 1652 he was astonished to find 'three rooms full of the King's pictures'. Returning from three years of self-imposed exile abroad, nothing could have prepared Symonds for the transformation he witnessed across the city, and nowhere were the changes more striking than in Austin Friars. Moving through the cramped, low-ceilinged rooms of de Critz's house, he looked at some of the finest examples of the dead king's collection – paintings by Titian, Giorgione, Correggio, Giulio Romano, Bassano, Orazio Gentileschi and Van Dyck that had once been displayed within the private inner chambers of Whitehall, exclusively reserved for the appreciation of the royal court and its supporters.

On his travels Symonds had seen some of the finest palaces in Europe, including the grandeur of the Palazzo Farnese in Rome, but this paled in comparison with the extraordinary concentration of masterpieces he saw in de Critz's three humble rooms.[1] He inspected Correggio's paintings *Allegory of Virtue* and *Allegory of Vice*, bought from Mantua and smuggled out of Venice over the Alps by Nicholas Lanier. Now here they were in a little house in a busy working suburb of London. In his notebooks Symonds described the two Correggios as 'about 3 foot & a quarter high. One Marsyas being flayed & one offers snakes towards him, a boy below smiling; a brave piece. The other of Pallas & others'. He also noted the staggering valuation placed upon the pictures: 'both prized at £1000 a piece'.[2]

Other marvels filled the room: a Virgin by Titian, a picture of Christ crowned with thorns by Bassano, and more pictures from Mantua, including Giulio Romano's adaptations of Ovid's *Metamorphoses* and his picture of 'Fortune Standing on a globe kept up by 2 Cupids',[3] previously hung at the end of the Long Gallery in Whitehall.[4] Now it was in Austin Friars, valued at £20. There were poignant reminders of the dead king's recent fall: a Goliath slain by David attributed to Giorgione, a portrait of the long-dead Duke of Buckingham attributed to Orazio Gentileschi and Van Dyck's group portrait of *The Five Eldest Children of Charles I*. The painting portrays Princess Mary and Prince James standing beside Prince Charles as he rests his hand on an enormous mastiff. To the prince's left his sister Princess Elizabeth holds the infant Princess Anne as she stretches out to reach the mastiff. During the 1630s, the picture of the King's children was hung amid the domestic tranquillity of the Whitehall breakfast chamber. But even in those happier times, Charles had queried Van Dyck's fee of £200, paying half that sum. There was little call now for pictures of the royal children, especially those featuring the Commonwealth's greatest foe, the fugitive Prince of Wales, now hailed as King Charles II by his exiled supporters, which partly explains the picture's further decline in value to £80, although de Critz had no scruples in offering it for sale to the highest bidder.

The greatest prize among de Critz's cluttered rooms was not, however, a painting. It was a bust that Symonds recorded as 'The King's head in white marble done by Bernino at Rome priced £400'.[5] During his exile in Rome Symonds admired Van Dyck's painting of King Charles seen from three different positions, designed to help Bernini to model the king's head.[6] Now he had the opportunity to admire the finished bust of the dead king, previously displayed at Greenwich Palace, now deposited in a corner of de Critz's rooms with a price on its head of £400. Symonds exhibited no apparent anger or disgust at this display of his late king's possessions. As a royalist he was horrified by Charles's downfall, but as a connoisseur he was seduced by the unprecedented access it gave him to such beautiful paintings and statues.

De Critz was only one among many Londoners to receive pictures from the king's collection in October 1651. Across the capital's parishes and suburbs ordinary people took possession of hundreds of paintings and statues in settlement of outstanding royal debts. In St-Martin-in-the-Fields Thomas Bagley, chief glazier to Charles I, received over thirty pictures, including Titians, Holbeins and Correggio's erotic *Education of Cupid*, valued at £800.[7] Symonds was there again, admiring a painting of Lucretia attributed to Titian, but criticizing the Holbein as 'far less than the life'.[8] In the Poultry district of the City of London the royal upholsterer Ralph Grynder proudly displayed Guido Reni's four panels of the *Labours of Hercules*,[9] Giulio Romano's *Nativity*,[10] valued at £500, and his '11 Caesars on horseback in long pieces of deal boards',[11] all originally from Mantua.

Elsewhere the king's Serjeant Plumber John Embree, who had been responsible for the maintenance of the royal buildings, picked up twenty-four paintings in lieu of debts of nearly £1,000, including a magnificent Titian. William Geere collected fourteen paintings, including several Van Dycks. South of the river in Southwark, the king's brewer Robert Houghton showed off his Van Dycks as well as the Titians he had acquired. Meanwhile the king's tailor, the Scot David Murray, received the erotic (and expensive) Correggio, *Venus with Satyr and Cupid*, reckoned to be worth £1,000.[12] He also acquired Dürer's exquisite self-portrait and painting of his father, brought back from Nuremberg by Arundel in 1636, now valued as a pair at just £100.[13] There were other remarkable bargains. Edward Bass, a minor functionary under Charles's rule, received Rembrandt's *Old Woman*, valued at just £4. Neither he nor the trustees seemed to have thought much of the painting, which was wrongly labelled as 'A Man's head'.[14]

In the space of just a few days in October 1651 almost 700 pictures were distributed among nearly 1,000 of Charles's creditors living in London's boroughs. It was a dramatic and unexpected situation. Widows, orphans, goldsmiths, soldiers, vintners, musicians, cutlers, drapers and tailors were allocated pictures by artists that included Titian, Raphael, Leonardo, Dürer, Rubens and Van Dyck. In some cases the pictures were valued at more than the average worker's lifetime salary. The size of many of the canvases, with their ornate gilt frames, dwarfed most people's dwellings. Ordinary Londoners could hold, examine, discuss, admire, buy and sell pictures and statues that, until then, had been destined exclusively for the pleasure and edification of the aristocracy, and, though many seized the opportunity to make a profit from their sudden ownership of some of the finest paintings of the Renaissance, for the first time in European history great works of art were in the private possession of the general public. It was a dramatic shift and one that would profoundly change English attitudes towards art.

This extraordinary dispersal was the direct result of the trustees' Second List, drawn up at the beginning of January 1651 'containing about 970 of the said Creditors & Servants, and presented the same to the Parliament'.[15] Ever vigilant, the Spanish ambassador, Cárdenas, learned of the trustees' plans through his network of parliamentary contacts and informed Haro of what he called 'appropriations instigated by the creditors of the late King'. He realized that the expectation surrounding the release of this new list would have a detrimental effect on the sale. Cárdenas shared most Londoners' disillusion with the Rump's political inertia. Sceptical of its ability to prioritize the publication of a new list of creditors and goods, he told Haro:

> I do not see Parliament making much haste in dispatching this. It is even being said that there is some doubt as to whether they will be announced at all, and that even when they are, they will exclude the best paintings and other things that were promised as for immediate sale. The consequence is that all those who were waiting for these appropriations to go out to buy at a good price are now wondering what to do. Some have decided, seeing how long this business is taking, to buy according to the set price, without making any discount.[16]

Cárdenas feared that Parliament would reserve the best pictures for its own use and that their delay would deter others from buying at the public sale until they discovered what pictures would go on the private market. The result was effectively to kill the sale. A few smaller buyers snapped up pictures at cost price, but most, like Cárdenas, decided to sit tight.

Although the sale went into abeyance, diplomatic observers in London were quick to report the success of Cárdenas's activities. In March 1651 the Venetian ambassador to the Spanish court noted that booty from the sale was starting to reach Madrid, including 'rich tapestries and very valuable paintings, the property of the unfortunate king, whose furniture is now being sold in London by public auction'. The ambassador was well informed about how the Spaniards were funding their acquisitions, observing, 'Don Luis [de Haro] has made considerable remittances to Cárdenas that he may purchase the best pictures, statues and arras. He has already begun to do so, one exquisite set of hangings having arrived, of incomparable design and delicacy, representing the *Acts of the Apostles*, which were sold as cheaply as if they had been made of plain cloth.'[17] But as the tapestries arrived in Madrid, back in London events took a turn for the worse. The sale was suspended pending a parliamentary investigation into obscure allegations that the trustees had acted irregularly. 'It would seem,' wrote Cárdenas, 'that they have greatly defrauded the state, and altered the valuations for their own benefit by having entered what has been sold at a lower price than the purchase price.'[18]

At this stage Cárdenas was concerned less with the allegations of deception than with the threatened closure of the sale. Ever resourceful, he went on to inform Haro that he was already making deals with a potential beneficiary of the Second List. 'I am now trying to reach an agreement with a party who, apparently, is to be among the first to receive a large part of the total. Up to now he is offering me a fifth of the set price as discount and, if I can get him up to a quarter, I shall conclude a deal with him.'[19] The two most plausible candidates were Edward Bass and the former royal brewer Robert Houghton. Bass was destined to become a major beneficiary of the Second List and, as a result, one of Cárdenas's biggest clients. Houghton had already helped Cárdenas acquire the *Acts of the Apostles* tapestries, and was an even more likely candidate as Cárdenas's contact, because he was subsequently involved in another scheme to buy pictures for the ambassador.

By May the sale resumed, but as the summer progressed, Cárdenas's correspondence reflected his growing nervousness at the deteriorating political situation and the implications of the publication of the new list. Now in his late fifties, the Spaniard had been in England for thirteen years. Weary and sick, he begged a recall to Madrid. He was also fearful of the increasing political belligerence of the Commonwealth. In July he reported the expulsion of the Portuguese ambassador and the hasty departure of an embassy from The Hague. An English embassy to The Hague also returned home 'dissatisfied with the Dutch' over plans for closer political and economic union.[20] Once again larger political events threatened to frustrate Cárdenas's plans to make a decisive strike on the sale.

Although Parliament continued to stall the release of the Second List, legislation to revise the original terms of the sale was nonetheless being prepared. On 17 July 1651 an act was passed that tilted the balance significantly in favour of the interests of the Council of State.[21] It declared that a further £10,000 worth of goods 'shall and may, by order and direction of the Council of State, be further reserved and appointed for the public service of the Commonwealth'.[22] It excluded significant parts of the royal estate from the sale (including the extensive collections held in the library of St James's Palace), effectively appropriating them for the benefit of Parliament, and aimed to enlarge the revenue from the sale by fining anyone concealing or removing royal goods double the value of the goods concerned. This was to prove especially problematic in relation to the act's most punitive and divisive measure: the encouragement of 'discoveries'. Any creditor who 'discovered' someone harbouring royal goods could report the culprit to the trustees and claim a percentage of their value. In a volatile climate where the line between royal and civic possession was increasingly blurred, it was a very dangerous initiative that could be easily abused. This was not an act designed to alleviate the grievances of an increasingly desperate and angry collection of creditors. It was a dangerous incitement to fraud and slander and a subtle act of political self-interest that suggested that the Rump was increasingly placing its own financial interests ahead of those it claimed to represent.

Just five days later Parliament finally released the Second List. It comprised the 970 creditors originally submitted in January, but the money available from the sale was simply not equal to their claims. The trustees audited claims from those on the list of £90,000, but over the next few months they released just £7,500 in cash.[23] Once again the onus was on the settlement of debts through the presentation of goods in kind, but the insufficiency of funds only led to further public anger and disillusionment.

In response to the publication of the Second List, the creditors made a valiant attempt to take matters into their own hands. Cárdenas gives the most graphic account of what happened next. As ever, the ambassador was watching events from the sidelines with an eye on the fate of the sale's paintings. He wrote to Haro to inform him:

> . . . of developments as regards the paintings, which are limited to the difficulties which have occurred in publishing the appropriations. This has meant that those best placed, or who pay the most, have chosen the most sought-after paintings and which are the easiest to sell. This has left to others the remainder – the ballast – those paintings of lesser value, and harder to dispose of.[24]

Cárdenas's comments reveal just how much money and political influence were now controlling the acquisition of the king's goods. He observed how, in some desperation, a group of creditors brokered a more equitable solution with the government:

> Consequently, interested parties went up to Parliament, and sent a representative group to find a way of dealing fairly with them all. Of the methods suggested, the one that was most favoured, and that they are trying to implement, was that those creditors whose debts did not exceed 15,000 *escudos* [£3,750] should form syndicates. Working from this figure, and in accordance with the asking prices, it was proposed that they should assemble sets of valuables of good quality.

They should then draw lots between fourteen dividends that
the creditors have created, and the winner should choose the
share that he desired.[25]

Although the scheme to take payment in goods via syndicates,
or so-called dividends, seemed like an effective way of involving as
many creditors as possible, in effect it concentrated power into the
hands of those in charge of the dividends. It also allowed Parliament to deflect any subsequent criticism of the sale on to the heads
of the dividends and the trustees. It was a sad indictment of the
initial aspirations of the Commonwealth. The sale of the king's
goods had literally turned into a lottery.

The squabbles over the creation of the dividends postponed
the distribution of the goods even longer. The delay was compounded by the political crisis precipitated by the return of Charles
II at the head of yet another Scottish army, this time intent on
leading the battle into England. By August 1651 Charles and his
forces had marched across the border and made their way to
Worcester, where they confronted Cromwell's army. As both sides
prepared for battle, Cárdenas was hastily organizing the shipment
of pictures by Titian, Van Dyck and Rubens. He reported with
apparent consternation that 'the sale has been closed' and due
to 'the circumstance that the King is in England, there is the
possibility that fate might bring him to London, thus making it
impossible to ship the paintings'.[26] It was a curious situation:
Cárdenas fearful of and irritated by the return to London of the
heir to the dead king whose pictures he was busily buying and
shipping back to Madrid.

However, Charles II was not to return to the capital quite
yet. By midnight on 3 September, exactly a year after Cromwell's
victory at Dunbar, Charles's Scottish army was decisively routed
at Worcester.[27] Charles himself managed to escape and fled to
France, but his hopes of regaining the crown while the apparently
invincible Cromwell stood in his way were at an end. The crisis
over, a relieved Cárdenas was free to resume his business, announcing just weeks later that the 'adjudication of the drawing of lots
among the creditors for the goods of the King that were in the sale
has taken place. Everything has therefore been distributed.'[28] The

English sources confirm that 'the Contractors, with the assistance of several of the said Creditors, did to the best of their skill equally divide all the said goods into Dividends, which were drawn by lot, & so made payment of the said List in Goods'.[29] The market was finally at the mercy of the Spaniard.

Before he could close in on the pictures, Cárdenas had to wait for their distribution among the newly created dividends. As his comments suggest, it was a slow and haphazard process. The dividends were consortia of creditors and there were fourteen in all, created without any parliamentary regulation. Each dividend appointed an individual from among its number who was responsible for receiving the goods allocated to his particular consortium. In consultation with 'several' creditors, the sale's contractors divided royal goods between all fourteen dividends. Subsequent events suggest that the creditors consulted put pressure on the contractors to ensure their dividends received some of the best allocation of goods, which included paintings. The dividends then agreed that lots would be drawn to divide the goods allocated between the individual creditors. They could then take away their goods, sell them on the open market or commission the leader of their dividend to sell the items for a percentage of the profit.

By the middle of October 1651, after an intensive period of haggling over which dividend received what in the division of the spoils, the harassed contractors were finally ready to release the king's goods. On 23 October lots were drawn at Somerset House allocating individual creditors their merchandise.[30] Each dividend received around £5,000 worth of former royal possessions, with individuals claiming goods valued at anything from a few shillings to hundreds of pounds. In just one day, the trustees wrote out credit notes for nearly 700 pictures to be distributed among the members of the fourteen dividends. Over the next few days many of the pictures which had been carted into Somerset House from Charles I's deserted palaces almost exactly two years previously were on the move again. It was the largest migration of art in London's history.

For most desperate creditors joining one of the fourteen dividends it was a last forlorn attempt to recover what they were owed. But Parliament did not attempt to put any equitable mechanism in place to ensure that individual creditors were given equal opportunity to profit from the sale of the goods allocated to their dividend. Once again the market was flooded with all manner of items from the royal palaces. Only the heads of the dividends, by acting on behalf of the poorer members, stood any realistic chance of making money from the scheme. It was a recipe for confusion and deception, with most minor creditors receiving broken, useless goods worth a fraction of their nominal price and hardly worth selling. As far as the state was concerned, their debt was officially settled, but for the creditors it was a doubly bitter betrayal, first by the royalist regime they had toppled, then by the parliamentary authorities who promised to redress their grievances.

For others, the division of the spoils simply came too late. Jan van Belcamp had succeeded as Keeper of the Cabinet Room at St James's following Abraham van der Doort's suicide in 1639. He had acted as one of the sale's most knowledgeable and enthusiastic trustees, while also claiming £2,210 owed to him from the previous regime. Unfortunately, in August 1651, before he could collect the pictures allocated to him in lieu of his debt, he died. Belcamp's executors picked up his share, including one of the finest pictures in the entire collection, Leonardo's *St John the Baptist*. As a painter and a conservator, Belcamp would have been delighted at his posthumous acquisition, but he never had the chance to savour it. Instead Symonds viewed what was left of Belcamp's career: 'At a merchant's in St Swithen's Lane, pictures which were of Belcamp lately dead who kept the king's picture'.[31]

For some, though, the Second List was another marvellous opportunity to profit from the sale of the king's goods. Just ten men headed the fourteen dividends. Most had already been involved in the sale prior to the announcement of the Second List. These included David Murray, the king's tailor, the royal upholsterer Ralph Grynder, glazier Thomas Bagley, the painter Emmanuel de Critz and Robert Houghton. Other prosperous businessmen and erstwhile creditors quickly established themselves at the heads of the other dividends. William Latham, formerly woollen draper to both King James and Charles, headed the fourth dividend, the royal embroiderer Edmund Harrison fronted the eleventh, while the lawyer John Jackson, acting for a consortium of more important creditors including Members of Parliament, took control of the twelfth.

The motivation of the two other dividend leaders encapsulated the radically polarized views of the late king's creditors. Edward Bass enthusiastically embraced the parliamentary cause after an undistinguished career as a minor royal official under King Charles. He headed no fewer than three dividends and made joint purchases with John Hunt, one of the sale's treasurers and former linen draper to Henrietta Maria. Bass appears to have relished his position and profited accordingly. The leader of the sixth dividend, on the other hand, was a surprising choice to participate in the break-up of the king's household. Captain John Stone[32] boasted a distinguished war record as a committed royalist. His father was the royal sculptor Nicholas Stone, which might explain why he was chosen to evaluate the sixty pictures his dividend received as part of its allocation on 23 October, valued at £1,614. Stone's subsequent actions suggest that financial profit was secondary to other motivations that led him to front his dividend.

The estimated value of the goods received by all fourteen dividends came to over £70,000. Pictures made up nearly a third of the total, with 684 valued at just over £20,000, distributed among the dividends. The creditors required expertise in the art market, which gave men like Captain Stone and Emmanuel de Critz a crucial advantage in shaping the dividends' fate. Like Edward Bass, de Critz fronted three of the fourteen dividends, and took responsibility for nearly £15,000 in royal possessions, including 154 pictures valued at just over £3,000.[33] As well as paintings by Titian, Van Dyck and Correggio, his dividends also took possession of nearly eighty classical statues, valued at £1,000, including the prized Bernini bust of King Charles which ended up in de Critz's house.[34]

No wonder Richard Symonds was overwhelmed when he glimpsed de Critz's fabulous haul in Austin Friars early in 1652. De Critz was the perfect front for his dividends. He was an established painter and well-connected businessman who knew the value of the goods he received. His political credentials as a deserving creditor were also impeccable. His father had painted King James's portrait and he personally acted as Serjeant-Painter to Charles I, although first Gentileschi and then Van Dyck quickly eclipsed his talent. If anyone could make his dividend a profit, it was Emmanuel de Critz, who began transforming his house into an art gallery. Leaders of the other dividends were quick to appreciate his expertise, and negotiated with him to sell their paintings in return for a percentage of the profits. William Latham, leader of the fourth dividend and more familiar with woollen stockings than paintings, placed his most valuable asset, Correggio's *Allegory of Vice*, priced at £1,000, in de Critz's house. More pictures allocated to the fourth dividend moved through de Critz's house, including paintings by Giulio Romano, Rubens, Brueghel, Mytens and even one attributed to Michelangelo.

Despite its obvious limitations, the Second List was more far-reaching in the dispersal of objects across a broad cross-section of ordinary working people. Although it is still possible to trace the circulation of the art objects through records and inventories, the lives of their owners are far more obscure. We know something of William Latham, the head of the fourteenth dividend. He also acted on behalf of another fourteen members of the dividend: William Aldridge, Andrew Halfepenny, Jane Dunsyne (acting on behalf of her husband, Alexander), Lydia Hope, Richard Dawning, John Arland, Katherine Bowers (representing her husband Vernon), Mabull Mackarill, Andrew Haitly, Dorothy Wingfeld, John Young and Henry Dawson. We know the fate of the objects that were supposed to alleviate their poverty – the Titians, Brueghels and Giulio Romanos. But little is known of what happened to these fourteen people or the scores of others who gambled on reclaiming their losses through the lottery of the dividend scheme. Surviving accounts briefly record the names of these unfortunate individuals as members of the various dividends. Otherwise, alas, the identities of the creditors soon faded amid the sale's detailed records of objects and valuations.

As the dividends picked over the spoils, Alonso de Cárdenas planned his next move. He drew up yet another list of pictures for Haro's consideration. His first memoranda were based upon the pictures offered for public sale of late 1649; he now listed twenty-four pictures 'in the possession of those to whom they were given and consigned, in payment of the debts of King Charles I'.[35]

Cárdenas's tastes were now firmly established and the list contained
the familiar mix of predominantly Italian, sixteenth-century painters, alongside a handful of northern European and contemporary
artists. There were four paintings by Correggio and Giulio
Romano, two by Raphael, Tintoretto, Mantegna and Palma, but,
primarily due to his popularity in the early months of the sale, only
one by Titian. Northern European art was barely represented,
apart from a handful of notable exceptions – Rubens's *Allegory
of Peace and War*, Van Dyck's *Five Eldest Children of Charles I* and
Holbein's exquisite *Portrait of Erasmus*.

Cárdenas knew almost every leader of the fourteen dividends
and decided to take his time in extracting the lowest possible
prices for whichever pictures Haro requested. Unfortunately for
the ambassador, his monopoly over such a phenomenal list was
about to end. In late November his supremacy was challenged by
the arrival in London of another Habsburg-sponsored art agent, the
Dutch painter David Teniers.[36] News of the Second List had
reached the Spanish-controlled Low Countries and its most senior
military commander, Alonso Pérez de Vivero, Count of Fuensaldaña. The Count was second-in-command to the Habsburg
Governor-General, Archduke Leopold-Wilhelm. Both men were
keen art collectors and eager to extend their favour with King
Philip and his first minister, Luis de Haro. It is possible that they
considered Cárdenas too slow in supplying Madrid with suitable
pictures, or perhaps they saw the opportunity to make a quick and
lucrative raid on the dividends before the best pictures disappeared.

Cárdenas obviously regarded Teniers as an interloper and on
24 November he wrote a measured letter to Haro about the artist's
sudden and mysterious arrival. The letter was a deliberate attempt
to undermine Tenier's activities in London. It explained that
Cárdenas had recently inspected the art collection of Van Dyck's
old patron, the recently deceased 4th Earl of Pembroke, which was
now on the market. However, Cárdenas dismissed the remaining
pictures, claiming that the new earl 'had withdrawn the best
items, reserving them for himself', and that 'of what was left, I did
not see anything worthwhile, nor did the painters I had accompany me'. He concluded grandly, 'I did not think it worthwhile to
give an account or send a memorandum to Your Worship of these

paintings, judging the whole business to be somewhat extra-ordinary.'

Having roundly condemned the quality of the remnants of the collection, the wily Cárdenas continued, 'Nevertheless, a painter [Teniers] sent by His Grace the Count of Fuensaldaña came here last week, took a fancy to some of them, bought them and returned so quickly that he only remained long enough for me to have them dispatched in my name at Customs.' Assuming a tone of wounded bewilderment at Teniers's actions, Cárdenas went on, 'I cannot tell Your Worship what the paintings are like because I did not see them. He only said to me that they were very dear, and with the haste he made to put them in the crate at his lodgings, he avoided showing me them.' Cárdenas's insinuation was clear: Teniers had bought inferior, expensive pictures and compounded his error by failing to consult the more experienced Cárdenas. Adding insult to injury, the Dutchman then left Cárdenas to dispatch the pictures using the cover of his diplomatic protection.

The ambassador then triumphantly claimed to have 'solved' the enigma surrounding Teniers' clandestine activities:

> After he had gone, I unravelled the mystery. The fact is he bought three or four of the paintings of the Duke of Pembroke and the rest of individual painters, his compatriots. He had bought them from the King's sale in order to sell them on, and as I was familiar with these paintings and he had told me that they were from the Pembroke estate, he did not see fit to show me them.[37]

According to this version of events, Teniers not only showed poor taste in pursuing Pembroke's pictures, but he also tried to deceive Cárdenas by disguising his acquisition of pictures from the royal collection, purchased via fellow Dutch painters in London. Cárdenas felt he owned exclusive rights to the royal sale and that Teniers was exploiting his London-based Dutch agents and generally undermining his own position.

To take instruction from a low-born Dutch painter must have been particularly galling for the aristocratic Cárdenas, but there was little option. Teniers was acting in the name of Cárdenas's superior, the Count of Fuensaldaña, who in turn supplied Haro and Philip with pictures. The implications were serious. Teniers could put Cárdenas out of business as a cultural emissary and damage his reputation back in Madrid. The ambassador also had good grounds to fear Teniers. He was ambitious and intelligent, with a better eye for a good picture. Teniers realized that if he could acquire some of King Charles's best paintings for his patron, Archduke Leopold-Wilhelm, his own reputation as Habsburg court painter and artistic adviser would be assured.

Much to Cárdenas's consternation, Teniers worked fast. By late November he had bought ten tapestries and over forty paintings at a cost of nearly £7,000. In just over a week he acquired more than Cárdenas had bought in over two years. Teniers went for quantity rather than quality. Many pictures came from other collections (including Pembroke's), but at least nine came from the royal collection, presumably through Teniers's connection with Flemish expatriates like Van Leemput.

Teniers understood that he was buying for the same conservative clientele that Cárdenas represented and his acquisitions reflected similar tastes: predominantly sixteenth-century Italian painting, including nine pictures by Tintoretto, eight by Veronese, five attributed to Titian and others by del Sarto, Bassano, Reni and Palma Vecchio.[38] However, the Antwerp-born Teniers also appreciated the value of works on offer from his compatriots and masters; this led him to buy eight pictures by Van Dyck, two by Rubens and one by Jan Roos. Richard Symonds recorded how Teniers and his Flemish compatriots established the value of Van Dyck's royal pictures, noting that 'in the years 1651 [and] 1652 ye things of Van Dyck were bought up by the Flemings at any rate'.[39]

As Cárdenas had feared, Teniers's negotiations with Flemish agents like Van Leemput had introduced him to the owners of more significant pictures, including an early buyer of some of the finest Titians, Colonel John Hutchinson. The colonel kept a low profile after his initial purchases from the sale, waiting for the right moment to sell his Titians. Unlike Cárdenas, Teniers was a buyer in a hurry with plenty of ready cash. By the time he left London he had paid Hutchinson £600 for the erotic *Venus and Cupid with an Organist*, for which the colonel paid just £165 in 1649.[40]

The deal was a coup for both parties. Teniers's eagerness to buy the picture was understandable. It was a Habsburg-commissioned picture, originally painted by Titian in the late 1540s as erotic entertainment for his imperial patron Charles V, moving between Venice, Augsburg and possibly even Prague before reaching Madrid.[41] Teniers appreciated the significance of taking credit for and returning the picture to the Spanish royal collection, liberating it from a godless colonel and a country ruled by the mob. For Hutchinson, the sale represented an excellent return on his investment. Unlike the trustees, the colonel understood how to manipulate the art market. Instead of selling his Titian to Cárdenas when the ambassador first entered the market, Hutchinson cleverly kept it back until Teniers appeared with less time and more money. This allowed him to quadruple his initial investment, and still keep hold of his finest Titian, the *Pardo Venus*. Cárdenas was reduced to making arrangements for the transportation of Teniers's purchases back to Spain and redoubled his own efforts to acquire pictures from the dividends. Thanks to the competition, there was a real urgency and purpose to Cárdenas's actions for the first time since he started buying in late 1649.

The ambassador responded to Teniers's raid by closing a deal on a series of the twelve Roman emperors by Titian. These were valued at £1,200 and allocated to the sixth dividend, led by Captain Stone. Cárdenas had dithered over their acquisition for two years. He listed them in one of his very first memoranda to Haro, but worried over the poor condition of six of the portraits. In November 1651 Cárdenas's agents informed him 'that nine of them' were now miraculously 'well-preserved', but unfortunately, 'one of them is by Van Dyck'. This apparent dilution of the series and the damage to two other portraits meant that, according to Cárdenas, 'this set of portraits is not highly valued by everyone'.[42] This gave him the leverage he needed to conclude one of his finest deals of the sale, buying the entire set from Stone for just over £600 – half their nominal value.

With Teniers's departure, Cárdenas was free once more to choose from the fourteen dividends' finest pictures and drive as hard a bargain as he wished. Still in search of Titians, he turned his attention to the second dividend, headed by David Murray, and its allocation of sixty-eight pictures. They included another titillating Titian, *Woman in a Fur Wrap*, brought from Madrid by Charles and valued at £100, as well as the two Dürer portraits, originally from Nuremberg. Cárdenas bought both Dürers for just £75 and the Titian for an undisclosed but presumably discounted figure.[43] The desperate creditors were in no position to refuse his cash offers, even though they halved the nominal value of particular pictures. Cárdenas also seemed to have learned a lesson from Teniers, buying both Titians previously held in the Habsburg collection and northern European portraiture by artists he previously ignored, like Dürer.

Cárdenas was seen regularly frequenting the makeshift galleries and shops established by dividend heads like de Critz in Austin Friars, haggling over the price of pictures. Richard Symonds painted a vivid picture of the cut-price deals Cárdenas was negotiating, noting that 'He has the famous Venus of Titians' bought from Hutchinson for £600, but 'for which the King was offered £2,500'. Perhaps there was an intimation of distaste here in the description of a republican selling art whose value, Symonds believed, was only appreciated by a king. Symonds certainly held the Council of State responsible for the sale of Titian's Roman emperors, claiming, 'The State gave him [Cárdenas] the 11 Caesars of Titian and ye 12th done by Van Dyck', which, he claimed, had 'cost the King £100 a piece for which he was offered 12 thousand pounds'. Although the official record suggests that the sixth dividend sold the series to Cárdenas, it is possible that official pressure was brought to bear on Stone to sell the Titians as Symonds seems to suggest.

Symonds watched Cárdenas approach the second dividend 'Of Murray ye Taylor and others' and bought '2 pieces of Titians', including the *Woman in a Fur Wrap*. He also witnessed Cárdenas's negotiations with another royal creditor that yielded one of his most impressive bargains. 'He has bought of Harrison the Woodmonger of the Kings, as many things as come to £500,' claimed Symonds, referring to Edmund Harrison, royal embroiderer, wood-monger and head of the eleventh dividend. In the first months of 1652 Cárdenas purchased at least eight masterpieces from Harrison. They included a pair of pictures by Palma of St Paul and David, *Pope Alexander* by Titian, a *Venus* by Reni, the

Allocution of the Marquis of Vasto by Titian, and the *Allegory of Peace and War* by Rubens.

It was a superb haul of magnificent pieces at a knockdown price, but there was an added poignancy to Cárdenas's acquisition of the *Allegory of Peace and War*. When Rubens completed the picture in London in 1629–30 it stood as a dramatic warning of what might happen if the Anglo-Spanish peace were to collapse. By 1652 its meaning had changed dramatically. The nightmare of violent chaos engulfing peace and order was now a political reality, but in ways that neither Rubens nor King Charles could ever have imagined. Europe was in turmoil and Minerva was in flight; Mars had triumphed. Only those like Cárdenas profited. Harrison received the painting, valued at £100, but with little interest in its relationship to wider international events, he sold it to Cárdenas for just £77.[44]

As Cárdenas continued to toil away in London, David Teniers returned to Brussels. Shortly after his arrival he painted a remarkable picture, *Gallery of the Archduke Leopold-Wilhelm*, which shows just some of Leopold-Wilhelm's vast art collection in the Coudenberg Palace. Leopold-Wilhelm stands in the middle of the scene, dressed in black, pointing to a canvas with his cane and talking to the Bishop of Ghent, another keen art collector. Further to the left are a group of Leopold-Wilhelm's art agents, examining a collection of prints and drawings spread out across a table. Next to the bishop stands the painter himself.

The paintings are exquisite renditions of some of the pictures bought from the Hamilton collection in the late 1640s. On the top row on the far left is Giorgione's *Three Philosophers*; on the third row down, second from the left, is Dosso Dossi's *St Jerome*; four along from the Dossi is Palma the Elder's *Virgin and Child with Saints*; and propped up on the floor to the right of the picture with a green drape over its corner is Raphael's famous *St Margaret*, all bought by Hamilton from the della Nave and Priuli collections in Venice and by this time in the possession of the proud archduke. Teniers's painting displayed his skill at copying the Old Masters, but it was primarily a celebration of his involvement in stripping the aristocratic art collections of England. Virtually none of Charles's pictures appear here because their public acquisition by another royal household would have been deemed insensitive. Those paintings acquired by Teniers were already on their way to Luis de Haro and the royal collection of Philip IV in Madrid.

The painting is more than just a bravura display of Teniers's ability to copy the Italian masters. It announces his skill as a buyer and dealer of paintings, vividly captured in the care taken to write the names of each painter on the pictures' frames. Today the painting looks like a scene of disinterested connoisseurship and self-conscious artistry. It is also a celebration of plunder, a shopping list delivered by the painter to his imperial client. A clue to its meaning can be found in the small equestrian statue of King Charles that stands on the table in the corner. Teniers's painting and so many others like it emerged from the relentless plunder of art that took place throughout the Thirty Years War, and which culminated in the dispersal of the great English collections of Arundel, Buckingham, Hamilton and King Charles I. The consequences of this massive redistribution of art are clear to see in Teniers's picture: the Habsburg Empire re-established itself as Europe's premier art-collecting dynasty, while the cities of the Low Countries confirmed their position as the global brokers of the seventeenth-century international art market.

❦

CHAPTER ELEVEN

WHILE STOCKS LAST

FOUR YEARS AFTER THE START of the sale of the king's art collection, one of its most expensive lots remained unsold. Andrea Mantegna's paintings of *The Triumphs of Caesar*, the subject of protracted negotiations between Daniel Nys and his Whitehall paymasters throughout 1629–30, had been bought from Mantua and hung in Hampton Court until Charles's departure from London in 1642. Seven years later the trustees valued them at a colossal £1,000.[1] They were put on public sale, but their price and poor condition deterred potential buyers, including the Spanish ambassador Cárdenas. The pictures were quietly withdrawn from the sale and reserved for the use of the state. By the spring of 1654 they adorned the chambers of the new ruler of England and part-time resident of Hampton Court: not a king, but the Lord Protector, Oliver Cromwell.[2]

Since the collapse of Charles II's military challenge to the new Commonwealth in the autumn of 1651, Cromwell had increasingly urged the Rump to 'proceed vigorously in reforming what was amiss in government, and to the settling of the Commonwealth upon a foundation of justice and righteousness'.[3] Over a year spent campaigning with his politically committed and fervently Puritan soldiers had convinced Cromwell that the Rump was unable or unprepared to deliver justice on his terms. With typical self-righteousness, he condemned the members for 'their delays of business, and designs to perpetuate themselves, and to continue the power in their own hands'.[4] In the spring of 1653 the Rump finally agreed to reform the increasingly moribund ruling executive and hold elections, the first for over a decade. However, unhappy at the restrictions placed on the voting, Cromwell dramatically marched into the House of Commons to dissolve Parliament in

April 1653.[5] The resulting Barebones Parliament also failed to live up to Cromwell's radical expectations and its perhaps inevitable collapse in the winter of 1653 effectively placed executive power directly in his hands. The army hastily drew up a new Instrument of Government, appointing Cromwell Lord Protector for life, ruling through a Council of State and Parliament, over which he held the power of assembly and dissolution – just like King Charles I. On 16 December 1653 Cromwell was sworn in at a solemn ceremony held in Westminster Hall as 'Lord Protector of the Commonwealth of England, Scotland and Ireland'.

While the creation of the Lord Protectorate effectively signalled the end of republican rule in England, it did not necessarily mean that Cromwell wanted to be crowned king of England. The year before his appointment as Lord Protector his friend Bulstrode Whitelocke reported that Cromwell asked him, 'What if a man should take upon him to be king?'[6] Whitelocke dismissed the idea, but Cromwell remained notoriously ambivalent on the matter, providing a series of contradictory statements on the possibility of his accepting the crown. Although many people were happy to see the back of King Charles, they still recognized and respected the ceremonies and customs associated with his office. Exhibiting a mixture of pragmatism, idealism and authoritarianism, Cromwell and his advisers realized that to survive they needed to appropriate the iconography of monarchy.[7] This did not necessarily mean an increase in expenditure, and it would be simplistic to accuse Cromwell of hypocrisy in assuming the luxury of royal authority. It was a strategic decision – and one that limited the amount spent on the protectoral household, which Parliament set at £64,000 a year, rising to £100,000 by 1657. This compared favourably with the upkeep of the royal household in the 1630s, estimated at approximately £250,000 a year, set against annual revenue of around £600,000. By contrast, the Commonwealth was operating on annual revenue of just under £2 million.[8]

Within days of Cromwell's assumption of the title of Lord Protector, arrangements were being made to provide him with the trappings of royal power. His portrait hung in the Royal Exchange, alongside the kings of England and also the decapitated statue of King Charles I seen by John Gibson in 1650.[9] A week after his accession in December 1653, it was reported that 'Whitehall is being prepared for his Highness to reside in',[10] and in the spring of the following year over £35,000 worth of furniture and works of art were allocated to Cromwell's two royal residences, Whitehall and Hampton Court, the latter where he stayed at weekends.[11] However, the number of goods withdrawn from the public sale by the trustees for the state's use caused rising public resentment. The removal of such a large quantity in the Protector's name was the biggest single redistributive act concerning the late king's goods – one which, bizarrely, involved everything remaining almost exactly where it was.

If Cromwell knew how to manipulate the symbols of the old regime that he had helped to destroy, he also appreciated the political damage the discredited sale was causing the Commonwealth. In January 1654, by refusing to allow the trustees to dispose of further goods, he finally brought the sale of the late king's goods to a characteristically discordant and confused end.[12] Those who profited from the sale quickly allied themselves with the new political dispensation, including John Embree, the dead king's Serjeant Plumber. Embree had been one of the largest creditors on the First List, published in 1651. Still in possession of a small but exquisite collection of Titians, Van Dycks and Bassanos, he was appointed Surveyor of Works to the Commonwealth in April 1653 on £300 a year. His responsibilities included the upkeep of Whitehall and Hampton Court. The day Cromwell took up residence in Whitehall in April 1654 Embree was paid £500 for repairs to the palace, claiming a further £1,200 just three months later.[13]

While Embree looked after the exteriors, Clement Kinnersley, Charles's former Yeoman of the King's Wardrobe and official contractor to the sale, was given the responsibility of requisitioning and maintaining the state's art collection. Just weeks after the sale's collapse in January 1654, Kinnersley manoeuvred himself into the more lucrative post of Wardrobe Keeper to the Protector. The position was in many ways an extension of his role as contractor, but bereft of the Rump's byzantine bureaucracy. Kinnersley was required to reserve and requisition pictures, statues, tapestries and furniture deemed suitable for the protectoral palaces, under the watchful eye of Sir Gilbert Pickering, member of the Council of State, director of the Mortlake tapestry factory and, since 1649, a member of the committee charged with the task of reserving goods for the state.

Tapestries valued at over £33,000 made up the vast bulk of the £35,497 16s 6d of furniture and works of art withdrawn from the sale and allocated to the protectoral residences.[14] This was the quickest way of establishing majestic splendour on a grand scale, which is what Cromwell and his advisers required. The Protectorate's decision to reserve tapestry rather than painting may have been a conservative choice, but it ensured that most of the royal collection's hangings remained in London, where they are to this day. The relative indifference towards pictures meant that very few were set aside. Instead many were sold off to private buyers and subsequently lost, or scattered across the private collections of Europe. Cromwell was not an iconoclastic 'hater of images',[15] as the royalists claimed. It was aesthetic indifference which prompted the dispersal of royal pictures under the Protectorate.

As the new ruler was repeatedly compared to biblical figures like David, Joshua, Gideon and Moses, care was taken to ensure that most of the tapestries reserved for Cromwell's use represented biblical scenes, many of which adorned his Hampton Court bedchamber. They included particularly expensive sets portraying the lives of Abraham, Joshua, Tobias and St Paul, some valued at as much as £8,000, as well as cheaper, smaller pieces portraying David, Samson, Samuel, Lazarus and the Seven Deadly Sins.[16] In May 1653, as Kinnersley took possession of a variety of tapestries including two pieces representing Joseph and the Pharaohs for just £5 17s, John Spittlehouse's *A Warning Piece Discharged* (May 1653) set out to 'compare our present General [Cromwell] to Moses', who 'has taken us from the power of our Egyptian Pharaoh [King Charles], and from the iron furnace of tyranny' into the Promised Land of the Protectorate.[17]

Paintings absorbed only a fraction of the £35,000 allocated to the protectoral renovations. Fewer than thirty pictures, valued at less than £2,000, were reserved for Cromwell's use. The unusual and often anonymous choice of painters and subject matter suggests that the Protectorate was generally indifferent to the style or significance of pictures. At this late stage of the sale, choice was clearly limited, as most of the finest paintings were either sold to private buyers or in the hands of creditors on the Second List. Nevertheless, little attempt was made to assemble an art collection consonant with the authority of a ruling head of state.

The Protectorate also showed little interest in obtaining pictures by established masters. There were works by Italian, Dutch and French painters – Del Sarto, Porcellis, Van Somer, Pordenone – although many of the reserved pictures had no attribution at all, suggesting they were chosen for their subject matter, not their artistic provenance. Pictures chosen included anonymous landscapes, shepherds and paintings of *A Madonna with Many Angels* (£20) and *Mary Ascension with the Apostles* (£10).[18] The latter is now entitled *The Assumption of the Virgin* and attributed to the Italian painter Luca Cambiaso, an employee of King Philip II who worked on the decoration of the Escorial in Madrid. Charles had acquired the painting from Mantua and it hung in Nonsuch Palace throughout the 1630s, where van der Doort described it as representing 'Our Lady in the clouds below a sepulchre full of flowers and the disciples kneeling about it'.[19] The reservation of such explicitly Catholic iconography for a resolutely Protestant ruler like Cromwell may seem surprising. However, Cromwell held no particular emotional, intellectual or financial investment in painting. There is no direct evidence that he made any personal choices from the reserved goods. Instead he seems to have left such matters to the more artistically experienced Pickering and Kinnersley. As a result, the subject matter or provenance of particular paintings appears to have been a matter of indifference to the Lord Protector.

Even Raphael's cartoons of *The Acts of the Apostles* were reserved in Whitehall primarily as designs for tapestries rather than as valuable paintings. Mantegna's *Triumphs of Caesar*, however, were displayed by Pickering and Kinnersley in the Long Gallery in Hampton Court to magnify the Lord Protector's own claims to political authority, which were still far from assured. Mantegna originally designed the series for the Gonzaga dynasty in the 1480s as a cheap alternative to woven tapestries. At over eight feet high and nine feet wide, each canvas was specifically designed to mimic the style and display of a monumental tapestry cycle, but at a fraction of the price. Pickering and Kinnersley were both experts in tapestry, holding key positions in the Mortlake tapestry factory and the royal wardrobe. As a result they both regarded pictures like Mantegna's as poor man's tapestry rather than what they really were: one of the greatest series of paintings of the Italian Renaissance. It was only for this reason, and their poor state of repair, as observed by Cárdenas, that the paintings were not sold off to one of the dividends.

The abiding power and achievement of Mantegna's paintings reside in their profoundly ambivalent portrayal of imperial power. The nine pictures represent Julius Caesar's triumphant entry into Rome following his success in the Gallic Wars. Each canvas parades a procession of soldiers, trumpeters and standard bearers, some leading humiliated captives alongside the cultural trophies of coin and plate looted from the wars. The final canvas portrays Caesar in his chariot, framed against a Roman triumphal arch, crowned by Victory with the laurel of military conquest. Mantegna's *Triumphs* provided a quintessentially Renaissance vision, drawing on the classical imperial past to validate the political and intellectual ambitions of aspirant Italian dynasties like the Gonzaga of Mantua. On closer inspection, Mantegna's paintings subtly question and subvert this imperial ideal through scenes of desolation, despoliation and melancholia. Soldiers march lost in thought, looking at the ground, exhausted from their labour, while the defeated are humbled and humiliated. With the bathetic appearance of Caesar in the final canvas, the paintings seem to ask if all the death and destruction were worth the glorification of this one overreaching individual.

Did Cromwell identify with Caesar when he strode past these pictures? His extraordinary military record throughout the 1640s and early 1650s meant that he could, with considerably more justification than Charles I, compare himself with Rome's greatest general. Contemporary poets seemed to agree. Marchamont Nedham claimed Cromwell was even greater than Caesar, exclaiming, 'Let the barbarian greatness of Caesar be silent,' because by 1654 'One greater than Caesar is present.'[20] Edmund Waller's sycophantic 'Panegyric to my Lord Protector' (1655)

went further, comparing Cromwell to Julius Caesar's imperial
successor, Augustus:

> As the vexed world, to find repose at last
> Itself into Augustus' arms did cast;
> So England now does, with like toil oppressed,
> Her weary head upon your bosom rest.[21]

Perhaps both poets saw the Mantegna canvases and grasped
their significance for Cromwell. Perhaps the Lord Protector lin-
gered over Mantegna's final scene himself, where the imperial
laurel hovers above Caesar's head. In March 1657 Parliament
presented Cromwell with the Humble Petition and Advice, a new
written constitution offering him the title of king. Like Caesar,
Cromwell spent several weeks agonizing over the offer, much to
the anger of die-hard republicans and army leaders like John
Lambert. Although Cromwell finally rejected the offer, his reign as
Lord Protector was running out of steam. He was as committed as
ever to the need for parliamentary reform and liberty of conscience
in religion, but his single-minded vision increasingly alienated both
radicals and conservatives. As Lord Protector he had taken the
country into an unpopular war with Spain and lost the backing of
many of his supporters in the army, including Lambert, who
refused to swear an oath of allegiance to his old friend.

Others turned to biblical analogies to combat what they saw as
Cromwell's shifting political position and his supposed seductions
by classical, 'pagan' icons. The Puritan Mary Netheway wrote to
Cromwell condemning the statues of Venus, Adonis, Apollo and
Cleopatra from Mantua erected at Hampton Court as 'monsters
which are set up as ornaments in the privy garden'. She begged
him to destroy the statues, 'for whilst they stand, though you see
no evil in them, yet there is much evil in it, for whilst the groves
and altars of the idols remained untaken away in Jerusalem, the
wrath of God continued against Israel'.[22] At the opening of his first
Protectorate Parliament in September 1654, Cromwell had compared the nation to the Israelites, who 'through unbelief, murmur-
ing, repining, and other temptations and sins' were still a long way
from the Promised Land.[23] Godly reformers like Mary Netheway
reminded the Lord Protector of the dangers of combining political

power with religious iconography – but this was a problem already experienced by Cromwell's predecessor, King Charles.

IN EARLY 1652, when the sale had already seemed to be on the verge of dissolution, few could have imagined it would last months, let alone years. The distribution of goods allocated to the fourteen dividends removed what remained of any significant value from the open sale at Somerset House, effectively bringing its public dimension to an end. The trustees continued to disburse goods and cash in settlement of debts on a small scale, but by this stage most deals were negotiated on the secondary market between private buyers and the heads of the dividends, or behind the closed doors of meetings between the trustees and contractors. Even Don Alonso de Cárdenas temporarily refrained from buying pictures. The sale records reveal that from January to December 1652 there were just six official cash purchases from largely unknown creditors and minor political functionaries that totalled a paltry £578.[24]

The public sale's collapse was initially due to the distribution of goods among the various dividends, but changing political circumstances also played their part. In October 1651 the passage of the Navigation Act reignited perennial Anglo-Dutch commercial rivalries. The act forbade the importation of goods except those carried in English ships or vessels belonging to the country where the goods were manufactured.[25] Over the next few months diplomatic tensions rose and commercial confidence waned as conflict loomed. Repeated naval skirmishes in the channel finally led to the outbreak of war in May 1652. The subsequent financial strain led the Rump to investigate avenues for reducing their expenditure.[26] With the sale bringing in negligible funds, Parliament quickly lost interest in it.

The public were already venting their anger at the Rump's continued refusal to institute domestic reforms and in particular the settlement of the claims of the king's debtors. One of the Rump's strongest critics was Colonel Thomas Pride, whose troops initially oversaw the creation of the Rump during Pride's Purge in 1648. Pride and his radical friend Samuel Chidley attacked Parliament for its inaction over the state's creditors.[27] Others turned to parody and ridicule to express their anger. J. B. Gent's *A Faire in Spittle Fields*, published in April 1652, satirized Parliament as being full of charlatans and necromancers, conjuring up the sale and making empty promises of public gain:

> . . . their predictions fail'd;
> Their tales prov'd fables, and the people rail'd
> Against these Jugglers, whose prevarications
> Had fill'd their minds with such vain expectations.[28]

Farce and dissimulation quickly accompanied satire and scorn. Con artists sprang up throughout London, importuning people for money on behalf of the creditors. In May the newsbook *Mercurius Democritus* warned the public, 'There is this week a new sect of old counterfeit knaves discovered, they are called Weepers, and have cheated many charitable persons under pretence of begging for the late king's servants and others that have been in prison and want.'[29] Absorbed in the war with the Dutch, the Rump continued to ignore such complaints.

With little left to sell and hardly any incoming revenue, the sale's trustees turned to the exploitation of one of the more controversial clauses in the act passed in July 1651 – 'discoveries'. The original terms of the act allowed creditors to report the discovery of royal goods and claim a percentage of their value. However, the failure to put in place any mechanisms to verify the royal provenance of 'discovered' goods meant that shrewder creditors could make claims against known royalists motivated by financial gain rather than the Commonwealth's greater good. 'The prosecution of discoveries', as one pamphleteer noted, would lead to 'many reproaches, scandals, clamours, disobligations, and vexations' over the next two years.[30]

Throughout 1652 the treasurers recorded a series of discoveries made against those allegedly harbouring former royal possessions. The majority of the claimants were heads of dividends or sale officials, and included Bass, Houghton, de Critz, Jackson and Kinnersley. Edward Bass was particularly quick to exploit the profitable possibilities of discoveries. Head of three dividends, he was already involved in selling artworks to Cárdenas and owned the jewel of the royal collection, Raphael's *Holy Family*. He soon learned from the trustees' mistakes and held on to his pictures in the hope of their subsequent appreciation in value. In the mean-time he pursued the more immediate satisfaction of claiming discoveries. In early November he 'discovered' a total of £154 8s 11d worth of 'diverse' items, including 'goods from Inigo Jones' valued at £21. It was a cynically opportunistic claim to make against the royalist architect, now poor and old, and apparently under scrutiny at the time from parliamentary supporters. Jones surrendered two insignificant pictures and one cheap brass figure just two days after Bass's claim. It was a poor return on a life-time's royal service, but Bass showed little mercy in making a claim that presumably left Jones with a fine to pay. Nevertheless, treasurers Hunt and Jones accepted Bass's claim and paid him £77 4s 5d.[31] Eight months later Jones died in his room in Somerset House, having watched much of the collection he was involved in amassing sold off around him in the last two years of his life.

Bass proceeded to form another consortium of creditors in pursuit of more lucrative discoveries. On 20 January, along with Robert Houghton, head of the fifth dividend and Cárdenas's agent, Bass made a claim for the discovery of royal plate valued at £981 4s 2d in the possession of one of the sale's most senior figures, Sir Henry Mildmay. Formerly Keeper of King Charles's Jewel House, Mildmay proved one of the more surprising, and many believed opportunistic, converts to the republican cause. He sat in judgement on the king during his trial, emerging as an enthusiastically militant member of both the Council of State and the Committee for the Reservation of Royal Goods.[32] Mildmay's position in the former royal household presented him with one of the most sensitive and lucrative roles in the entire sale – valuing the royal plate and jewels. His inventory of the goods in the upper jewel house of the Tower of London, which included the king's crown, valued at £1,110, came to £6,771.[33] His involvement in its dismantling and sale earned him the nickname 'Knave of Diamonds', as well as satirical denunciation in John Crouch's lampoon of the sale, *New Market Fayre*.[34] However, in November 1651 Mildmay was voted off the Council, leaving him politically exposed and vulnerable to charges of opportunism, corruption – and withholding the king's possessions.[35]

Just ten days after this first allegation in January, Mildmay faced yet another, this time from a different consortium claiming the discovery of £820 worth of royal plate in the former councillor's possession.[36] This brought the total value of plate allegedly concealed by Mildmay to a staggering £1,800 – nearly half of the final amount of £3,926 raised from all recorded discoveries.[37] That the treasurers promptly paid out on both discoveries suggests that the claims were legitimate; even Mildmay's brother Anthony signed the receipt authorizing settlement of the discovery. Mildmay was required to pay what must have been a crippling fine, equal to the value of the concealed plate, while Bass and Houghton received £490 for their first claim, another handsome reward on top of the substantial profits both men made selling paintings and tapestries to Alonso de Cárdenas.

The lucrative rewards of discoveries partly explain Cárdenas's puzzling withdrawal from the market in paintings throughout 1652. Apart from his acquisition of eight paintings from Harrison in the spring, he did not buy another picture until a year later. Unfortunately his letters to Haro between 1652 and 1653 have not survived. However, the actions of Bass and Houghton suggest that his sudden withdrawal was not from want of trying. Most of the finest pictures from the public sale were now in the hands of prosperous heads of dividends with little need to sell immediately at a discounted price in a buyers' market. Many were making money on discoveries and appreciated the importance of holding on to their pictures until economic conditions improved or Cárdenas' monopoly was broken by the appearance of rival buyers. Withholding their prized possessions proved an astute decision. In December 1652 competition duly arrived in the shape of Antoine de Bordeaux-Neufville, French ambassador to England.

Bordeaux arrived with the delicate task of officially recognizing the new republican regime and resolving a rapidly escalating seaborne conflict between England and France. Just two months earlier General Robert Blake had attacked and captured a French flotilla in the Channel attempting to relieve the Spanish siege of

Dunkirk. France was outraged, but the Rump demanded formal recognition of the Commonwealth before it considered returning the vessels. Bordeaux's predicament was compounded by the politically weakened state of the French royal family. France was not only harbouring Henrietta Maria and her eldest son, Charles, but also engulfed in its own civil war.[38] Just days before the execution of King Charles in London in January 1649, the French queen regent, Anne of Austria, and her son, the future King Louis XIV, fled Paris after increasingly violent clashes with the French Parlement. For the next four years Anne and Louis battled to assert their control over a range of competing factions.

Cardinal Jules Mazarin, Anne's leading minister, successfully resisted calls from royalists on both sides of the Channel to declare war on the Commonwealth, while also skilfully frustrating attempts by English republicans to support the more militant French anti-monarchical factions. However, trying to juggle a civil war, maritime conflict with England and war with Spain proved too much for even the skilful Mazarin. In agreeing to dispatch Bordeaux to recognize the English Commonwealth, the shrewd, art-loving cardinal soon realized that he could turn this potentially humiliating embassy into a chance to capitalize on the final stages of the dispersal of the late king's art collection.

Throughout the winter of 1652–3 Bordeaux and Cárdenas were too occupied with vying for the Rump's political favour to worry about art. Both realized that an English decision to side with one could spell political disaster for the other.[39] Unfortunately there was little time for the Rump to enjoy the success of its aggressive foreign policy. War with the Dutch was going badly and there were further calls for an investigation into the proceedings of the sale of the king's goods. On 25 January 1653 Parliament finally acted. It established a committee to 'examine the abuses and misdemeanours of any Trustees, Contractors, or other Officers or Clerks, to any committee of Parliament, or any other under the Parliament, in taking any bribes, rewards or fees, not allowed unto them; and to report the same to the House'.[40]

Investigating allegations of corruption within the labyrinthine accounting practices of the sale's officers was a commendable act, but by this stage it was too little too late. The sale required comprehensive reform of its structure and practices. However, by now most of the goods were in the hands of private owners. Blaming individuals was pointless, but this is precisely what the Rump did. It identified a scapegoat among the minor sale officials, resolving 'to examine the business touching the charge of corruption against Mr. Beauchamp, Clerk to the Trustees for sale of the late king's goods'.[41]

In his capacity as clerk-register, Thomas Beauchamp spent over three years painstakingly transcribing and circulating the royal inventories. He received a meagre and irregular portion of the seven shillings in every pound of royal goods sold allocated to the trustees' officers. Like many of the trustees and contractors, he supplemented his paltry earnings by speculating on the fringes of the sale, but his purchases were painfully modest. They included seven paintings at the lowest end of the market – a copy after Caravaggio for £4, a still life by the Spanish painter Labrador, and a surviving *Virgin Mary* taken from Somerset House chapel, his most expensive acquisition for £21. Beauchamp was more interested in the domestic detritus of the king's household – carpets, cheap tapestries, linen, cabinets and tables. He bought one bed, a pile of stone from Scotland Yard, £100 worth of brass kitchen utensils (including pots, pans, spits and spoons), a £10 organ and five pairs of stag's antlers at 5s a pair.[42]

Beauchamp was not a connoisseur – he obviously lacked the education and income to invest in grander paintings. Even so, he appreciated the modest but guaranteed profit of investing in staple items (beds, pots and pans) as opposed to the riskier acquisition of pictures. However, none of his behaviour was technically fraudulent. Many sale officials spent substantial amounts on a variety of royal goods. So who accused Beauchamp of corruption? The records remain frustratingly silent. Perhaps he was a central player in a carefully organized group of buyers and dealers, taking money to reduce the valuations and sell goods at a reduced price, but the scrupulously annotated inventories, as well as the sales throughout 1652, provide few clues. The evidence suggests that Beauchamp was another victim of 'discoveries', like his superior Sir Henry Mildmay, under investigation for withholding royal goods at the same time as Beauchamp's arraignment for corruption. Throughout 1652 Beauchamp was involved in consortia claiming discoveries against the estates of royalists including the earls of Holland and Dorset. The syndicate demanding £537 of Dorset's goods included Bass, Houghton and another avid hunter of discoveries, the regicide and parliamentary finance commissioner Cornelius Holland.[43] Beauchamp acted as assignee for other members of the consortium, taking his percentage of the moneys claimed from his superiors, the treasurers Humphrey Jones and John Hunt. In the midst of this complicated insider trading, Beauchamp could have put a foot wrong. Perhaps he took a larger percentage than agreed, or alienated one of the more powerful members of the consortium.

There is one further possibility. Beauchamp apparently remained loyal to the royalist cause, despite profiting from aristocratic 'discoveries'. It is possible that a more hard-line member of the sale team doubted his political commitment, but considering the atmosphere of the period, it is equally likely to have been an obscure squabble over money. Whatever the real reason behind the accusation, like many attempts to address the sale's limitations, it soon petered out. No action was taken against Beauchamp and he continued his active involvement in the sale.

As the sting went out of the accusations against Beauchamp, Antoine de Bordeaux made his first moves on the royal collection. By March 1653 he reached deals on all of Mazarin's diplomatic initiatives – recognition of the Commonwealth, negotiations for a lasting peace and the restoration of Anglo-French trade. He now turned to satisfying Mazarin's other great passion: collecting. Like Cárdenas, Bordeaux realized that his diplomatic posting provided him with an excellent prospect of satisfying both the political and the aesthetic demands of his superior. But by the time he arrived in London, the art market had changed dramatically. The public sale was effectively over, buyers were dealing with private owners and prices were on the rise. To make matters worse, having competed with his Spanish rival Cárdenas for English diplomatic approval, Bordeaux now faced the prospect of fighting with the Spaniard over what remained of the royal art collection.

Mazarin's first written instructions were to purchase English horses and tapestries. However, there were few decent tapestries left in the public sale, and Bordeaux confessed there was 'no great likelihood of finding fine tapestries here, nor cheaply', although he promised to enquire as requested about tapestries portraying the *History of David*. He could only recommend 'a Flemish hanging of sixty ells, done in silk, very fine', of a riding school based on Rubens cartoons, but this was already in the private hands of dividend holders, who valued it at a staggering £10,000.[44] Ever the diplomat, Bordeaux pointed out to Mazarin that 'if however trade were to be re-established, as seems very likely, this might fall by a third, which is why there would be advantage in delaying the purchase'. Bordeaux understood that a trade agreement between the two countries was crucial for the successful acquisition of cheap, top-quality art, especially now that the dividends were inflating their prices.

There was better news on the *History of David* series. Bordeaux obtained five *David* tapestries 'from the hands of an officer to whom they had been given in payment by Parliament'. The seller was William Latham, former royal draper and head of the fourth dividend, who took possession of 'five pieces of arras hangings of King David', valued at £994, in October 1651.[45] Bordeaux omitted to mention the cost of the tapestries, but by 1661 an inventory of Mazarin's art collection valued them at an incredible £12,000.

Bordeaux concluded his report on their acquisition by recommending to Mazarin that 'If your Eminence should think fit to send me a letter of compliments for Mr Cromwell it might have some effect'[46] in swiftly expediting the purchase and safe passage of the tapestries. It was a characteristically shrewd and prescient suggestion. Less than four weeks later, on 20 April 1653, Cromwell marched into the House of Commons with an armed troop to denounce Parliament and proclaim its immediate dissolution.[47] The move delighted Bordeaux. Cromwell was a pragmatist who supported the resumption of peace and unrestricted trade with France, both of which now seemed a distinct possibility. The royal creditors also expected much of Cromwell. Both were exasperated at the Rump's failure to institute wide-ranging financial and civic reform, and the creditors' now hoped for speedy redress from Cromwell's interim ruling council.

Just three days after the dissolution of the Rump, one of its

most vociferous critics published a pamphlet calling for the immediate disbursement of the creditors' outstanding claims. Samuel
Chidley's *A Remonstrance to the Valiant and Well Deserving Soldier, and to
the rest of the Creditors of the Commonwealth* called on the new regime
to provide 'free and speedy passage'[48] for an act to settle the
creditors' outstanding financial claims. Chidley invoked the emotive issue of the sacrifices made during the Civil War: 'many of the
said Creditors have ventured their lives; many of them lost their
blood'. Having 'panted a long time for justice . . . concerning the
monies due unto many of them', the Rump's dissolution now
offered an opportunity for financial redress. According to Chidley,
this 'sudden change will work a more speedy settlement of security,
and general satisfaction to all the good people of England'.[49] He
reserved his most ferocious language for the Rump's councillors:

> No truth or constancy was found in them; for amongst 30 or
> 40 Orders gotten with much ado, from them, for the Public
> faith, they kept but a tenth part of them; and those three or
> four which they observed were altogether ineffectual by their
> dilatory proceedings, clothing justice with sack-cloth, and
> turning judgment to wormwood and gall.[50]

Chidley railed against 'corrupt Lawyers, and other mercenary
self seekers' within Parliament, arguing that the Rump's unpopularity stemmed from what he saw as corruption. The failure to
settle the creditors' debts led him to mutter darkly 'the chambers
of the world are hang'd with discontent'.[51] It was a telling image
of the fate of the sale and its pictures. Instead of bringing prosperity
and unity, for most people the sale produced only frustration
and discord. According to Chidley, Cromwell was the sole figure
capable of resolving the situation. At the end of the *Remonstrance*,
he 'wished for some man, like Job, who sat as a King in the Army
. . . to relieve the fatherless'. This man was Cromwell, the saviour
of the state and its creditors, but, as Chidley warned, 'his is the
Nation's expectation'.[52]

Others also expected much of Cromwell. On 23 May an
anonymous pamphlet, *A Remonstrance Manifesting the Lamentable Miseries of the Creditors and Servants of the Late King, Queen, & Prince*, called

on the new regime to settle the creditors' debts on the terms stipulated in the original act of June 1649:

> ... the survivors, with the widows and orphans of the rest deceased, have just cause to hope, that his Excellency the Lord Gen. Cromwell, Major. Gen. Harrison, and others, who were instrumental in procuring the said Act, will likewise in all reason, equity, and compassion see it fulfilled; seeing God hath given them power, authority, and opportunity to do many such just, and needful acts, for preventing the ruin of hundreds of poor families.[53]

The *Remonstrance* held the Rump to blame for what it saw as 'the great injustice, tedious delays, and unexpected obstructions' experienced by the creditors. Understandably, the consequences of the Second Act of July 1651 came in for particularly scathing criticism. The *Remonstrance* condemned the act's exclusion of hundreds of deserving creditors and its withdrawal of royal goods for its own use worth thousands of pounds, leaving those creditors eligible for disbursements with 'but the one half of their said debts'. More seriously the pamphlet alleged that unnamed figures 'have taken from the use of the said Creditors and Servants £2,800 in ready money, and about £40,000 worth of the best of the goods'.[54] Such claims bear little relationship to the final accounts, but that they were made at all reveals the suspicion and hostility with which the sale was regarded in its last few months and also throws some doubt on the veracity of its final accounting practices.

Cárdenas and Bordeaux's correspondence verified one allegation – the sale of artworks that never reached their buyers. The *Remonstrance* defined these as 'goods which are not reserved, but sold to the Creditors, which as yet they cannot receive, as the Statues in Whitehall garden, hangings, &c in use at the Parliament house, for the entertainment of Ambassadors'.[55] The implication was that tapestries, statues and pictures allocated to creditors were retained by the state for both ceremonial diplomatic display and, as far as the Spanish and French ambassadors were concerned, bids from outside interests.

The pamphlet's recommendations made yet another attempt

to settle the creditors' financial plight. They included the immediate sale of the remaining reserved goods, a further disbursement
of merchandise to those excluded from the Second List and the
enlargement of the trustees' power to make discoveries of royal
goods. The recommendations were hardly original and in many
instances threatened to reproduce or even magnify established
problems, but they reflected the desire of the sale's officials to
deflect public criticism of their actions and seek the favour of the
new political dispensation.

These disputes between Whitehall and its officials made little
impact on Bordeaux and Cárdenas. As the trustees struggled for
political survival, the ambassadors moved in on the dividends'
pictures. While Bordeaux may have gained the diplomatic upper
hand over Cárdenas, he now confronted the daunting prospect of
outbidding the vastly more experienced Spaniard in the acquisition
of art. He also faced tough negotiations with private owners who,
unlike the trustees, had a vested interest in obtaining the highest
possible price from their pictures and statues.

Bordeaux unwisely started with two of the most expensive
paintings on offer. Cárdenas was already after both of them. On
5 May the Frenchman informed Mazarin, 'There are two very
beautiful paintings; one, by Raphael, is a *Virgin Mary*' for which
'on an earlier occasion the Spanish ambassador attempted to pay
£12,000; at present it will scarcely cost £10,000'.[56] The naive
ambassador was being hoodwinked. Edward Bass and his tenth
dividend received the Raphael, valued at £2,000, in October
1651. Cárdenas was then offered the picture for £2,250 following its initial reduction from £3,000, but thought it too expensive
and declined. The scheming Bass was now exploiting the arrival
of a new buyer with no experience of the original public sale and
its valuations. To Bordeaux the price was five times the original
valuation, including a bogus 'discount' of £2,000.

Bordeaux fared no better in his appraisal of the second picture,
'a Correggio, larger, very well preserved, which shows a Satyr
uncovering a woman, for which they are asking £6,000. They
refused my offer of £4,000 when I first arrived in the country.'[57]
This time it was David Murray, head of the second dividend and
recipient of the Correggio, who showed no mercy. Having received

the picture in 1651, valued at £1,000, he now marked it at six times the original price. He even felt confident enough to reject Bordeaux's initial offer of £4,000.

At this point Cárdenas realized the need to move quickly, before prices rocketed and Bordeaux appreciated what was happening and learned to manipulate the dividends. For over three years Cárdenas had watched the movement of three of the finest pictures in the royal collection. Finally, in August, using all his negotiating skills and local knowledge, he concluded a series of deals with the dividends for all of them. He bought Correggio's *Education of Cupid* from the eighth dividend of Thomas Bagley and George Green for just £400 – exactly half its original sale valuation.[58] He then paid another £400 for a Raphael *Madonna*, despite dismissing it three years earlier when viewing it at Somerset House as 'pleasing to few, nor is it considered to be worth the price placed upon it'.[59] As the finest pictures began to disappear, Cárdenas hastily revised his opinion of the Raphael. He apologized to Haro that his initial inspection of the picture was obscured because 'it was hanging high up and was covered in dust and I couldn't examine it with the care that I did when I came to buy it',[60] an echo of Lodewijck Huygens's own complaint about the sale's poor conditions. Cárdenas bought the painting from Robert Houghton's third dividend, which received it in lieu of goods worth £800.[61] Houghton's only possible reason for letting the picture go so cheaply was that he was still in Cárdenas's pay, having brokered the ambassador's acquisition of the *Acts of the Apostles* in October 1650.

But without doubt Cárdenas's finest coup was the acquisition of Raphael's *Holy Family*. In a letter to Haro dated 11 August, he proudly announced, 'Thanks be to God, I have also bought the large Raphael painting of Our Lady, Her Son, St John and St Anne, life-size, and St Joseph, in small, in perspective, that was valued at 8000 *escudos* [£2,000].' To his delight, Cárdenas announced, 'I have it now for 4000 [£1,000], which is half.' This was also a fraction of the figure Bordeaux claimed to have offered Bass for the painting. To buy the jewel of the collection at half its original valuation in the face of competition was a magnificent achievement and Cárdenas knew it. He talked up the picture's beauty and importance, while also acknowledging that its rarity stemmed from its place at the heart of the dead king's collection. 'This is held to be the best in Europe today' he claimed, 'and is renowned amongst the painters the finest painting in the world; there is no doubt that there is no equal to it in the works of King Charles.'[62]

Only the accumulated experience of three years' dealing with (and paying off) various members of the dividends allowed Cárdenas to negotiate such reductions and close such impressive deals. Although he bought sparingly over the years, he always optimized the timing of his acquisitions to coincide with a weakness in the market. By August 1653 he exploited one of the dividends' patent dilemmas: did they hold out for higher offers from other buyers or assuage the demands of their members and accept cash deals lower than their pictures' nominal value? Cárdenas guessed correctly, gambling that the dividends needed cash.

However, private owners had no need to refer bids to a consortium and drove a much harder bargain. Cárdenas tried and failed to obtain a reduction on a pair of Mantegnas from the shrewd Jan Baptist Gaspars. The ambassador reported that Gaspars wisely bought Mantegna's *Death of the Virgin* and *Virgin and Child with Saints* before the announcement of the dividends, and 'paid a proper price for them, and so not only gave less than the asking price but wanted to make a small profit' on his investment of £17 10s. If Haro wanted the pictures, Cárdenas admitted, 'I could try and get them for the best possible price', but he clearly knew that Gaspars would drive a hard bargain. And so he did. Eventually Cárdenas agreed to pay £105 for the Mantegnas, a huge profit for Gaspars but a significant acquisition for the ambassador.[63] He also acknowledged the growing rivalry with Bordeaux, who was also bidding for Correggios. Cárdenas reported, 'I am trying to buy Venus, Cupid and Mercury, which is not as irreverent as the other, Venus Asleep and the Satyr', which would eventually go to his French rival. Even the Spaniard had to admit that, although this was 'an irreverent painting, it is still a piece of great art worth for the delicacy and art with which it is painted'. However, Cárdenas sensed that time was running out. He counselled Haro, 'There are few of the king's pictures that are left here and there are more buyers than there used to be and so it is necessary for Your Excellency to make a rapid decision about whether to buy.'[64]

Cárdenas lost no time in utilizing his parliamentary connections to dispose of his impressive haul as quickly as possible. Towards the end of August the parliamentary Commissioners of Customs granted Cárdenas a warrant allowing him to export duty-free 'twenty-four chests with paintings, tapestries and other furnishings' acquired over the past two years.[65] This was the fourth and final consignment of artworks dispatched from London to Madrid. It was the culmination of Cárdenas's extraordinary four-year relationship with the sale of King Charles's art collection, and for most of the pictures and tapestries involved, it represented the final voyage in their already chequered and much-travelled history.

As Cárdenas predicted, the market was overheating, primarily due to Bordeaux's initially naive forays into the art market. Unlike Cárdenas, he possessed few contacts in the London art world and had very little grasp of its protocol. By offering excessive prices from the very beginning, he created a sellers' market, encouraging the dividends to hike their prices and play him off against Cárdenas. In the autumn of 1653, as prices rose and the quality of pictures fell, Cárdenas prepared to withdraw from the sale he had dominated for nearly four years.

CHAPTER TWELVE

SETTLING ACCOUNTS

BY THE END OF 1653 Alonso de Cárdenas conceded that he had finally lost the political initiative to his French counterpart, Bordeaux. In reality, the Spaniard was powerless to stop the change in the diplomatic climate. Cromwell was already moving towards a pro-French foreign policy in order to thwart any potential Stuart invasion from across the English Channel. However, if Cárdenas had lost the diplomatic battle, his achievements as Philip of Spain's art agent were unrivalled. His scrupulous accounts reveal that during his time in London he bought over fifty of the finest paintings in the royal collection, including three Titians that Charles had brought back from Madrid in 1623.[1] The total cost came to just under £6,000. A further £4,000 was spent on various tapestries, hangings and statues, including the enormous *Acts of the Apostles* series. Haro was delighted and presented many of the best pictures to King Philip, who hung them in the Escorial in Madrid. In sharp contrast, the exiled English royalists were outraged. Few of Charles II's retinue commented directly on the sale of the king's pictures – in the early 1650s there were more pressing matters for them to deal with – but Edward Hyde, Earl of Clarendon, later angrily denounced what he saw as Cárdenas's unprincipled behaviour, complaining that 'that ambassador (who had always a great malignity towards the King) bought as many pictures and other precious goods appertaining to the Crown' as he could, before shipping them to Spain and 'thence to Madrid upon eighteen mules'.[2]

Clarendon was equally scathing in his condemnation of Bordeaux, characterizing him as Mazarin's lackey, sent to England 'as a merchant to traffic in the purchase of the royal goods and jewels of the rifled Crown'.[3] Clarendon feared the sale was a violation of the nobility of monarchy that debased the crown and reduced it to the norms and values of the marketplace. To some extent he was right, but unfortunately Bordeaux still hadn't learned his lesson. As Cárdenas prepared to dispatch his rich haul of pictures in the autumn of 1653, Bordeaux had yet to buy a single painting. His letters to Mazarin during this period betray his inexperience and growing sense of anxiety. Discussing the availability of a series of *Abraham* tapestries (which he failed to buy), Bordeaux asked Mazarin 'to enquire of some Englishman what it may be worth and let me know how far I may go, for fear that my offers should exceed what you would wish to pay'. He goes on to say, 'Apart from the Spanish ambassador, who is buying many paintings and curious furnishings . . . there is no-one in England able to buy.'⁴ Although this presented Bordeaux with a great opportunity, it also weighed on him as a heavy responsibility. At least the Frenchman had established how Cárdenas was buying his pictures. He informed Mazarin that 'those who wish to buy customarily negotiate with the creditors, settling their bills for less than half their value'.⁵ The problem was that the dividend holders were hugely inflating their 'bills' and pushing up the prices.

On 23 October Bordeaux wrote again to Mazarin. Things looked bleak. Mazarin had enquired about the *Apostles* tapestries and Bordeaux now informed him that they were already in Madrid. The Raphael *Holy Family* 'was bought by the Spanish ambassador three months ago, on my refusing it'. Raphael's *Madonna of the Rose*? Already 'out of the country', on its way to Spain. What of pictures by Mantegna, Parmigianino and Correggio? Predictably, 'the first were sold long ago, and the others since some little time, to the said Spanish Ambassador'. Even worse, few good modern tapestries remained and, according to Bordeaux, the classical statues 'do not appear to me to be so rare, despite their age'.⁶ He could only hope that his attempts to buy a Giulio Romano *St Jerome* and Correggio's *Allegory of Vice* would meet with some success.

Just four days later the relieved ambassador notified Mazarin of his purchase of both paintings. But it had not been easy. Bordeaux explained that the *St Jerome* 'cost £1,300; if I had delayed even a moment the Spanish Ambassador would have carried them off, and indeed I had the second from the very hands of a painter who had bought it on his behalf'.[7] Bordeaux was learning how to get ahead of Cárdenas in the unscrupulous world of the dividends, but he was still no match for the likes of Edward Bass and Emmanuel de Critz when it came to agreeing prices. He was now negotiating with some of the shrewdest veterans of the sale, whose only allegiance was to their profit margins. Edmund Harrison, owner of the £200 *St Jerome*, had little compunction selling to Bordeaux as the highest bidder, despite having sold Cárdenas one of his finest hauls of pictures in early 1652. The painter who reneged on his agreement with Cárdenas and sold the Correggio to Bordeaux was the cunning Emmanuel de Critz, who had displayed the picture in his house in the autumn of 1651 with a £1,000 price tag. It is not clear how much Bordeaux paid for the Correggio, or to what extent Harrison and de Critz manufactured Cárdenas's rivalry to maximize their profit. However, there is a delicious irony in the fact that the painting which prompted all this fraudulence and deceit was entitled the *Allegory of Vice*.

Unfortunately for the hapless Bordeaux, just as he worked out how to outsmart one rival, another appeared. The ambassador failed to acquire Correggio's *Allegory of Virtue* because, as he informed Mazarin, a French merchant by the name of Oudancour bought it for £4,000 on behalf of Everard Jabach, the Cologne-based banker and art dealer to Louis XIV.[8] Jabach's representatives, including Oudancour, quietly bought up over twenty of the dividends' best paintings. Richard Symonds watched Ralph Grynder's dividend selling pictures to one of Jabach's agents, probably Oudancour. They included Titian's *Christ at Emmaus* and a Giulio Romano *Nativity*, purchased at nearly half their sale values of between £500 and £600. Symonds noted the kind of cut-price deals Grynder's dividend was forced to make to raise money. They held a painting of Mary Magdalene valued at £80, 'but they'll take £40. £35 has been offered.'[9] This corroborates Bordeaux's claim that most of the dividends were accepting offers on paintings at half their valuation by the trustees – not that the ambassador managed to obtain such reductions with his own purchases.

Other dividend holders were also eager to sell, including de Critz, although if Bordeaux's figures are accurate Oudancour needed to pay twice the original valuation of the *Allegory of Virtue*. Jabach's acquisitions included five Titians, paintings by Sebastiano del Piombo and Rosso Fiorentino, as well as the best Caravaggio in the collection, the *Death of the Virgin*.[10] But without doubt his finest moment was the acquisition of the only original Leonardo in the royal collection, *St John the Baptist*. Having passed to his executors following Jan van Belcamp's death in 1651, the Leonardo languished in St Swithen's Lane before Oudancour snapped it up for an undisclosed figure and returned it to France.

It transpired that Jabach was also buying for Mazarin, although unlike Bordeaux he was selling artworks on to the cardinal for a profit. This meant that his London representatives needed to buy as cheaply as possible. Bordeaux, on the other hand, was under no such restrictions and spent much of his time advising Mazarin on how to transfer money as quickly and cheaply as possible to cover his extravagant offers. On 23 October he told Mazarin:

> I have made enquiries of a number of bankers as to how one might save on the exchange, which today stands at 54 per cent, no-one wishing to do business in France, for fear of a rupture in relations. They advise me to have *louis d'argent* or heavy Mexican *reals* sent here, there being a saving of 10% to be made.[11]

Bordeaux also lamented the need for money, because 'payment for the pictures cannot be deferred'. Unlike the relatively prosperous 1630s, when most royal households bought paintings on credit, the English dividends now preferred the security of silver or gold pieces rather than bills of exchange that could fail in the rapidly changing political and economic climate.

Mazarin's only response was impatience and exasperation at Bordeaux's failure to match Cárdenas's purchasing power. He encouraged the ambassador to buy a specific Correggio, but warned him 'on no account let it go to the Spanish ambassador'. Behaving with the classical instincts of the obsessive collector, Mazarin ignored Bordeaux's recent achievements, instead focusing on the next tantalizing acquisition. 'I would also wish to have portraits by Van Dyck, of which they have very many in England,' he told Bordeaux, adding peremptorily, 'I would ask you to make haste in this.'[12]

Before Bordeaux could turn his attention to Van Dycks, he needed to conclude two pressing deals: a Raphael portrait and a second Correggio, the *Venus with Satyr and Cupid*, in the possession of David Murray. He finally secured the Correggio for £4,300, despite the fact that, as Murray agreed terms, 'the Spanish Ambassador immediately intervened, offering him 500 pounds if he would go back on his agreement' – this, despite Cárdenas's initial dismissal of the picture as too profane for his tastes. Fortunately for Bordeaux, Murray inexplicably refused, but Bordeaux's acceptance of Cárdenas's actions as a matter of course suggests just how cutthroat the situation had become. After all, Bordeaux employed exactly the same tactic in obtaining Correggio's *Allegory of Vice*.

The fact that deferred credit was only grudgingly accepted by dealers like Bass and Houghton made Bordeaux's life even harder, as he conceded in his subsequent letter to Mazarin about the purchase of the Correggio: 'if I had waited for the money from Calais, the Spanish Ambassador would have carried it off, the English being unable to resist the least profit. With a little credit I managed the business.' His decision to borrow money was motivated by his growing interest in another jewel of the collection that was now up for sale – Titian's *Pardo Venus*.

It is little surprise that its shrewd owner, Colonel Hutchinson, chose this moment to sell his last Titian. Ever since his first acquisitions at the public sale in 1649, Hutchinson had exhibited a remarkable ability to buy and sell at just the right time. Having already made nearly 400 per cent profit selling his Titian of *Venus and Cupid with an Organist* to Teniers, he now enticed Bordeaux with the offer of this last erotic Venus. Bordeaux first came across the picture in October, when he noted, 'the finest piece remaining here is in the possession of a colonel; but he has a very high price on it'. By December he was eager to conclude the purchase and ship the painting to France, 'but the colonel selling it does not wish to come down' from the initial purchase price of nearly a thousand pounds – according to Hutchinson. In fact, the picture cost Hutchinson £600 in the sale. Instead of questioning Hutchinson's inflated claims, Bordeaux was swayed by his team of artistic 'advisers', who 'esteem it highly'.

By 18 December the ambassador agreed terms with Hutchinson, but in just three days the price went up even higher for:

> ... a Venus given by the King of Spain to the late King of England, the work of Titian, fairly well preserved, very large, and generally held to be of great price. So as not to lose it, I was today obliged to finalise the purchase of 7,000 livres [£1,200]; ... the same price at which it was sold to this army officer after the death of the King. I have promised 2,000 livres for Monday and the remainder three weeks later.[13]

Hutchinson was running rings round the unfortunate ambassador, increasing his price and also demanding an immediate down payment. The colonel's moves were exemplary. Of course he did not want to reveal just how much he had paid for the painting, hence the shift in price. As one of the centrepieces of first the Spanish Habsburg and then the English Stuart collections, imagine the coup of presenting it to Cardinal Mazarin. A decision was urgently required. Bordeaux knew that Cárdenas was waiting to reclaim the picture for the Spanish because 'he haggles for all the fine pieces', which meant that 'the sale must be agreed before he becomes aware of it'. Bordeaux was being panicked into buying pictures even before Cárdenas had heard of their sale. The Frenchman tried to justify the purchase, admitting that 'although this painting of Venus is dear, the painters and dealers who know about these things advised me not to let it go'.[14] It was a painfully credulous belief in the aesthetic judgement of a group of people whose own involvement in the sale and its dividends hopelessly compromised their ability to offer independent advice on pictures. If the behaviour of some of the sale's officials was anything to go by, Bordeaux's advisers were probably in league with sellers like Hutchinson, taking their own cut for encouraging the Frenchman to buy at such inflated prices.

The half a dozen paintings Bordeaux had purchased by the end of 1653 cost more than Cárdenas spent in total on pictures in over four years. The Spaniard obtained nearly ten times the number of paintings and avoided the uncomfortable position in which Bordeaux now found himself – in debt to the dividends. The Frenchman requested money to settle payment for the *Pardo Venus* within three weeks, while also reminding Mazarin, 'I still owe money for the last Correggio.' Bordeaux sent even worse news: 'All the sales of the King's goods and tapestries are to be halted until further notice.' Just four days later, Cromwell was formally appointed Lord Protector.

Throughout the autumn months both the collapse of the sale and the restoration of political rule by a single leader looked increasingly likely. In August Parliament requested a full financial account of the sale, 'what goods are sold, and what yet remains unsold, and where and in whose hands those goods remain, and how the proceeds of that hath been sold and disposed of'. Gilbert Pickering was also asked to head a committee to decide 'what hangings and other household stuff are fit to be made use of and to reserve for the service of the State'.[15] It was an attempt to placate the sale's critics, like Chidley, while also broadening the state's right to reserve royal goods, particularly tapestries. It suggested that the sale was finally reaching its culmination. For Bordeaux, these developments unintentionally frustrated his attempts to buy tapestries. While most of the king's best pictures were now in private hands, many exceptional tapestries remained on sale in the royal palaces, too cumbersome and expensive to interest most buyers. Mazarin wanted tapestries, and could pay the prices involved. Unfortunately, Bordeaux reported, as a result of these parliamentary initiatives the trustees were suspending the sale in order to re-evaluate the tapestries and choose which ones to reserve, preventing him from bidding for the ones Mazarin wanted. It was another blow for the hapless French ambassador.

Together with the remaining royal creditors, Bordeaux hoped that the new Protectorate would decide to sell off its tapestries, but he soon realized this was unlikely to happen. In his first letter of 1654 he told Mazarin, 'I do not yet know with certainty if any of the King's tapestries are to be sold,' but he suspected that 'as all the unsold goods have been given to the Protector and he is to lodge in the royal palace, all these furnishings are needed by him'. Mazarin immediately saw that a consummate politician like

Cromwell would not sacrifice such grand tapestries in the face of dwindling public criticism. 'Do not concern yourself any longer with the tapestries,' he informed Bordeaux brusquely, 'for assuredly they will be of use to the Protector.' Bordeaux forlornly agreed, providing an insight into how the Protectorate's initial promise of financial settlement soon evaporated: 'The Protector gives hope of satisfaction to those who are pursuing the sale of the King's goods, but I have difficulty in believing that he will let go the fine tapestries.'[16] This showed that in matters of state Bordeaux was as shrewd as ever; it was only in the ruthless London art world that his judgement and experience failed him.

The sale may officially have ended but private buyers still offered pictures and Mazarin wanted Van Dycks. Annoyed at Bordeaux's failure to obtain the right kind of pictures by April, Mazarin told him, 'You will remember, please, that it is Van Dyck's portraits that are esteemed, and not the other paintings' like those that poor Bordeaux had agonized over for weeks before finally buying, and which he was now compelled to return to the seller. The sophisticated and increasingly demanding cardinal also warned his ambassador 'not to allow oneself to be deceived, for it is difficult to distinguish a copy from an original'.[17] It was wise counsel. Artists like Geldorp, Van Leemput and the late Jan van Belcamp were all renowned for their skill in copying Van Dycks, especially the royal portraits. Under Charles, the view of copies shifted from their initial status as respectable reproductions of unobtainable pictures, to dreaded forgeries passed on to buyers by unscrupulous art dealers. Now that buying pictures was no longer the exclusive preserve of the royal elite, new standards of authenticity were developed to retain the prestige value of acquiring Old Masters.[18] Allowing a copy to enter your collection also reflected badly on your judgement as a virtuoso, as William Sanderson pointed out in his *Graphice* (1658). 'Originals have a natural force of grace rising,' he argued, but, anticipating modern sensibilities, he believed that 'copies seem to have only an imperfect and borrowed comeliness'.[19] Poor Bordeaux was now required to buy original Van Dycks from a group of dealers who specialized in copying his work. The results were fairly predictable.

It took the ambassador months before he 'found a fair number of portraits of Van Dyck', but even the usually profligate Bordeaux confessed 'the prices are so high that I am most reluctant to buy them'.[20] It wasn't until October 1654 that he finally agreed to purchase eight. He persuaded Mazarin to take some classical and biblical scenes – a *Psyche* sold by Houghton and a *St Sebastian* – as well as the prized portraits 'of ladies of rank', including 'the head of Van Dyck's mistress', Margaret Lemon, in the possession of Gaspars. According to Bordeaux, it was 'considered to be one of his best works', probably because it was heavily indebted to Titian's *Girl in a Fur Wrap*, purchased by the late king in Madrid. Bordeaux was probably unaware that Gaspars had 'finished' the picture while it was in his possession, which only further clouded its attribution as an 'original' Van Dyck.[21]

Mazarin's desire for Van Dycks was partly driven by the popularity of the painter among the royalist exiles living in France, for whom Van Dyck's portraits captured the glory of the Stuart dynasty just before its collapse. When Henrietta Maria arrived in The Hague in 1642, her Bohemian relatives were shocked at her appearance. Her sister-in-law Elizabeth's daughter, Sophia of Bohemia, confessed that 'Van Dyck's portraits had so accustomed me to thinking that all English women are beautiful that I was amazed to find a small creature, with skinny arms and teeth like defence works'.[22] The tragic glamour of Van Dyck's paintings gained a certain cachet in the royal courts of Europe, but they also caused some problems, as his portraits often depicted dead, imprisoned or exiled members of the Stuart royal family. This made Bordeaux's acquisition of the group portrait 'representing the three children of the late King of England when they were children' particularly delicate. Colonel Webb, one of the sale's biggest early spenders, bought the painting for £60 in October 1649. Like Hutchinson, he now resurfaced to cash in on his investment, selling it to Bordeaux for £100.[23] It was a rewarding deal for Webb, but a surprisingly tactless one on Bordeaux's part. A painting of the queen's dead and exiled children was a particularly insensitive picture to send back to Paris, where Henrietta Maria still held court. Even Cárdenas generally avoided such politically insensitive acquisitions, although his more conservative, Italianate tastes also limited his interest in Van Dycks.

The only other person who benefited from such convoluted transactions was the dead artist. The sale created a gradual revival of Van Dyck's value and international reputation. At the beginning of the sale his portraits sold for as little as £20. By the point at which Bordeaux concluded his expensive acquisitions, the cost of a Van Dyck had more than quadrupled. This was partly due to the aura of lost majesty associated with his royal portraits, but it also reflected the sudden dispersal and circulation of a small but significant number of his pictures throughout the royal courts and public art markets of Europe. In death, the reputations of both the king and his court painter reached new heights.

By April 1655 Mazarin decided he no longer wanted all his Van Dyck portraits. He gave no reason, but the return of the portrait of Margaret Lemon suggests he realized that some of the portraits were copies, studio works or, as with the canvas of Van Dyck's mistress, retouched by their previous owners, in this instance the painter Jan Baptist Gaspars, acting on behalf of a consortium of painters. Almost six months after buying the portraits, Bordeaux was left in the invidious position of returning them to Gaspars and asking for a refund. Once again he was hoodwinked. He informed Mazarin:

> I have spoken to the painters who sold me the paintings by Van Dyck; they are happy to have them back in exchange; but I do not see with them any works by good painters and I can assure Your Eminence that if the said portraits had not been considered to be by Van Dyck and in good taste, I would not have sent them.[24]

Bordeaux's dealers claimed to have no decent pictures to offer in exchange for the returned Van Dycks. It seemed that, at last, the sale of the late king's goods was finally at an end. Bordeaux was left trying to justify his purchases to an ominously silent Mazarin. It was his last recorded transaction in England and a typically bad-tempered and unsuccessful conclusion to the ambassador's participation in the sale.

A Van Dyck that eluded everyone was *Charles I with M. de St*

Antoine. Sold from one dealer to another, it finally ended up in the hands of the artist's protégé and one of Cárdenas's London dealers, Remigius Van Leemput. Hoping to cash in on the king's growing status as a martyr to the royalist cause, Van Leemput took the painting to Antwerp, but he failed to get his asking price and brought it back to England.[25] While European buyers were obviously reluctant to purchase such a defining image of a martyred sovereign, the English Protectorate was eager to appropriate its iconography in the service of its new leader.

In July 1655 the French artist and renowned Van Dyck copyist Pierre Lombart was paid £20 'for presenting several portraits of his Highness to the Council'. One of his engravings of Cromwell was a direct copy of Van Dyck's equestrian portrait. The crucial difference was that Lombart replaced the dead king's head with Cromwell's.[26] This was a striking example of how easily Charles's image could be manipulated, but it was hardly a ringing endorsement of Cromwell; the Protectorate was still reliant upon copying images of a king it executed but failed to destroy. Charles's head was replaced but his image endured. A subsequent 'headless' version of the engraving was executed following the death of Cromwell, reflecting the ease with which the next incumbent could be drawn on to the portrait, ready to take up the reins of power regardless of their political ideology.

Bordeaux missed the defining picture of King Charles's collection, but he eventually prevailed over his Spanish adversary, Cárdenas. In October 1655 Cromwell declared war on Spain after launching an attack on the Spanish colony of Hispaniola earlier in the year. Although the assault failed, Cromwell settled for the annexation of Jamaica and a formal peace and trade treaty with France. Cárdenas was expelled from London, but Bordeaux stayed to oversee the growing commercial and military alliance between England and France. After his traumatic experience of London's ruthless art world, he was relieved to return to the relatively straightforward world of international diplomacy. Although he remained in post to witness the restoration of King Charles II, he never bought another picture during the remainder of his time in London.[27]

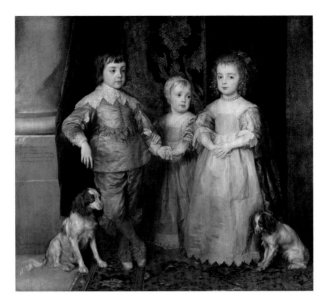

30. Van Dyck's touching family portrait *The Three Eldest Children of Charles I*
(Charles, James and Mary) hung in Somerset House before being sold in the sale for £60.
After the French ambassador rejected it, Peter Lely briefly owned it before returning it
to Charles II, who appears in the picture aged just five.

31. Van Dyck asked for £200 for completion of *The Five Eldest Children of Charles I*;
he received £100. During the sale this picture was valued at £120, and was passed
between various dealers before Colonel Hawley retrieved it in 1661.

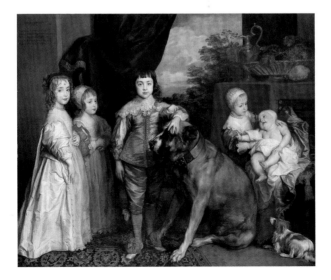

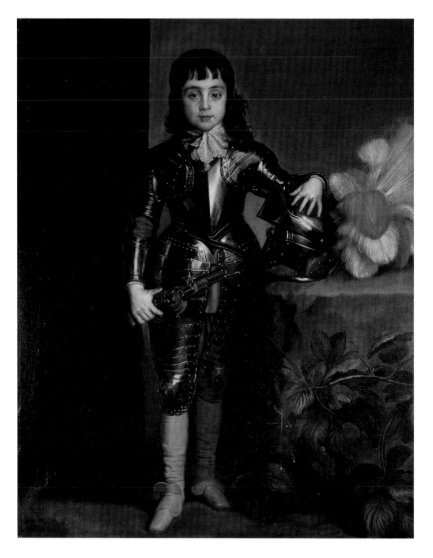

32. Van Dyck's studio produced this portrait of *Charles II as Prince of Wales* to show off the young heir to the Stuarts' Spanish Habsburg relatives.

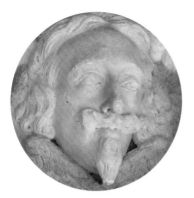

33. Plaster cast after Gianlorenzo Bernini's bust of King Charles.

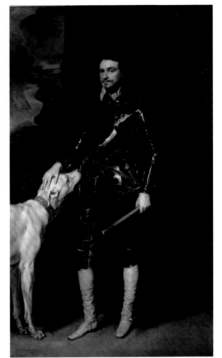

34. Anthony Van Dyck's imposing portrait of his patron Thomas Wentworth, 1st Earl of Strafford, King Charles's doomed political confidant.

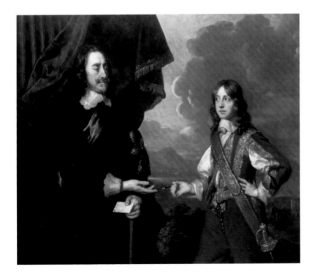

35. Peter Lely's portrait of the defeated Charles I with his son James, Duke of York, was commissioned by one of the Commonwealth's most discerning collectors, the Earl of Northumberland.

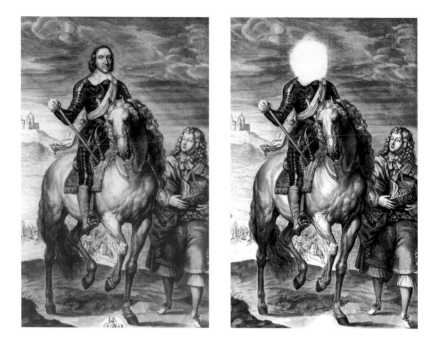

36 a & b. Pierre Lombart's remarkable engravings based on Van Dyck's equestrian portrait of King Charles. The first replaces the king's head with Oliver Cromwell's; the second, completed after Cromwell's death, erases Cromwell's face, presumably in anticipation of his successor.

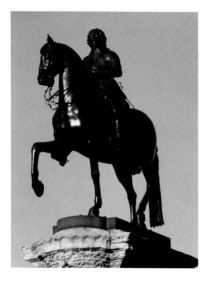

37. Hubert le Sueur's *Charles I on Horseback*. Cast in the 1630s and hidden throughout the civil war, the statue now stands in Charing Cross looking towards the Banqueting House, where Charles was executed in 1649.

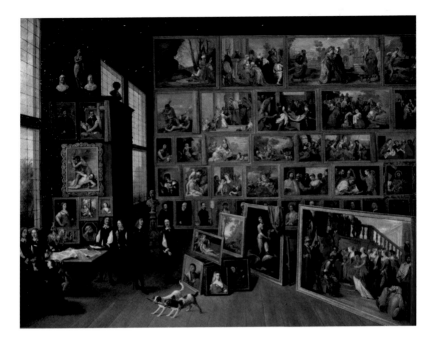

38. Teniers's *The Gallery of the Archduke Leopold-Wilhelm* shows off the Habsburg acquisitions from the English collections during the Commonwealth.

39. Titian's erotic *Venus and Cupid with Organist*, bought from the sale by the republican Colonel Hutchinson, who made a fortune selling it back to the Spanish after the sale.

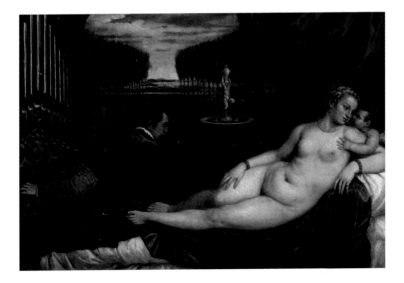

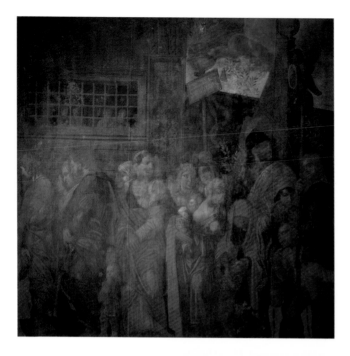

40. One of Andrea Mantegna's *The Triumphs of Caesar*, bought by King Charles from Mantua, but by the 1650s a symbol of Cromwell's new regime.

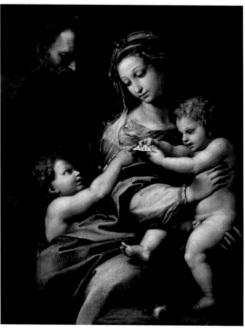

41. Raphael's *Madonna of the Rose*, another picture repossessed by the Spanish ambassador Cárdenas.

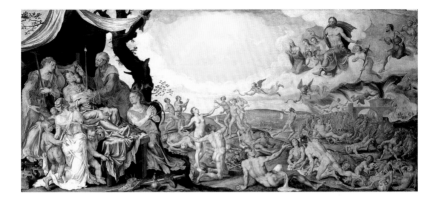

42. Heemskerck's apocalyptic *The Four Last Things*, part of Charles II's attempt to restock the royal collection. It also marked a renewed royal interest in northern European art.

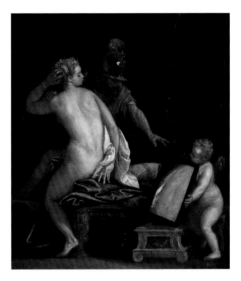

43. Veronese's studio painting of *Venus, Mars and Cupid with a Mirror*, probably in Charles I's collection, and sold back to his son in the 1660s.

44. Giovanni Cariani's *Reclining Venus*, given to Charles II by the Dutch as a replacement for the Titians disbanded during the sale.

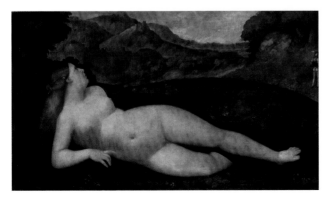

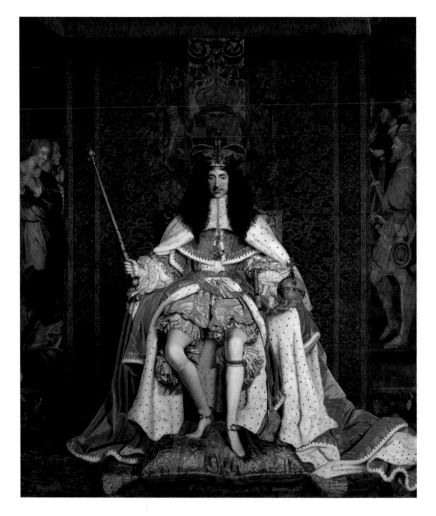

45. John Michael Wright's coronation portrait of King Charles II, complete with hastily repaired and redesigned royal regalia.

LOOKING BACK ON the dispersal of King Charles' art collection in the late 1660s, Edward Hyde, the Earl of Clarendon, concluded:

> In this manner did the neighbour princes join to assist Cromwell with very great sums of money, whereby he might be enabled to prosecute and finish his wicked victory over what yet remained unconquered, and to extinguish monarchy in this renowned kingdom; whilst they enriched and adorned themselves with the ruins and spoils of the surviving heir.[28]

For Clarendon, like many subsequent historians, the sale was a sordid monetary transaction. It provided the Commonwealth and Protectorate with capital to resist a royalist restoration and maintain republican rule, and left its participants morally compromised, with blood on their hands and looted pictures in their galleries. However, the final accounts for the sale tell a rather different story.

Considering the double-dealing and insider trading that took place, it is not surprising that the surviving financial records are somewhat opaque, but taken together they provide a reasonably comprehensive official account of the sale's history. *The Treasurer's Accompte of their disbursements of the Money raysed by Sale of the late King Queene & princes goods & personal Estate*, completed around 1658, lists over 1,100 transactions beginning in May 1650 and concluding as late as 1658, when smaller sums were paid out and outstanding debts (some of many years' standing) were finally settled. It calculated that 'the total of all payments made by Treasurers for the proceeds of the late King, Queen's and Prince's goods' came to £134,383 5s 4d. Of this figure £26,500 went to the navy, as specified in the parliamentary act of 1649, although there is no evidence the money was ever returned as initially stipulated. A further £10,000 went on the salaries and allowances claimed by the trustees, contractors and treasurers. Estimates vary as to exactly how much money the creditors finally received, primarily because of the difficulty of assessing the value of the goods provided in lieu of debts. The final figure was somewhere between £96,000 and £118,000.[29]

The nominal value of all the inventoried goods came to over

£180,000, although only a fraction of this figure was realized as cash. The balance sheet also recorded income of £4,800 from Scottish estates and a paltry £3,900 from the infamous discoveries, despite all the controversy and scandal that surrounded Beauchamp and ultimately destroyed Mildmay. One of the most revealing figures represented 'the goods in public use & not sold[30] – in other words, reserved goods. By the end of the sale £53,700 worth of former royal possessions were in the state's possession, including Raphael's cartoons, Mantegna's *Triumphs* and the tapestry cycles Bordeaux tried in vain to acquire throughout his time in London. These goods represented over a quarter of the entire monetary value of the inventoried goods and approximately half the final amount used to settle the creditors' debts. It was a revealing figure that vindicated the sale's more radical critics in condemning the bias towards the state rather than the creditors.

The figures involving paintings are even more surprising. Approximately 1,300 pictures were sold or assigned in lieu of debts, valued at a total of over £33,000. This represented nearly a third of all payments made by the treasurers, dwarfing the income from any other single source of revenue. Their public display and subsequent dispersal among the dividends in 1651 represented an unprecedented moment when Londoners took the opportunity to buy, sell or own some of the finest pictures of the European Renaissance. It was the dividends' leaders, figures like de Critz, Bass and Houghton, who finally benefited most from the sale, rather than either the Commonwealth or the Protectorate. By timing their sales and exploiting rivalries between buyers like Cárdenas, Teniers and Bordeaux, they made lucrative profits on their investments, capital that never found its way into the treasury. Colonel Hutchinson played the market as well as anyone. Having spent £765 on his two Titian Venuses, he sold them for nearly £2,000. This figure alone is an indictment of the trustees' missed opportunities. Simply on these grounds the sale can be described as a failure, although many of its more spectacular beneficiaries would undoubtedly have demurred.

Nor were the buyers and recipients of the pictures predominantly ignorant commoners or unscrupulous foreigners. Buyers like colonels Hutchinson, Webb and Wetton showed exceptional taste and judgement in both what they bought and when they sold. For these individuals the pictures represented excellent investments, regardless of the fact that their own ostensible religious convictions seemed at variance with the subject matter. Unlike many of the destitute creditors, the colonels seemed to understand how to match painter and picture to a particular buyer at just the right moment, showing a remarkably sophisticated appreciation of the workings of art and its market. At the opposite end of the ideological spectrum, aristocratic collectors turned government supporters like Lisle and Northumberland took full advantage of the sale with few qualms at profiting from the king's death. Both peers bought extensively on the public and secondary market. As with Webb and Hutchinson, their purchases appear unfettered by religious or political loyalties. For these flexible political individuals, pictures were a source of both aesthetic and political value, admired for their beauty but also sound financial investments as and when it proved expedient to sell them.

The other undoubted winners in the sale were the cosmopolitan artists, dealers and merchants like de Critz, Houghton, Gaspars, Bass, Geldorp and Van Leemput. They were the real specialists in money and art, employed by all sides – crown, republic, dividends and foreign embassies – that took the opportunity to buy, sell, value and in some cases even repaint pictures for their own individual profit. Many had experience of working for royalty before the sale in the acquisition of pictures. To them, it was only natural to work as advisers and agents for international buyers like Cárdenas, Teniers, Bordeaux and Jabach, who in turn entered the sale primarily at the behest of their political paymasters. For such men, mostly commoners, loyalty to religion or nation took second place to the pursuit of profit, and this is what the sale of the late king's goods meant to them. It also proved to such entrepreneurs the potentially lucrative financial value of trading art works like paintings and statues on the international market, as prices rose uniformly in comparison with Prince Henry's early acquisitions and Charles's subsequent purchase of the Mantuan collection in the late 1620s.

The losers were without doubt King Charles's creditors. Some profited from the sale, like William Clarke of St Martin's Lane and the widow Mrs Elizabeth Hunt, who both visited the sale in its early months and came away with a clutch of cheap paintings and tapestries. However, many more were frustrated and disillusioned by Parliament's byzantine bureaucracy and growing indifference to their plight. The introduction of the First and Second Lists led to a greater distribution of goods, but also placed power in the hands of a small group of influential and well-connected individuals like de Critz, Bass and Houghton. The lists left the most desperate creditors regarding paintings, statues and tapestries as capital goods – commodities given arbitrary cash values that most individuals cashed in as quickly as possible. Nevertheless, some ordinary men and women were given the opportunity, however briefly, to assess and evaluate artworks in terms of size, style, genre and quality, a practice previously the preserve of the late king's privately appointed *virtuosi*.

Politically, the sale can hardly be judged a success, although its outcomes need to be measured against the complex and contradictory motives that inspired it. As an attempt to swell the coffers of the Commonwealth, it was an unquestionable failure. Even taking into account the £26,500 that went towards the funding of the navy, the sale's contribution to the Commonwealth's international security was negligible. By the time the regime collapsed in 1660 the naval debt stood at £694,112.[31] Nor did the sale succeed in erasing all traces of the Stuart monarchy by disposing of many of its visible symbols of power and authority. The circulation of royal possessions among creditors, dealers and aristocrats only encouraged popular reflection on the fate of the monarchy, providing delight and personal profit for some, but horror and anger for others. The Protectorate found it politically expedient to appropriate many of the finest artworks in the collection, but paradoxically this bequeathed a powerful and lasting legacy to future English monarchs.

However, the sale was not the act of barbaric cultural vandalism by a bunch of iconoclastic zealots assumed by many subsequent royal historians and dismayed connoisseurs. Ironically, instead of embracing popular calls for the destruction of royal icons and greater redistribution of Stuart land and goods, first the Rump and then the Protectorate retained substantial numbers of paintings, tapestries and statues. True, the republican regime was largely indifferent to pictures, preferring tapestries, but this reflected a more traditional demand measured in silk and gold rather than oil and canvas. Such preferences were not based on religious conviction, just the pragmatic politics of an administration that understood the magnificence and authority that tapestry conferred upon its owner.

As for the artists involved, both living and dead, the sale enhanced some reputations but diminished others. It was a severe if somewhat artificial test of how Charles's connoisseurship would measure up to the judgement of the marketplace. Artists like Titian, Raphael, Rubens and Correggio already possessed a certain amount of international currency and were immediate targets for buyers who knew they could either sell on the European market or offer their purchases directly to other royal collections. Van Dyck triumphed posthumously for his skilfully cultivated association with the glamour and nostalgia of the lost Stuart court. Others were not so lucky. Royal favourites like Polidoro da Caravaggio and Palma Giovane, who produced copious studio works and authorized copies, were already widely available; both artists emerged from the sale with little cultural cachet or rarity value. As a result, they attracted very little international attention, and with hardly anything to distinguish them beyond their royal association, many of their pictures sold for as little as £10.[32] It was only much later that such pictures would be judged and valued by recognizably modern stylistic and aesthetic criteria.

The sale was also responsible for establishing painting's pre-eminence over all the other forms of artistic creativity represented among the collection. This was partly due to issues of size and scale. As Cárdenas soon realized, moving such a large amount of goods presented serious logistical problems. Paintings were far more portable than large tapestries or heavy statues, many of which were sold off in bulk. While many of the tapestries were reserved for Cromwell's use, international buyers like Cárdenas and Bordeaux were generally unimpressed by the quality of royal statuary. Instead, as the sale drifted towards its inconclusive end in the late 1650s, it became increasingly clear that nobody emerged from the sale with very much dignity, apart from the paintings themselves. In the end it was not monarchy, republicanism or religion that benefited from the sale of Charles I's goods; it was painting that triumphed.

✣

CHAPTER THIRTEEN

LIKE FATHER, LIKE SON?

RECORDING THE EVENTS OF Friday 16 March 1660 in his diary, Samuel Pepys wrote that after a busy day of business he headed off to Westminster:

> ... where I heard how the Parliament had this day dissolved themselves, and did pass very cheerfully through the Hall, and the Speaker without his mace. The whole Hall was joyful thereat, as well as themselves; and now they begin to talk loud of the King. To-night I am told that yesterday, about five a-clock in the afternoon, one came with a ladder to the great Exchange, and wiped with a brush the inscription that was upon King Charles, and that there was a great bonfire made in the Exchange, and people called out 'God bless King Charles the Second!'[1]

It was typical of the curious Pepys to capture not only the final death throes of parliamentary republicanism in England but also the popular reaction on the streets of London. The man on his ladder outside the Royal Exchange, later identified as Michael Darby, a painter to the Company of Mercers, was painting over the graffiti daubed underneath the decapitated statue of King Charles I back in 1650: *Exit Tyrannus Regum ultimus*. A popular ballad entitled 'An Exit to the Exit Tyrannus' commemorated the event, lamenting:

> Oh CHARLES that Exit which they put
> Up o'er thy statue's head was but
> An entrance to our woe,
> That fatal axe which thee divorc'd
> From us, our happiness hath forc'd
> Into the grave to go.[2]

The ballad hoped that from Darby's act 'the kingdom may recover strength' by ushering in a new king. It was a poignant public moment in the remarkable rehabilitation of the Stuart family that concluded less than two months later with the triumphant entry into London of Charles II as king of England.

Some two years earlier, in the summer of 1658, the political restoration of Charles II had seemed highly unlikely. Throughout the 1650s, as Cromwell inexorably strengthened his grip on political and military power in England, Charles wandered the courts of Europe, his attempts to re-create a viable military challenge to first Parliament and then Protectorate looking increasingly forlorn. Spain and France's official recognition of the regime responsible for his father's death was a bitter blow to the young Charles, but worse was to follow. By 1653 the French authorities were so embarrassed at Charles's presence in Paris that they settled his claim for a pension on condition that he left the country immediately. He travelled to Spa, then Aachen and Cologne, where his finances were so parlous that he suffered the indignity of food and washing rations. In his attempt to court an anti-Cromwell alliance with the Spanish in 1656, he moved his court to first Brussels, then Bruges and Antwerp, but with little realistic expectation of regaining his father's crown. Then suddenly, in September 1658, news came that changed everything. Oliver Cromwell was dead.

Over the next eighteen months, republican rule in England gradually unravelled. Cromwell's son Richard assumed the title of Lord Protector, but he was unequal to the task, lacking his father's combination of political guile and religious passion. The army was demanding payment for its soldiers and Cromwell had little choice but to recall Parliament. The elections held over the winter of 1658–9 returned predominantly conservative and moderate members, who sat alongside republican veterans of the Rump. Both groups successfully frustrated Cromwell's rule as Lord Protector, a campaign that only increased the army's disillusion with both the new Protector and Parliament. When Cromwell resisted calls from senior military officers to dissolve Parliament in April 1659, the army deserted him. The Protectorate was effectively at an end. Cromwell agreed to dissolve Parliament and retire into private life, leaving the army in control. Their immediate response was to return to what they knew, recalling the Rump Parliament that they had forcibly dissolved in 1653.

The Rump began where it had left off, promising radical reform but implementing very little and, in the process, antagonizing the army. By October 1659 John Lambert, the architect of the Protectorate who had fought so brilliantly alongside Cromwell throughout the Civil War, led the army back into Westminster to dissolve the Rump for a second time, less than six months after its first sitting. This was effectively a military coup. The only problem for Lambert was that General George Monck, head of the English army in Scotland, refused to accept the dissolution of the Rump. What motivated Monck's decision is unclear: certainly personal animosity towards Lambert, a reluctant acceptance of the rule of Parliament and possibly even sympathy for the restoration of Charles II. Throughout the winter of 1659–60 Monck played a brilliant waiting game, holding his army together, threatening to march on London and watching as the internecine squabbles between radicals and conservatives gradually paralysed Lambert.

Confidence in the interim authorities collapsed so quickly that by December 1659 the Rump was recalled for a third time to prevent the descent into anarchy. When Monck arrived in London at the head of his army in February 1660, it was with the intention of holding free elections. In March the dissolution of Parliament reported by Pepys presaged the elections that took place the following month. The Upper House of the Lords was restored, and with it a House of Commons overwhelmingly in favour of the return of the monarchy. On 7 May a new statue of Charles I appeared in its niche in the Royal Exchange and on the following day Parliament finally proclaimed the Restoration of the monarchy. Charles prepared to return to England after nearly two decades in the political wilderness.[3]

On 9 May, the day after the official declaration of the Restoration, the reunited House of Lords ordered the appointment of a committee to consider and receive information on the whereabouts of the late king's goods, jewels and pictures.[4] The committee comprised the earls of Berkshire, Dorset, Northumberland and Oxford, and barons Maynard, Hunsdon, Morley and Grey. Two days later they were empowered to order the seizure of all such goods that were 'discovered to their Lordships to be concealed'.[5] It was patently clear to the new Parliament that political restoration was a meaningless gesture without the material restitution of the trappings of royal power – property, land, money and, of course, pictures and statues. On 12 May it was ordered that 'all persons that have any of the King's Goods, Jewels, or Pictures, shall bring them in to the Committee for the King's Goods, &c. within seven days after the date' – this despite the fact that it had taken the Commonwealth nearly five years to disperse Charles's possessions.[6]

The submission of lists of royal goods was almost immediate, although they represented only a fraction of the original collection. On the same day as the first demand for returns, George Geldorp, one of the sale's most energetic buyers and agents, presented a 'Memorando of diverse pictures and statues and rarities belonging to the king'. The document listed some of the most prominent buyers and their acquisitions. These included fellow dealers and painters like Van Leemput and de Critz. Geldorp identified Van Leemput as owning several pictures of Charles I. They included 'the king upon a white horse, with Sir Anthony holding a head piece, stood at St James in the gallery', Van Dyck's portrait of *Charles I with M. de St Antoine*, now back in the country after Van Leemput's failure to sell it abroad.[7] Geldorp also identified more publicly significant buyers, including General Monck's old adversary John Lambert, one of the few individuals still capable of mustering military opposition to the royalist Restoration. Geldorp claimed, 'My Lord Lambert hath diverse rare pictures', and that an unnamed Dutch painter who served Lambert 'has had divers pictures and sold and stolen some'. He also indentified Colonel Hutchinson as owning 'one Madonna of Titian and diverse other pictures and one naked boy of marble very rare'.[8]

Members of the committee had tipped off Geldorp to cooperate as quickly as possible to save his own career, although it is unlikely that his submission was motivated by loyalty to the royalist cause. He significantly failed to record the royal goods he bought in the early 1650s, although it is possible that he had disposed of them by 1660. As a vulnerable foreigner, he saw the opportunity of profiting by assisting in the restoration of the royal collection. His list was more political than aesthetic, based on an attempt to discredit key members of the Commonwealth, regardless of which royal goods they actually possessed.

As the committee grasped the scale of their task, they banned any further dispersal of the royal goods. Two days after Geldorp's submission the Lords ordered that the export of all royal pictures and statues cease immediately.[9] The order came too late for the pictures, tapestries and statues purchased by Cárdenas, Teniers, Bordeaux and Jabach, now scattered across Europe, but for anyone still hoping to sell pictures on the Dutch art market, the opportunity had passed.

Those keenest to collaborate with the new regime included functionaries involved in the sale who were originally employed by Charles II's father, and whose loyalty to the Commonwealth was always questionable, to say the least. Thomas Beauchamp, former clerk to the sale's trustees, was ordered to surrender his inventories of all goods and transactions undertaken during his appointment to the new royal surveyor, John Webb.[10] Eager to please and obtain a profitable position, Beauchamp hastily drew up a petition addressed to the Lords, describing the bare outline of the sale and attempting to justify his own participation:

> £110,000 or thereabouts in goods were according to their appraisement distributed amongst the servants and creditors by special order of Parliament in payment for so much debt due to the said servants and creditors ... their debts were taken in and discharged and the said goods were daily bought up by agents from beyond the seas and so were transported, diverse pictures and statues were bought by the petitioner which he refused to transport, and has preserved them, and restored and amended the breakings and other defacings done thereunto by Colonel Pride's soldiers and others.[11]

It was a broadly accurate if partial account of the sale and Beauchamp's involvement. It argued for the impossibility of complete accountability – after all, so much had left the country – as well as his own heroic refusal to dispose of goods or support the iconoclastic activities of Colonel Pride. Unfortunately there is little evidence to support either of Beauchamp's claims. What really concerned him was 'the money he is out of purse, as for part of the goods he is still indebted'. Not surprisingly, there was no disclosure of the substantial sums of money Beauchamp pocketed from the proceeds of royal 'discoveries', nor was there any mention of the clerk's meagre royal acquisitions.

An even greater source of information also stepped forward to offer his services. Clement Kinnersley, Cromwell's Keeper of the Wardrobe, former contractor to the Commonwealth sale and another covert royalist, ranked as one of the sale's most opportunistic protagonists. As a trustee he signed inventories, pursued discoveries and sold off the royal crowns, plate and jewels, as well as investing his own money in a substantial cache of royal possessions. He also lobbied for reinstatement as keeper to the state's wardrobe. In the winter of 1652–3 he accused the incumbent, William Legge, of sympathizing with royalists and arming the king's attendants from the royal wardrobe back in 1642. It was an audacious allegation coming from one of the dead king's most intimate servants, but it cleverly targeted Legge, who had spent 1647–8 attending the renegade King Charles I during his time on the Isle of Wight. The allegations worked. Legge was dismissed and Kinnersley reinstated.[12]

Kinnersley retained his post as Keeper of the Wardrobe under the interim Convention Parliament and felt secure enough under the restored monarchy to submit one of the more audacious petitions for compensation in the autumn of 1660. Pointing to his loyal service in the royal household since birth, he claimed to have preserved a staggering £500,000 worth of the late king's possessions from sale or embezzlement during the Commonwealth and Protectorate periods. He even demanded backdated salary arrears of £7,000, most of which related to the Commonwealth period.[13]

Other members of the royal household recounted lurid stories of loyal heroism in the face of republican iconoclasm. Richard Meredith, Keeper of the Whitehall Volery chambers, originally designed as an aviary, claimed he 'preserved a brazen statue in the said Volery from being demolished by a Quaker who had already defaced those in the Privy Gardens'. The zealous Quaker 'had broken one door to come at this [statue] which had been formerly sold at Somerset House & rebought by Oliver Cromwell'.

Meredith's solution was to buy the statue for £50. He now threw himself on the mercy of the committee, requesting settlement of lost salary to 'rescue him from imminent ruin'.[14] There is no record that he ever received any recompense for his efforts.

Some who submitted inventories of goods in the first few days had more to fear from the Restoration. Many were enthusiastic supporters of the Commonwealth who had bought heavily from the sale and profited from the dividends. They were now in a potentially embarrassing situation, and the only solution seemed to be an admission of guilt before the king returned. Their dilemma was captured by the Venetian resident in London, who observed that 'many of his Majesty's enemies are now trying to curry favour with him by excuses and justifications', adding wryly that 'all are becoming men of sobriety and integrity'.[15] In a volatile political climate where republicans hoped for reconciliation but feared retribution, this was no time to deny possession of paintings marked with the royal brand of the new king's dead father. For over a decade the brand had promised financial gain; now it threatened social exclusion and professional ruin.

Two of the first individuals to acknowledge possession of royal paintings had also profited more than most under the sale and dividends. John Embree, still officially Surveyor of Works, submitted a petition listing 'some pictures in my hands which I had from the Committee at Somerset House, in place of a great debt due to me for works done and materials delivered for his late Majesties use towards the repairing the houses belonging to his Majesty'.[16] It was a reasonable defence intended to retain his post within the reformed royal household, but his nine pictures represented just over a third of the number he actually received, of which at least one (Titian's *St Margaret*) had been sold to Cárdenas. One of the most expensive was Bassano's *The Flood*, bought from Mantua by Charles I, valued now at just £60. He radically undervalued his list at just £174, compared to the twenty-four pictures he received during the sale, which were valued at £484.[17]

One of the most successful of all the sale's buyers, Edmund Harrison, former royal embroiderer, conceded brusquely that he 'hath in his possession certain goods that were delivered by the Trustees at Somerset House about 9 years since for settlement of his debt due from his Late Majestie and fifty three other credi-tors',[18] who constituted the eleventh dividend. As its head, Harrison had acquired sixty-one of the collection's finest pictures. They included works by Rubens, Titian, Mantegna and Van Dyck that he sold to both Cárdenas and Bordeaux, returning a substantial profit on their original valuation of £1,821. It is a measure of his success in disposing of his royal goods that in May 1660 he named just six royal pictures, including an undistinguished Tintoretto, *Portrait of a Knight of Malta*, valued in 1651 at £15, nine years later priced at just £12. Harrison's entire submission of pictures came to just £93.

The petitions of the dozens of others who owned pictures, statues and tapestries ranged from the loyal and confused to the fearful and indignant. The royalist veteran John Stone claimed that he had hoarded many of the goods allocated to his sixth dividend in 1651 in anticipation of the Restoration. He filed a list totalling £1,565 12s 6d, including statues valued at over £1,000, and a mixed collection of thirty-eight pictures valued at £370. It comprised some of Charles's finest pieces, including the remaining fragments of Perino's *Deposition* altarpiece, listed by Stone as 'The two thieves', Dismas and Gestas. Unlike many others, Stone's submission remained faithful to their original valuations. He listed his Perinos at their 1651 cost: £40 the pair. He also recorded Palma Giovane's dramatic *Expulsion of Heresy*, listed at its 1651 value of just £10.[19]

Peter Lely, a minor court painter to Charles I during the Civil War and a successful dealer during the Commonwealth sale, was also keen to ingratiate himself with the new regime. On 18 May he registered ten paintings and four statues, most of which he bought from dividend holders, including the marble *Crouching Venus*. Two of his finest paintings were Van Dycks: *Cupid and Psyche* and *The Three Eldest Children of Charles I*, the latter acquired from Colonel Webb. Bordeaux had offered Mazarin both pictures, but he rejected them as too expensive and, in the case of the portrait of the dead king's offspring, politically inappropriate. Lely now hastily acknowledged possession of the paintings as he prepared to petition the returning monarch for Van Dyck's title of Principal Painter to the King.[20] As well as keeping on the right side politically, Lely was also making a shrewd artistic move by returning these paintings, suggesting that, as the self-appointed heir to Van Dyck, he no longer needed his mentor's pictures.

Others acknowledged possession but resisted returning royal goods before they were compelled to do so by specific legislation. Tradesman John Cade, working near the Royal Exchange, submitted a detailed 'Note of such pictures in my hands which I suppose belonged to his Late Majesty Charles the First King of England and the prices at which I bought them'. He proceeded to list an exquisite collection of nineteen pictures that provide a miniature snapshot of the royal collection and suggests that he – or his buyer – had a very good eye. His purchases included two Holbeins and 'Nine large pieces of saints' painted in Mantua by the Roman mannerist Domenico Fetti.[21] Cade boasted of the cheapness of his acquisitions, claiming that his £240 worth of pictures were 'bought of the creditors at an undervalue'. This suggests that Cárdenas and Bordeaux were not the only buyers who profited from the desperation of the dividends.

Cade's most controversial submission was one of the more contemporary paintings, the Van Dyck studio portrait of *Charles II When Prince of Wales*. By 1660 its image of the boy prince brandishing a pistol evoked darker memories of the Civil War. Colonel Webb had bought the picture in the first weeks of the public sale in October 1649 and sold it to Cade, who valued the repossessed picture of his new king at £25.[22] It was a sign of the changes undergone in English political life that a London merchant could now traffic in pictures of his monarch. Just twenty years earlier such a transaction would have been unthinkable. It seemed appropriate that as Cade was putting a price on Charles's portrait, the king was busily cutting financial deals with Parliament that would ensure his restoration but would also limit his absolute political authority. Even if the country was eager for the return of the monarchy (although many people were not), the Stuart dynasty would never re-establish the power it had taken for granted in either politics or collecting during the first half of the seventeenth century.

The pro-parliamentary Anglo-Dutch tobacco merchant Nicholas Corsellis was more indignant at the claim on what he regarded as 'his' pictures. As an enthusiastic supporter of mercantile trade

with Ireland and America, Corsellis was understandably hostile to
the Restoration, and was unprepared to hand over his possessions
based on the demand of an interim committee, insisting that they
'shall be forthcoming when lawfully demanded'.[23] The pictures
were initially dispersed to settle debts incurred by the Stuart royal
family and then sold on the open market, so it seemed unjust to
demand their return without offering any financial recompense.
Many like Corsellis hoped that once Charles returned he might
waive his right to former royal possessions, having weightier
matters on his mind than the reacquisition of pictures and statues.
Royalists like Robert Leslie, the newly appointed Master of the
King's Cabinets, realized that Corsellis had a point. Leslie complained to the committee that the returns could not keep up with
official decrees, as individuals 'have offered me pictures and other
things which I could not receive without an order from this
honourable committee'.[24]

The most politically embarrassing admissions came from those
members of the aristocracy who had switched sides during the
Civil War. The earls of Northumberland and Peterborough and
Viscount Lisle all bought pictures and statues either from the sale
itself or from its dividend holders. Their choices provide a fascinating insight into the changing attitudes towards art during the
Commonwealth, and reflect the tastes of those who were ideologically sympathetic to Parliament but took a more independent line
to the Civil War, prepared to attack the king's authority but
opposed to his execution.

Northumberland and Peterborough declared to the House
'That they conceived that they might have some Statues and
Pictures that were formerly His late Majesty's; and that their
Lordships would keep them in safety for his Majesty's use, and to
present them unto him if He pleased to accept them'.[25] Both men
were, under the circumstances, understandably circumspect. Peterborough had less to worry about, confessing that he owned just
'four or five pictures that possibly did belong to the king'.[26]
Northumberland was more reticent, and not only because of his
larger investment in the late king's collection. One of the period's
great political survivors, he was also compromised by his position

on the committee appointed to restore the collection.[27] Having opposed the execution of King Charles in 1649, he had refused to profit directly from the initial public sale. However, unable to resist the bargains on sale from the dividends, he bought antique statues from de Critz and Beauchamp and three paintings from Jerome Lanier.[28] Like so many dividend sellers, Lanier sold to Northumberland at a loss. For just £120 Northumberland acquired an astonishing collection of key royal pictures, including the Correggio studio painting of *St John the Baptist*, brought back from Madrid by Charles in 1623, Giulio Romano's *Sacrifice of a Goat to Jupiter*, bought from Mantua, and Polidoro da Caravaggio's *Psyche Abandoned on a Rock*, bought by Charles from William Frizell.

On 19 May Viscount Lisle, Northampton's nephew, made his own submission. The Lords were informed that 'the Lord Viscount Lisle conceiving that some pictures and statues are in his custody which might be the late King's Majesty's, that he would keep them in safety, and be ready at His Majesty's command, or at the command of this House, to deliver them as he shall be directed'.[29] It was another grudging admission of guilt, but of an even greater magnitude than the returns of either Peterborough or Northumberland. Using a network of dealers and intermediaries, Lisle had amassed over 120 paintings, statues and gems throughout the course of the sale. At a cost of over £3,000, he had spent more than any other English aristocrat participating in the sale.[30]

Although Lisle had avoided buying directly from the sale and lacked the purchasing power of buyers like Cárdenas or Bordeaux, he had nonetheless amassed an outstanding collection that included works by Holbein, Mantegna, Gentileschi, Bassano and Rubens. To some extent, Lisle's acquisitions reflected established Caroline tastes. They were overwhelmingly Italian, sixteenth-century, with a sprinkling of northern artists. However, compared with earlier Stuart collections, there were hardly any portraits, no pictures of women and very few biblical scenes. The emphasis was much more on classical scenes of personal temperance and political virtue. Although not necessarily explicitly republican in its outlook, Lisle's collection marked a distinct shift in post-war English aristocratic taste, moving away from the celebration of individuals and potentially controversial religious works and towards a more geo-graphically diverse collection of artists with an interest in classical and historical subject matter.[31]

While Peterborough, Northumberland and Lisle all announced their intention to surrender their pictures, none were immediately forthcoming. They were all waiting to see how the new king would react to those who had – as had they – changed allegiance during the Civil War. Until the court declared its hand, they were not prepared to surrender any of their goods, regardless of their previous royal provenance.

As ENGLAND PREPARED FOR the restoration of the Stuart mon-archy, Charles left Brussels and moved to the city of Breda to plan his return. It was an astute decision, turning his back on Spanish influence and negotiating with key parliamentarians and military officers from a Protestant, republican stronghold. On 4 April he issued the Declaration of Breda, granting 'a free and general pardon' to all those who publicly pledged allegiance to the king's authority, 'liberty to tender consciences' of any religious persuasion and 'full satisfaction of all arrears due to the officers and soldiers of the army'. Parliament was to settle all outstanding grants, sales and purchases of royal possessions.[32] The declaration paved the way for the Commons to invite Charles to take the throne on 8 May and undoubtedly contributed to the stream of royal goods returned over the next fortnight.

The day before Charles endorsed the Declaration of Breda, he signed another agreement smoothing his path to the English throne. He agreed to buy seventy-two paintings from the art dealer William Frizell for the considerable sum of £2,086.[33] This was a substantial investment at a time when Charles still had very little money and suggests that his court regarded public art as vital to the definition of majesty, especially at such a crucial moment as its restoration. Frizell was a logical choice to act as the royal art dealer, having spent most of the 1630s in Italy buying pictures for Arundel and Charles I before reappearing in Antwerp in the late 1640s to broker the sale of Buckingham's collection. It was another shrewd move on Charles's part. The purchase created a vision of political and aesthetic continuity between father and son, a fact reinforced by the pictures chosen.

The seventy-two pictures would have fitted seamlessly into the royal collection Charles last saw in the early 1640s. However, by 1660 the Breda acquisition was a small gesture intended to replace what the exiled royal party assumed was the complete dispersal of the collection. Prince Charles chose many of his father's favourite artists, including Tintoretto, Reni, Bassano, del Sarto and Veronese, plus paintings ascribed to Titian.[34] He was embracing his father's varied taste in art, although his choice of subject matter gave little away regarding his own religious beliefs. His choices were those of a typically well-educated Englishman.

Nevertheless, Charles's selection also exhibits the influence of his painful years of dispossession and exile, as well as his imminent restoration. One of his father's favourite Dutch painters, Marten van Heemskerck, was represented by two apocalyptic paintings: *The Flood* and *The Four Last Things*. In the latter, Death, Judgement, Paradise and Hell are all depicted in one of Heemskerck's most powerful Counter-Reformation paintings. The dead are resurrected as Christ descends from on high, while to the right the damned are dragged into Hell, with skulls and skeletons littering the foreground. Absolution is offered in the figure of the dying man ministered to by a priest accompanied by Faith, Hope and Charity, the same values espoused in Charles's declaration of restoration and toleration. Separated by nation, religion and history, Heemskerck and Charles offered a surprisingly similar message: the time of sin and chaos was coming to an end. Paradise was there for the taking, but for some it would require searching judgement, possibly even death and damnation.

A Bassano imitator's *Flight into Egypt* would have appealed to the itinerant prince as he prepared to return home, while Pedro Orrente's *Betrayal of Christ* drew parallels with the execution of his father, a comparison assiduously exploited by the royalist party. Pieter Brueghel's masterpiece *The Massacre of the Innocents* also evoked the darker side of recent events. In the desolate cruelty of Brueghel's painting, the biblical scene is transposed on to the brutal occupation of the Low Countries in the late sixteenth century by the Spanish army. After witnessing many years of fighting and despoliation on both his home soil and across Europe, Charles must have found added resonance in the scene of an occupying army brutalizing a local community.

The Frizell acquisition shows that the new king's tastes were markedly different from those of his late father. Having been alternatively sheltered and spurned by both Catholic powers, Charles clearly found it politic to return to England with as few French and Spanish paintings as possible. On the other hand, northern European artists made up nearly half of his purchases, and included Dürer, Heemskerck, Brueghel, Brill and Beuckelaer. To some extent this was circumstantial; Frizell bought and sold in the Dutch Republic, and this was reflected in the pictures he offered the king. Nevertheless, Charles's new pictures showed that the balance of power in the art market had decisively shifted to the Low Countries. Landscapes, domestic interiors and still lifes had rarely attracted his father's more Italianate eye.

While the motives behind the Breda purchase seemed honourable and noble – to confer an aura of majesty upon the young king – what drove the sale was not royal patronage but a straightforward cash transaction. Times had changed since Frizell's dealings with Charles's father in the 1630s. The European art world was no longer centred on royal courts but on salerooms and auction houses, and this was partly due to the sale of Charles I's collection. Each painting was carefully priced in Frizell's inventory, from Heemskerck's biblical scene, valued at £120, to Hans Rottenhammer's £15 *St Christopher*. The prices were broadly comparable to those listed under the terms of the sale of the late king's goods, exploding the assumption made by many art historians that the English collection was sold too cheaply under the Commonwealth, and suggesting the establishment of a growing uniformity of prices and apprehension of aesthetic value across the European markets.

Frizell conceded that some of his pictures were stolen or plundered. 'These pieces,' he wrote of the Heemskercks and the Brueghel, 'were taken at Prague & from Sweden', where they were 'brought hither by the Queen of whom I had them'.[35] Originally part of the celebrated collection of the Habsburg emperor Rudolf II, the pictures were looted in 1648 during Queen Christina of Sweden's siege of Prague. Over 500 paintings were forcibly removed from the imperial palaces and sent back to Stockholm. In 1654, to the shock of the courts of Europe, Christina abdicated, converting to Roman Catholicism and selling off much of her collection to dealers, among them Frizell.[36] In restocking the collection of one fallen monarch, Frizell had few scruples in purchasing from another; in fact, as far as he was concerned, the Prague connection was a selling point. In the pursuit of fine painting, one monarch's misfortune was another's opportunity.

It is uncertain if Frizell also profited by selling Charles pictures from his dead father's collection. The descriptions of at least four paintings in his list closely match those sold in the early stages of the sale, including the beautiful little Veronese studio piece *Venus, Mars and Cupid with a Mirror*.[37] If Frizell dealt in plundered pictures from Prague, as well as the sale of Buckingham's pictures to the Habsburgs, the chances are that he also trafficked in paintings sold in London under the Commonwealth, and that Charles was unwittingly spending money buying pictures he regarded as his by birth.

The king-in-waiting was shrewd enough to realize that returning to England laden down with crates of paintings would not create a good impression. Although eager to capitalize on his father's martyrdom, he did not intend to repeat his father's mistakes as he sought to consolidate his political restoration. Charles II was not drawn to pictures and statuary on the same scale as his father, who had often acquired works of art regardless of the financial and political cost. In contrast, his son bought, commissioned and graciously accepted paintings and statues based on the anticipated political capital they would confer on his new reign. As a result, he was prepared to bide his time before displaying his newly acquired pictures. At the end of Frizell's inventory, Charles scribbled, 'Frizell, keep these pictures till I send for them at Breda.' Less than two months later, on 29 May 1660, his thirtieth birthday, King Charles II entered London to claim his throne.

CHAPTER FOURTEEN

∽

THE ART OF RESTORATION

CHARLES RETURNED TO THE CITY he had fled eighteen years earlier a conquering hero, riding in state through the streets of London like a Roman emperor. Republicans, like the poet John Milton and Lucy Hutchinson, lamented his return, but the diarist John Evelyn was ecstatic. He recorded that the new king's path was 'strewed with flowers, the bells ringing, the streets hung with tapestry, fountains running with wine . . . the windows and balconies all set with ladies; trumpets, music and myriads of people flocking the streets'. Evelyn 'stood in the Strand, and beheld it and blessed God'. The return was all the more remarkable because, as Evelyn pointedly concluded, it took place 'without one drop of blood, and by that very army, which rebelled against him'.[1] It was an auspicious start to the Restoration.

If Charles thought he was returning to a capital bereft of the symbols of his father's rule, he was wrong. Throughout the last weeks of May the committee for both the restoration of the royal goods and the new king's reception worked frantically to restore what remained of his father's collection. On 23 May the new Royal Surveyor, John Webb, requested a list of all the returned paintings available for hanging throughout the royal palaces. It was pitifully thin. Three days later the Lords handed the cache of returned goods to Clement Kinnersley and gave him just three days to hang, arrange and display them throughout the rooms of the royal residences.[2] His task was complicated by the reserved goods that never left the royal residences. This was royal interior design on an epic scale. One can only imagine the chaos involved in transporting the bulky tapestries, statues, pictures and cloth of state, then mixing and matching them to maximum political and aesthetic effect, and minimum royal embarrassment.

While Kinnersley rushed to refurbish Whitehall, the other royal palaces were redecorated, having experienced two decades as army barracks. Hugh Woodward, Housekeeper to St James, renovated the palace's ravaged gardens. Down on the Strand Henry Browne, Housekeeper of Somerset House, spent £345 on the grounds of the queen's former residence, lamenting that the gardens where so many of Charles I's classical statues once stood were now 'utterly spoiled and defaced, and many great dunghills made there, by the three regiments that lately have quartered there'.[3] All three received handsome rewards for their hard work, particularly Kinnersley, who received £211 for his efforts on the eve of Charles's return.[4] By the time that Charles entered London the following day, the royal residences were partially restored to their former splendour.

It is one of the great paradoxes of the Restoration that the royal grandeur inherited by Charles II was largely due to the one man who spent over two decades of his life trying to destroy the Stuart monarchy: Oliver Cromwell. With hardly any returned possessions to work with, Kinnersley was reduced to rearranging the paintings, statues and tapestries reserved by Cromwell during his time as Lord Protector. Kinnersley tacitly conceded as much in his May inventory of what remained in the palaces, composed entirely of the goods reserved for Cromwell's use. There were fifteen sets of 'rich hangings of Arras with gold in the drapery', valued at £34,000, including a series of the lives of Caesar and Pompey worth £5,022, the defeat of the Spanish Armada and the life of Abraham, valued at £8,206.[5] As well as 220 other tapestries, Kinnersley listed thirty-one pictures, plus Mantegna's *Triumphs*. The total came to £40,758 18s 6d. This was still well down on the earlier accounts of over £53,000 worth of goods reserved for the state, but puts into perspective the size of the legacy inadvertently bequeathed to the new king by the republican regime.

The king settled into his refurbished Whitehall apartments in the first weeks of June 1660 and set about one of his first tasks: appointing a new political administration. His Privy Council was careful to represent the political and religious perspectives of the various interest groups that still defined his divided nation. Edward Hyde retained his post as Lord Chancellor and Sir Edward Nicholas remained as Secretary of State, reward for their loyal service to Charles in exile. Former Cromwell supporters were also included, most prominently General Monck, appointed Captain-General of the armed forces. Wartime parliamentarians who opposed the regicide found favour as well, including the Earl of Northumberland, who was briefly appointed Lord High Constable.[6]

As Charles and his advisers manufactured a new political consensus, he was required to settle an avalanche of outstanding petitions from individuals requesting preferment, promotion and restitution. They included old royalists pleading for reinstatement or recompense for lost revenues and salaries, and republicans now eager to curry royal favour. Many of these petitions shed colourful light on the fate of the royal goods. Carew Hervy *alias* Mildmay, former Yeoman of the Jewel House in the Tower of London, asked for reinstatement, beseeching Charles to take 'pity and favour upon your father's old servant'. Mildmay claimed that when Charles I fled London it was agreed 'one officer should stay behind to look to the treasure that was left in the said office which fell to your petitioner's lot'. When the sale's trustees arrived to inventory the jewel house, they demanded Mildmay 'deliver up the keys of the said office, which your petitioner refusing to do, they broke open the office doors and took away in gold and silver plate to the value of £7,000 beside what was in the Upper Jewel House'.[7] Despite his dramatic plea, there is no record that Mildmay received any restitution for his loyalty.

Even more revealing was the audacious petition of Emmanuel de Critz, who, in mid-May, submitted one of the largest lists of royal goods, valued at £1,576. It included twenty-four paintings and, more significantly, 'that incomparable head in marble of the late king's': Bernini's bust of King Charles I.[8] De Critz's inventory offered a fascinating glimpse of his activities as head of the first, fifth and fourteenth dividends in 1651. He made complicated distinctions between those pictures he 'possessed solely', those he held in common with others and those entrusted to him by others.

As with so many pictures dispersed among the dividends in the 1650s, possession was an ambiguous matter. Like all the other returnees, de Critz kept quiet about the massive profits he had made selling pictures to Cárdenas, Jabach and Bordeaux. Instead he claimed that the paintings 'have been ever since preserved by him [de Critz] with great care and danger'. This was a lie, and one that the usually assured dealer told because he failed to sell the pictures before the king's return. That the Giulio *Europa* turned out to be a poor imitation by an inferior artist was little comfort to de Critz. As the son of James I's Serjeant-Painter John de Critz, Emmanuel now claimed his father's position, £4,000 in backdated salary, and a further £1,200 for the money spent on buying pictures and statues, especially Bernini's statue, 'having used all manner formerly to convey it to your Majesty, but could not'.[9] It was a remarkably audacious claim, only partly justified by de Critz's reference to his brother's death at Oxford fighting for the royalist cause.

Pepys's diaries reveal just how quickly dealers and collectors like de Critz and Northumberland moved to retrieve royal favour. Visiting Whitehall on 30 June 1660 with his friend Edward Montagu, Earl of Sandwich, Pepys 'saw a great many fine antique heads of marble, that my Lord Northumberland had given the king. Here meeting with Mr De Critz, he looked over many of the pieces in the gallery with me and told me whose hands they were, with great pleasure.'[10] Not only had Northumberland hastily returned royal statues obtained during the sale, but de Critz was also back at the heart of the royal collection, showing admiring visitors like Pepys around what remained. Pepys was clearly impressed by the smooth-talking painter; he borrowed Peter Lely's portrait of Montagu and paid de Critz to make a copy.

Neither de Critz nor any of the other petitioners received immediate satisfaction of the claims because, throughout the first months of his reign, Charles was embroiled in the complex and fraught process of forging a new political and religious settlement. Controversy raged in particular over the proposed Act of Indemnity and Oblivion. Under the terms of the Declaration of Breda unconditional pardons were offered to any republicans who promised to accept Charles's authority. The king insisted that it was up to Parliament to establish the specific terms of the act, but this proved more difficult than expected. Many in Charles's Parliament demanded capital punishment for those involved in the late king's execution, while others felt it was more important to address losses of money, property and life during the Civil War, all of which the proposed Act of Indemnity broadly disregarded.[11]

Opportunistic members of the previous regime were already experiencing Parliament's wrath. For the Knave of Diamonds, Sir Henry Mildmay, rechristened 'Sir Reverence Henry Bauble',[12] it was the end of a long and eventful career as both royalist and rebel. When questioned about his involvement in the sale of the crown jewels, he tried to flee the country but was captured at Rye and brought before the House of Commons. He was committed to the Tower and sentenced to the humiliation of being annually paraded through London's streets on the anniversary of the king's execution with a rope tied round his neck. Calmer heads prevailed and the sentence was commuted to exile in Tangier, but Mildmay died en route in Antwerp. His fate suggested that, despite the promises of toleration, for some the Restoration would also bring its share of retribution.

On 29 June orders allowing royalists to repossess goods taken from them under the Commonwealth were issued. Meanwhile, the Privy Council turned its attention back to the recovery of royal property, empowering Clement Kinnersley, the former Lord Protector's Wardrobe Keeper, to submit a list to the Lord Chamberlain, the Earl of Manchester, 'of all such plate Jewels and other Goods as belong to his Majesty' in his possession.[13] The list did not include a single picture. This was a serious embarrassment for the council, which immediately reconvened to take action. With the king in attendance, the Attorney General, Sir Geoffrey Palmer, issued a proclamation instructing all those in possession of royal goods 'that they should forthwith bring them in, or make discovery thereof under the penalty of his Majesties high displeasure'.[14]

The council also moved to act on information already supplied on the whereabouts of some of the royal possessions. They had heard of a Lieutenant-Colonel Cox, living at the Swan in Dowgate. Cox knew 'where to discover diverse trunks or bails of goods and household stuff belonging to [Richard] Cromwell; the most part whereof is conceived to be hangings and other moveables, which are his Majesty's'. Clement Kinnersley took charge of the case himself, raiding the Cromwell household and repossessing 'all that he found pertaining to his Majesty' held by both Richard and

Oliver's widow, Elizabeth.[15] It was no accident that one of the first forcible removals of royal merchandise targeted Oliver Cromwell's surviving family. Just as the public sale of 1649 was an explicitly political act aimed at the appropriation and dispersal of the symbols of monarchy, so the 1660 restoration of the royal collection provided political justification for the punishment of those involved in the death of the king and the sale of his possessions.

The publication of Attorney General Palmer's *Proclamation for the Restoring and Discovering his Majesty's Goods* on 14 August 1660 spelled out the new regime's position in no uncertain terms. Those in possession of the goods 'which did belong to our late dear Father' and 'have been purloined and embezzled, or upon pretences seized, taken and received' were instructed to deliver them to the Earl of Sandwich, Master of the Great Wardrobe, by 29 September, 'under the penalty of our high displeasure, and as they will answer the contrary at their peril'. As with the Commonwealth sale, the new government promised 'that we will reasonably reward any of our well affected subjects or others who shall discover unto us any of the said Goods wilfully concealed'.[16] Informants were entitled to 20 per cent of the value of all returned goods, a lucrative enticement but also one that, as with the Commonwealth sale, could only encourage fraud and corruption.

The proclamation unleashed one of the great unsung villains of the history of the royal collection, the royalist Colonel William Hawley. Since early May he and his accomplice, Colonel Hercules Lowe, had been quietly sequestering pictures marked with Charles I's brand, having been appointed by the Lords to secure concealed royal possessions and deliver them to Kinnersley in preparation for the return of the king.[17] By August 1660 Hawley was finally given the legal authority to requisition royal assets, together with an eager team of repossession men. Armed with detailed inventories, Clement Kinnersley's enthusiastic support back in Whitehall, the able assistance of his fellow enforcer Colonel Lowe and a network of avaricious informers, Hawley began the arduous but profitable task of commandeering concealed royal assets.

Many people eager for a slice of the rewards offered for concealed possessions needed little prompting from the likes of Hawley. Christopher Clapham, secretary to the 1st Earl of Sussex,

Thomas Savile, wrote to the Chancellor of the Exchequer, Sir Anthony Ashley Cooper, just a week after the publication of the proclamation, regarding his late master. Savile had been elevated to the peerage and Privy Chamber by Charles I but, like so many peers involved in the sale, had wavered between committing himself to either king or Parliament, which led to his imprisonment by both sides in the 1650s.[18] Although there is no official record of Savile's involvement in the royal sale, Clapham wrote to Cooper regarding 'those pictures of the late king's which my Lord of Sussex bought at Somerset House'. Clapham claimed that he was with Sussex when he spent the unlikely sum of £2,500 for some of the finest, sadly unspecified, pictures in the sale, and that he made Savile promise to return the pictures upon the restoration of the king.[19]

Admitting that he was unable to gain access to the pictures because they were locked in a room in Savile's Howley Hall residence, Clapham went on to accuse other parliamentary sympathizers associated with Savile of not only buying but stealing pictures from the royal collection. According to the garrulous Clapham, 'My Lady Temple, Sir Richard Temple's mother, at that very time stole a picture out of the Queen's closet and tied it to her lath under her petticoat which was valued at £20', presumably referring to the cost of the picture, not the petticoat. The Temples were a pro-parliamentary family that included regicides among its kin, making them obvious targets for opportunists like Clapham, who insisted, 'I never was any informer before, but in this I conceive I do but the will of the dead and the duty and obedience I owe to my prince.' Even Clapham thought better of pursuing pictures hidden in Lady Temple's petticoats, but on Cooper's authority he wrote to Savile's widow, Lady Sussex, demanding that she return her dead husband's twenty paintings to the king.[20] There is no record of any subsequent returns, but Clapham was apparently after his 20 per cent share of £2,500 worth of restored pictures – a lucrative £500. His grasping submission set the tone for the subsequent trail of deceitful, fraudulent and politically motivated claims and repossessions.

While Christopher Clapham pursued the Earl of Sussex's pictures, Lowe and Thomas Beauchamp went after another nobleman with links to the former Commonwealth – Philip, Lord Viscount Lisle. Beauchamp travelled down to Lisle's Sheen residence to inventory and repossess the 120 pictures, statues and gems formerly in the royal collection. Beauchamp recorded that he 'was appointed to attend the Lord Viscount Lisle to demand the aforesaid goods all which were accordingly received' and returned to Whitehall.[21] What Beauchamp omitted to mention was that in the mid-1650s he had sold Lisle some of the same statues that he now reclaimed on behalf of the crown. Beauchamp had acted in a similar capacity for Lisle's uncle, the Earl of Northumberland, but the shrewd High Constable, mindful of his position in the new administration, hastily paid for copies of his royal pictures and statues, dispatching the originals to join those Pepys had seen in Whitehall, before Beauchamp or Hawley came knocking.[22]

As Hawley, Lowe and Beauchamp went about their work during the autumn of 1660, King Charles received an unexpected addition to his depleted collection. On the eve of his departure from Scheveningen in May, the states of Holland and West Friesland had pledged to dispatch a suitable gift once Charles was reinstalled in England. The States had a long record of sending pictures as diplomatic gifts to the Stuart family, including the presentation of maritime paintings to the young Prince Henry in 1610 and the less successful presentation of old altarpieces and cows to Charles I and Henrietta Maria in 1636. By 1660 the Dutch art market was infinitely more sophisticated in its sensitivity to international demand, partly because of the sheer volume of high-quality pictures that now passed through its cities.[23] Many of the king's former paintings, as well as those of his fellow collectors Arundel, Buckingham and Hamilton, were sold through Dutch dealers, and this gave the States a good idea of which pictures to choose with the deliberate intention of replacing those sold off under the Commonwealth.

To avoid embarrassment, the States sought to establish the new king's artistic tastes. Their intelligence revealed that his official tastes remained similar to that of his father: he would welcome Italian painting and classical sculpture in preference to modern northern European artists.[24] The States accordingly acquired twenty-four paintings and twelve statues from the collection of the merchant brothers Gerard and Jan Reynst. The pictures were first-rate Italian masterpieces purchased by the brothers while on business in Venice from the collection of one of the city's most distinguished collectors, Andrea Vendramin, following his death in 1629. The States paid 80,000 guilders for the paintings and statues, which perfectly fitted King Charles's requirements. However, the States were proud of the new style of contemporary Dutch artists painting landscapes, domestic interiors and architectural scenes, and could not resist supplementing the Reynst pictures with works by Gerrit Dou and Pieter Saenredam, despite admonitions against sending modern works.

By November the gift was in London, where it was bestowed on the king at a special ceremony held at the Banqueting House. The Dutch ambassadors presented 'an excellent collection of pictures of the most famous, ancient and modern masters, with a great number of statues of white marble and excellent sculpture'. Charles addressed the ambassadors and 'heartily thanked them for so worthy a present, and expressed his willingness to enter into a nearer alliance with them'.[25] The envoys were gratified to observe that Charles was particularly pleased with the works of Dou and Saenredam, as well as the more obvious favourites like Tintoretto, Schiavone, Lotto, Bassano and, of course, Titian. John Evelyn expressed the shifting taste of the new regime when he visited Whitehall a few weeks later. He was impressed by the striking realism of Dou's works, especially the two-year-old domestic interior *The Young Mother*, praising 'those two rare pieces of drolerie, or rather a Dutch kitchen, painted by Douce [Dou] so finely as hardly to be at all distinguished from enamel'.[26] Despite the condescending reference to the pictures as 'drolerie', or comical paintings, Evelyn's and the king's diplomatic admiration of the Dutch pieces marked a new departure for the royal collection's interest in Dutch art.

What immediately struck the restored royal court was how the carefully chosen pictures were meant to replace particular works sold off under the Commonwealth. A Cariani *Reclining Venus* bore more than a passing resemblance to Titian's *Pardo Venus*, by then in Paris, and a painting of *Christ on a Lamb, the Virgin and St Joseph* by a member of the School of Raphael (since lost) was closely based on Raphael's *La Perla*, already on show in the Spanish royal collection in Madrid.[27] The Dutch gift also tried to make up for the loss of all Charles I's Titians by presenting his son with three paintings attributed to the Venetian master. To this day the *Portrait of Jacopo Sannazaro* remains the only original undisputed Titian in the royal collection.[28]

Other pictures designed to settle political debts also arrived from the Low Countries. On Thursday 15 November Pepys called on de Critz to collect the commissioned portrait of the Earl of Sandwich. Pepys was soon absorbed and 'stayed and did see him give some finishing touches to my Lord's picture, so that at last it was complete to my mind, and I leave mine with him to copy out another for himself, and took the original by a porter with me to my Lord's'. It is a fascinating glimpse into the evolving Restoration art market: Pepys overseeing the completion of the portrait to his liking, not only being 'well pleased with it and the price' of £3 10s, but also allowing de Critz to reproduce the copy while returning the borrowed Lely portrait to the earl. However, by the time Pepys arrived at the earl's residence there was an even better picture to discuss. 'My Lord did this day show me the King's picture,' reported Pepys, 'which was done in Flanders, that the king did promise my Lord before he ever saw him, and that we did expect to have had at sea before the King came to us; but it came but to-day, and indeed it is the most pleasant and the most like him that ever I saw picture in my life.'[29] Once again, pictures were being traded as political currency, but this time within a very specific market economy.

In the autumn of 1660, Charles presided over the trial and execution of the regicides Parliament had insisted should be exempted from the original Act of Indemnity. John Milton narrowly escaped the hangman, but in October ten convicted regicides were publicly hung, drawn and quartered at Charing Cross. Evelyn did not watch the executions, 'but met their quarters mangled and cut and reeking as they were brought from the gallows'.[30] The stench of burned flesh was so powerful that the locals complained the air was becoming putrefied.[31] The decision to execute the men in such a fashion tainted what had been until then a seemingly harmonious period of political transition.

Restitution quickly gave way to the settling of old scores.

Encouraged by the prospect of receiving a fifth of the value of all returns, Hawley and his associates began to employ increasingly heavy-handed tactics. They raided the Cromwell household again, causing Elizabeth to lodge a formal complaint, requesting 'protection from unwarranted searching through her possessions for the Late King's goods, of which she is willing to swear she knows nothing'.[32] John Embree was summarily dismissed as Serjeant Plumber to the royal household for acting under 'the usurping powers',[33] and to add insult to injury Hawley confiscated his pictures. Quakers and Anabaptists were also targeted, often falsely accused of concealing royal assets. Hawley's agents went to extraordinary lengths to recover possessions. William Bell, another republican supporter, complained that his kitchen floor was dug up in search of nonexistent royal plate, but he received no compensation for the vandalism.[34] The former republican mayor of London and architect of the original sale of Charles I's goods, John Ireton, was forced to surrender plate and jewels that, it was claimed, belonged to the king, and suffered repeated periods of imprisonment in the Tower of London.

Hawley and his team were spinning out of control. John Cottrell and William Hubbard petitioned Parliament for permission to 'break up six houses in London' where they believed £12,000 worth of royal goods were concealed.[35] The victims of these increasingly arbitrary raids started to hit back. Lucy Needham petitioned the Privy Council for restoration of 'the greatest part of her household stuff, together with four or five hampers of books', which were forcibly removed by Hawley and Lowe, 'but no part of all of which belonged to His Majesty, but given to her by her father'. The council found in Needham's favour and ordered Hawley to return the purloined goods.[36]

Many were not as fortunate as Lucy Needham. They suffered removal of and destruction to property, fines and in some cases even imprisonment. One of the king's earlier petitioners, Carew Hervy *alias* Mildmay, encapsulated public outrage at Hawley's activities in his second petition, dated 3 April 1661. Mildmay reiterated his loyal service under Charles's father. He pointed out that the sale's trustees had partially settled his outstanding salary of over £1,000 with a gift of £250 worth of plate. However:

... since his Majesty's restoration Colonel Hawley and Colonel Lowe procured a Warrant to seize the said plate (which was long since sold for the Petitioner's present subsistence) who took from the Petitioner £150 ready money for his Majesty, until his Royal pleasure were further known. And in regard, it hath pleased his Majesty, by the late Act of Indemnity, to forgive and confirm all such of his late Majesty's goods and chattels as were sold or disposed of to any of his late Majestie's servants or Creditors towards satisfaction of their debts or wages. Prayed that he may enjoy the benefit of the said Act & restitution of the said £150, taken from him by the said Colonel Hawley and Colonel Lowe.[37]

Mildmay argued that under the terms of the Act of Indemnity the plate rightly belonged to him. By fining Mildmay £150 for failure to return the plate, Hawley and Lowe were in effect refusing to recognise debts incurred by the king's deceased father. At least the Commonwealth had attempted to reimburse creditors for outstanding royal debts; Charles II was not only ignoring his loyal subjects' claims for compensation but also beggaring them in the most humiliating way possible.

Charles and his ministers only decided to rein in Hawley because they were anxious to forestall any threats to their popular appeal in the run-up to parliamentary elections beginning in March and the ensuing royal coronation, planned for St George's Day, 23 April, 1661. When Thomas Garrett of Norwich submitted a petition contesting his summary fine of £700 and subsequent imprisonment at the hands of Hawley and Lowe, the Privy Council immediately annulled Hawley's authority. The king personally demanded 'that the said William Hawley and Hercules Lowe do speedily deliver over by true & perfect Inventory into the custody of Mr Kinnersley Yeoman of his Majesties Wardrobe all such Goods, Hangings, Pictures, Books and other things as they have seized upon and are now in their custody'.[38] It was the first serious attempt to hold Hawley and his team accountable for their harsh and unjust actions.

On 23 April Charles was finally invested as King Charles II of England, Scotland and Ireland, in a spectacular coronation ceremony held at Westminster that closely replicated the style and language of his father's investiture back in 1626.[39] Because most of the royal regalia had been destroyed or sold off during the Interregnum, Charles commissioned a new set at the cost of over £31,000.[40] The imperial crown had survived, and was hastily repaired and embellished. Charles required a dazzling visual affirmation of his restoration to royal power and it was provided by John Michael Wright's coronation portrait showing him arrayed in the robes of both Parliament and the Garter, his father's favourite royal order. Behind him hangs a recovered tapestry of the Judgement of Solomon, intended to express Charles's pious wisdom, as well as a subtle nod towards the legacy of that earlier self-styled Solomon, his grandfather, King James I. It was a powerful symbol of majesty, but many who admired it could also see that it was composed of a tarnished assortment of objects salvaged from Cromwell and the impoverished royal creditors.

By August 1661 Colonel Hawley had completed his inventory. Entitled 'A Booke conteining severall of his Maties goods brought into his Maties closset and wardrop by Col. Wm. Hawley, by the order of a Committee of Lords, in April 1660', it was a remarkable vindication of his crude but effective methods.[41] It provided a description of every item he collected, listed by date of acquisition, although it omitted details of previous owners, and nominal values. Having stockpiled items throughout the previous eighteen months, Hawley's list was finally long enough to submit as an impressive testament to his nefarious activities.

For 16 August Hawley listed the official return of over 600 pictures and 203 statues.[42] This was the largest movement of an English art collection since 23 October 1651, when the allocation of the dividends under the Rump Parliament dispersed over 700 art works to its creditors. Even more remarkably, the majority of the paintings originally carted out of the royal residences in 1651 now found themselves right back where they had started. Without further information it is impossible to match all of Hawley's returns alongside either the sale's inventory or van der Doort's original catalogue of the royal collection, but this was probably a deliberate decision. By omitting names of previous owners, Hawley avoided charges of taking goods that never belonged to the king. However, most of the royal pieces listed earlier in May 1660 were now back in Whitehall, including those briefly owned by de Critz, Embree, Harrison, Stone and the Earl of Northumberland.

Back came scores of paintings of the royal family and their relatives, most of whom were now dead or dispersed across Europe. There were also pictures ascribed to what Hawley referred to as 'The rarest masters in the world': Titian, Raphael, Correggio, Holbein and Tintoretto.[43] Unfortunately, as with many previous functionaries who had tried to catalogue the royal collection, Hawley was duped by the brilliance of anonymous copiers of the Old Masters. Not a single picture by the undisputed hand of Titian, Raphael or Correggio was returned.[44] Works by these artists previously owned by Charles I were now in private collections scattered across Europe. In place of his father's lost Titians, Charles II had to settle for the two pictures attributed to the Venetian master presented to him by the Dutch states.

Paintings that were returned constituted the bulk of Charles I's original collection. Hawley listed no fewer than fourteen paintings by Van Dyck, five of which are still held in the current royal collection. These paintings provided a virtual pictorial inventory of Charles II's childhood. They included two portraits of his dead father, in his robes of state and on horseback, and the particularly emotive portraits featuring the young Prince Charles in the bosom of his family, so many of whom were now dead: *The Five Eldest Children of Charles I* and the towering *Great Piece*.

For Charles, the emotional power of seeing such paintings again must have been profound, but, always quick to exploit an opportunity, he immediately maximized their political potential. He put *The Great Piece* back in the Long Gallery in Whitehall, exactly where it had hung during his father's reign. It was an obvious way of acknowledging his father while also affirming his own natural succession to the throne he now occupied. There he stood at his father's knee, the heir apparent; Van Dyck's prophecy had come to pass. By the early 1660s, however, the message of Van Dyck's painting underwent a subtle transformation from its original intention. The king is dead, the painting now seemed to suggest; long live the king.

The strategic rehanging of *The Great Piece* was in notable contrast to the fate of the restored equestrian portrait *Charles I with*

M. de St Antoine, which focused exclusively on the new king's father. The exact nature of its return remains shrouded in mystery, although a later eighteenth-century commentator claimed that, following Remigius Van Leemput's failure to sell the painting in Antwerp, it was 'taken from him by due course of law', probably by Hawley.[45] When it arrived back in the royal collection, Charles II hung it at Hampton Court, a suitable act of filial piety, although one that remained at a discreet distance from where such political gestures really mattered, in Whitehall.

Charles's approach towards art and collecting was pragmatic. Brought up observing his father's ruling passion for art and with his aesthetic judgement sharpened by the time spent in exile at the French court, Charles appreciated the importance of defining his restored majesty through the acquisition of a splendid collection of paintings. This is why he risked popular opprobrium in supporting Hawley and his henchmen in their crooked pursuit of royal goods, gratefully accepted the Dutch gift, spent over £2,000 on Frizell's pictures when he could ill afford it and relaxed moribund laws forbidding the importation of pictures.[46] But he never gambled on his political or financial security by pursuing a large collection of paintings, as his father had done when buying the Mantua collection.

Charles was more financially constrained than his father, but he remained largely indifferent to the talents of his officially appointed Principal Painter, Peter Lely, and left the serious connoisseurship and patronage of the arts to his brother James, Duke of York. Some of his subjects were openly contemptuous of his interest in the arts. Anne Oliver, widow of the miniaturist Isaac Oliver, refused Charles's offer of an annuity in exchange for her husband's miniatures, claiming they would only be squandered on his bastards and strumpets.[47] The king's artistic patronage does suggest that he was far more interested in commissioning portraits of his mistresses than of Roman emperors, but at least this was in keeping with his political stature within Europe and lacked the imperial hubris and political bad faith of his father.[48]

Charles's attitude towards collecting comes across in his sanguine response to Hawley's success in returning such an impressive haul of pictures and statues. It was a vindication of the colonel's crooked methods and the king had little compunction about allowing Hawley to carry on with his work, however distasteful it appeared. To the dismay of his many enemies, the colonel became not only unassailable but also a very rich man based on the percentages he claimed from the returned goods. Over the next four years he continued to execute his role with relish, receiving repeated payments from the grateful and admiring Secretary of State, Sir Henry Bennet.[49]

Hawley's position was secured by his appointment in 1662 to a royal committee for the recovery of Charles I's belongings, appointed to interrogate the trustees, contractors and treasurers involved in the Commonwealth sale of the king's estate and demand financial or material restitution from those still in possession of royal assets. Hawley was not the only opportunistic member of the committee. It included his accomplices Thomas Beauchamp, Francis Rogers, William Rumbold, Thomas Chiffinch, the Keeper of the Privy Closet, and one final member, Elias Ashmole.

Ashmole was an obsessive antiquarian who made a name for himself after the Civil War by cataloguing John Tradescant's collection of rarities known as the 'Ark'. The new king employed him to catalogue the royal coins, medals and gems, and act as Windsor Herald. At the time of his appointment to the new committee, he was embroiled in a legal battle with John Tradescant's widow, Hester, over possession of her husband's collection.[50] Ashmole won his case in Chancery, taking possession of the collection and denying Tradescant's widow her only potential source of income. Poor Hester drowned herself in despair, but Ashmole flourished. He was an assiduous bibliophile and offered his ill-gotten gains to Oxford University on the condition that they were housed in a suitably grand building. His gift provided the basis for the creation of today's Ashmolean Museum. The story of Ashmole's deceitful behaviour underlines the fact that the current royal art collection was not the only great English cultural institution to benefit from the nefarious activities of royal servants during the Restoration.

By the summer of 1662 Charles II was politically and financially secure. His marriage to Catherine of Braganza and the sale of Dunkirk to King Louis XIV for £290,000 enabled him to finally settle his debt to William Frizell of £2,860 and incorporate another seventy-two pictures into the resurrected royal collection.[51] However, his matrimonial and foreign policy seriously alienated the Spanish king, Philip IV. In June 1662 the Council of State in Madrid instructed its London ambassador, Baron Batteville, that 'if anything is proposed to you about the restitution of the paintings and tapestries that some ministers bought when the Parliamentarians sold the treasures of the deceased King Charles, you will excuse yourself that you have notice of this matter'.[52] This was as much a political as an aesthetic decision, as Spain prepared to launch undeclared war on England over the West Indies. As Edward Hyde argued in his assessment of those who profited from the Commonwealth sale, 'not one of all these princes ever restored any of their unlawful purchases to the King after his blessed restoration'.[53]

In many ways, the Spanish decision made little difference. By 1666, when Thomas Chiffinch completed his inventory of pictures held at Whitehall and Hampton Court, the royal collection was mostly restored. Many of its finest pictures by Titian, Raphael and Correggio were gone for ever, but Hawley's enthusiastic recovery of royal goods and the addition of Frizell's collection and the Dutch gift compensated for these losses in quantity if not exact quality.[54] The inventory taken in 1666 of the paintings on display in Whitehall and Hampton Court gives some indication of the scale of the restoration of the royal collection. The gaps in the manuscript suggest that Hawley was still busy repossessing pictures, but even by 1666 the returns were impressive, especially when compared to the size of the collection prior to the sale. Hampton Court contained 204 items, including Mantegna's *Triumphs*, while Whitehall held the bulk of the collection with 645 items. This represented nearly 200 more artworks than van der Doort had recorded in 1639. Unfortunately there are no inventories of the other royal palaces and the sheer number of pictures reveals that Charles II was even more intent on concentrating his collection within Whitehall than his father had been. Nevertheless, the final tally suggests that subsequent claims about the collection's irreparable dispersal were seriously exaggerated.

Comparisons between the 1666 inventory and van der Doort's reveal some departures but also remarkable continuities in the palace's decor between the fall of Charles I and the restoration of his son. In 1639 the Long Gallery, the centrepiece of the palace, boasted 103 pictures. Under Charles II it contained eighty-one. These included Van Dyck's *The Great Piece*, as well as pictures by Giulio Romano and Andrea del Sarto, and no less than twenty paintings by Fetti, many of them former Mantua pieces recovered from John Cade. Charles also displayed his new acquisitions – the Titian and Schiavone presented by the States-General, as well as several Dutch pictures. The king's Privy Gallery remained very similar to its appearance in 1639, when it had contained seventy-three pictures, mainly dynastic portraits. Under Charles II the gallery contained sixty-three pictures, including portraits of Henry VIII, Mary Queen of Scots, Frederick V and King Charles I again. However, once more the new king added his own acquisitions, including contemporary Dutch paintings and pictures bought from Frizell – Heemskerck's *Landscape with a Bridge*, Saenredam's *Haarlem Church* and Brueghel's *Massacre of the Innocents*.

Under Charles I, the Second Privy Lodging Room had been decorated with just nineteen erotic and mythological paintings by Polidoro da Caravaggio, Giulio Romano and Titian, the last of whom contributed its voluptuous centrepiece, the *Pardo Venus*. Charles II took a more sober approach to the room, but packed it with seventy paintings, retaining some Giulios but adding more dynastic portraits, including Holbeins, as well as copies of the lost Titians, significantly modifying the room's tenor. A similar process was repeated throughout the rest of the palace. Charles II's Cabinet Room featured 600 objects, mainly pictures, closely modelled on almost exactly the same number of pieces in his father's cabinet. The king's bedchamber also copied that of his father, containing just seven portraits, including Charles II's mother, Henrietta Maria, his wife, Catherine, his sister, Minette and Prince Henry, and one final nostalgic but also mischievously erotic reminder of his father's reign, Van Dyck's *Cupid and Psyche*.[55]

The restoration of Charles I's collection was almost complete, but there remained one final peculiar twist to the story, overlooked by those who remain more interested in the artistic activities of kings and princes than queens and princesses. Old before her time and plagued with illness, Charles II's mother, Queen Henrietta Maria, spent her years in exile experiencing repeated humiliation at the hands of a French court increasingly eager to make peace with the English Commonwealth and reluctant to pursue her claims for a dower income as Charles's royal widow. During her exile she found herself alienated from both her sons, Charles and James. Charles refused to accept his mother's counsel, for fear of being too closely identified with her Catholic, pro-French position. As hopes for Charles's restoration grew in the late 1650s, the queen took an increasing interest in the political fortunes of both her eldest children, although many in England still regarded her as a deeply divisive influence. Throughout the 1660s the queen and her entourage, which included the young deputy surveyor Christopher Wren, travelled back and forth between London and her Colombes residence outside Paris, advising and demurring over her children's marriages and sexual indiscretions.[56]

In December 1668 Henrietta Maria left her adopted country for the last time and returned to France. With Charles II's blessing, she took with her a dozen pictures from the recently restored royal collection. By this stage, the queen possessed little except her memories and her faith, both of which defined the pictures she selected. They included two Van Dycks from happier days: the painting of her *Three Eldest Children*, passed between Colonel Webb, Bordeaux and Peter Lely, and the portrait of *Charles II when Prince of Wales*, a copy of which still hung in Philip IV's collection in Madrid. Bought by Webb in the sale and returned by John Cade, the portrait was now back in the possession of the painted subject's mother.[57] In addition to paintings by her old court painter and religious compatriot, Henrietta Maria also chose the more explicitly religious work of another artist she and her husband had patronized in the 1630s, Orazio Gentileschi's *Joseph and Potiphar's Wife*. This picture, commissioned back in 1633–4 to hang in the Queen's House in Greenwich, contained bittersweet memories for Henrietta.[58] She also chose a portrait of her dead husband's brother, Prince Henry, as well as one of the first pictures to enter the fledgling Stuart art collection, Tintoretto's *Portrait of Marco Grimani*.[59]

The queen had less than a year to enjoy her pictures. She died at Colombes on 10 September 1669. When the news reached King Charles one of his first responses was to dispatch his French ambassador, Ralph Montague, to recover them.[60] Montague sent in a team to inventory Henrietta Maria's pictures and return them to London. When they entered the dead queen's apartments they found over seventy pictures, from the Van Dyck of Charles as a boy hanging in the vestibule to the picture of her son James, Duke of York, hanging in her bedroom. The most poignant discovery came when the officials entered the queen's most intimate room, the cabinet adjoining her bedroom. There they discovered a small case containing a 'miniature of the King when he was Prince of Wales'.[61]

As they moved through the queen's residence, the team appraised the paintings for both their provenance and their ease of removal. Cataloguing a painting by Guido Reni, they noted that 'this is an excellent picture, brought from England the last time, also fixed over the chimney, but 'tis thought removable'. The rule was simple: if it was not nailed down it went, or, in the prosaic language of the inventory, 'the pictures not fixed to be sent hither'.[62] The team's house clearance also ensured that Charles's royal collection actually gained several pictures originally owned outright by his mother, most significantly an extremely rare painting of the Resurrection, Hans Holbein's *Noli Me Tangere*.[63] It was typical of Charles to allow his mother to walk away with some of the finest paintings in his restored collection and then repossess them with interest after her death. When John Evelyn revisited the Whitehall galleries in 1680 the painting he admired more than any other was 'the *Noli me tangere* of our Blessed Saviour to Mary Magdalen, after his Resurrection, of Hans Holbeins', claiming, 'in my life, I never saw so much reverence & kind of heavenly astonishment expressed in picture'.[64] It is unlikely that Evelyn realized that the picture represented a further repossession on the part of his king.

By the end of Charles II's reign the royal collection boasted nearly 1,100 pictures and over 100 statues, composed primarily of pictures formerly owned by his father and repossessed in the first ten years of the Restoration. Estimates vary as to how many paintings were irretrievably lost to international buyers and domestic creditors. This is partly due to the sketchy records kept under the Restoration, especially when compared to the meticulous efforts of van der Doort and his Commonwealth counterparts. However, based on the figures available, the collection probably lost fewer than 300 pictures. In contrast to the breaking up of other seventeenth-century collections – for example, in Prague – this was hardly the cultural catastrophe claimed by subsequent commentators on the royal collection.

THE MOST POIGNANT SYMBOL of the political and artistic restoration of Charles II remains in the very heart of London. At the top of Whitehall, on the site of the city's ancient Charing Cross, stands Hubert Le Sueur's equestrian statue. Astride the horse sits the figure of King Charles I, gazing down Whitehall towards Inigo Jones's Banqueting Hall. Every year on 30 January a wreath is placed at the base of the statue, a discreet commemoration of the king's public execution just over 100 yards down the road.

The bizarre story of the statue's installation in Whitehall started in 1630, when Lord Treasurer Weston commissioned it from Charles I's French sculptor. In 1633 Henry Peacham admired 'the great horse with his Majesty upon it, twice as great as the life, and now well-nigh finished', claiming that it 'will compare with that of the New-Bridge at Paris, or those others at Florence and Madrid, though made by Sueur his Master, John de Bolonia that rare worke-man, who not long since lived at Florence'.[65] Later that year the statue was completed, but Weston died before it could be erected.[66] It was subsequently forgotten and, during the Civil War, was stored in the crypt of St Paul's in Covent Garden to escape the destruction aimed at other public statues of the king.

When the sale reached an impasse in 1650, the Council of State attempted to secure the statue, first discussing the whereabouts of the 'Brass Horse' and then dispatching officers to discover who owned it.[67] In 1655 an order was issued 'to state the matter of fact touching a statue in the churchyard of Covent Garden', where it was finally recovered. Parliament ordered the sale of

Charles 'for the rate of old brass, by the pound rate'[68] and terms were agreed with Mr John Rivett, a brazier from Holborn, on the strict condition that he agreed 'to break the said statue in pieces to the end that nothing might remain in memory of his said majesty'.[69]

By the spring of 1660, as former creditors started to return royal goods, the Earl of Portland, son of the late Lord Treasurer Weston, claimed the statue from Rivett, insisting that it 'belongs to him, and there being no Courts of Justice now open wherein he can sue for it, doth humbly desire the Lords to be pleased to order that it may not be removed from the place where it now is, nor defaced nor otherwise disposed of, till the Title may be determined in Law to whom it belongs'.[70] Rivett was ordered to surrender the statue to the Portland family only for it to be offered by Weston's widow, the Countess of Portland, to Charles II in 1671 at a cost of £1,500.

It was a shrewd proposal that provided Charles with the opportunity to acknowledge publicly his martyred father, while also basking in the reflected political glory of such a monument. However, he had reason to be sensitive about the erection of public statues. As he prepared to return to England in the spring of 1660, the Venetian ambassador reported that in place of the Royal Exchange's decapitated and defaced statue of Charles I, London's merchants were eager to erect a statue to General Monck, 'as a sign of their gratitude for what he has done, as he may truly be called the prime mover of the tranquillity this distressed nation is to enjoy again'.[71] Charles was clearly unprepared to countenance the elevation of such a potentially dangerous political rival and the public scheme was quietly forgotten. Nevertheless it was a telling episode in the initial struggle between the monarchy and the military on the eve of the Restoration and explains why Charles was eager to pay so much for Le Sueur's statue. Better piously to install a statue of his father than one of Cromwell's former lieutenants.

By 1674 Charles had agreed to pay the countess the sum of £1,600 for the statue, and ordered its installation at Charing Cross, a particularly emotive location. In 1647 the public cross at Charing had been pulled down as part of Parliament's religious 'reformation' of public monuments and in October 1660 the same site witnessed the execution of the regicides.[72] By placing his father's statue there, Charles II was ensuring that Charles I would posthumously ride in triumph over the religious and political opponents of his rule. In May 1675 Sir Christopher Wren was paid £2 to create designs for the stone pedestal upon which the statue would stand, but progress was once again delayed due to lack of funds. In his poem 'On King Charles the First his Statue', Andrew Marvell asked:

> What can the mystery be why Charing Cross
> These five months continue still blinded with board?

Work on the statue was finally completed towards the end of 1676, at a cost of £681, and it was unveiled to the public for the first time since Le Sueur cast it forty-three years before.

It is one of the many paradoxes of Charles I's art collection that the most public artwork associated with the king was neither commissioned by him nor displayed until nearly thirty years after his death. As with the restoration of the rest of the royal art collection, the completion of the statue said more about the political rise of Charles II than about the fall of his father, Charles I. Edmund Waller marked this in his epitaph 'On the Statue of King Charles I at Charing Cross', written in 1675:

> That the First Charles does here in triumph ride,
> See his son reign where he a martyr died,
> And people pay that reverence as they pass,
> (Which then he wanted!) to the sacred brass,
> Is not the effect of gratitude alone,
> To which we owe the statue and the stone;
> But heaven this lasting monument has wrought,
> That mortals may eternally be taught
> Rebellion, though successful, is but vain,
> And kings so killed rise conquerors again.
> This truth the royal image does proclaim,
> Loud as the trumpet of surviving fame.[73]

King Charles's 'surviving fame' was not what Waller or Le Sueur ever imagined. Today, the statue stands as a monument to the calamitous rule of a king who declared war on his elected Parliament: a move that limited for ever the absolute authority of the royal family and led to the greatest sale of royal art that England has ever seen.

EPILOGUE

About 4 this afternoon a fire broke out at Whitehall in Colonel
Stanley's lodgings near the waterside, which got such a head,
that notwithstanding all the care that was taken with playing
of Engines, and blowing up of part of buildings, the king's
apartments, with the lodgings adjoining, and part of the new
Long Gallery, and the other way the old Presence Chamber,
and as far as the chapel, are burned down.[1]

THE DISASTROUS FIRE that took place on 4 January 1698 was the
second to consume Whitehall in less than a decade. Scores of
paintings and tapestries restored during Charles II's reign were
destroyed. The greatest loss was Bernini's statue of King Charles I,
along with many of the Mantuan statues bought in 1629. It was
fire, and not republican fury, that ignominiously robbed the royal
collection of many of its finest pieces.

And what of the fate of those who spent much of their time
buying and selling Charles I's art collection? Endymion Porter
passed most of the war years in France, returning to England only
to find his goods confiscated and Charles on the verge of execution;
he died penniless in August 1649. Inigo Jones died poor and alone
in Somerset House in 1653, while Lord Cottington took a final
posting to Spain under Charles's government in exile, dying there
a confirmed Catholic in 1652. Emmanuel de Critz's petition for
restoration as Serjeant-Painter failed and he succumbed to the
plague in 1665. The bankrupt Burlamachi was briefly imprisoned
by Parliament and died in such penury in 1644 that his daughters
were forced into service. The irrepressible Gerbier tried to reinvent
himself as a republican under the Commonwealth, but when his
Bethnal Green academy (effectively a school for spies) failed, he

left to launch a mining operation in Guiana. While travelling to the colony, his daughter Katherine, depicted by Rubens in the *Allegory of Peace and War*, was murdered. The scheme collapsed and Gerbier returned to England, offering dubious artistic advice to a new generation of Stuart courtiers,[2] but failing to gain preferment under Charles II. He died in 1667.

Others fared better under King Charles II's regime. Nicholas Lanier had gone into exile in the 1640s but was reappointed master of the king's music. He ended his days playing at parties attended by Samuel Pepys. Other well-connected figures also flourished. Basil, Lord Feilding, who had switched sides and fought with distinction for Parliament, went on to oppose the king's execution and received a pardon from Charles II, dying peacefully in 1675. Northumberland also died quietly on his estate at Petworth in October 1668, one of the five wealthiest peers in England. Sir Peter Lely prospered as court painter, dying a popular portraitist and rich man in Covent Garden in 1680.

By the time of Charles II's death in 1685, London's art market was one of the busiest in Europe. This was partly due to the restored king's attitudes towards art and commerce. Unlike his father, Charles II avoided imposing rapacious taxes on the mercantile classes, stimulating economic confidence and growth. He was also more moderate in his approach to art, seeing it as something that enhanced his majesty but in no way defined it. Faced with the delicate process of political restoration and mindful of the criticism levelled at his father's collecting, he pursued a more tactful line, which contributed to a reign eight years longer, and a good deal less troubled. Under Charles II, most things – from mistresses to paintings – had a price. As a result, the trade in pictures boomed. Sales and even auctions became regular events in the fashionable district of Covent Garden, and between 1669 and 1692 over 35,000 oil paintings went through London's salerooms, involving twenty named noblemen, twenty dealers and over 100 'commoners'.[3] Following Peter Lely's death in 1680, public auctions of his collection of over 500 paintings raised more than £26,000; many of the pictures went to Dutch as well as English buyers.[4] Both Samuel Pepys and John Evelyn attended auctions, often held in the Banqueting House and Somerset House, the latter the location of the original sale. The international interest sparked by the trading in Charles I's collection meant that buyers were now eagerly participating in the sale and auction of a mass of art previously owned by bankrupt royalists, politically embarrassed republicans and individuals living beyond their means. By embracing an emerging credit economy, Charles II created the conditions for a thriving London art world, and it was the impact of the sale of his late father's goods that was primarily responsible for the new belief in the possibility of making profits from paintings.

Nevertheless, history has clung to the myth of the original sale as the philistine act of religious iconoclasts eager to squander the country's heritage in the name of godly reformation. It is a familiar but partisan story, part of a broader attempt to create an image of King Charles as a royal martyr, destroyed for his taste as much as for his politics. Restoration writers understandably heaped opprobrium upon the sale, but many later eighteenth-century historians embellished the myth, castigating the Commonwealth for destroying what they regarded as the first flowering of sensibility among the polite arts in England. Horace Walpole claimed that throughout history 'the mob have vented their hatred to tyrants on the pomp of tyranny. The magnificence the people have envied, they grow to detest, and mistaking consequences for causes, the first objects of their fury are the palaces of their masters . . . This was the case in the contests between Charles and his parliament.'[5] Like many other connoisseurs of his day, Walpole viewed the consequences of the sale through the prism of prevailing eighteenth-century conventions of taste and sensibility. From this perspective, Charles I was the great connoisseur in advance of his times and Parliament the representative of the uncultured mob. Once established, such beliefs proved remarkably enduring.

But was the sale really a cultural catastrophe? To focus on the breaking up of the collection ignores the remarkable act of artistic restitution that took place under Charles II, which saw the return of the majority of the dead king's pictures and statues, and was carried out with the same disregard for individual distress as that displayed by those involved in the initial dispersal. The sale itself transformed the royal paintings into worldly commodities, destroying for ever their royal exclusivity removing them from the privacy of the royal palace and releasing them into the world of the public sale. Italian Renaissance painting became more widely available and sought after than ever before, encouraging a more cosmopolitan style among subsequent English-born artists.[6] The loss and destruction of artworks was minimal and the finest pictures, sold to buyers like Cárdenas, Bordeaux and Jabach, are today on view in public museums and art galleries in cities including Paris, Madrid and Vienna. It is often easier to see these pictures in Europe than many of those still held in the British royal collection. The brief residence in Whitehall of paintings like Raphael's *La Perla* was just one part of its long, rich history and Van Dyck's *Charles I with M. de St Antoine*, for example, would not necessarily have retained its popularity without the colourful narrative of disappearance, theft and dramatic rediscovery that now accompanies it.

Claims that a group of cultural vandals perpetrated the sale simplify the complex and highly sophisticated responses to art on the part of those who opposed Charles I. These responses ranged from the iconoclastic anger of William Prynne to the deft connoisseurship of buyers like Colonel Hutchinson. The sale captured an abiding English ambivalence towards art, established since the Protestant Reformation, and this ambivalence manifested itself in various ways, one of which was to pull art away from church and palace, and push it towards the marketplace. Thus the sale gave the pictures a new lease of life, as their circulation and exchange among merchants, creditors, diplomats and international dealers created new definitions of their financial, political and aesthetic value throughout Europe.

With a relatively unregulated art market still in its infancy, it was difficult to establish the value of a Titian or a Dürer (partly because royal patrons and keepers like van der Doort refused to put a price on them). As a result, buyers, dealers, merchants and artists employed criteria other than the reputation of the artist and the quality of the creative object to judge aesthetic and financial value. Taking the example of Raphael's *Apostles* cartoons, the early eighteenth-century essayist Bernard Mandeville claimed:

The value that is set on paintings depends not only on the name of the Master and the time of his age he drew them in, but likewise in a great measure on the scarcity of his works, and what is still more unreasonable, the quality of the persons in whose possession they are as well as the lengths of time they have been in great families; and if the Cartoons now at Hampton Court were done by a less famous hand than that of Raphael, and had a private person for their owner, who would be forc'd to sell them, they would never yield the tenth part of the money which with all their gross faults they are now esteemed to be worth.[7]

Mandeville appreciated that the 'social life'[8] of the picture was central to its value. Where it came from, who owned it and where it hung were as important as who painted it and what it represented.

Once the sale of Charles I's collection had unleashed pictures on to the market, they followed circuitous social pathways in excess of what Parliament initially intended. Just as in the hands of King Charles I the collection failed to shore up his royal authority, so throughout the 1650s it failed to satisfy the financial demands of the royal creditors or the Commonwealth that ordered the king's death. Political pragmatists like Cromwell and Charles II learned to avoid making too many emotional or political investments in their art collections, with the result that their pictures served them well.

THE KINGS – and their republican enemies – perished, but the paintings endured. Today, the dispersed pictures can be seen in public galleries and museums across the world. At the heart of many of the great public art collections of Europe – the Louvre in Paris, the Prado in Madrid, the Kunsthistorisches Museum in Vienna – lie paintings originally owned by King Charles I. The departure of such pictures from seventeenth-century England represented one small step on the road to the creation of the public art gallery. With the subsequent collapse of the great European dynasties in the eighteenth and nineteenth centuries, the new industrial and financial elite took possession of the Old Masters. A more utilitarian approach to art emerged, stressing its educative dimension and calling for the creation of public national art collections. This development divested art of its aura of majesty and mystery, but provided artists with a previously unimaginable level of professional security and creative autonomy.

In England these developments might have taken place much earlier had the Commonwealth's short-lived period of republican rule successfully pursued its official policy of redistributing King Charles's art collection among its war-weary people. As it was, the experiment disintegrated amid political compromise, mismanagement and mutual recriminations. Most of the restored collection went back into the royal palaces. A fraction of the original Stuart collection is today on public display at Windsor, Hampton Court and Buckingham Palace. 'By definition,' according to a recent keeper of the collection, 'the royal collection is a private collection, held in trust by each monarch in turn for those who will succeed to the throne.' However, in the words of another twentieth-century keeper, its aim is also 'to make available to the public, in appropriately worthy surroundings (and only on deserving occasions) as many pictures as possible'.[9] This ambiguity is a direct legacy of the events that took place between 1642 and 1660 and the Collection remains, in large part, as inaccessible to the general populace as that of Charles I.

Afterword

DESPITE BEING one of the seventeenth century's greatest collectors, King Charles I had very little to say about art. He did, however, make one remark in 1638 that would prove more prophetic than even he could ever have realized. Speaking to his Keeper of Pictures, the king observed that paintings were the 'lasting monuments remaining to posterity'.[1] Like many seventeenth-century monarchs Charles assumed that an art collection was an enduring physical memorial to future generations of a monarch's magnificence. Little did he know just how prescient his remark would prove. The king's involvement in a protracted civil war from 1642, his execution in January 1649, the subsequent dispersal of his art collection under the Commonwealth (1649–60) and its partial restitution under his son Charles II, have all traditionally seen him celebrated as a royal martyr whose commitment to art and collecting was a 'lasting monument' to the taste and sensibility of a reign cut violently short by Puritan republicans personified in the figure of Oliver Cromwell. But there is another lasting monument to Charles's collection, and that has been the divided legacy of modern public art in this country. The partial and bitterly contested restitution of the king's collection under Charles II provided the foundation of the modern royal collection, one of the largest in the world. But with such foundations forged in political revolution and royal restoration came some enduringly awkward questions: was it a private collection bought and therefore owned by the monarchy, or a public and national one acquired with crown revenue? It was this ambiguous lasting legacy, or 'monument', that came to define *The Sale of the Late King's Goods* in the eleven years since its publication in April 2006.

At the heart of the book was the extraordinary story of the collection and the colourful cast of characters responsible for its creation, sale and restoration. Never before or since had paintings and politics, art and warfare come together in such a compelling mix. Despite widespread scholarly interest in the fate of Charles's art collection, nobody had written a book-length study of its seventeenth-century history from formation through dispersal to restitution, and for reasons that soon became clear to me. Art historians were wary of the political dimensions of the story, especially with the collection's sale under the Commonwealth regime; historians were likewise reluctant to engage with the complexities of aesthetics, iconography and collecting in explaining how the dispersal of the collection became a feature of Commonwealth and Protectorate policy. I was fortunate that my academic training was what is called 'interdisciplinary': in other words, I crossed literature, history, art and the specific field of Renaissance Studies, loosely understood as the period *c.* 1450–1650 that encompassed both Charles I's reign and the Old Master paintings he acquired. It enabled me to tell the story by combining disciplines and documents without any institutional involvement or academic commitment, something that would prove significant in the subsequent reception of the book.

It was only in the book's final paragraphs that I raised the thorny issue of the peculiar legacy of Charles's collecting and its impact on today's royal collection within the wider history of European art collecting. Yet it was this subject more than any other that came to define the book's impact. The revolutions that swept away so many of Europe's monarchies from 1789 also gave birth to the great public art collections like the Louvre in Paris, the Uffizi in Florence, the Hermitage in St Petersburg and the Kunsthistorisches Museum in Vienna that inherited the royal art of the Bourbon, Medici, Romanov and Habsburg dynasties. In England, the collapse of the Commonwealth and restoration of the monarchy under Charles II ensured that with the restitution of the royal collection no such transfer of royal art into the public domain would ever happen. It was not until the 1820s that London's National Gallery was founded, primarily thanks to private donors, despite unheeded calls for the royal collection to form the basis of a national one. As a result, despite the iconic status of the National Gallery, its permanent collection of around 2,500 paintings is nearly a third smaller than the

National Gallery of Ireland, and is dwarfed by comparable collections in Paris, Madrid and St Petersburg.

The political conditions that ensured the separation between the current royal and national collections also created perennial ambiguity over the former's ownership. Even before the book was published questions had been raised as to who owned what. In May 2002, the *Guardian* reported that 'as with most crown assets, the ownership status of the royal collection and the crown jewels has been muddied by time and different people's interpretations'.[2] When *The Sale of the Late King's Goods* was first published, the royal collection's website described its estimated 7,000 paintings, 500,000 prints and 30,000 watercolours and drawings (with an estimated worth of anything up to £10 billion) as 'the largest private collection of art in the world'. Since the book's publication the website has been amended and now insists '[t]he royal collection is not owned personally by the Queen, but is held in trust by her as Sovereign for her successors and the nation'. The Treasury deems the collection 'crown property', although statements by members of the royal family suggest they believe the Queen is technically at liberty to sell any of the pieces, should she so wish. Such confusion is compounded by the fact that, remarkably, for a major international collection of its size, the collection still has no complete inventory.

The royal collection's history is a classic English fudge, an unsatisfactory compromise between the royal elite that created it and the dissenting radicalism that tried, unsuccessfully, to dismantle it. The result is a divided collection, the national sitting in Trafalgar Square, the royal one dispersed across palaces throughout England and Scotland, with no inventory, and little sense why the fraction that *is* on display is shown as it is; hardly any paintings hang where they would have been displayed in the reign of Charles I, giving the lie to the 'appropriateness' of their settings. As many curators also confessed to me on condition of absolute anonymity, the royal collection lent very little, offered arbitrary reasons when they refused to loan and would clearly look askance at subsequent loan requests from anyone that openly criticized them.

Back in 2006 when my book was first published, it was well reviewed as a historical account of the collection's creation under Charles I, but it almost immediately generated controversy about the collection's role today. Some journalists questioned the collection's policy of public access and accountability, with one arguing that the royal family's 'excessive act of possession adds nothing to the prestige of royalty. Worse, it gets in the way of public appreciation of some of the world's supreme art'. Others like Brian Sewell defended the collection as a 'bargain', doubting that 'any government would be willing to double what it spends annually on museums and galleries, but that is what taking over the royal collection would mean'.[3] When I interviewed Sewell before the publication of this book I asked him how the royal collection would respond to criticism regarding public access. He was dismissive, saying they had 'heard them all before' and would not respond in the belief that they would 'go away'. To some extent he was right. The collection refused to engage with me in any meaningful public debate about its status before and after the book's publication (despite one of their curators haranguing me after a public talk at the National Gallery, which led to a letter of profuse apology from the then Keeper, Desmond Shawe-Taylor).

Over the last decade little has changed. In November 2006, the royal collection announced that it had reattributed a painting bought by Charles I in 1637 as a Caravaggio (rather than a copy, as had been assumed for 400 years).[4] *The Calling of Saints Peter and Andrew* has since been authenticated as by Caravaggio's hand and, instead of being worth tens of thousands of pounds, is now valued somewhere in the region of £50 million. It was a wonderful discovery, but it begged the question of how much more might be discovered in the collection given public transparency regarding access. As no inventory exists and it is unclear how many of the collection's paintings have been catalogued and properly analysed by conservators, more discoveries lie in wait in what the *Daily Telegraph* called 'the Queen's Storeroom'.

The question of scholarly and curatorial access to the royal collection was raised again early in 2008 when one of the National Gallery's trustees invited me to lunch. Would it be possible, he asked, or even desirable, to approach the Royal Collection Trust with a view to bringing its collection under the control of a future plan for the National Gallery's expansion? The V&A currently exhibits the royal collection's priceless series of Raphael cartoons of the *Acts of the Apostles* on permanent loan. Surely a similar arrangement could be reached whereby the royal collection 'gifted' its paintings to the nation, to create the greatest national collection in the world? It seemed an eminently sensible plan that would leave the royal family still nominally in possession of the collection while allowing it to be seen and studied in the more appropriate context of a national collection with all its attendant resources. Although the will and support was ultimately lacking in 2008, I still hope that such an arrangement could be reached, as I maintain that it would transform not only the National Gallery but also the nation's approach to Old Master paintings. No longer the provenance of palaces and royal retreats, the royal collection's finest pieces could be appreciated alongside the other great art works in the National Gallery. Indeed, to put one of the royal collection's greatest pieces, Andrea Mantegna's iconic *Triumphs of Caesar*, on show alongside the National Gallery's Italian Renaissance would transform our understanding of both and place the nation's Old Master collection back at the heart of English national culture.

In 2013, another book on Charles I's art collection was published, albeit posthumously. Francis Haskell's *The King's Pictures: The Formation and Dispersal of the Collections of Charles I and his Courtiers* was based on his 1994 Paul Mellon Lectures, which covered similar ground to *The Sale of the Late King's Goods*. Although we never met (Haskell died in 2000 just before I began my research), we were in broad agreement about the details of the formation and dispersal of the collection. Situating the history of English art collecting within the context of Charles I's collection, Haskell concluded that 'English collecting in the early seventeenth century was an anomaly, the outcome of a historical accident. It lacked a real substructure, such as was characteristic, in varying degrees, of the formation of other private – and ultimately national – collections'.[5] Haskell understood that Charles I's collecting was the peculiar passion born of one man's fatal insecurities, rather than part of a longer sustained English tradition of commissioning and acquiring art, of the kind that characterized other early modern dynasties like the Habsburg, Valois or Medici. The legacy of this 'historical accident' remains with us to this day in the peculiar role that the royal collection plays in the nation's cultural life.

Two years ago, while having lunch with a senior figure at the Royal Academy, I learned about the arrangements to celebrate the Academy's 250th anniversary in 2018 with the forthcoming exhibition in collaboration with the royal collection entitled 'Charles I: King and Collector'. It would show around 100 of the finest paintings acquired by Charles I, many borrowed from the Louvre, Prado and Kunsthistorisches museums, where they ended up after being sold off in the Commonwealth sale. Reconstituting Charles's collection in this way is a remarkable achievement and promises to be a defining moment in our understanding of its history. Quite how the exhibition deals with the debate surrounding public access to the royal collection remains to be seen, although my conversations at the Royal Academy hardly filled me with confidence.[6]

Public museums and art galleries play a vital role within modern culture and society. As institutions that are publicly accessible to all groups in our society – at least in theory – they can play a binding role within the nation state, telling a collective historical story of who we are and in turn shaping modern collective identities. In contrast the history of Charles I's royal art collection was one of exclusivity and division, created in the midst of enormous economic inequality and political conflict for a tiny elite. For all its beauty and glamour, its story was symptomatic of a deeply divided seventeenth-century England. Today, England is yet again struggling to understand itself in relation to Europe and within an increasingly divided United Kingdom reminiscent of Charles I's own political difficulties. Exhibiting Old Masters may not solve our political difficulties, but it is to be regretted that the nation's art collections remain as divided and opaque as our current political discourse.

Notes

Abbreviations

APC Acts of the Privy Council
BL British Library
CSPD Calendar of State Papers, Domestic
CSPV Calendar of State Papers, Venice
HLRO House of Lords Records Office
JHC Journals of the House of Commons
JHL Journals of the House of Lords
RCHM Seventh Report of the Royal Commission on Historical Manuscripts, Part 1 Report and Appendix (London, 1879)
TNA (PRO) The National Archives, Kew, London

Introduction: The King's Head

1 Gudrun Raatschen, 'Van Dyck's "Charles I on horseback with M. de St Antoine"', in Hans Vlieghe (ed.), *Van Dyck 1599–1999: Conjectures and Refutations* (Turnhout, 2001), pp. 139–50.

2 Quoted in B. Graeme, *The Story of St James's Palace* (London, 1929), p. 107.

3 Ibid., pp. 106–7.

4 Oliver Millar (ed.), 'Abraham van der Doort's catalogue of the collections of King Charles I', *Walpole Society*, 37 (1958–60), p. 226.

5 W. N. Sainsbury (ed.), *Original Unpublished Papers Illustrative of the Life of Sir Peter Paul Rubens* (London, 1859), p. 350.

6 His brother Jacob painted Charles I's portrait in 1625, the same year that Abraham was officially appointed Keeper of the Cabinet Room. See Karen Hearn (ed.), *Dynasties* (London, 1995), p. 224.

7 See John Peacock, 'The politics of portraiture', in Kevin Sharpe and

Peter Lake (eds), *Culture and Politics in Early Stuart England* (London, 1994), pp. 199–228. Also Peacock, 'The visual image of Charles I', in Thomas Corns (ed.), *The Royal Image: Representations of Charles I* (Cambridge, 1999), pp. 176–239.

8 Millar (ed.), 'Abraham van der Doort's catalogue of the collections of King Charles I', p. 226.

9 William Sanderson, *Graphice: The Use of the Pen and Pencil* (London, 1658), p. 6.

10 Not be confused with Agnolo Bronzino (1503–72), whose work can also be found in Charles's collection. See John Shearman, *The Early Italian Pictures in the Collection of Her Majesty the Queen* (Cambridge, 1983), pp. 6–8, 58–9.

11 Werner Muensterberger, *Collecting: An Unruly Passion* (Princeton, 1994), pp. 3, 48.

12 Henry Perrinchief, *The Royal Martyr* (London, 1676), p. 253. This story was associated with various European rulers, including the sixteenth-century Habsburg emperor Charles V.

13 Claude Philips, *The Picture Gallery of Charles I* (London, 1896), p. 6.

14 John Michael Montias, *Art at Auction in Seventeenth-Century Amsterdam* (Amsterdam, 2002).

15 R. Malcolm Smuts, *Court Culture and the Origins of the Royalist Tradition in Early Stuart England* (Philadelphia, 1987), pp. 60, 130–31; David Howarth, *Images of Rule: Art and Politics in the English Renaissance, 1485–1649* (London, 1997), pp. 9–10.

16 Oliver Millar (ed.), 'The inventories and valuation of the king's goods, 1649–1651', *Walpole Society*, 43 (1970–72).

17 Quoted in Per Palme, *Triumph of Peace: A Study of the Whitehall Banqueting House* (London, 1957), p. 83.

18 Quoted in Edward Chaney (ed.), *The Evolution of English Collecting: The Reception of Italian Art in the Tudor and Stuart Periods* (New Haven, 2003), pp. 59–60.

19 Arjun Appadurai, 'Introduction: commodities and the politics of value', in Arjun Appadurai (ed.), *The Social Life of Things: Commodities in Cultural Perspective* (Cambridge, 1986), pp. 3–58.

20 Quoted in Millar, 'Abraham van der Doort's catalogue of the collections of King Charles I', p. xvi.

21 Horace Walpole, *Anecdotes of Painting in England*, 4 vols (London, 1762), Vol. 2, p. 51. Walpole took his story from Sanderson, *Graphice*, pp. 14–15.

22 See Jonathan Brown and J. H. Elliott (eds), *The Sale of the Century: Artistic Relations between Spain and Great Britain, 1604–1655* (New Haven, 2002).

ONE: DEATH OF A PRINCE

1 Francis Bacon, 'The Praise of Henry, Prince of Wales', in Joseph Devey (ed.), *The Moral and Historical Works of Lord Bacon* (London, 1852), p. 493.

2 Attr. Charles Cornwallis, *An Account of the Baptism, Life, Death and Funeral, of the Most Incomparable Prince Frederick Henry, Prince of Wales* (London, 1751), p. 26. In *Henry Prince of Wales and England's Lost Renaissance* (London, 1986), Roy Strong argues that this account was written by John Hawkins.

3 Cornwallis, *An Account of the Baptism, Life, Death and Funeral, of the Most Incomparable Prince Frederick Henry, Prince of Wales*, p. 35.

4 Oliver Millar (ed.), 'Abraham van der Doort's catalogue of the collections of King Charles I', *Walpole Society*, 37 (1958–60), p. 92.

5 Cornwallis, *An Account of the Baptism, Life, Death and Funeral, of the Most Incomparable Prince Frederick Henry, Prince of Wales*, pp. 36–7.

6 Ibid., p. 38.

7 Ibid., p. 45.

8 CSPV 1610–1613, p. 521.

9 CSPV 1610–1613, p. 472.

10 Cornwallis, *An Account of the Baptism, Life, Death and Funeral, of the Most Incomparable Prince Frederick Henry, Prince of Wales*, p. 48.

11 Ibid., p. 92.

12 Ibid., p. 56.

13 John Webster, *A Monumental Column erected to the living memory of the ever-glorious Henry, late Prince of Wales* (London, 1613).

14 A. J. Smith (ed.), *John Donne: The Complete English Poems* (London, 1971), pp. 253–5.

15 CSPV 1603–1607, pp. 162–3.

16 Quoted in Pauline Gregg, *King Charles I* (London, 1981), p. 8.

17 Ibid., p. 10.

18 Ibid., p. 11.

19 Hamon L'Estrange, *The Reign of King Charles. An History* (London, 1656), p. 1.

20 Leeds Barroll, *Anna of Denmark, Queen of England: A Cultural Biography* (Philadelphia, 2001), p. 100.

21 Quoted in Ralph Winwood, *Memorials of Affairs of State in the Reign of Queen Elizabeth and King James I* (London, 1725), p. 44.

22 Quoted in Richard Williams, 'Collecting and religion in late sixteenth-century England', in Edward Chaney (ed.), *The Evolution of English*

Collecting: The Reception of Italian Art in the Tudor and Stuart Periods (New Haven, 2003), p. 162.

23 See Lucy Gent, *Picture and Poetry 1560–1620* (Leamington, 1981).

24 Iain Pears, *The Discovery of Painting: The Growth of Interest in the Arts in England, 1680–1768* (New Haven, 1988), p. 52.

25 Martin Havran, *Catholics in Caroline England* (London, 1962), pp. 116–17.

26 Mary Edmond, 'Limners and picturemakers: new light on the lives of miniaturists and large-scale portrait-painters working in London in the sixteenth and seventeenth centuries', *Walpole Society*, 47 (1978–80), pp. 63–5; Susan Foister; 'Foreigners at court: Holbein, Van Dyck and the Painter-Stainers', in David Howarth (ed.), *Art and Patronage in the Caroline Courts* (Cambridge, 1993), p. 39.

27 Edmond, 'Limners and picturemakers', pp. 140–62.

28 Quoted in Alan Stewart, *The Cradle King: A Life of James VI and I* (London, 2003), p. 172.

29 Karen Hearn (ed.), *Dynasties* (London, 1995), p. 186.

30 Arthur Wilson, *The History of Great Britain, Being the Life and Reign of King James the First* (London, 1653), p. 52.

31 On these figures see Roy Strong, *Henry Prince of Wales and England's Lost Renaissance* (London, 1986), Ch. 1.

32 Kathryn Barron, 'The collecting and patronage of John, Lord Lumley', in Chaney (ed.), *The Evolution of English Collecting*, pp. 125–58; Sears Jayne and Francis Johnson (eds), *The Lumley Library: The Catalogue of 1609* (London, 1956).

33 Lionel Cust 'The Lumley inventories', *Walpole Society*, 6 (1918), p. 22.

34 Oliver Impey and Arthur MacGregor (eds), *The Origins of Museums: The Cabinet of Curiosities in Sixteenth- and Seventeenth-Century Europe* (Oxford, 1985); Krzysztof Pomian, *Collectors and Curiosities: Paris and Venice, 1500–1800* (Oxford, 1990).

35 Barbara Gutfleisch and Joachim Menzhausen, ' "How a Kunstkammer should be formed": Gabriel Kaltemarckt's advice to Christian I of Saxony on the formation of an art collection', *Journal of the History of Collections*, 1, 1 (1989), pp. 3–32; Ronald Lightbrown, 'Charles I and the tradition of princely collecting', in Arthur MacGregor (ed.), *The Late King's Goods: Collections, Possessions and Patronage in the Light of the Commonwealth Sale Inventories* (Oxford, 1989), pp. 53–72.

36 Rosalys Coope, 'The "long gallery": its origins, development, use and decoration', *Architectural History*, 29 (1986), pp. 43–84.

37 Quoted in Rosalys Coope, 'The gallery in England: names and meaning', *Architectural History*, 27 (1984), p. 450.

38 Quoted in Linda Levy Peck, *Northampton: Patronage and Policy at the Court of James I* (London, 1982), p. 8.

39 Ibid., p. 74.

40 E. P. Shirley, 'An inventory of the effects of Henry Howard, K.G., Earl of Northampton, taken on his death in 1614, together with a transcript of his will', *Archaeologia*, 42 (1869), pp. 347–78.

41 Ibid., pp. 357–8.

42 Ibid., p. 360.

43 Ibid., p. 355.

44 Arthur Wilson, quoted in *Miscellany of the Abbotsford Club* (Edinburgh, 1837), p. 80.

45 MacGregor (ed.), *The Late King's Goods*, p. 27.

46 Raymond Needham and Alexander Webster, *Somerset House: Past and Present* (London, 1905).

47 CSPV 1617–19, p. 81.

48 M. T. W. Payne, 'An inventory of Queen Anne of Denmark's "ornaments, furniture, householde stuffe, and other parcels" at Denmark House', *Journal of the History of Collections*, 13, 1 (2001), pp. 23–44.

49 Quoted in Timothy Wilks, 'The Court Culture of Henry, Prince of Wales, 1603–1613', D.Phil. thesis (Oxford, 1987), p. 293.

50 On James's relationship with Cecil, see Pauline Croft, 'Robert Cecil and the early Jacobean court', in Linda Levey Peck (ed.), *The Mental World of the Jacobean Court* (Cambridge, 1991), pp. 134–47, esp. 139.

51 Quoted in Hearn (ed.), *Dynasties*, p. 175.

52 On Cecil's collections, see E. Auerbach and C. K. Adams, *Paintings and Sculpture at Hatfield House* (London, 1971).

53 On Cecil's collection, see Susan Bracken, 'The early Cecils and Italianate taste', in Chaney (ed.), *The Evolution of English Collecting*, pp. 201–20.

54 Logan Pearsall Smith (ed.), *The Life and Letters of Sir Henry Wotton*, 2 vols (Oxford, 1907), Vol. 1, p. 49.

55 Ibid., p. 359.

56 Ibid., p. 412.

57 Ibid., p. 419.

58 Ibid., pp. 419–20.

59 Quoted in J. Irene Whalley, 'Italian art and English taste: an early seventeenth-century letter', *Apollo*, 94 (1971), p. 184.

60 CSPV 1603–07, pp. 513–14.

61 Historical Manuscripts Commission 9: *Calendar of the Manuscripts of the Most Honourable The Marquess of Salisbury*, Vol. 21 (London, 1970), p. 39.

62 Wilks, 'The Court Culture of Henry, Prince of Wales, 1603–1613', p. 129. His accession brought with it lucrative rights to land and industries, including tin mining.

63 Strong, *Henry Prince of Wales and England's Lost Renaissance*, pp. 87–91. On Oliver, see Roy Strong, *The English Renaissance Miniature* (London, 1983), pp. 142–85.

64 Strong, *Henry Prince of Wales and England's Lost Renaissance*, pp. 66–73.

65 Quoted in Wilks, 'The Court Culture of Henry, Prince of Wales, 1603–1613', p. 181.

66 Ibid., p. 175; Strong, *Henry Prince of Wales and England's Lost Renaissance*, p. 195, n. 11.

67 Quoted in J. G. Van Gelder, 'Notes on the Royal Collection IV – the "Dutch gift" of 1610 to Henry, Prince of "Whalis", and some other presents', *Burlington Magazine*, 105 (1963), p. 543.

68 Ibid.

69 Wilks, 'The Court Culture of Henry, Prince of Wales, 1603–1613', p. 91.

70 Gelder suggests that this was a painting by Porcellis, one of Vroom's pupils.

71 Quoted in Gelder, 'Notes on the Royal Collection IV', p. 544.

72 Thomas Birch, *The Life of Henry, Prince of Wales* (London, 1760), p. 486.

73 Quoted in Samuel R. Gardiner, *History of England 1603–1642*, 10 vols (London, 1883–4), Vol. 2, p. 57.

74 Katharine Watson and Charles Avery, 'Medici and Stuart: a grand ducal gift of "Giovanni Bologna" bronzes for Henry Prince of Wales (1612)', *Burlington Magazine*, 115 (1973), p. 501.

75 Strong, *Henry Prince of Wales and England's Lost Renaissance*, p. 144; Wilks, 'The Court Culture of Henry, Prince of Wales, 1603–1613', p. 168.

76 Quoted in Strong, *Henry Prince of Wales and England's Lost Renaissance*, p. 148.

77 CSPV 1610–13, p. 116.

78 A. V. Judges, 'Philip Burlamachi: a financier of the Thirty Years War', *Economica*, 6, (1926), pp. 285–300.

79 Quoted in Smith, *The Life and Letters of Sir Henry Wotton*, Vol. 2, pp. 7–8; Vol. 1, p. 454.

80 CSPV 1610–13, p. 106.

81 Quoted in Strong, *Henry Prince of Wales and England's Lost Renaissance*, p. 145.

82 Roy Strong, 'England and Italy: the marriage of Henry Prince of Wales', in Richard Ollard and Pamela Tudor-Craig (eds), *For Veronica Wedgwood These* (London, 1986), pp. 59–87.

83 Quoted in Watson and Avery, 'Medici and Stuart', p. 501.

84 Aristotle, 'The Nicomachean Ethics', in J. Barnes (ed.), *The Complete Works of Aristotle*, Vol. 2 (Princeton, 1984), pp. 1,771–2.

85 Quoted in Maurice Lee (ed.), *Dudley Carleton to John Chamberlain, 1603–1624: Jacobean Letters* (New Brunswick, NJ, 1971), p. 136.

Two: Debts and Discredits

1 Timothy Wilks, 'The Court Culture of Henry, Prince of Wales, 1603–1613', D.Phil. thesis (Oxford, 1987), p. 240.

2 Oliver Millar (ed.), 'Abraham van der Doort's catalogue of the collections of King Charles I', *Walpole Society*, 37 (1958–60), p. 154.

3 Wilks, 'The Court Culture of Henry, Prince of Wales, 1603–1613', p. 194.

4 N. E. McClure (ed.), *The Letters of John Chamberlain*, 2 vols (Philadelphia, 1939), Vol. 1, p. 391.

5 Quoted in Wilks, 'The Court Culture of Henry, Prince of Wales, 1603–1613', p. 162.

6 See Timothy Wilks, 'Art collecting at the English court from the death of Henry, Prince of Wales, to the death of Anne of Denmark', *Journal of the History of Collections*, 9, 1 (1997), pp. 31–48; M. T. W. Payne, 'An inventory of Queen Anne of Denmark's "ornaments, furniture, householde stuffe, and other parcels" at Denmark House', *Journal of the History of Collections*, 13, 1 (2001), pp. 23–44.

7 Hamon L'Estrange, *The Reign of King Charles. An History* (London, 1656), p. 1.

8 Quoted in Pauline Gregg, *King Charles I* (London, 1981), p. 33.

9 McClure (ed.), *The Letters of John Chamberlain*, Vol. 1, p. 394.

10 CSPD 1611–18, p. 160.

11 Gregg, *King Charles I*, p. 32.

12 David Howarth, *Lord Arundel and his Circle* (London, 1985), pp. 38–9.

13 Beverly Louise Brown (ed.), *The Genius of Rome 1592–1623* (London, 2001); Howarth, *Lord Arundel and his Circle*, Ch. 2.

14 Jeremy Wood, 'Taste and connoisseurship at the court of Charles I: Inigo Jones and the work of Giulio Romano', in Eveline Cruickshanks

(ed.), *The Stuart Courts* (Stroud, 2000), pp. 118–40; John Harris and Gordon Higgott, *Inigo Jones: Complete Architectural Drawings* (London, 1989), pp. 52–7.

15 *The Winter's Tale*, V.ii. 87–8.

16 Quoted in Wood, 'Taste and connoisseurship at the court of Charles I', p. 132.

17 Ibid., pp. 131, 134.

18 Alastair Bellany, *The Politics of Court Scandal in Early Modern England: News Culture and the Overbury Affair* (Cambridge, 2002), Ch. 1.

19 David Lindley, *The Trials of Frances Howard: Fact and Fiction at the Court of King James I* (London, 1993), p. 95.

20 Quoted in A. R. Braunmuller, 'Robert Carr, Earl of Somerset, as collector and patron', in Linda Levey Peck (ed.), *The Mental World of the Jacobean Court* (Cambridge, 1991), p. 231.

21 Ibid., p. 232.

22 Ibid.

23 See Robert Hill, 'The ambassador as art agent: Sir Dudley Carleton and Jacobean collecting', in Edward Chaney (ed.), *The Evolution of English Collecting: The Reception of Italian Art in the Tudor and Stuart Periods* (New Haven, 2003), pp. 241–55.

24 Braunmuller, 'Robert Carr, Earl of Somerset, as collector and patron', pp. 231–9; Howarth, *Lord Arundel and his Circle*, pp. 60–63; W. N. Sainsbury (ed.), *Original Unpublished Papers Illustrative of the Life of Sir Peter Paul Rubens* (London, 1859), pp. 269–99.

25 Ibid., pp. 275–8.

26 See François Portier, 'Prices paid for Italian pictures in the Stuart age', *Journal of the History of Collections*, 8, 1 (1996), p. 56.

27 Timothy Wilks, 'The picture collection of Robert Carr, Earl of Somerset (c. 1587–1645), reconsidered', *Journal of the History of Collections*, 1, 2 (1989), p. 171; Sainsbury (ed.), *Original Unpublished Papers Illustrative of the Life of Sir Peter Paul Rubens*, pp. 273–4.

28 Quoted in Bellany, *The Politics of Court Scandal in Early Modern England*, p. 68.

29 Quoted in Sainsbury (ed.), *Original Unpublished Papers Illustrative of the Life of Sir Peter Paul Rubens*, p. 270.

30 Ibid.

31 Ibid., p. 351.

32 Quoted ibid., p. 271.

33 Quoted ibid., p. 272.

34 Quoted ibid., pp. 272–3.

35 One example of Arundel's haul was Bassano's *The Beheading of St John the Baptist*, which was sold in Amsterdam in 1684. See Wilks, 'The picture collection of Robert Carr, Earl of Somerset (c. 1587–1645), reconsidered', pp. 174–5.

36 Hill, 'The ambassador as art agent: Sir Dudley Carleton and Jacobean collecting', p. 248.

37 Quoted in Sainsbury (ed.), *Original Unpublished Papers Illustrative of the Life of Sir Peter Paul Rubens*, p. 301.

38 Ibid., p. 273.

39 Quoted in Roger Lockyer, *Buckingham: The Life and Political Career of George Villiers, First Duke of Buckingham* (London, 1981), p. 33.

40 Dr Godfrey Goodman, *The Court of King James the First*, ed. John Brewer, 2 vols (London, 1839), Vol. 1, p. 225.

41 Quoted in Lockyer, *Buckingham*, p. 43.

42 Quoted ibid., p. 20.

43 Charles Richard Cammell, *The Great Duke of Buckingham* (London, 1939).

44 Horace Walpole, *Anecdotes of Painting in England* (London, 1762), Vol. 2, p. 124.

45 Edward Chaney (ed.), *The Evolution of English Collecting: The Reception of Italian Art in the Tudor and Stuart Periods* (New Haven, 2003), p. 53.

46 Sainsbury (ed.), *Original Unpublished Papers Illustrative of the Life of Sir Peter Paul Rubens*, p. 23; Jeffrey Muller, *Rubens: The Artist as Collector* (Princeton, 1989), pp. 57–8, 82–7.

47 Quoted in Ruth Magurn (ed.), *The Letters of Peter Paul Rubens* (Cambridge, Mass., 1971), p. 101.

48 Portier, 'Prices paid for Italian pictures in the Stuart age', claims an English sovereign was worth five florins and eighteen stivers in 1610.

49 Magurn (ed.), *The Letters of Peter Paul Rubens*, p. 102.

50 Ibid., pp. 102–3.

51 Ibid.

52 Quoted ibid., p. 104.

53 Quoted in Sainsbury (ed.), *Original Unpublished Papers Illustrative of the Life of Sir Peter Paul Rubens*, p. 37.

54 Quoted in Magurn, *The Letters of Peter Paul Rubens*, pp. 106, 109.

55 Muller, *Rubens*, p. 77.

56 Magurn, *The Letters of Peter Paul Rubens*, p. 109.

57 Quoted in Sainsbury (ed.), *Original Unpublished Papers Illustrative of the Life of Sir Peter Paul Rubens*, p. 59, n. 86.

58 Quoted in Per Palme, *Triumph of Peace: A Study of the Whitehall Banqueting House* (London, 1957), pp. 2–3.

59 Harris and Higgott, *Inigo Jones*, pp. 108–23.

60 Quoted in Palme, *Triumph of Peace*, p. 3.

61 Quoted in Sainsbury (ed.), *Original Unpublished Papers Illustrative of the Life of Sir Peter Paul Rubens*, p. 48.

62 Ibid., p. 49.

63 Quoted ibid., p. 50; Muller, *Rubens*, p. 148.

64 David Howarth, 'William Trumbull and art collecting in Jacobean England', *British Library Journal*, 20 (1994), pp. 140–62.

65 Sainsbury (ed.), *Original Unpublished Papers Illustrative of the Life of Sir Peter Paul Rubens*, p. 53.

66 Ibid., p. 57.

67 Anon., 'Madame the Queen's Death, and Maner thereof', in *Miscellany of the Abbotsford Club*, Vol. 1 (Edinburgh, 1837), p. 81.

68 Payne, 'An inventory of Queen Anne of Denmark's "ornaments, furniture, householde stuffe, and other parcels" at Denmark House', pp. 36–40.

69 Ibid., pp. 57–58.

70 Ibid., pp. 60–61.

71 Quoted in David Howarth, 'Rubens's "owne pourtrait"', *Apollo*, 132 (1990), pp. 238–41.

THREE: MR SMITH IN MADRID

1 CSPV 1621–23, p. 452.

2 Quoted in W. B. Patterson, *King James VI and I and the Reunion of Christendom* (Cambridge, 1997), pp. 35–6. I am grateful to Kevin Sharpe for bringing this to my attention.

3 Of the many recent studies, see Christopher Durston and Jacqueline Eales (eds), *The Culture of English Puritanism, 1560–1700* (Basingstoke, 1996).

4 Edward Chaney, 'Notes towards a biography of Sir Balthazar Gerbier', in Edward Chaney, *The Evolution of the Grand Tour* (London, 1998), pp. 215–25.

5 William Sanderson, *Graphice: The Use of the Pen and Pencil* (London, 1658), p. 15.

6 Quoted in Lita-Rose Betcherman, 'Balthazar Gerbier in seventeenth-century Italy', *History Today*, 11 (1961), p. 325.

7 Lita-Rose Betcherman, 'The York House collection and its keeper', *Apollo*, 92 (1970), p. 251.

8 Balthazar Gerbier, *Subsidium Peregrinantibus* (Oxford, 1665), pp. 95–6.

9 Beverly Louise Brown (ed.), *The Genius of Rome 1592–1623* (London, 2001).

10 Balthazar Gerbier, *The Interpreter of the Academie* (London, 1649), pp. 161–3.

11 See Harold Wethey, *The Paintings of Titian*, 3 vols (London, 1975), Vol. 1, pp. 79–80.

12 Betcherman, 'Balthazar Gerbier in seventeenth-century Italy', p. 331.

13 See *Carolus: Charles Quint 1500–1558* (Ghent, 2000) and *Felipe II: Un monarca y su época* (Madrid, 1999).

14 James Howell, *Epistolae Ho-Elianae: Familiar Letters Domestic and Foreign* (London, 1645), p. 52.

15 Quoted in Roger Lockyer, *Buckingham: The Life and Political Career of George Villiers, First Duke of Buckingham* (London, 1981), p. 109.

16 Glyn Redworth, *The Prince and the Infanta: The Cultural Politics of the Spanish Match* (New Haven, 2003), p. 51.

17 Quoted in Glyn Redworth, 'Of pimps and princes: three unpublished letters from James I and the Prince of Wales relating to the Spanish match', *Historical Journal*, 37 (1994), p. 408.

18 Quoted in Redworth, *The Prince and the Infanta*, p. 54.

19 Howell, *Epistolae Ho-Elianae*, p. 49.

20 See J. H. Elliott, *The Count–Duke of Olivares: The Statesman in an Age of Decline* (London, 1986), pp. 203–14.

21 Quoted in Redworth, *The Prince and the Infanta*, p. 74.

22 Quoted in Samuel R. Gardiner, *History of England 1603–1642*, 10 vols, (London, 1883–4), Vol. 5, p. 5.

23 Quoted in W. G. Thomson, *A History of Tapestry* (London, 1906), p. 281.

24 John Shearman, *Raphael's Cartoons in the Collection of Her Majesty the Queen* (London, 1972).

25 Arthur Wilson, *The History of Great Britain, Being the Life and Reign of King James the First* (London, 1653), p. 225.

26 Lockyer, *Buckingham*, p. 139.

27 Howell, *Epistolae Ho-Elianae*, p. 71.

28 Quoted in Gardiner, *History of England 1603–1642*, Vol. 5, p. 10.

29 Andrés de Almansa y Mendoza, 'A Relation of the Departure of the most Illustrious Prince of Wales, from Madrid the Ninth of September, this present Yeare. 1623', in *A Second Collection of Scarce and Valuable Tracts* (London, 1750), Vol. 1, p. 231.

30 Quoted in Thomas Cogswell, *The Blessed Revolution: English Politics and the Coming of War, 1621–24* (Cambridge, 1989), p. 36.

31   Quoted in Redworth, *The Prince and the Infanta*, p. 76.

32   Ibid.

33   See Jonathan Brown, *The Golden Age of Painting in Spain* (New Haven, 1991), pp. 52–67; Glyn Redworth and Fernando Checa, 'The Courts of the Spanish Habsburgs 1500–1700', in John Adamson (ed.), *The Princely Courts of Europe* (Weidenfeld and Nicolson, 1999), pp. 43–65; José Manuel Barbeito, 'Felipe II y la arquitectura', in *Felipe II: Un monarca y su época* (Madrid, 1999).

34   Quoted in Charles Petrie (ed.), *The Letters, Speeches and Proclamations of King Charles I* (London, 1935), pp. 10–11.

35   Quoted in G. P. V. Akrigg (ed.), *Letters of King James VI and I* (Berkeley, 1984), p. 388.

36   John Digby, Earl of Bristol, *A True Relation and Journal, or the Manner of the Arrival . . .* (London, 1623), pp. 19–20.

37   Ibid., p. 26.

38   Sir Francis Cottington, 'The Account Book of Sir Francis Cottington, Madrid, 1623', National Library of Scotland, MS 1879, p. 2. I am grateful to Glyn Redworth for allowing me to consult his forthcoming edition of this manuscript.

39   W. N. Sainsbury (ed.), *Original Unpublished Papers Illustrative of the Life of Sir Peter Paul Rubens* (London, 1859), p. 355.

40   Quoted in Shearman, *Raphael's Cartoons in the Collection of Her Majesty the Queen*, p. 146.

41   Mary Hervey, *The Life, Correspondence and Collections of Thomas Howard, Earl of Arundel* (Cambridge, 1921), p. 226.

42   Anon., *A Continuation of a Former Relation Concerning the Entertainment given to the Prince . . .* (London, 1623), p. 7.

43   Lisa Jardine and Jerry Brotton, *Global Interests: Renaissance Art between East and West* (London, 2000), Ch. 2.

44   *A Continuation of a Former Relation Concerning the Entertainment given to the Prince . . .* , p. 5.

45   Cottington, 'The Account Book of Sir Francis Cottington, Madrid, 1623', p. 6.

46   Brown, *The Golden Age of Painting in Spain*, pp. 209–11.

47   Quoted in Carl Justi, 'Die Spanische Brautfahrt Carl Stewarts', in *Miscellaneen aus drei Jahrhunderten Spanischen Kunstlebens*, 2 vols (Berlin, 1908), Vol. 2, p. 323.

48   Vicente Carducho, *Diálogos de la pintura* (Madrid, 1633), ed. Francisco Calvo Serraller (Madrid, 1979), p. 435.

49   Quoted in Edward L. Goldberg, 'Artistic relations between the Medici

and the Spanish courts, 1587–1621: part I', *Burlington Magazine*, 134 (1996), pp. 108–9.

50 Quoted in Carducho, *Diálogos de la pintura*, p. 422.

51 Jonathan Brown and J. H. Elliott (eds), *The Sale of the Century: Artistic Relations between Spain and Great Britain, 1604–1655* (New Haven, 2002), p. 53.

52 Carducho, *Diálogos de la pintura* p. 438.

53 See Brown and Elliott (eds), *The Sale of the Century*, pp. 201–4.

54 Quoted in Goldberg, 'Artistic relations between the Medici and the Spanish courts, 1587–1621: part I', p. 113.

55 Quoted in Redworth, *The Prince and the Infanta*, p. 88.

56 Oliver Millar (ed.), 'Abraham van der Doort's catalogue of the collections of King Charles I', *Walpole Society*, 37 (1958–60), p. 16.

57 See Wethey, *The Paintings of Titian*, Vol. 3, pp. 127–8.

58 See Thomson, *A History of Tapestry*, p. 282.

59 Petrie (ed.), *The Letters, Speeches and Proclamations of King Charles I*, p. 11.

60 Ibid., p. 13.

61 Patterson, *King James VI and I and the Reunion of Christendom*, pp. 323–4.

62 Gardiner, *History of England 1603–1642*, Vol. 5, pp. 37–8.

63 See Roy Strong, *Art and Power: Renaissance Festivals 1450–1650* (Woodbridge, 1984), pp. 78–81.

64 Cottington, 'The Account Book of Sir Francis Cottington, Madrid, 1623', p. 5.

65 Quoted in Patterson, *King James VI and I and the Reunion of Christendom*, p. 326.

66 Millar (ed.), 'Abraham van der Doort's catalogue of the collections of King Charles I', pp. 183–4.

67 Carducho, *Diálogos de la pintura*, p. 436. Wethey suggests the fire occurred in 1604 (Wethey, *The Paintings of Titian*, Vol. 3, p. 161).

68 See the list of 'Presents given by the king of Spain to the Prince of Wales', TNA (PRO) 94/28, fol. 223.

69 Petrie (ed.), *The Letters, Speeches and Proclamations of King Charles I*, p. 395.

70 Howell, *Epistolae Ho-Elianae*, p. 76.

71 Redworth, *The Prince and the Infanta*, pp. 174–83.

72 Gerbier, *Subsidium Peregrinantibus*, p. 112.

73 Cottington, 'The Account Book of Sir Francis Cottington, Madrid, 1623', pp. 41, 47.

74 Ibid., p. 50.

75 Petrie (ed.), *The Letters, Speeches and Proclamations of King Charles I*, p. 31.

76 Almansa y Mendoza, 'A Relation of the Departure of the most

Illustrious Prince of Wales, from Madrid the Ninth of September, this present Yeare. 1623', p. 238.

77 Edward L. Goldberg, 'Artistic relations between the Medici and the Spanish courts, 1587–1621: part II', *Burlington Magazine*, 138 (1996), pp. 529–30.

78 Quoted in Sarah Walker Schroth, 'Charles I, the duque de Lerma and Veronese's Edinburgh *Mars and Venus*', *Burlington Magazine*, 139 (1997), p. 550.

79 Sainsbury (ed.), *Original Unpublished Papers Illustrative of the Life of Sir Peter Paul Rubens*, p. 355; Timothy Wilks, 'Art collecting at the English court from the death of Henry, Prince of Wales, to the death of Anne of Denmark', *Journal of the History of Collections*, 9, 1 (1997), pp. 33–4.

80 Sainsbury (ed.), *Original Unpublished Papers Illustrative of the Life of Sir Peter Paul Rubens*, p. 349.

81 Quoted in Krzysztof Pomian, *Collectors and Curiosities: Paris and Venice, 1500–1800* (Oxford, 1990), p. 161.

82 Lockyer, *Buckingham*, Chs 6–7; Cogswell, *The Blessed Revolution*.

83 Henry Peacham, *The Compleat Gentleman* (2nd edition, London, 1634), p. 108.

Four: The Italian Job

1 David Howarth, ' "Mantua peeces": Charles I and the Gonzaga collections', in David Chambers and Jane Martineau (eds), *Splendours of the Gonzaga* (London, 1981), p. 95; Lucy Whitaker, 'L'accoglienza della collezione Gonzaga in Inghilterra', in Raffaella Morselli (ed.), *Gonzaga: La Celeste Galeria* (Milan, 2002), pp. 233–49. I am grateful to Ms Whitaker for sharing her work with me.

2 Lorraine Madway, ' "The most conspicuous solemnity": the coronation of Charles I', in Eveline Cruickshanks (ed.), *The Stuart Courts* (Stroud, 2000), pp. 141–57; Roger Lockyer, *Buckingham: The Life and Political Career of George Villiers, First Duke of Buckingham* (London, 1981), pp. 308, 334.

3 Quoted in James Larkin, *Stuart Royal Proclamations*, Vol. 2, *Royal Proclamations of King Charles I, 1625–1646* (Oxford, 1983), p. 37.

4 David Howarth, *Lord Arundel and his Circle* (London, 1985), Ch. 6.

5 Michael Levey, *The Later Italian Pictures in the Collection of Her Majesty the Queen* (London, 1964), p. 12.

6 David Howarth, *Images of Rule: Art and Politics in the English Renaissance, 1485–1649* (London, 1997), pp. 96–7, 251–2.

7 Jeffrey Muller, *Rubens: The Artist as Collector* (Princeton, 1989), pp. 58, 78.

8 Quoted in David Howarth, 'Rubens's "owne pourtrait"', *Apollo*, 132 (1990), p. 238.

9 R. W. Bissell, *Orazio Gentileschi and the Poetic Tradition in Caravaggesque Painting* (Pennsylvania, 1981), pp. 50–62; Gabriele Finaldi (ed.), *Orazio Gentileschi at the Court of Charles I* (London, 1999).

10 See Michael Wilson, *Nicholas Lanier: Master of the King's Musick* (Aldershot, 1994).

11 W. N. Sainsbury (ed.), *Original Unpublished Papers Illustrative of the Life of Sir Peter Paul Rubens* (London, 1859), pp. 321–2.

12 Quoted in Wilson, *Nicholas Lanier*, p. 85; see TNA (PRO) SP90/26, fol. 168.

13 TNA (PRO) SP 84/134, fols 196–7.

14 Quoted in Alessandro Luzio, *La Galleria dei Gonzaga Vendutta all'Inghilterra nel 1627–28* (Milan, 1913), p. 137.

15 Quoted ibid.

16 Chambers and Martineau (eds), *Splendours of the Gonzaga*, pp. 51–64; Alison Cole, *Art of the Italian Renaissance Courts* (London, 1995), pp. 160–68.

17 See Pamela Askew, 'Ferdinando Gonzaga's patronage of the pictorial arts: the Villa Favorita', *Art Bulletin*, 60 (1978), pp. 274–96.

18 On Pope Urban, see Francis Haskell, *Patrons and Painters: Art and Society in Baroque Italy* (2nd edition, London, 1980). On music, see Rossella Vodret and Claudio Strinati, 'Painted music: "A new and affecting manner"', in Beverly Louise Brown (ed.), *The Genius of Rome 1592–1623* (London, 2001), pp. 90–115.

19 Quoted in Luzio, *La Galleria dei Gonzaga Vendutta all'Inghilterra nel 1627–28*, p. 137.

20 David Parrott, 'The Mantuan succession, 1627–31: a sovereignty dispute in early modern Europe', *English Historical Review*, 112 (1997), pp. 20–65.

21 Quoted in Luzio, *La Galleria dei Gonzaga Vendutta all'Inghilterra nel 1627–28*, p. 138.

22 Ibid., p. 139.

23 Sainsbury (ed.), *Original Unpublished Papers Illustrative of the Life of Sir Peter Paul Rubens*, p. 326.

24 Quoted in Luzio, *La Galleria dei Gonzaga Vendutta all'Inghilterra nel 1627–28*, pp. 140–41.

25 Ibid., pp. 141–2.

26 CSPV 1626–28, p. 241; Sainsbury (ed.), *Original Unpublished Papers Illustrative of the Life of Sir Peter Paul Rubens*, p. 322, n. 51.

27 Luzio, *La Galleria dei Gonzaga Vendutta all'Inghilterra nel 1627–28*, p. 142.

28 A. V. Judges, 'Philip Burlamachi: a financier of the Thirty Years War', *Economica*, 6, (1926), p. 293; APC, Jan–Aug 1627, p. 412; Lockyer, *Buckingham*, p. 397.

29 TNA (PRO) SP16/79, fol. 123.

30 TNA (PRO) SP16/79, fol. 123, reproduced in Sainsbury (ed.), *Original Unpublished Papers Illustrative of the Life of Sir Peter Paul Rubens*, p. 323.

31 Ruth Magurn (ed.), *The Letters of Peter Paul Rubens* (Cambridge, Mass., 1971), p. 212.

32 Quoted in Luzio, *La Galleria dei Gonzaga Vendutta all'Inghilterra nel 1627–28*, p. 143.

33 Sainsbury (ed.), *Original Unpublished Papers Illustrative of the Life of Sir Peter Paul Rubens*, pp. 327–8.

34 Quoted in Luzio, *La Galleria dei Gonzaga Vendutta all'Inghilterra nel 1627–28*, p. 143.

35 Ibid., pp. 145–6.

36 Quoted in Sainsbury (ed.), *Original Unpublished Papers Illustrative of the Life of Sir Peter Paul Rubens*, p. 328.

37 Parrott, 'The Mantuan succession, 1627–31', p. 49.

38 TNA (PRO) 85/6, fol. 42.

39 Quoted in Luzio, *La Galleria dei Gonzaga Vendutta all'Inghilterra nel 1627–28*, p. 153.

40 Parrott, 'The Mantuan succession, 1627–31', pp. 52, 58.

41 Sainsbury (ed.), *Original Unpublished Papers Illustrative of the Life of Sir Peter Paul Rubens*, pp. 325–7; Howarth, ' "Mantua peeces" ', p. 97.

42 Quoted in Sainsbury (ed.), *Original Unpublished Papers Illustrative of the Life of Sir Peter Paul Rubens*, p. 325.

43 Ibid., p. 327.

44 Ibid., p. 325.

45 Quoted ibid., p. 326; Luzio, *La Galleria dei Gonzaga Vendutta all'Inghilterra nel 1627–28*, pp. 154–5.

46 Quoted in Wilson, *Nicholas Lanier*, p. 131.

47 Quoted in Luzio, *La Galleria dei Gonzaga Vendutta all'Inghilterra nel 1627–28*, p. 158.

48 Quoted in Sainsbury (ed.), *Original Unpublished Papers Illustrative of the Life of Sir Peter Paul Rubens*, pp. 328–9.

49 Ibid., p. 329.

50 See A. H. Scott-Elliott, 'The statues from Mantua in the collection of King Charles I', *Burlington Magazine*, 101 (1959), pp. 218–27.

51 Magurn (ed.), *The Letters of Peter Paul Rubens*, p. 297.

52 Sainsbury (ed.), *Original Unpublished Papers Illustrative of the Life of Sir Peter Paul Rubens*, p. 331.

53 J. H. Elliott, *The Count–Duke of Olivares: The Statesman in an Age of Decline* (London, 1986), p. 367.

54 Quoted in Magurn (ed.), *The Letters of Peter Paul Rubens*, p. 298.

55 Luzio, *La Galleria dei Gonzaga Vendutta all'Inghilterra nel 1627–28*, pp. 162–3.

56 Quoted ibid., pp. 164–5.

57 Quoted ibid., p. 165.

58 Quoted in Sainsbury (ed.), *Original Unpublished Papers Illustrative of the Life of Sir Peter Paul Rubens*, p. 332.

59 Ibid., p. 333.

60 TNA (PRO) SP99/28, fols 301–2.

61 TNA (PRO) SP99/28, fol. 301v–301r.

62 Sainsbury (ed.), *Original Unpublished Papers Illustrative of the Life of Sir Peter Paul Rubens*, pp. 334–5.

63 Ibid., p. 335.

64 CSPD 1629–31, p. 323.

65 CSPD 1629–31, pp. 325, 336.

66 Quoted in Sainsbury (ed.), *Original Unpublished Papers Illustrative of the Life of Sir Peter Paul Rubens*, p. 335.

67 Ibid., p. 336.

68 Ibid., p. 321.

69 Ibid., pp. 336–7; Scott-Elliott, 'The statues from Mantua in the collection of Charles I', p. 220.

70 Parrott, 'The Mantuan succession, 1627–31', p. 64; Elliott, *The Count–Duke of Olivares*, pp. 400–401.

71 For later estimates of just over 100 pictures acquired from Mantua, see Luzio, *La Galleria dei Gonzaga Vendutta all'Inghilterra nel 1627–28*, pp. 168–76. For estimates of the number of statues and busts, see Jonathan Scott, *The Pleasures of Antiquity: British Collectors of Greece and Rome* (New Haven, 2003), pp. 26–7.

72 Oliver Millar (ed.), 'Abraham van der Doort's catalogue of the collections of King Charles I', *Walpole Society*, 37 (1958–60), p. 173.

73 Sainsbury (ed.), *Original Unpublished Papers Illustrative of the Life of Sir Peter Paul Rubens*, pp. 321, 336–7; Howarth, '"Mantua peeces"', p. 100.

74 Quoted in Judges, 'Philip Burlamachi: a financier of the Thirty Years War', p. 286.

75 Robert Ashton, 'The disbursing official under the early Stuarts: the cases of Sir William Russell and Philip Burlamachi', *Bulletin of Institute of Historical Research*, 30 (1957), pp. 162–73.

76 Quoted in Wilson, *Nicholas Lanier*, p. 128.

77 William Prynne, *Histrio-mastix, The Player's Scourge or Actor's Tragedie* (London, 1633), p. 901.

78 Henry Peacham, *The Compleat Gentleman* (2nd edition, London, 1634), pp. 107–8.

79 Clair Pace, 'Virtuoso to connoisseur: some seventeenth-century English responses to the visual arts', *The Seventeenth Century*, 2 (1987), pp. 166–88; Walter Houghton, 'The English virtuoso in the seventeenth century', *Journal of the History of Ideas*, 3 (1942), pp. 51–73.

Five: Lasting Monuments to Posterity

1 Quoted in Kevin Sharpe, *The Personal Rule of Charles I* (New Haven, 1992), p. 55.

2 W. N. Sainsbury (ed.), *Original Unpublished Papers Illustrative of the Life of Sir Peter Paul Rubens* (London, 1859), p. 125.

3 Sharpe, *The Personal Rule of Charles I*, pp. 65–75.

4 Ruth Magurn (ed.), *The Letters of Peter Paul Rubens* (Cambridge, Mass., 1971), pp. 285–7.

5 CSPV 1629–32, pp. 84–5.

6 Magurn (ed.), *The Letters of Peter Paul Rubens*, pp. 299–306.

7 Quoted ibid., p. 320.

8 Quoted ibid., p. 314.

9 Quoted ibid., p. 322.

10 Roy Strong, 'Queen Elizabeth I and the order of the garter', in *The Tudor and Stuart Monarchy: Pageantry, Painting and Iconography*, Vol. II, *Elizabethan* (Woodbridge, 1995), pp. 55–86.

11 Erica Veevers, *Images of Love and Religion: Queen Henrietta Maria and Court Entertainments* (Cambridge, 1989), pp. 187–91.

12 Quoted in Wolfgang Adler, *Corpus Rubenianum Ludwig Burchard: I Landscape and Hunting Scenes* (London, 1982), p. 122.

13 Quoted in Sainsbury (ed.), *Original Unpublished Papers Illustrative of the Life of Sir Peter Paul Rubens*, p. 142.

14 Quoted in Christopher White, *Peter Paul Rubens* (New Haven, 1987), p. 223.

15 David Howarth, 'The Entry Books of Sir Balthazar Gerbier: Van Dyck, Charles I and the Cardinal-Infante Ferdinand', in Hans Vlieghe (ed.), *Van Dyck 1599–1999: Conjectures and Refutations* (Turnhout, 2001), pp. 77–97.

16 Quoted in William Hookham Carpenter, *Pictorial Notices: Consisting of a Memoir of Sir Anthony Van Dyck* (London, 1844), p. 62.

17 Hookham Carpenter, *Pictorial Notices*, p. 59.

18 Ibid., p. 62.

19 See Rosemary Weinstein, 'London at the outbreak of the civil war', in Stephen Porter (ed.), *London and the Civil War* (London, 1996), pp. 31–44; R. Malcolm Smuts, *Court Culture and the Origins of the Royalist Tradition in Early Stuart England* (Philadelphia, 1987), esp. p. 57.

20 See Mary Edmond, 'Limners and picturemakers: new light on the lives of miniaturists and large-scale portrait-painters working in London in the sixteenth and seventeenth centuries', *Walpole Society*, 47 (1978–80); Jeremy Wood, 'Orazio Gentileschi and some Netherlandish artists in London: the patronage of the Duke of Buckingham, Charles I and Henrietta Maria', *Simiolus*, 28, 3 (2000–2001), pp. 103–28.

21 Ibid., pp. 116–17, 124–6.

22 G. E. Aylmer, *The King's Servants: The Civil Service of Charles I, 1625–1642* (London, 1961), Ch. 4.

23 Wood, 'Orazio Gentileschi and some Netherlandish artists in London', pp. 115–16.

24 Sainsbury (ed.), *Original Unpublished Papers Illustrative of the Life of Sir Peter Paul Rubens*, p. 319; Hookham Carpenter, *Pictorial Notices*, pp. 66–8.

25 Susan Foister; 'Foreigners at court: Holbein, Van Dyck and the Painter-Stainers', in David Howarth (ed.), *Art and Patronage in the Caroline Courts* (Cambridge, 1993), pp. 32–3.

26 David Howarth, *Images of Rule: Art and Politics in the English Renaissance, 1485–1649* (London, 1997), p. 279.

27 Quoted in W. N. Sainsbury, 'Artist's quarrels', *Notes and Queries*, 8 (13 August 1859), p. 121.

28 Hookham Carpenter, *Pictorial Notices*, pp. 66–8; Zirka Zaremba Filipczak, *Picturing Art in Antwerp, 1550–1700* (Princeton, 1987), pp. 95–6.

29 Quoted in Alison Plowden, *Henrietta Maria* (Stroud, 2001), p. 145.

30 Quoted in Raymond Needham and Alexander Webster, *Somerset House:*

Past and Present (London, 1905), p. 114; Veevers, *Images of Love and Religion*, p. 167.

31 Jeremy Wood, 'Van Dyck: a Catholic artist in Protestant England, and the notes on painting compiled by Francis Russell, 4th Earl of Bedford', in Vliege (ed.), *Van Dyck 1599–1999*, pp. 167–98.

32 Arthur Wheelock, 'The queen, the dwarf and the court: Van Dyck and the ideals of the English monarchy', ibid., pp. 151–66; Nick Page, *Lord Minimus: The Extraordinary Life of Britain's Smallest Man* (New York, 2002).

33 William Prynne, *Histrio-mastix, The Player's Scourge or Actor's Tragedie* (London, 1633), p. 901.

34 Henry Peacham, *The Gentleman's Exercise* (London, 1634), pp. 11–12.

35 Richard Montagu, *A Gag for the New Gospel? No, a New Gag for an Old Goose* (London, 1624), p. 299.

36 Ibid., p. 318.

37 See David Brown et al. (eds), *Lorenzo Lotto: Rediscovered Master of the Renaissance* (Washington, 1997), pp. 175–7.

38 Edmund Waller, 'To Vandyck' in G. Thorn Drury (ed.), *The Poems of Edward Waller* (London, 1893), p. 45.

39 Quoted in Ronald Lightbown, 'The journey of the Bernini bust of Charles I to England', *Connoisseur*, 169 (1968), p. 220; Ronald Lightbrown, 'Bernini's busts of English patrons', in Moshe Barasche and Lucy Freeman Sandler (eds), *Art, the Ape of Nature* (New York, 1981), pp. 439–76; Gudrun Raatschen, 'Bernini's busts of Charles I, *Burlington Magazine*, 138 (1996), pp. 813–16.

40 Christopher Brown and Hans Vleighe (eds), *Van Dyck, 1599–1641* (London, 1999), p. 293.

41 Gordon Albion, *Charles I and the Court of Rome* (London, 1935), p. 398.

42 Quoted in Howarth, *Images of Rule*, p. 147.

43 Quoted in Mary Hervey, *The Life, Correspondence and Collections of Thomas Howard, Earl of Arundel* (Cambridge, 1921), p. 393.

44 Quoted in R. Wittkower, 'Inigo Jones – "Puritanissimo Fiero"', *Burlington Magazine*, 90 (1948), p. 51.

45 Quoted in *The Personal Rule of Charles I*, p. 181.

46 Sainsbury (ed.), *Original Unpublished Papers Illustrative of the Life of Sir Peter Paul Rubens*, p. 187.

47 Ibid., p. 186.

48 Ibid., p. 197.

49 CSPD 1635, p. 492.

50 Roy Strong, 'Britannia Triumphans: Inigo Jones, Rubens and the

Whitehall Banqueting House', in *The Tudor and Stuart Monarchy: Pageantry, Painting and Iconography*, Vol. III, *Jacobean and Caroline* (Woodbridge, 1998), p. 132.

51 Gregory Martin, 'The Banqueting House ceiling: two newly discovered projects', *Apollo*, 139 (1994), pp. 29–34.

52 On the Banqueting House, see Strong, 'Britannia Triumphans'; Oliver Millar, *Rubens: The Whitehall Ceiling* (London, 1958).

53 Graham Parry, *The Golden Age Restor'd: The Culture of the Stuart Court, 1603–42* (Manchester, 1981), p. 36.

54 Strong, 'Britannia Triumphans', pp. 150–54.

55 Magurn (ed.), *The Letters of Peter Paul Rubens*, p. 400.

56 Martin, 'The Banqueting House ceiling', p. 32.

57 Francis Haskell, *Patrons and Painters: Art and Society in Baroque Italy* (2nd edition, London, 1980), p. 33.

SIX: WHATEVER THE COST

1 Samuel R. Gardiner, *History of England 1603–1642*, 10 vols (London, 1883–4), Vol. 4, p. 221.

2 Susan Maddocks Lister, '"Trumperies brought from Rome": Barberini gifts to the Stuart court in 1635', in Elizabeth Cropper (ed.), *The Diplomacy of Art: Artistic Creation and Politics in Seicento Italy* (Milan, 2000), p. 175; Francis Haskell, 'Charles I's collection of pictures', in Arthur MacGregor (ed.), *The Late King's Goods: Collections, Possessions and Patronage in the Light of the Commonwealth Sale Inventories* (Oxford, 1989), p. 221.

3 Elizabeth du Gue Trapier, 'Sir Arthur Hopton and the interchange of paintings between Spain and England in the seventeenth century: Part 1', *Connoisseur*, 164 (1967), pp. 239–43.

4 Quoted in W. N. Sainsbury (ed.), *Original Unpublished Papers Illustrative of the Life of Sir Peter Paul Rubens* (London, 1859), p. 353.

5 Enriqueta Harris, 'Velazquez and Charles I: antique busts and modern paintings from Spain for the royal collection', *Journal of the Warburg and Courtauld Institutes*, 30 (1967), pp. 414–20.

6 Simon Thurley, *Whitehall Palace: An Architectural History of the Royal Apartments, 1240–1690* (New Haven, 1999), p. 93.

7 Oliver Millar (ed.), 'Abraham van der Doort's catalogue of the collections of King Charles I', *Walpole Society*, 37 (1958–60), pp. 76–154.

8 Ibid., pp. 57, 60; Christopher White, The *Dutch Pictures in the Collection of Her Majesty the Queen* (Cambridge, 1982), pp. xxxvi–viii, 101–2.

9 See Francis Springell, *Connoisseur and Diplomat: The Earl of Arundel's Embassy to Germany in 1636* (London, 1963).

10 Ibid., pp. 105–8.

11 Quoted in Mary Hervey, *The Life, Correspondence and Collections of Thomas Howard, Earl of Arundel* (Cambridge, 1921), pp. 365–6.

12 Quoted in Paul Shakeshaft, ' "To much bewitched with those intysing things": the letters of James, third Marquis of Hamilton, and Basil, Viscount Feilding, concerning collecting in Venice 1635–1639', *Burlington Magazine*, 128 (1986), pp. 114–32.

13 Springell, *Connoisseur and Diplomat*, p. 257; Hervey, *The Life, Correspondence and Collections of Thomas Howard, Earl of Arundel*, p. 377.

14 Quoted ibid., p. 394.

15 Jeremy Wood, 'Van Dyck and the Earl of Northumberland: taste and collecting in Stuart England', in Susan Barnes and Arthur Wheelock Jr (eds), *Van Dyck 350: Studies in the History of Art 46* (Washington, 1994), pp. 281–324. On Northumberland, see George A. Drake, 'Percy, Algernon, tenth earl of Northumberland (1602–1668)', *Oxford Dictionary of National Biography* (Oxford, 2004).

16 Oliver Millar, 'Strafford and Van Dyck', in Richard Ollard and Pamela Tudor-Craig (eds), *For Veronica Wedgwood These* (London, 1986), pp. 109–23.

17 Hervey, *The Life, Correspondence and Collections of Thomas Howard, Earl of Arundel*, pp. 473–500.

18 Quoted ibid., p. 399.

19 Quoted ibid.

20 Quoted ibid., pp. 399–400.

21 Millar (ed.), 'Abraham van der Doort's catalogue of the collections of King Charles I', p. 79.

22 Ibid., p. 89.

23 J. Bruyn and Oliver Millar, 'Notes on the royal collection – III: the "Dutch gift" to Charles I', *Burlington Magazine*, 104 (1962), pp. 291–4.

24 Shakeshaft, ' "To much bewitched with those intysing things" ', p. 123.

25 Ibid., p. 123.

26 Quoted in Charles Petrie (ed.), *The Letters, Speeches and Proclamations of King Charles I* (London, 1935), pp. 81–2.

27 Shakeshaft, ' "To much bewitched with those intysing things" ', p. 125.

28 Ibid., p. 125.

29 Ibid.

30 Brian Reade, 'William Frizell and the royal collection', *Burlington Magazine*, 89 (1947), pp. 70–75; John Shearman, *The Early Italian*

Pictures in the Collection of Her Majesty the Queen (Cambridge, 1983), pp. 196–200.

31 Shakeshaft, ' "To much bewitched with those intysing things" ', p. 129.

32 Ibid., p. 131.

33 Ibid., p. 116; Cecilia, Countess of Denbigh, *Royalist Father and Roundhead Son, being the Memoirs of the First and Second Earls of Denbigh 1600–1675* (London, 1915), pp. 133–4.

34 Millar (ed.), 'Abraham van der Doort's catalogue of the collections of King Charles I', p. 82.

35 Quoted ibid., p. 135.

36 See Maurice Lee, *The Road to Revolution: Scotland under Charles I, 1625–37* (Chicago, 1985); David Stevenson, *The Scottish Revolution 1637–44* (Newton Abbot, 1973).

37 Quoted in Conrad Russell, *The Crisis of Parliaments* (Oxford, 1971), p. 326.

38 Quoted in Samuel R. Gardiner, *The Constitutional Documents of the Puritan Revolution* (3rd edition, Oxford, 1906), pp. 202–32.

39 R. Ward Bissell, *Artemisia Gentileschi and the Authority of Art* (Pennsylvania, 1999), pp. 58–61; Sainsbury (ed.), *Original Unpublished Papers Illustrative of the Life of Sir Peter Paul Rubens*, p. 235.

40 Quoted in Gardiner, *History of England 1603–1642*, 10 vols (London, 1883–4), Vol. 10, p. 140.

41 For an overview of the period, see Conrad Russell, *The Fall of the British Monarchies 1637–1642* (Oxford, 1991).

SEVEN: CLOUDED MAJESTY

1 Oliver Millar, *The Age of Charles I* (London, 1972), pp. 99–101.

2 David Stevenson, *The Scottish Revolution 1637–44* (Newton Abbot, 1973), pp. 283–6.

3 See Austin Woolrych, *Britain in Revolution 1625–1660* (Oxford, 2002), pp. 335–40.

4 CSPV 1655–56, p. 124.

5 Quoted in Samuel R. Gardiner, *History of the Great Civil War*, 4 vols (London, 1901), Vol. 4, pp. 220–21.

6 David Underdown, *Pride's Purge: Politics in the Puritan Revolution* (Oxford, 1971).

7 Quoted in W. C. Abbott (ed.), *The Writings and Speeches of Oliver Cromwell*, 4 vols (Harvard, 1937–47), Vol. 1, p. 691.

8   Valerie Pearl, *London and the Outbreak of the Puritan Revolution* (London, 1961), pp. 237–75.

9   Sean Kelsey, 'Clotworthy, John, first Viscount Massereene (d. 1665)', *Oxford Dictionary of National Biography* (Oxford, 2004).

10 Quoted in Albert J. Loomie, 'The destruction of Rubens's "Crucifixion" in the Queen's chapel, Somerset House', *Burlington Magazine*, 140 (1998), pp. 680–81.

11 Oliver Millar (ed.), 'The inventories and valuation of the king's goods, 1649–1651', *Walpole Society*, 43 (1970–72), p. xi; Julie Spraggon, *Puritan Iconoclasm during the English Civil War* (Woodbridge, 2003), pp. 73–8.

12 Jacqueline Eales, *Puritans and Roundheads: The Harleys of Brampton Bryant and the Outbreak of the English Civil War* (Cambridge, 1990).

13 *Mercurius Aulicus* (16–22 June 1644), p. 1040.

14 Quoted in Spraggon, *Puritan Iconoclasm during the English Civil War*, pp. 259–60.

15 Ibid., pp. 88–96.

16 Ibid., p. 212.

17 Quoted in David Howarth, *Lord Arundel and his Circle* (London, 1985), p. 212.

18 Quoted in Philip McEvansoneya, 'The sequestration and dispersal of the Buckingham collection', *Journal of the History of Collections* 8, 2 (1996), pp. 135–6.

19 Jeremy Wood, 'Van Dyck and the Earl of Northumberland: taste and collecting in Stuart England', in Susan Barnes and Arthur Wheelock Jr (eds), *Van Dyck 350: Studies in the History of Art 46* (Washington, 1994), pp. 281–4.

20 Jonathan Brown, *Kings and Connoisseurs: Collecting Art in Seventeenth-Century Europe* (New Haven, 1995), pp. 60, 161.

21 McEvansoneya, 'The sequestration and dispersal of the Buckingham collection', pp. 141–2.

22 Jeremy Wood, 'Van Dyck's "Cabinet de Titien": the contents and dispersal of his collection', *Burlington Magazine*, 132 (1990), pp. 680–96.

23 Wood speculates that *The Three Children of Charles I* was commissioned by the king, not Northumberland (Wood, 'Van Dyck and the Earl of Northumberland', p. 295).

24 For a brilliant analysis of this painting and Lovelace's poetic response, see James Loxley, *Royalism and Poetry in the English Civil Wars* (London, 1997), pp. 155–68.

25 Quoted in Albert J. Loomie, 'New light on the Spanish ambassador's purchases from Charles I's collection 1649–53', *Journal of the Warburg and Courtauld Institutes*, 52 (1989), p. 258.

EIGHT: WHO BIDS MOST?

1 JHC VI, pp. 127–8.

2 JHC VI, p. 129.

3 Bernard Capp, *Cromwell's Navy: The Fleet and the English Revolution, 1648–1660* (Oxford, 1989), pp. 42–72.

4 JHC VI, pp. 132–33; Samuel R. Gardiner, *History of the Commonwealth and Protectorate*, 4 vols (London, 1903; revised edition, 1988), Vol. 1, p. 3.

5 David Underdown, *Pride's Purge: Politics in the Puritan Revolution* (Oxford, 1971), p. 205.

6 JHC VI, p. 148.

7 JHC VI, p. 172.

8 CSPV 1647–52, p. 92.

9 JHC VI, p. 172.

10 The committee was composed of 'Mr. *Holland*, Sir *Gilbert Pickering*, Commissary General *Ireton*, and Mr. *Robinson* . . . And the care thereof is especially recommended to Mr. *Holland*, and Mr. *Allen*' (ibid.).

11 R. Malcolm Smuts, 'Art and the material culture of majesty', in R. Malcolm Smuts (ed.), *The Stuart Court and Europe* (Cambridge, 1996), pp. 86–112.

12 See Sean Kelsey, *Inventing a Republic: The Political Culture of the English Commonwealth, 1649–1653* (Stanford, 1997), p. 29, on payments to Kinnersley of £100 in spring 1649 to furnish Whitehall.

13 C. H. Firth and R. S. Rait (eds), *Acts and Ordinances of the Interregnum*, 3 vols (London, 1911), Vol. 2, p. 160.

14 Ibid., p. 167.

15 Ibid., p. 160.

16 Ibid., pp. 164–5.

17 Ibid., p. 167.

18 Ibid., p. 168.

19 Kelsey, *Inventing a Republic*, p. 164; TNA (PRO) SP25/62, fols 544, 624, and SP25/63, fols 33, 91, 115.

20 See Michelle O'Callaghan, 'Wither, George (1588–1667), poet', *Oxford Dictionary of National Biography* (Oxford, 2004).

21 Peter Heylyn, *Cyprianus Anglicus* (London, 1671), pp. 147–8.

22 Anon., *A Deep Sigh Breath'd Through the Lodgings at Whitehall, Deploring the Absence of the Court* (London, 1642), fol. A2.

23 Ibid., fols A2–A3.

24 Oliver Millar (ed.), 'The inventories and valuation of the king's goods, 1649–1651', *Walpole Society*, 43 (1970–72), pp. 20–21.

25 Ibid., p. 380.

26 Ibid., pp. 343–4.

27 Ibid., p. 396.

28 Ibid., p. 125.

29 Quoted in Simon Thurley, *Whitehall Palace: An Architectural History of the Royal Apartments, 1240–1690* (New Haven, 1999), p. 22.

30 John Shearman, *The Early Italian Pictures in the Collection of Her Majesty the Queen* (Cambridge, 1983), p. 217.

31 Ibid., pp. 196–7.

32 Ibid., pp. 192–3.

33 Ibid., pp. 128–30, 131–2, 121–2.

34 Ibid., p. 215.

35 Millar (ed.), 'Abraham van der Doort's catalogue of the collections of King Charles I', p. 9.

36 Shearman, *The Early Italian Pictures in the Collection of Her Majesty the Queen*, p. 274.

37 Ibid., pp. 80–81.

38 Ibid., pp. 268–9.

39 Ibid., pp. 69–72.

40 Millar (ed.), 'Abraham van der Doort's catalogue of the collections of King Charles I', p. 35.

41 Ibid., p. 36.

42 John Crouch, *A Tragi-Comedy, called New Market Fayre or a Parliament Out-Cry of State-Commodities Set to Sale* (London, 1649), pp. 3–4. For a modern edition arguing that the play was performed, see Paul Werstine, 'New Market Fayre', *Analytical and Enumerative Bibliography*, 6.2 (1982), pp. 71–101.

43 Crouch, *A Tragi-Comedy, called New Market Fayre or a Parliament Out-Cry of State-Commodities Set to Sale*, pp. 3–6.

44 Ibid.

45 Quoted in Raymond Needham and Alexander Webster, *Somerset House: Past and Present* (London, 1905), p. 127.

46 Quoted in Stephen Porter, 'The economic and social impact of the civil

war upon London', in Stephen Porter (ed.), *London and the Civil War*, p. 191.

47 R. G. Collmer (ed.), *Lodweijk Huygens: The English Journal* (Leiden, 1982), p. 61.

48 Millar (ed.), 'The inventories and valuation of the king's goods, 1649–1651', p. 310.

49 Ibid., p. 64

50 Ibid., p. 308.

51 Ibid., p. 304.

52 Ibid., p. 70.

53 Ibid., p. 306; Oliver Millar, *The Tudor, Stuart and Early Georgian Pictures in the Collection of Her Majesty the Queen* (London, 1963), pp. 98–9.

54 Millar (ed.), 'The inventories and valuation of the king's goods, 1649–1651', pp. 67, 69, 316.

55 Ibid., p. 71.

56 Ibid., p. 318. He also bought another Van Dyck, described in the inventories as 'Mary. Christ & Many Angells danceing done by Vandyke' at a cost of £40, £30 for a picture of 'King Henry ye 8. at Length' and 'Christ by ye well wth ye Samaretan. woman' from the workshop of the early sixteenth-century Italian painter Bonifazio di Marzio de' Pitati for £50 (ibid., p. 319).

57 Shearman, *The Early Italian Pictures in the Collection of Her Majesty the Queen*, p. 131; Millar (ed.), 'The inventories and valuation of the king's goods, 1649–1651', pp. 61, 298–9, 317.

58 Ibid., p. 305.

59 On Lisle, see Hilary Maddicott, 'A collection of the interregnum period: Philip, Lord Viscount Lisle, and his purchases from the "late king's goods", 1649–1660', *Journal of the History of Collections*, 11, 1 (1999), pp. 1–24.

60 Ibid., p. 6.

61 Millar (ed.), 'The inventories and valuation of the king's goods, 1649–1651', pp. 65, 276–7.

62 Ibid., p. 298.

63 Ibid., pp. 299, 305.

64 Maddicott, 'A collection of the interregnum period', p. 15.

65 Lucy Hutchinson, *Memoirs of the Life of Colonel Hutchinson* (London, 1904), p. 348.

66 Millar (ed.), 'The inventories and valuation of the king's goods, 1649–1651', pp. 302, 318.

67 Ibid., pp. 299, 310.
68 See Jeremy Wood, 'Van Dyck's "Cabinet de Titien": the contents and
    dispersal of his collection', *Burlington Magazine*, 132 (1990), p. 685, for
    other examples.
69 John Gibson, *Commonplace Book*, BL Add. MS 37719, *c.* 1656, fol. 198v.

NINE: THE FIRST LIST

 1 JHC VI, p. 382; W. L. F. Nuttall, 'King Charles I's pictures and the
    commonwealth sale', *Apollo*, 81 (1965), p. 303. Receipted payments
    listed in TNA (PRO) SP 28/282. See also Anon., *A Remonstrance
    Manifesting the Lamentable Miseries of the Creditors and Servants of the Late King,
    Queen, & Prince* (London, 1653).
 2 Mary Beal, *A Study of Richard Symonds* (London, 1984), p. 311.
 3 Ibid., p. 312.
 4 Oliver Millar (ed.), 'The inventories and valuation of the king's goods,
    1649–1651', *Walpole Society*, 43 (1970–72), pp. 198, 205, 261, 310, 311,
    394.
 5 See Peter Barber, 'Gambling in wartime: the rise and fall of William
    Geere (1589/90–1652), *Camden History Review*, 19 (1995), pp. 17–20.
 6 Millar (ed.), 'The inventories and valuation of the king's goods,
    1649–1651', p. 73.
 7 Ibid., p. 126.
 8 Ibid., p. 287.
 9 Ibid., pp. 64–5, 312.
10 Ibid., pp. 269, 316.
11 Quoted in Dr Godfrey Goodman, *The Court of King James the First*, ed.
    John Brewer, 2 vols (London, 1839), Vol. I, p. 369.
12 Millar (ed.), 'The inventories and valuation of the king's goods,
    1649–1651', p. xv, citing TNA (PRO) SP 25/62, fol. 547, and 25/16,
    fol. 43.
13 Attr. Balthazar Gerbier, *The None-Such Charles his Character* (London,
    1651), pp. 2–3.
14 Ibid., pp. 5, 133, 158.
15 Ibid., p. 56.
16 Ibid., p. 84.
17 Ibid., pp. 84–5.
18 Ibid., p. 87.

19 Albert J. Loomie, 'Alonso de Cárdenas and the Long Parliament', *English Historical Review*, 97 (1982), pp. 289–307.

20 Quoted in Jonathan Brown and J. H. Elliott (eds), *The Sale of the Century: Artistic Relations between Spain and Great Britain, 1604–1655* (New Haven, 2002), p. 36.

21 Albert J. Loomie, 'New light on the Spanish ambassador's purchases from Charles I's collection 1649–53', *Journal of the Warburg and Courtauld Institutes*, 52 (1989), p. 295.

22 Quoted ibid., p. 259.

23 Quoted ibid.

24 In *The Rump Parliament 1648–1653* (Cambridge, 1974), Blair Worden points out that many of the revolutionary members of the Rump Parliament had incomes under £500 a year (p. 53). See David Underdown, *Pride's Purge: Politics in the Puritan Revolution* (Oxford, 1971), p. 245.

25 Loomie, 'New light on the Spanish ambassador's purchases from Charles I's collection 1649–53', pp. 262–3; Millar (ed.), 'The inventories and valuation of the king's goods, 1649–1651', pp. 298, 304, 319; Jonathan Brown, *Kings and Connoisseurs: Collecting Art in Seventeenth-Century Europe* (New Haven, 1995), p. 76.

26 Loomie, 'New light on the Spanish ambassador's purchases from Charles I's collection 1649–53', pp. 26–63.

27 Quoted in Jerry Brotton and David McGrath, 'The Spanish acquisition of King Charles I's paintings: the letters of Alonso de Cárdenas, 1649–51', *Journal of the History of Collections* (forthcoming). This article translates the original Spanish correspondence held in Madrid, which was transcribed by Beatrice Mariño and published as an appendix in Brown and Elliot (eds), *The Sale of the Century*.

28 Quoted ibid.

29 Oliver Millar, *The Tudor, Stuart and Early Georgian Pictures in the Collection of Her Majesty the Queen* (London, 1963), pp. 116–19.

30 Loomie, 'New light on the Spanish ambassador's purchases from Charles I's collection 1649–53', pp. 263–4.

31 Quoted in Brotton and McGrath, 'The Spanish acquisition of King Charles I's paintings: the letters of Alonso de Cárdenas, 1649–51'.

32 On Veronese, see Millar (ed.), 'The inventories and valuation of the king's goods, 1649–1651', p. 205. On Van Dyck, see Millar, *The Tudor, Stuart and Early Georgian Pictures in the Collection of Her Majesty the Queen*, p. 101. On Mantegna, see Millar (ed.), 'The inventories and valuation

of the king's goods, 1649–1651', p. 266; Oliver Millar (ed.), 'Abraham van der Doort's catalogue of the collections of King Charles I', *Walpole Society*, 37 (1958–60), p. 81.

33 Worden, *The Rump Parliament 1648–1653*, pp. 222–6.

34 Quoted in Loomie, 'New light on the Spanish ambassador's purchases from Charles I's collection 1649–53', p. 260.

35 Quoted in Brotton and McGrath, 'The Spanish acquisition of King Charles I's paintings: the letters of Alonso de Cárdenas, 1649–51'.

36 See Millar (ed.), 'The inventories and valuation of the king's goods, 1649–1651', p. 5; Brotton and McGrath, 'The Spanish acquisition of King Charles I's paintings: the letters of Alonso de Cárdenas, 1649–51'.

37 Quoted ibid.

38 Quoted ibid.

TEN: REAPING DIVIDENDS: THE SECOND LIST

1 See Anne Brookes, 'Richard Symonds and the Palazzo Farnese, 1649–50', *Journal of the History of Collections*, 10, 2 (1998), pp. 139–57.

2 Quoted in Mary Beal, *A Study of Richard Symonds* (London, 1984), p. 308.

3 Ibid.

4 Oliver Millar (ed.), 'Abraham van der Doort's catalogue of the collections of King Charles I', *Walpole Society*, 37 (1958–60), p. 60.

5 Beal, *A Study of Richard Symonds*, p. 309; see Ronald Lightbrown, 'The journey of the Bernini bust of Charles I to England', *Connoisseur*, 169 (1968), pp. 217–20.

6 Oliver Millar, *The Tudor, Stuart and Early Georgian Pictures in the Collection of Her Majesty the Queen* (London, 1963), p. 96.

7 Oliver Millar (ed.), 'The inventories and valuation of the king's goods, 1649–1651', *Walpole Society*, 43 (1970–72), p. 323. Purchased with others on 23 October 1651, Cárdenas got it for £400. See Jonathan Brown, *Kings and Connoisseurs: Collecting Art in Seventeenth-Century Europe* (New Haven, 1995), p. 81.

8 Beal, *A Study of Richard Symonds*, p. 305.

9 Millar (ed.), 'The inventories and valuation of the king's goods, 1649–1651', p. 274.

10 Ibid., p. 72.

11 Beal, *A Study of Richard Symonds*, p. 307.

12 W. L. F. Nuttall, 'King Charles I's pictures and the commonwealth

sale', *Apollo*, 81 (1965), p. 308; Millar (ed.), 'The inventories and valuation of the king's goods, 1649–1651', p. 305.

13 Ibid., p. 259.

14 Ibid., p. 265.

15 Anon., *A Remonstrance Manifesting the Lamentable Miseries of the Creditors and Servants of the Late King, Queen, & Prince* (London, 1653), p. 2.

16 Quoted in Jerry Brotton and David McGrath, 'The Spanish acquisition of King Charles I's paintings: the letters of Alonso de Cárdenas, 1649–51', *Journal of the History of Collections* (forthcoming).

17 CSPV 1647–52, p. 175.

18 Quoted in Brotton and McGrath, 'The Spanish acquisition of King Charles I's paintings: the letters of Alonso de Cárdenas, 1649–51'.

19 Ibid.

20 Blair Worden, *The Rump Parliament 1648–1653* (Cambridge, 1974), p. 254.

21 C. H. Firth and R. S. Rait (eds), *Acts and Ordinances of the Interregnum*, 3 vols (London, 1911), Vol. 2, pp. 546–8. On the significance of the changes, see Sean Kelsey, *Inventing a Republic: The Political Culture of the English Commonwealth, 1649–1653* (Stanford, 1997), pp. 164–5.

22 Quoted in Firth and Rait (eds), *Acts and Ordinances of the Interregnum*, p. 547.

23 See Kelsey, *Inventing a Republic*, p. 155; Anon., *A Remonstrance Manifesting the Lamentable Miseries of the Creditors and Servants of the Late King, Queen, & Prince*, pp. 4–5.

24 Quoted in Brotton and McGrath, 'The Spanish acquisition of King Charles I's paintings: the letters of Alonso de Cárdenas, 1649–51'.

25 Quoted ibid.

26 Quoted ibid.

27 Austin Woolrych, *Britain in Revolution 1625–1660* (Oxford, 2002), pp. 497–500.

28 Quoted in Brotton and McGrath, 'The Spanish acquisition of King Charles I's paintings: the letters of Alonso de Cárdenas, 1649–51'.

29 Anon., *A Remonstrance Manifesting the Lamentable Miseries of the Creditors and Servants of the Late King, Queen, & Prince*, pp. 4–5.

30 RCHM, p. 90.

31 Beal, *A Study of Richard Symonds*, p. 309.

32 There is some confusion over John/Robert Stone. Nuttall, 'King Charles I's pictures and the commonwealth sale', refers to Capt John Stone; Millar (ed.), 'The inventories and valuation of the king's goods, 1649–1651', refers to Capt Robert Stone. The Bodleian Rawlinson MS

lists 'Robert Stone of Barbican' as purchaser at sale, and John Stone as head of the sixth dividend (attr. Elias Ashmole, 'Persons who bought the King & Queenes Goods', Bodleian Library, Oxford, MS Rawlinson D. 695 (*c.* 1659), fol. 1v).

33 Nuttall, 'King Charles I's pictures and the commonwealth sale', p. 308. See Bodleian Rawlinson MS, fols 10–11.

34 Millar (ed.), 'The inventories and valuation of the king's goods, 1649–1651', pp. 131–3, 139, 155.

35 Quoted in Brotton and McGrath, 'The Spanish acquisition of King Charles I's paintings: the letters of Alonso de Cárdenas, 1649–51'.

36 W. Alexander Vergara, 'The Count of Fuensaldaña and David Teniers: their purchases in London after the civil war', *Burlington Magazine*, 131 (1989), pp. 127–32.

37 Quoted in Brotton and McGrath, 'The Spanish acquisition of King Charles I's paintings: the letters of Alonso de Cárdenas, 1649–51'.

38 Vergara, 'Fuensaldaña', p. 128.

39 Beal, *A Study of Richard Symonds*, p. 310.

40 Millar (ed.), 'The inventories and valuation of the king's goods, 1649–1651', p. 299.

41 Harold Wethey, *The Paintings of Titian*, 3 vols (London, 1975), Vol. 3, pp. 196–200.

42 Quoted in Brotton and McGrath, 'The Spanish acquisition of King Charles I's paintings: the letters of Alonso de Cárdenas, 1649–51'.

43 The title of the piece is subject to confusion, so its provenance is slightly unclear. See Vergara, 'The Count of Fuensaldaña and David Teniers', p. 264, n. 54, on its acquisition.

44 Millar (ed.), 'The inventories and valuation of the king's goods, 1649–1651', p. 70; Vergara, 'The Count of Fuensaldaña and David Teniers', p. 265.

Eleven: While Stocks Last

1 Oliver Millar (ed.), 'The inventories and valuation of the king's goods, 1649–1651', *Walpole Society*, 43 (1970–72), p. 186.

2 Andrew Martindale, *The Triumphs of Caesar by Andrea Mantegna in the Collection of Her Majesty the Queen at Hampton Court* (London, 1979); Roy Sherwood, *The Court of Oliver Cromwell* (London, 1977), pp. 27–9.

3 Quoted in David L. Smith, *The Stuart Parliaments, 1603–1689* (London, 1999), p. 137.

4 Quoted in Ivan Roots (ed.), *Speeches of Oliver Cromwell* London, 1989, p. 209.

5 Blair Worden, *The Rump Parliament 1648–1653* (Cambridge, 1974), Chs 14–16; J. S. A. Adamson, 'Oliver Cromwell and the Long Parliament', in John Morrill (ed.), *Oliver Cromwell and the English Revolution* (Harlow, 1990), Ch. 3.

6 Quoted in Roots (ed.), *Speeches of Oliver Cromwell*, p. 210.

7 See Kevin Sharpe, ' "An image doting rabble": the failure of republican culture in seventeenth-century England', in *Remapping Early Modern England: The Culture of Seventeenth-Century Politics* (Cambridge, 2000), pp. 223–65.

8 Austin Woolrych, *Britain in Revolution 1625–1660* (Oxford, 2002), p. 595.

9 Nicola Smith, *The Royal Image and the English People* (Aldershot, 2001), p. 75.

10 Quoted in Sherwood, *The Court of Oliver Cromwell*, p. 21.

11 Ibid., p. 25.

12 See W. L. F. Nuttall, 'King Charles I's pictures and the commonwealth sale', *Apollo*, 81 (1965), p. 305.

13 Sherwood, *The Court of Oliver Cromwell*, p. 105; TNA (PRO) SP18/73, fol. 15; CSPD 1653–4, p. 415; CSPD 1654, pp. 394–5.

14 CSPD 1654, p. 360.

15 John Cleveland, *The Character of a London Diurnall* (Oxford, 1645), p. 6.

16 Millar (ed.), 'The inventories and valuation of the king's goods, 1649–1651', p. 158; Sherwood, *The Court of Oliver Cromwell*, pp. 26–7.

17 On the tapestry, see Millar (ed.), 'The inventories and valuation of the king's goods, 1649–1651', p. 378; Spittlehouse, quoted in John Morrill, 'Cromwell and his contemporaries', in John Morrill (ed.), *Oliver Cromwell and the English Revolution* (London, 1990), p. 272; J. Spittlehouse, *A Warning Piece Discharged* (London, 1653), p. 10.

18 Millar (ed.), 'The inventories and valuation of the king's goods, 1649–1651', pp. 416–17.

19 Oliver Millar (ed.), 'Abraham van der Doort's catalogue of the collections of King Charles I', *Walpole Society*, 37 (1958–60), p. 186. See also John Shearman, *The Early Italian Pictures in the Collection of Her Majesty the Queen* (Cambridge, 1983), pp. 63–4.

20 Quoted in Laura Lunger Knoppers, *Constructing Cromwell: Ceremony, Portrait, and Print, 1645–1661* (Cambridge, 2000), p. 78.

21 Quoted ibid., p. 104.

22 Quoted in Sherwood, *The Court of Oliver Cromwell*, p. 31.

23 Quoted in Roots (ed.), *Speeches of Oliver Cromwell*, p. 39.

24 Attr. Elias Ashmole, 'Persons who bought the King & Queenes Goods', Bodleian Library, Oxford, MS Rawlinson D. 695 (*c.* 1659), fols 10r–11v.

25 Samuel R. Gardiner, *The Constitutional Documents of the Puritan Revolution* (3rd edition, Oxford, 1906), pp. 468–71. On the Dutch War, see Charles Wilson, *Profit and Power: A Study of England and the Dutch Wars* (London, 1957); Steven Pincus, *Protestantism and Patriotism: Ideologies and the Making of English Foreign Policy* (Cambridge, 1996).

26 Worden, *The Rump Parliament 1648–1653*, p. 306.

27 Ibid., pp. 318–19.

28 J. B. Gent, *A Faire in Spittle Fields where all the Knick Knacks of Astrology are Exposed to Open Sale* (London, 1652), p. 4.

29 Quoted in Sean Kelsey, *Inventing a Republic: The Political Culture of the English Commonwealth, 1649–1653* (Stanford, 1997), p. 156.

30 Anon., *A Remonstrance Manifesting the Lamentable Miseries of the Creditors and Servants of the Late King, Queen, & Prince* (London, 1653), p. 9.

31 TNA (PRO) SP 28/284, fol. 53. On Jones's surrendered pictures, see Millar (ed.), 'The inventories and valuation of the king's goods, 1649–1651', pp. 414–15.

32 J. T. Peacey, 'Mildmay, Henry (*c.* 1594–1664/5?)', *Oxford Dictionary of National Biography* (Oxford, 2004); Worden, *The Rump Parliament 1648–1653*, p. 38; Sherwood, *The Court of Oliver Cromwell*, p. 25.

33 Millar (ed.), 'The inventories and valuation of the king's goods, 1649–1651', p. 48.

34 CSPD 1649–50, p. 276.

35 Worden, *The Rump Parliament 1648–1653*, p. 281.

36 TNA (PRO) SP 28/284, fol. 71.

37 Attr. Ashmole, 'Persons who bought the King & Queenes Goods', fol. 11r, although this may represent half the amount of discoveries. In other words, half the money is given to those claiming the discoveries, so the actual figure could be £7,800.

38 Philip Knachel, *England and the Fronde* (Ithaca, 1967).

39 Ibid., p. 186, n. 18.

40 JHC VII, p. 251.

41 JHC VII, pp. 250–51.

42 See Millar (ed.), 'The inventories and valuation of the king's goods, 1649–1651', p. 437, for Beauchamp's purchases.

43 TNA (PRO) SP 28/285, fol. 340. On Holland's accumulated claims of over £1,000, see TNA (PRO) SP 28/283, fols 1,225, 1,202.

44 Quoted in Le Comte de Cosnac (Gabriel-Jules), *Les Richesses du Palais Mazarin* (Paris, 1885), pp. 170–71.

45 Millar (ed.), 'The inventories and valuation of the king's goods, 1649–1651', p. 73, but note pp. 4 and 362 for other *David* tapestries acquired by Bass.

46 Quoted in Cosnac, *Les Richesses du Palais Mazarin*, p. 171.

47 For an account of the events and motivations surrounding the dissolution, see Worden, *The Rump Parliament 1648–1653*, Ch. 15.

48 Samuel Chidley, *A Remonstrance to the Valiant and Well Deserving Soldier, and to the rest of the Creditors of the Commonwealth* (London, 1653), p. 8. On Chidley, see Ian Gentles, 'London Levellers in the English revolution: the Chidleys and their circle', *Journal of Ecclesiastical History*, 29 (1978), pp. 281–309.

49 Chidley, *A Remonstrance to the Valiant and Well Deserving Soldier, and to the rest of the Creditors of the Commonwealth*, pp. 3–4.

50 Ibid., p. 7.

51 Ibid., p. 16.

52 Ibid.

53 Anon., *A Remonstrance*, Preface, unpaginated.

54 Ibid., pp. 8–9.

55 Ibid., p. 4.

56 Quoted in Cosnac, *Les Richesses du Palais Mazarin*, p. 175.

57 Quoted ibid.

58 Millar (ed.), 'The inventories and valuation of the king's goods, 1649–1651', p. 323.

59 Quoted in Jerry Brotton and David McGrath, 'The Spanish acquisition of King Charles I's paintings: the letters of Alonso de Cárdenas, 1649–51', *Journal of the History of Collections* (forthcoming).

60 Quoted in H. Léonardon, 'Une dèpêche diplomatique relative à des tableaux acquis en Angleterre pour Philippe IV', *Bulletin Hispanique*, 2 (1900), p. 28.

61 Millar (ed.), 'The inventories and valuation of the king's goods, 1649–1651', p. 205.

62 Quoted in Léonardon, 'Une dépêche diplomatique relative à des tableaux acquis en Angleterre pour Philippe IV', pp. 28–9. See also Jonathan Brown, *Kings and Connoisseurs: Collecting Art in Seventeenth-Century Europe* (New Haven, 1995), pp. 87–90.

63 Quoted in Léonardon, 'Une dépêche diplomatique relative à des tableaux acquis en Angleterre pour Philippe IV', p. 30.

64 Quoted ibid., pp. 30, 33.
65 Quoted in Albert J. Loomie, 'New light on the Spanish ambassador's purchases from Charles I's collection 1649–53', *Journal of the Warburg and Courtauld Institutes*, 52 (1989), p. 267.

TWELVE: SETTLING ACCOUNTS

1 Albert J. Loomie, 'New light on the Spanish ambassador's purchases from Charles I's collection 1649–53', *Journal of the Warburg and Courtauld Institutes*, 52 (1989), p. 266.
2 Edward Hyde, Earl of Clarendon, *The History of the Rebellion and Civil Wars in England*, ed. W. Dunn Macray, 6 vols (Oxford, 1888), Vol. 4, p. 498.
3 Ibid.
4 Quoted in Le Comte de Cosnac (Gabriel-Jules), *Les Richesses du Palais Mazarin* (Paris, 1885), p. 182.
5 Quoted ibid., p. 184.
6 Quoted ibid., pp. 187–8.
7 Quoted ibid., pp. 188–9.
8 W. N. Sainsbury (ed.), *Original Unpublished Papers Illustrative of the Life of Sir Peter Paul Rubens* (London, 1859), pp. 205–7; David Howarth, *Lord Arundel and his Circle* (London, 1985), p. 212.
9 Mary Beal, *A Study of Richard Symonds* (London, 1984), p. 308.
10 Jonathan Brown, *Kings and Connoisseurs: Collecting Art in Seventeenth-Century Europe* (New Haven, 1995), p. 92.
11 Quoted in Cosnac, *Les Richesses du Palais Mazarin*, p. 188.
12 Quoted ibid., p. 195.
13 Quoted ibid., pp. 200–203.
14 Quoted ibid., p. 203.
15 TNA (PRO) SP25/70, fols 299–300.
16 Quoted in Cosnac, *Les Richesses du Palais Mazarin*, p. 207.
17 Quoted ibid., p. 218.
18 Arjun Appadurai (ed.), *The Social Life of Things: Commodities in Cultural Perspective* (Cambridge, 1986), pp. 44–5.
19 William Sanderson, *Graphice: The Use of the Pen and Pencil* (London, 1658), p. 16.
20 Quoted in Cosnac, *Les Richesses du Palais Mazarin*, p. 226.
21 Quoted ibid., p. 231.

22 Quoted in Ellis Waterhouse, *Painting in Britain 1530–1700* (New Haven, 1953; 5th edition, 1994), p. 49.

23 Oliver Millar (ed.), 'The inventories and valuation of the king's goods, 1649–1651', *Walpole Society*, 43 (1970–72), p. 306; Oliver Millar, *The Tudor, Stuart and Early Georgian Pictures in the Collection of Her Majesty the Queen* (London, 1963), pp. 98–9, claims that Bordeaux rejected the picture, but Cosnac notes that Colbert's inventory lists the picture as no. 169. However, this could be the small copy Millar identifies in the Louvre (p. 99).

24 Quoted in Cosnac, *Les Richesses du Palais Mazarin*, p. 236.

25 Millar, *The Tudor, Stuart and Early Georgian Pictures in the Collection of Her Majesty the Queen*, p. 93.

26 See G. S. Layard, *The Headless Horseman* (London, 1922); Anthony Griffiths, *The Print in Stuart Britain 1603–1689* (London, 1988), p. 181.

27 Austin Woolrych, *Britain in Revolution 1625–1600* (Oxford, 2002), pp. 631–7; Jonathan Brown and J. H. Elliott (eds), *The Sale of the Century: Artistic Relations between Spain and Great Britain, 1604–1655* (New Haven, 2002), p. 38.

28 Clarendon, *The History of the Rebellion and Civil Wars in England*, Vol. 4, p. 498.

29 TNA (PRO) SP28/350, fol. 9.

30 Attr. Elias Ashmole, 'Persons who bought the King & Queenes Goods', Bodleian Library, Oxford, MS Rawlinson D. 695 (*c.* 1659), fol. 12v.

31 CSPD 1659–60, p. 383.

32 Millar (ed.), 'The inventories and valuation of the king's goods, 1649–1651', pp. 171–4, 196–9.

Thirteen: Like Father, Like Son?

1 Robert Latham and William Matthews (eds), *The Diary of Samuel Pepys*, 11 vols (London, 1970), Vol. 1, p. 89; CSPV 1659–61, p. 132.

2 Anon., 'An Exit to the Exit Tyrannus . . .' (London, 1660).

3 See Ronald Hutton, *The Restoration: A Political and Religious History of England and Wales, 1658–1667* (Oxford, 1985); Godfrey Davies, *The Restoration of Charles II, 1658–1660* (Oxford, 1955).

4 JHL XI, p. 19. See also Stephen Gleissner, 'Reassembling a royal art collection for the restored king of Great Britain', *Journal of the History of Collections*, 6, 1 (1994), pp. 103–15.

5 JHL XI, p. 23.

6 JHL XI, p. 26; BL Thomason Tract 669 fol. 25 (20).

7 The manuscripts dealing with the returns are held at the HLRO. I am grateful to Jennie Lynch for her help identifying these records. For Geldorp's memorandum, see HLRO, Main Papers, May 1660, HL/PO/JO/10/1/285, fol. 80. See also Oliver Millar, *The Tudor, Stuart and Early Georgian Pictures in the Collection of Her Majesty the Queen* (London, 1963), p. 93. A calendar of the returns is collected in RCHM, pp. 88–92.

8 HLRO, Main Papers, May 1660, HL/PO/JO/10/1/285, fol. 80.

9 JHL XI, p. 27.

10 JHL XI, p. 31.

11 HLRO, Main Papers, May 1660, HL/PO/JO/10/1/285, fol. 90.

12 Roy Sherwood, *The Court of Oliver Cromwell* (London, 1977), pp. 120–21; Lisa Jardine, *On a Grander Scale: The Outstanding Career of Sir Christopher Wren* (London, 2002), pp. 14–18.

13 CSPD 1660–61, p. 396.

14 HLRO, Main Papers, May 1660, HL/PO/JO/10/1/285, fol. 85.

15 CSPV 1659–61, p. 137.

16 HLRO, Main Papers, May 1660, HL/PO/JO/10/1/285, fol. 68.

17 W. L. F. Nuttall, 'King Charles I's pictures and the commonwealth sale', *Apollo*, 81 (1965), p. 306.

18 HLRO, Main Papers, May 1660, HL/PO/JO/10/1/285, fol. 70.

19 HLRO, Main Papers, May 1660, HL/PO/JO/10/1/285, fol. 83; John Shearman, *The Early Italian Pictures in the Collection of Her Majesty the Queen* (Cambridge, 1983), pp. 187–8, 171–2.

20 RCHM, p. 90; Millar, *The Tudor, Stuart and Early Georgian Pictures in the Collection of Her Majesty the Queen*, pp. 98–9, 104–5.

21 Michael Levey, *The Later Italian Pictures in the Collection of Her Majesty the Queen* (London, 1964), p. 78.

22 Millar, *The Tudor, Stuart and Early Georgian Pictures in the Collection of Her Majesty the Queen*, pp. 105–6.

23 HLRO, Main Papers, May 1660, HL/PO/JO/10/1/285, fol. 75. On Corsellis's commercial activities, see Robert Brenner, *Merchants and Revolution* (Princeton, 1993), pp. 160, 176, 183, 193, 617.

24 HLRO, Main Papers, May 1660, HL/PO/JO/10/1/285, fol. 71.

25 JHL XI, p. 33.

26 HLRO, Main Papers, May 1660, HL/PO/JO/10/1/285, fol. 76.

27 Jeremy Wood, 'Van Dyck and the Earl of Northumberland: taste and collecting in Stuart England', in Susan Barnes and Arthur

Wheelock Jr (eds), *Van Dyck 350: Studies in the History of Art 46* (Washington, 1994).

28 Ibid., pp. 297–8; Oliver Millar (ed.), 'The inventories and valuation of the king's goods, 1649–1651', *Walpole Society*, 43 (1970–72), pp. 298, 303, 315.

29 JHL XI, p. 34.

30 Hilary Maddicott, 'A collection of the interregnum period: Philip, Lord Viscount Lisle, and his purchases from the "late king's goods", 1649–1660', *Journal of the History of Collections*, 11, 1 (1999), p. 1.

31 For speculation on the political interpretation of Lisle's purchases, see ibid., pp. 12–15.

32 'The Declaration of Breda', in Samuel R. Gardiner, *The Constitutional Documents of the Puritan Revolution* (3rd edition, Oxford, 1906), pp. 465–7. See also Hutton, *The Restoration*, pp. 108–9.

33 See Brian Reade, 'William Frizell and the royal collection', *Burlington Magazine*, 89 (1947), pp. 70–75; Gleissner, 'Reassembling a royal art collection for the restored king of Great Britain', pp. 109–14.

34 BL Add. MS 23199, fols 28, 30–31. For a transcription, see Gleissner, 'Reassembling a royal art collection for the restored king of Great Britain', pp. 112–13; Reade, 'William Frizell and the royal collection', pp. 73–4.

35 BL Add. MS 23199, fol. 30.

36 On the history of Christina's collection, see Görel Cavalli-Björkman, 'La collection de la reine Christine à Stockholm', in *1648: Paix de Westphalie – l'art entre la guerre et la paix* (Münster and Paris, 1999), pp. 295–306.

37 Reade, 'William Frizell and the royal collection', p. 74; Shearman, *The Early Italian Pictures in the Collection of Her Majesty the Queen*, pp. 291–2.

FOURTEEN: THE ART OF RESTORATION

1 Quoted in E. S. de Beer (ed.), *The Diary of John Evelyn*, 6 vols (Oxford, 1955), Vol. 3, p. 246.

2 JHL XI, p. 43.

3 HLRO, Main Papers, May 1660, HL/PO/JO/10/1/285, fols 104, 106.

4 JHL XI, p. 44.

5 HLRO, Main Papers, May 1660, HL/PO/JO/10/1/285, fols 109–10.

6 On the composition of the Council, see Ronald Hutton, *The Restoration:*

    A Political and Religious History of England and Wales, 1658–1667 (Oxford, 1985), pp. 126–8.

7 TNA (PRO) SP29/2, fol. 123.

8 HLRO, Main Papers, May 1660, HL/PO/JO/10/1/285, fol. 87.

9 TNA (PRO) SP29/1, fol. 119v; CSPD 1660–61, p. 6; Mary Edmond, 'Limners and picturemakers: new light on the lives of miniaturists and large-scale portrait-painters working in London in the sixteenth and seventeenth centuries', *Walpole Society*, 47 (1978–80), pp. 159–60.

10 Robert Latham and William Matthews (eds), *The Diary of Samuel Pepys*, 11 vols (London, 1970), Vol. 1, pp. 188–9.

11 Hutton, *The Restoration*, pp. 132–4.

12 Anon., *Lucifer's Life-Guard* (London, 1660), p. 32.

13 TNA (PRO) PC2/54, fols 54–5.

14 TNA (PRO) PC2/54, fol. 100.

15 TNA (PRO) PC2/54, fols 100, 106.

16 Sir Geoffrey Palmer, 'A Proclamation for the Restoring and Discovering his Majesties Goods' (London, 1660).

17 HLRO, Main Papers, May 1660, HL/PO/JO/10/1/285, fols 84, 100.

18 See Andrew J. Hopper, 'Savile, Thomas, first earl of Sussex (bap. 1590, d. 1657–9)', *Oxford Dictionary of National Biography* (Oxford, 2004).

19 TNA (PRO) SP29/11, fol. 40v.

20 TNA (PRO) SP29/11, fol. 40v; CSPD 1660–61, pp. 200–201.

21 Quoted in Hilary Maddicott, 'A collection of the interregnum period: Philip, Lord Viscount Lisle, and his purchases from the "late king's goods", 1649–1660', *Journal of the History of Collections*, 11, 1 (1999), p. 18.

22 Ibid., p. 9; Jeremy Wood, 'Van Dyck and the Earl of Northumberland: taste and collecting in Stuart England', in Susan Barnes and Arthur Wheelock Jr (eds), *Van Dyck 350: Studies in the History of Art 46* (Washington, 1994), pp. 297–9.

23 See John Michael Montias, *Art at Auction in Seventeenth-Century Amsterdam* (Amsterdam, 2002).

24 Anne-Marie S. Logan, *The 'Cabinet' of the Brothers Gerard and Jan Reynst* (Amsterdam, 1979), p. 75; Denis Mahon, 'Notes on the "Dutch Gift" to Charles II: parts I, II and III', *Burlington Magazine*, 91 (1949), pp. 303–5, 349–50, and *Burlington Magazine*, 92 (1950), pp. 12–18.

25 Quoted in Logan, *The 'Cabinet' of the Brothers Gerard and Jan Reynst*, p. 81. See CSPD 1659–60, pp. 218–19.

26 Quoted in de Beer (ed.), *The Diary of John Evelyn*, Vol. 3, p. 262.

27 Logan, *The 'Cabinet' of the Brothers Gerard and Jan Reynst*, pp. 117–18, 138–9.

28 John Shearman, *The Early Italian Pictures in the Collection of Her Majesty the Queen* (Cambridge, 1983), pp. 251–3.

29 Latham and Matthews (eds), *The Diary of Samuel Pepys*, Vol. 1, p. 292.

30 Quoted in de Beer (ed.), *The Diary of John Evelyn*, Vol. 3, p. 259.

31 John Miller, *Charles II* (London, 1991), p. 47.

32 Quoted in Stephen Gleissner, 'Reassembling a royal art collection for the restored king of Great Britain', *Journal of the History of Collections*, 6, 1 (1994), p. 108. See also CSPD 1660–61, p. 374.

33 CSPD 1661–62, pp. 25, 59.

34 Gleissner, 'Reassembling a royal art collection for the restored king of Great Britain', p. 108.

35 Ibid., p. 115, n. 34.

36 Quoted ibid., p. 108.

37 TNA (PRO) PC2/55, fols 192–93.

38 TNA (PRO) PC2/54, fols 49–50.

39 See Lorraine Madway, ' "The most conspicuous solemnity": the coronation of Charles I', in Eveline Cruickshanks (ed.), *The Stuart Courts* (Stroud, 2000), pp. 141–57.

40 Oliver Millar, *The Tudor, Stuart and Early Georgian Pictures in the Collection of Her Majesty the Queen* (London, 1963), p. 129.

41 BL Add. MS 17916.

42 William Hawley, 'A Booke conteining severall of his Maties goods brought into his Maties closset and wardrop by Coll. Wm. Hawley, by the order of a Committee of Lords, in April 1660', BL Add. MS 17916, fols 7–113. The exact number of pictures listed is difficult to assess as Hawley often describes the same painting twice or even more.

43 BL Add. MS 17916, fol. 78r.

44 The one debatable exception is *A Boy with a Pipe*, attributed to Titian although also believed to be by Giorgione. Hawley lists 'A shepheard with a pipe' in his inventory (BL Add. MS 17916, fol. 12v) without ascribing it to Titian. On the disputed provenance of the painting, see Shearman, *The Early Italian Pictures in the Collection of Her Majesty the Queen*, pp. 253–6.

45 Quoted in Millar, *The Tudor, Stuart and Early Georgian Pictures in the Collection of Her Majesty the Queen*, p. 93.

46 Iain Pears, *The Discovery of Painting: The Growth of Interest in the Arts in England, 1680–1768* (New Haven, 1988), pp. 52–3. On other

commissions celebrating Charles's restoration, see David Solkin, 'Isaac Fuller's "Escape of Charles II": A Restoration Tragicomedy', *Journal of Warburg and Courtauld Studies*, 62 (1999), pp. 199–240.

47 Quoted in Edmond, 'Limners and picturemakers: new light on the lives of miniaturists and large-scale portrait-painters working in London in the sixteenth and seventeenth centuries', p. 93.

48 See Michael Wenzel, 'The *Windsor Beauties* by Sir Peter Lely and the collection of paintings at St James's Palace, 1674', *Journal of the History of Collections*, 14, 2 (2002), pp. 205–13.

49 See TNA (PRO) SP44/22, fol. 182.

50 On the committee, see TNA (PRO) SP44/7, fol. 134. See C. H. Josten (ed.), *Elias Ashmole (1617–1692): His Autobiographical and Historical Notes, his Correspondence, and Other Contemporary Sources Relating to his Life and Work*, 5 vols (Oxford, 1966), Vol. 1, pp. 144–5, and Vol. 3, pp. 856–7; Lisa Jardine, *Ingenious Pursuits: Building the Scientific Revolution* (London, 1999), pp. 253–62.

51 Hutton, *The Restoration*, pp. 158–60, 184–5, 187–8; Brian Reade, 'William Frizell and the royal collection', *Burlington Magazine*, 89 (1947), p. 73.

52 Quoted in Jonathan Brown, *Kings and Connoisseurs: Collecting Art in Seventeenth-Century Europe* (New Haven, 1995), p. 93.

53 Edward Hyde, Earl of Clarendon, *The History of the Rebellion and Civil Wars in England*, ed. W. Dunn Macray, 6 vols (Oxford, 1888), Vol. 4, p. 499.

54 MS in Surveyor of Queen's Pictures Collection, St James's Palace. I am grateful to Sir Christopher Lloyd for providing me with access to this inventory.

55 Attr. Thomas Chiffinch, 'Charles II's Inventory of pictures at Whitehall and Hampton Court, *c.* 1665–66', Surveyor's Office, St James's Palace, fols 1–26.

56 See Lisa Jardine, *On a Grander Scale: The Outstanding Career of Sir Christopher Wren* (London, 2002), pp. 239–47.

57 'An inventory of all the goods, plate and household stuff belonging to the late Queen the King's Mother, begun to be taken at Colombes the last of October 1669 and finished the first of November 1669' (TNA [PRO] SP78/128, fols 209–25).

58 Michael Levey, *The Later Italian Pictures in the Collection of Her Majesty the Queen* (London, 1964), pp. 13, 82; TNA (PRO) SP78/128, fol. 209r.

59 TNA (PRO) SP78/128, fols 211v, 209v; Shearman, *The Early Italian Pictures in the Collection of Her Majesty the Queen*, p. 247.

60 CSPD 1668–89, p. 503.

61 TNA (PRO) SP78/128, fol. 220r.

62 TNA (PRO) SP78/128, fols 211v, 209r.

63 TNA (PRO) SP78/128, fol. 219v; Millar, *The Tudor, Stuart and Early Georgian Pictures in the Collection of Her Majesty the Queen*, p. 61.

64 Quoted in de Beer (ed.), *The Diary of John Evelyn*, Vol. 3, pp. 216–17.

65 Henry Peacham, *The Compleat Gentleman* (2nd edition, London, 1634), p. 107.

66 Ronald Lightbown, 'Isaac Besnier, sculptor to Charles I, and his work for court patrons *c.* 1624–1634', in David Howarth (ed.), *Art and Patronage in the Caroline Courts* (Cambridge, 1993), pp. 132–67.

67 D. G. Denoon, 'The statue of King Charles I at Charing Cross', *Transactions of the London and Middlesex Archaeological Society*, new series 6 (1933), p. 466; JHC III, p. 690.

68 Denoon, 'The statue of King Charles I at Charing Cross', p. 466.

69 Quoted in R. M. Ball, 'On the statue of King Charles at Charing Cross', *Antiquaries Journal*, 67 (1987), pp. 99–100.

70 JHL XI, p. 29.

71 CSPV 1659–61, p. 137.

72 Nicola Smith, *The Royal Image and the English People* (Aldershot, 2001), pp. 37–64.

73 Quoted in Arthur MacGregor (ed.), *The Late King's Goods: Collections, Possessions and Patronage in the Light of the Commonwealth Sale Inventories* (Oxford, 1989), p. 109.

Epilogue

1 TNA (PRO) SP32/9, fol. 6.

2 Jeremy Wood, 'Gerbier, Sir Balthazar (1592–1663/1667)', *Oxford Dictionary of National Biography* (Oxford, 2004).

3 Denys Sutton, 'London as an art centre II', *Apollo*, 114 (1981), pp. 298–313.

4 Diana Dethloff, 'Lely, Sir Peter (1618–1680)', *Oxford Dictionary of National Biography* (Oxford, 2004).

5 Horace Walpole, *Anecdotes of Painting in England*, 4 vols (London, 1762), Vol. 3, p. 1.

6 Jeremy Wood, 'Taste and connoisseurship at the court of Charles I: Inigo Jones and the work of Giulio Romano', in Eveline Cruickshanks (ed.), *The Stuart Courts* (Stroud, 2000), p. 131.

7 Quoted in Neil de Marchi and Hans J. Van Miegroet, 'Art, value and market practices in the Netherlands in the seventeenth century', *Art Bulletin*, 76 (1994), p. 454.

8 Arjun Appadurai (ed.), *The Social Life of Things: Commodities in Cultural Perspective* (Cambridge, 1986), pp. 3–58.

9 Quoted in Christopher Lloyd, *The Queen's Pictures: Royal Collectors through the Centuries* (London, 1991), pp. 10, 27.

AFTERWORD

1 Quoted in Kevin Sharpe, *The Personal Rule of Charles I* (New Haven, 1992), p. 181.

2 *Guardian*, 30 May 2002, 'The convenient fiction of who owns priceless treasure', https://www.theguardian.com/uk/2002/may/30/jubilee. education.

3 Charlotte Higgins, 'Buried Treasure', *Guardian*, 20 April 2006, accessed at: https://www.theguardian.com/artanddesign/2006/apr/20/art. monarchy. Jonathan Jones, 'Why is the world's best art being detained at Her Majesty's Pleasure?', *Guardian*, 5 August 2006, accessed at: https://www.theguardian.com/artanddesign/jonathanjonesblog/2013/ aug/05/art-royal-collection-leonardo-da-vinci, Brian Sewell, 'The Queen Mum had better taste than this', *Evening Standard*, 17 August 2006, accessed at: http://www.standard.co.uk/arts/the-queen-mum-had-better-taste-than-this-7387962.html.

4 Nigel Reynolds, 'The Queen Finds a Caravaggio in her Storeroom', *Daily Telegraph*, 10 November 2006, accessed at: http://www.telegraph. co.uk/news/uknews/1533759/The-Queen-finds-a-Caravaggio-in-her-storeroom.html.

5 Francis Haskell, *The King's Pictures: The Formation and Dispersal of the Collections of Charles I and his Courtiers* (New Haven, 2013), p. 193.

6 Perhaps the fact that the current Chief Executive wrote a positive review of *The Sale of the Late King's Goods* should allay my fears. See Charles Saumarez Smith, 'Treasure Going Cheap', *Literary Review*, April 2016.

Bibliography

Abbott, W. C. (ed.), *The Writings and Speeches of Oliver Cromwell*, 4 vols. (New Haven, 1937–47)

Adamson, J. S. A., 'Oliver Cromwell and the Long Parliament', in John Morrill (ed.), *Oliver Cromwell and the English Revolution* (Harlow, 1990)

Adler, Wolfgang, *Corpus Rubenianum Ludwig Burchard: I Landscape and Hunting Scenes* (London, 1982)

Akrigg, G. P. V. (ed.), *Letters of King James VI and I* (Berkeley, 1984)

Albion, Gordon, *Charles I and the Court of Rome* (London, 1935)

Almansa y Mendoza, Andrés de, 'A Relation of the Departure of the most Illustrious Prince of Wales, from Madrid the Ninth of September, this present Yeare. 1623', in *A Second Collection of Scarce and Valuable Tracts* (London, 1750), Vol. I, pp. 231–43

Anon., *A Continuation of a Former Relation Concerning the Entertainment given to the Prince . . .* (London, 1623)

——— *A Deep Sigh Breath'd Through the Lodgings at Whitehall, Deploring the Absence of the Court* (London, 1642)

——— *A Remonstrance Manifesting the Lamentable Miseries of the Creditors and Servants of the Late King, Queen, & Prince* (London, 1653)

——— 'An Exit to the Exit Tyrannus . . .' (London, 1660)

——— *Lucifer's Life-Guard* (London, 1660)

——— 'An inventory of all the goods, plate and household stuff belonging to the late Queen the King's Mother, begun to be taken at Colombes the last of October 1669 and finished the first of November 1669', TNA, PRO SP78/128, fols 209–25

——— 'Madame the Queen's Death, and Maner thereof', in *Miscellany of the Abbotsford Club*, Vol. I (Edinburgh, 1837), pp. 77–84

Appadurai, Arjun (ed.), *The Social Life of Things: Commodities in Cultural Perspective* (Cambridge, 1986)

Aristotle, 'The Nicomachean Ethics', in J. Barnes (ed.), *The Complete Works of Aristotle*, Vol. 2 (Princeton, 1984)

Attr. Ashmole, Elias, 'Persons who bought the King & Queenes Goods',
    Bodleian Library, Oxford, MS Rawlinson D. 695 (*c.* 1659)

Ashton, Robert, 'The disbursing official under the early Stuarts: the cases of
    Sir William Russell and Philip Burlamachi', *Bulletin of the Institute of
    Historical Research* 30 (1957), pp. 162–73

Askew, Pamela, 'Ferdinando Gonzaga's patronage of the pictorial arts: the
    Villa Favorita', *Art Bulletin*, 60 (1978), pp. 274–96

Auerbach, E., and Adams, C. K., *Paintings and Sculpture at Hatfield House*
    (London, 1971)

Aylmer, G. E., *The King's Servants: The Civil Service of Charles I, 1625–1642*
    (London, 1961)

Bacon, Francis, 'The Praise of Henry, Prince of Wales', in Joseph Devey
    (ed.), *The Moral and Historical Works of Lord Bacon* (London, 1852),
    pp. 493–5

Ball, R. M., 'On the statue of King Charles at Charing Cross', *Antiquaries
    Journal*, 67 (1987), pp. 97–101

Barbeito, José Manuel, 'Felipe II y la arquitectura', in *Felipe II: Un monarca y
    su época* (Madrid, 1999)

Barber, Peter, 'Gambling in wartime: the rise and fall of William Geere
    (1589/90–1652)', *Camden History Review*, 19 (1995), pp. 17–20

Barnes, Susan J., and Wheelock Jr, Arthur (eds), *Van Dyck 350: Studies in the
    History of Art 46* (Washington, 1994)

Barnes, Susan J., et al. (eds), *Van Dyck: A Complete Catalogue of the Paintings*
    (New Haven, 2004)

Barroll, Leeds, *Anna of Denmark, Queen of England: A Cultural Biography*
    (Philadelphia, 2001)

Barron, Kathryn, 'The collecting and patronage of John, Lord Lumley', in
    Edward Chaney (ed.), *The Evolution of English Collecting: The Reception of
    Italian Art in the Tudor and Stuart Periods* (New Haven, 2003), pp. 125–58

Beal, Mary, *A Study of Richard Symonds* (London, 1984)

Beer, E. S. de (ed.), *The Diary of John Evelyn*, 6 vols (Oxford, 1955)

Bellany, Alastair, *The Politics of Court Scandal in Early Modern England: News
    Culture and the Overbury Affair* (Cambridge, 2002)

Betcherman, Lita-Rose, 'Balthazar Gerbier in seventeenth-century Italy',
    History Today, 11 (1961), pp. 325–31

——— 'The York House collection and its keeper', *Apollo*, 92 (1970),
    pp. 250–59

Birch, Thomas, *The Life of Henry, Prince of Wales* (London, 1760)

Bissell, R. Ward, *Orazio Gentileschi and the Poetic Tradition in Caravaggesque
    Painting* (Pennsylvania, 1981)

———— *Artemisia Gentileschi and the Authority of Art* (Pennsylvania, 1999)

Bracken, Susan, 'The Patronage of Robert Cecil, 1st Earl of Salisbury' (Courtauld MA report, 1993)

———— 'The early Cecils and Italianate taste', in Edward Chaney (ed.), *The Evolution of English Collecting: The Reception of Italian Art in the Tudor and Stuart Periods* (New Haven, 2003), pp. 201–20

Braunmuller, A. R., 'Robert Carr, Earl of Somerset, as collector and patron', in Linda Levy Peck, (ed.), *The Mental World of the Jacobean Court* (Cambridge, 1991), pp. 230–50

Brenner, Robert, *Merchants and Revolution* (Princeton, 1993)

Brookes, Anne, 'Richard Symonds and the Palazzo Farnese, 1649–50', *Journal of the History of Collections*, 10, 2 (1998), pp. 139–57

Brotton, Jerry, 'The art of restoration: King Charles II and the restitution of the English royal art collection', *The Court Historian* (forthcoming)

———— 'Buying the Renaissance: Prince Charles' art purchases in Madrid, 1623', in Alex Samson (ed.), *The Spanish Match: Prince Charles' Journey to Madrid, 1623* (Aldershot, forthcoming, 2006)

Brotton, Jerry, and McGrath, David, 'The Spanish acquisition of King Charles I's paintings: the letters of Alonso de Cárdenas, 1649–51', *Journal of the History of Collections* (forthcoming)

Brown, Beverly Louise (ed.), *The Genius of Rome 1592–1623* (London, 2001)

Brown, Christopher, and Vleighe, Hans (eds), *Van Dyck, 1599–1641* (London, 1999)

Brown, David, et al. (eds), *Lorenzo Lotto: Rediscovered Master of the Renaissance* (Washington, 1997)

Brown, Jonathan, *The Golden Age of Painting in Spain* (New Haven, 1991)

———— *Kings and Connoisseurs: Collecting Art in Seventeenth-Century Europe* (New Haven, 1995)

Brown, Jonathan, and Elliott, J. H. (eds), *The Sale of the Century: Artistic Relations between Spain and Great Britain, 1604–1655* (New Haven, 2002)

Bruyn, J., and Millar, Oliver, 'Notes on the royal collection – III: the "Dutch gift" to Charles I', *Burlington Magazine*, 104 (1962), pp. 291–4

Cammell, Charles Richard, *The Great Duke of Buckingham* (London, 1939)

Capp, Bernard, *Cromwell's Navy: The Fleet and the English Revolution, 1648–1660* (Oxford, 1989)

Carducho, Vicente, *Diálogos de la pintura*, ed. Francisco Calvo Serraller (Madrid, 1979)

Carolus: Charles Quint 1500–1558 (Ghent, 2000)

Carpenter, William Hookham, *Pictorial Notices: Consisting of a Memoir of Sir Anthony Van Dyck* (London, 1844)

Cavalli-Björkman, Görel, 'La collection de la reine Christine à Stockholm', in *1648: Paix de Westphalie – l'art entre la guerre et la paix* (Münster and Paris, 1999)

Chambers, David, and Martineau, Jane (eds), *Splendours of the Gonzaga* (London, 1981)

Chaney, Edward, 'Notes towards a biography of Sir Balthazar Gerbier', in Edward Chaney, *The Evolution of the Grand Tour* (London, 1998), pp. 215–25

Chaney, Edward (ed.), *The Evolution of English Collecting: The Reception of Italian Art in the Tudor and Stuart Periods* (New Haven, 2003)

Chidley, Samuel, *A Remonstrance to the Valiant and Well Deserving Soldier, and to the rest of the Creditors of the Commonwealth* (London, 1653)

Attr. Chiffinch, Thomas, 'Charles II's inventory of pictures at Whitehall and Hampton Court, *c.* 1665–66', Surveyor's Office, St James's Palace, fols 1–26

Clarendon, Edward Hyde, Earl of, *The History of the Rebellion and Civil Wars in England*, ed. W. Dunn Macray, 6 vols (Oxford, 1888)

Cleveland, John, *The Character of a London Diurnall* (Oxford, 1645)

Cogswell, Thomas, *The Blessed Revolution: English Politics and the Coming of War, 1621–24* (Cambridge, 1989)

Cole, Alison, *Art of the Italian Renaissance Courts* (London, 1995)

Collmer, R. G. (ed.), *Lodewijk Huygens: The English Journal* (Leiden, 1982)

Coope, Rosalys, 'The gallery in England: names and meaning', *Architectural History*, 27 (1984), pp. 446–55

—— 'The "long gallery": its origins, development, use and decoration', *Architectural History*, 29 (1986), pp. 43–84

Corns, Thomas (ed.), *The Royal Image: Representations of Charles I* (Cambridge, 1999)

Attr. Cornwallis, Charles, *An Account of the Baptism, Life, Death and Funeral, of the Most Incomparable Prince Frederick Henry, Prince of Wales* (London, 1751)

Cosnac, Le Comte de (Gabriel-Jules), *Les Richesses du Palais Mazarin* (Paris, 1885)

Cottington, Sir Francis, 'The Account Book of Sir Francis Cottington, Madrid, 1623', National Library of Scotland, MS 1879

Coward, Barry, *Cromwell* (London, 1991)

Croft, Pauline, 'Robert Cecil and the early Jacobean court', in Linda Levy Peck (ed.), *The Mental World of the Jacobean Court* (Cambridge, 1991), pp. 134–47

Crouch, John, *A Tragi-Comedy, called New Market Fayre or a Parliament Out-Cry of State-Commodities Set to Sale* (London, 1649)

Cruickshanks, Eveline (ed.), *The Stuart Courts* (Stroud, 2000)

Cust, Lionel, 'The Lumley inventories', *Walpole Society*, 6 (1918), pp. 15–35

Davies, Godfrey, *The Restoration of Charles II, 1658–1660* (Oxford, 1955)

Davies, Randall, 'An inventory of the Duke of Buckingham's pictures, etc at York House in 1635', *Burlington Magazine*, 10 (1906–7), pp. 376–83

Denbigh, Cecilia, Countess of, *Royalist Father and Roundhead Son, being the Memoirs of the First and Second Earls of Denbigh 1600–1675* (London, 1915)

Denoon, D. G., 'The statue of King Charles I at Charing Cross', *Transactions of the London and Middlesex Archaeological Society*, new series 6 (1933), pp. 460–86

Digby, John, Earl of Bristol, *A True Relation and Journal, or the Manner of the Arrival . . .* (London, 1623)

Drury, G. Thorn (ed.), *The Poems of Edward Waller* (London, 1893)

Durston, Christopher, and Eales, Jacqueline (eds), *The Culture of English Puritanism, 1560–1700* (Basingstoke, 1996)

Eales, Jacqueline, *Puritans and Roundheads: The Harleys of Brampton Bryant and the Outbreak of the English Civil War* (Cambridge, 1990)

Edmond, Mary, 'Limners and picturemakers: new light on the lives of miniaturists and large-scale portrait-painters working in London in the sixteenth and seventeenth centuries', *Walpole Society*, 47 (1978–80), pp. 60–242

Elliott, J. H., *The Count-Duke of Olivares: The Statesman in an Age of Decline* (London, 1986)

Englefield, W. A. D., *The History of the Painter-Stainers Company of London* (Dublin, 1924)

Felipe II: Un monarca y su época (Madrid, 1999)

Filipczak, Zirka Zaremba, *Picturing Art in Antwerp, 1550–1700* (Princeton, 1987)

Finaldi, Gabriele (ed.), *Orazio Gentileschi at the Court of Charles I* (London, 1999)

Firth, C. H., and Rait, R. S. (eds), *Acts and Ordinances of the Interregnum*, 3 vols (London, 1911)

Foister, Susan, 'Foreigners at court: Holbein, Van Dyck and the Painter-Stainers', in David Howarth (ed.), *Art and Patronage in the Caroline Courts* (Cambridge, 1993), pp. 32–50

Gardiner, Samuel R., *History of England 1603–1642*, 10 vols (London, 1883–4)

——— *History of the Great Civil War*, 4 vols (London, 1901)

——— *History of the Commonwealth and Protectorate*, 4 vols (London, 1903)

———— *The Constitutional Documents of the Puritan Revolution* (3rd edition, Oxford, 1906)

Gelder, J. G. Van, 'Notes on the Royal Collection IV – the "Dutch gift" of 1610 to Henry, Prince of "Whalis", and some other presents', *Burlington Magazine*, 105 (1963), pp. 541–4

Gent, J. B., *A Faire in Spittle Fields where all the Knick Knacks of Astrology are Exposed to Open Sale* (London, 1652)

Gent, Lucy, *Picture and Poetry 1560–1620* (Leamington, 1981)

Gentles, Ian, 'London Levellers in the English revolution: the Chidleys and their circle', *Journal of Ecclesiastical History*, 29 (1978), pp. 281–309

Gerbier, Balthazar, *The Interpreter of the Academie* (London, 1649)

———— *Subsidium Peregrinantibus* (Oxford, 1665)

Attr. Balthazar Gerbier, *The None-Such Charles his Character* (London, 1651)

Gibson, John, *Commonplace Book*, BL Add. MS 37719, *c.* 1656

Gleissner, Stephen, 'Reassembling a royal art collection for the restored king of Great Britain', *Journal of the History of Collections*, 6, 1 (1994), pp. 103–15

Goldberg, Edward L., 'Artistic relations between the Medici and the Spanish courts, 1587–1621: part I', *Burlington Magazine*, 134 (1996), pp. 105–14

———— 'Artistic relations between the Medici and the Spanish courts, 1587–1621: part II', *Burlington Magazine*, 138 (1996), pp. 529–40

Goldthwaite, Richard, *Wealth and the Demand for Art in Italy, 1300–1600* (Baltimore, 1993)

Goodman, Dr Godfrey, *The Court of King James the First*, ed. John Brewer, 2 vols (London, 1839)

Graeme, B., *The Story of St James's Palace* (London, 1929)

Gregg, Pauline, *King Charles I* (London, 1981)

Griffiths, Anthony, *The Print in Stuart Britain 1603–1689* (London, 1988)

Gutfleisch, Barbara, and Menzhausen, Joachim, ' "How a kunstkammer should be formed": Gabriel Kaltemarckt's advice to Christian I of Saxony on the formation of an art collection', *Journal of the History of Collections*, 1, 1 (1989), pp. 3–32

Harris, Enriqueta, 'Velazquez and Charles I: antique busts and modern paintings from Spain for the royal collection', *Journal of the Warburg and Courtauld Insitutes*, 30 (1967), pp. 414–20

Harris, John, and Higgott, Gordon, *Inigo Jones: Complete Architectural Drawings* (London, 1989), pp. 52–7

Haskell, Francis, *Patrons and Painters: Art and Society in Baroque Italy* (2nd edition, London, 1980)

—— 'Charles I's collection of pictures', in Arthur MacGregor (ed.), *The Late King's Goods: Collections, Possessions and Patronage in the Light of the Commonwealth Sale Inventories* (Oxford, 1989)

Havran, Martin, *Catholics in Caroline England* (London, 1962)

Hawley, William, 'A Booke conteining severall of his Maties goods brought into his Maties closset and wardrop by Coll. Wm. Hawley, by the order of a Committee of Lords, in April 1660', BL Add. MS 17916

Hearn, Karen (ed.), *Dynasties* (London, 1995)

Hervey, Mary, *The Life, Correspondence and Collections of Thomas Howard, Earl of Arundel* (Cambridge, 1921)

Heylyn, Peter, *Cyprianus Anglicus* (London, 1671)

Hill, Robert, 'The ambassador as art agent: Sir Dudley Carleton and Jacobean collecting', in Edward Chaney (ed.), *The Evolution of English Collecting: The Reception of Italian Art in the Tudor and Stuart Periods* (New Haven, 2003), pp. 241–55

Historical Manuscripts Commission 9: *Calendar of the Manuscripts of the Most Honourable The Marquess of Salisbury*, Vol. 21 (London, 1970)

Houghton, Walter, 'The English virtuoso in the seventeenth century', *Journal of the History of Ideas*, 3 (1942), pp. 51–73

Howarth, David, *Lord Arundel and his Circle* (London, 1985)

—— *Images of Rule: Art and Politics in the English Renaissance, 1485–1649* (London, 1997)

—— '"Mantua peeces": Charles I and the Gonzaga collections', in David Chambers and Jane Martineau (eds), *Splendours of the Gonzaga* (London, 1981), pp. 95–100

—— 'The Entry Books of Sir Balthazar Gerbier: Van Dyck, Charles I and the Cardinal-Infante Ferdinand', in Hans Vlieghe (ed.), *Van Dyck 1599–1999: Conjectures and Refutations* (Turnhout, 2001), pp. 77–97

—— 'Rubens's "owne pourtrait" ', *Apollo*, 132 (1990), pp. 238–41

—— 'William Trumbull and art collecting in Jacobean England', *British Library Journal*, 20 (1994), pp. 140–62

Howell, James, *Epistolae Ho-Elianae: Familiar Letters Domestic and Foreign* (London, 1645)

Hutchinson, Lucy, *Memoirs of the Life of Colonel Hutchinson* (London, 1904)

Hutton, Ronald, *The Restoration: A Political and Religious History of England and Wales, 1658–1667* (Oxford, 1985)

Impey, Oliver, and MacGregor, Arthur (eds), *The Origins of Museums: The Cabinet of Curiosities in Sixteenth- and Seventeenth-Century Europe* (Oxford, 1985)

Jardine, Lisa, *Ingenious Pursuits: Building the Scientific Revolution* (London, 1999)

—— *On a Grander Scale: The Outstanding Career of Sir Christopher Wren* (London, 2002)

Jardine, Lisa, and Brotton, Jerry, *Global Interests: Renaissance Art between East and West* (London, 2000)

Jayne, Sears, and Johnson, Francis (eds), *The Lumley Library: The Catalogue of 1609* (London, 1956)

Josten, C. H. (ed.), *Elias Ashmole (1617–1692): His Autobiographical and Historical Notes, his Correspondence, and Other Contemporary Sources Relating to his Life and Work*, 5 vols (Oxford, 1966)

Judges, A. V., 'Philip Burlamachi: a financier of the Thirty Years War', *Economica*, 6, (1926), pp. 285–300

Justi, Carl, 'Die Spanische Brautfahrt Carl Stewarts', in *Miscellaneen aus drei Jahrhunderten Spanischen Kunstlebens*, 2 vols (Berlin, 1908)

Kelsey, Sean, *Inventing a Republic: The Political Culture of the English Commonwealth, 1649–1653* (Stanford, 1997)

Knachel, Philip, *England and the Fronde* (Ithaca, 1967)

Knoppers, Laura Lunger, *Constructing Cromwell: Ceremony, Portrait, and Print, 1645–1661* (Cambridge, 2000)

Larkin, James, *Stuart Royal Proclamations Vol. II: Royal Proclamations of King Charles I 1625–1646* (Oxford, 1983)

Latham, Robert, and Matthews, William (eds), *The Diary of Samuel Pepys*, 11 vols (London, 1970)

Layard, G. S., *The Headless Horseman* (London, 1922)

Lee, Maurice, *The Road to Revolution: Scotland under Charles I, 1625–37* (Chicago, 1985)

Lee, Maurice (ed.), *Dudley Carleton to John Chamberlain, 1603–1624: Jacobean Letters* (New Brunswick, NJ, 1971)

L'Estrange, Hamon, *The Reign of King Charles. An History* (London, 1656)

Léonardon, H., 'Une dépêche diplomatique relative à des tableaux acquis en Angleterre pour Philippe IV', *Bulletin Hispanique*, 2 (1900), pp. 25–34

Levey, Michael, *The Later Italian Pictures in the Collection of Her Majesty the Queen* (London, 1964)

Lightbown, Ronald, 'Bernini's busts of English patrons', in Moshe Barasche and Lucy Freeman Sandler (eds) *Art, the Ape of Nature* (New York, 1981), pp. 439–76

—— 'Charles I and the tradition of princely collecting', in Arthur MacGregor (ed.), *The Late King's Goods: Collections, Possessions and Patronage in the Light of the Commonwealth Sale Inventories* (Oxford, 1989), pp. 53–72

—— 'Isaac Besnier, sculptor to Charles I, and his work for court patrons *c.* 1624–1634', in David Howarth (ed.), *Art and Patronage in the Caroline Courts* (Cambridge, 1993), pp. 132–67

—— 'The journey of the Bernini bust of Charles I to England', *Connoisseur*, 169 (1968), pp. 217–20

Lindley, David, *The Trials of Frances Howard* (London, 1993)

Lister, Susan Maddocks, '"Trumperies brought from Rome": Barberini gifts to the Stuart court in 1635', in Elizabeth Cropper (ed.), *The Diplomacy of Art: Artistic Creation and Politics in Seicento Italy* (Milan, 2000), pp. 151–75

Lloyd, Christopher, *The Queen's Pictures: Royal Collectors through the Centuries* (London, 1991)

Lockyer, Roger, *Buckingham: The Life and Political Career of George Villiers, First Duke of Buckingham* (London, 1981)

Logan, Anne-Marie S., *The 'Cabinet' of the Brothers Gerard and Jan Reynst* (Amsterdam, 1979)

Loomie, Albert J., 'Alonso de Cárdenas and the Long Parliament', *English Historical Review*, 97 (1982), pp. 289–307

—— 'New light on the Spanish ambassador's purchases from Charles I's collection 1649–53', *Journal of the Warburg and Courtauld Institutes*, 52 (1989), pp. 257–67

—— 'The destruction of Rubens's "Crucifixion" in the Queen's chapel, Somerset House', *Burlington Magazine*, 140 (1998), pp. 680–82

Loomie, Albert J. (ed.), *Ceremonies of Charles I: The Notebooks of John Finet* (New York, 1987)

Loxley, James, *Royalism and Poetry in the English Civil Wars* (London, 1997)

Luzio, A., *La Galleria dei Gonzaga Venduta all'Inghilterra nel 1627–28* (Milan, 1913)

McClure, N. E. (ed.), *The Letters of John Chamberlain*, 2 vols (Philadelphia, 1939)

McEvansoneya, Philip, 'Vertue, Walpole and the documentation of the Buckingham collection', *Journal of the History of Collections*, 8, 1 (1996), pp. 1–14

—— 'The sequestration and dispersal of the Buckingham collection', *Journal of the History of Collections*, 8, 2 (1996), pp. 133–54

MacGregor, Arthur (ed.), *The Late King's Goods: Collections, Possessions and Patronage in the Light of the Commonwealth Sale Inventories* (Oxford, 1989)

Maddicott, Hilary, 'A collection of the interregnum period: Philip, Lord Viscount Lisle, and his purchases from the "late king's goods", 1649–1660', *Journal of the History of Collections*, 11, 1 (1999), pp. 1–24

Madway, Lorraine, ' "The most conspicuous solemnity": the coronation of Charles I', in Eveline Cruickshanks (ed.), *The Stuart Courts* (Stroud, 2000), pp. 141–57

Magurn, Ruth (ed.), *The Letters of Peter Paul Rubens* (Cambridge, Mass., 1971)

Mahon, Denis, 'Notes on the "Dutch Gift" to Charles II: parts I, II and III', *Burlington Magazine*, 91 (1949), pp. 303–5, 349–50, and *Burlington Magazine*, 92 (1950), pp. 12–18

Marchi, Neil de, and Miegroet, Hans J. Van, 'Art, value and market practices in the Netherlands in the seventeenth century', *Art Bulletin*, 76 (1994), pp. 451–64

Martin, Gregory, 'The Banqueting House ceiling: two newly discovered projects', *Apollo*, 139 (1994), pp. 29–34

Martindale, Andrew, *The Triumphs of Caesar by Andrea Mantegna in the Collection of Her Majesty the Queen at Hampton Court* (London, 1979)

Millar, Oliver, *Rubens: The Whitehall Ceiling* (London, 1958)

——— *The Tudor, Stuart and Early Georgian Pictures in the Collection of Her Majesty the Queen* (London, 1963)

——— *The Age of Charles I* (London, 1972)

——— 'Strafford and Van Dyck', in Richard Ollard and Pamela Tudor-Craig (eds), *For Veronica Wedgwood These* (London, 1986), pp. 109–23

Millar, Oliver (ed.), 'Abraham van der Doort's catalogue of the collections of King Charles I', *Walpole Society*, 37 (1958–60), pp. 1–243

——— 'The inventories and valuation of the king's goods, 1649–1651', *Walpole Society*, 43 (1970–72)

Miller, John, *Charles II* (London, 1991)

Montagu, Richard, *A Gag for the New Gospel? No, a New Gag for an Old Goose* (London, 1624)

Montias, John Michael, *Art at Auction in Seventeenth-Century Amsterdam* (Amsterdam, 2002)

Morill, John, *The Nature of the English Revolution: Essays* (London, 1993)

Morrill, John (ed.), *Oliver Cromwell and the English Revolution* (London, 1990)

Muensterberger, Werner, *Collecting: An Unruly Passion* (Princeton, 1994)

Muller, Jeffrey, *Rubens: The Artist as Collector* (Princeton, 1989)

Needham, Raymond, and Webster, Alexander, *Somerset House: Past and Present* (London, 1905)

Nuttall, W. L. F., 'King Charles I's pictures and the commonwealth sale', *Apollo*, 81 (1965), pp. 302–9

Pace, Clair, 'Virtuoso to connoisseur: some seventeenth-century English responses to the visual arts', *The Seventeenth Century*, 2 (1987), pp. 166–88

Page, Nick, *Lord Minimus: The Extraordinary Life of Britain's Smallest Man* (New York, 2002)

Palme, Per, *Triumph of Peace: A Study of the Whitehall Banqueting House* (London, 1957)

Palmer, Sir Geoffrey, *A Proclamation for the Restoring and Discovering his Majesties Goods* (London, 1660)

Parrott, David, 'The Mantuan succession, 1627–31: a sovereignty dispute in early modern Europe', *English Historical Review*, 112 (1997), pp. 20–65

Parry, Graham, *The Golden Age Restor'd: The Culture of the Stuart Court, 1603–42* (Manchester, 1981), p. 36

Patterson, W. B., *King James VI and I and the Reunion of Christendom* (Cambridge, 1997)

Payne, M. T. W., 'An inventory of Queen Anne of Denmark's "ornaments, furniture, householde stuffe, and other parcels" at Denmark House', *Journal of the History of Collections*, 13, 1 (2001), pp. 23–44

Peacham, Henry, *The Compleat Gentleman* (2nd edition, London, 1634)
―――― *The Gentleman's Exercise* (London, 1634)

Peacock, John, 'The politics of portraiture', in Kevin Sharpe and Peter Lake (eds), *Culture and Politics in Early Stuart England* (London, 1994), pp. 199–228
―――― 'The visual image of Charles I', in Thomas Corns (ed.), *The Royal Image: Representations of Charles I* (Cambridge, 1999), pp. 176–239

Pearl, Valerie, *London and the Outbreak of the Puritan Revolution* (London, 1961)

Pears, Iain, *The Discovery of Painting: The Growth of Interest in the Arts in England, 1680–1768* (New Haven, 1988)

Peck, Linda Levy, *Northampton: Patronage and Policy at the Court of James I* (London, 1982)

Peck, Linda Levy (ed.), *The Mental World of the Jacobean Court* (Cambridge, 1991)

Perrinchief, Henry, *The Royal Martyr* (London, 1676)

Petrie, Charles (ed.), *The Letters, Speeches and Proclamations of King Charles I* (London, 1935)

Peyton, Sir Edward, *The Divine Catastrophe of the Kingly Family of the House of Stuarts* (London, 1652)

Philips, Claude, *The Picture Gallery of Charles I* (London, 1896)

Pincus, Steven, *Protestantism and Patriotism: Ideologies and the Making of English Foreign Policy* (Cambridge, 1996)

Plowden, Alison, *Henrietta Maria* (Stroud, 2001)

Pomian, Krzysztof, *Collectors and Curiosities: Paris and Venice, 1500–1800* (Oxford, 1990)

Porter, Stephen (ed.), *London and the Civil War* (London, 1996)

Portier, François, 'Prices paid for Italian pictures in the Stuart age', *Journal of the History of Collections*, 8, 1 (1996), pp. 55–69

Prynne, William, *Histrio-mastix, The Player's Scourge or Actor's Tragedie* (London, 1633)

Raatschen, Gudrun, 'Van Dyck's "Charles I on horseback with M. de St Antoine"', in Hans Vlieghe (ed.), *Van Dyck 1599–1999: Conjectures and Refutations* (Turnhout, 2001), pp. 139–50

———— 'Bernini's busts of Charles I', *Burlington Magazine*, 138 (1996), pp. 813–16

Reade, Brian, 'William Frizell and the royal collection', *Burlington Magazine*, 89 (1947), pp. 70–75

Redworth, Glyn, The *Prince and the Infanta: The Cultural Politics of the Spanish Match* (New Haven, 2003)

———— 'Of pimps and princes: three unpublished letters from James I and the Prince of Wales relating to the Spanish Match', *Historical Journal*, 37, 2 (1994), pp. 401–9

Redworth, Glyn, and Checa, Fernando, 'The Courts of the Spanish Habsburgs 1500–1700', in John Adamson (ed.), *The Princely Courts of Europe* (London, 1999), pp. 43–65

Roots, Ivan (ed.), *Speeches of Oliver Cromwell* (London, 1989)

Russell, Conrad, *The Crisis of Parliaments* (Oxford, 1971)

———— *The Fall of the British Monarchies 1637–1642* (Oxford, 1991)

Sainsbury, W. N., 'Artist's quarrels', *Notes and Queries*, 8 (13 August 1859), pp. 121–2

Sainsbury, W. N. (ed.), *Original Unpublished Papers Illustrative of the Life of Sir Peter Paul Rubens* (London, 1859)

Sanderson, William, *Graphice: The Use of the Pen and Pencil* (London, 1658)

Schroth, Sarah Walker, 'Charles I, the duque de Lerma and Veronese's Edinburgh *Mars and Venus*', *Burlington Magazine*, 139 (1997), pp. 548–50

Scott, Jonathan, *The Pleasures of Antiquity: British Collectors of Greece and Rome* (New Haven, 2003)

Scott-Elliott, A. H., 'The statues from Mantua in the collection of King Charles I', *Burlington Magazine*, 101 (1959), pp. 218–27

Shakeshaft, Paul, '"To much bewitched with those intysing things": the letters of James, third Marquis of Hamilton, and Basil, Viscount Feilding, concerning collecting in Venice 1635–1639', *Burlington Magazine*, 128 (1986), pp. 114–32

Sharpe, Kevin, *The Personal Rule of Charles I* (New Haven, 1992)
———— ' "An image doting rabble": the failure of republican culture in seventeenth-century England', in *Remapping Early Modern England: The Culture of Seventeenth-Century Politics* (Cambridge, 2000), pp. 223–65
Shearman, John, *Raphael's Cartoons in the Collection of Her Majesty the Queen* (London, 1972)
———— *The Early Italian Pictures in the Collection of Her Majesty the Queen* (Cambridge, 1983)
Sherwood, Roy, *The Court of Oliver Cromwell* (London, 1977)
Shirley, E. P., 'An inventory of the effects of Henry Howard, K.G., Earl of Northampton, taken on his death in 1614, together with a transcript of his will', *Archaeologia*, 42 (1869), pp. 347–78
Smith, A. J. (ed.), *John Donne: The Complete English Poems* (London, 1971)
Smith, David L., *The Stuart Parliaments, 1603–1689* (London, 1999)
Smith, Logan Pearsall (ed.), *The Life and Letters of Sir Henry Wotton*, 2 vols (Oxford, 1907)
Smith, Nicola, *The Royal Image and the English People* (Aldershot, 2001)
Smuts, R. Malcolm, *Court Culture and the Origins of the Royalist Tradition in Early Stuart England* (Philadelphia, 1987)
———— 'Art and the material culture of majesty', in R. Malcolm Smuts (ed.), *The Stuart Court and Europe* (Cambridge, 1996), pp. 86–112
Solkin, David, 'Isaac Fuller's "Escape of Charles II": A Restoration Tragicomedy', *Journal of Warburg and Courtauld Studies*, 62 (1999), pp. 199–240
Spittlehouse, J., *A Warning Piece Discharged* (London, 1653)
Spraggon, Julie, *Puritan Iconoclasm during the English Civil War* (Woodbridge, 2003)
Springell, Francis, *Connoisseur and Diplomat: The Earl of Arundel's Embassy to Germany in 1636* (London, 1963)
Stevenson, David, *The Scottish Revolution 1637–44* (Newton Abbot, 1973)
Stewart, Alan, *The Cradle King: A Life of James VI and I* (London, 2003)
Strong, Roy, *The English Renaissance Miniature* (London, 1983)
———— *Art and Power: Renaissance Festivals 1450–1650* (Woodbridge, 1984)
———— *Henry Prince of Wales and England's Lost Renaissance* (London, 1986)
———— *The Tudor and Stuart Monarchy: Pageantry, Painting and Iconography*, Vol. II, *Elizabethan* (Boydell, 1995)
———— 'England and Italy: the marriage of Henry Prince of Wales', in Richard Ollard and Pamela Tudor-Craig (eds), *For Veronica Wedgwood These* (London, 1986), pp. 59–87
———— 'Britannia Triumphans: Inigo Jones, Rubens and the Whitehall

Banqueting House', in Roy Strong, *The Tudor and Stuart Monarchy: Pageantry, Painting and Iconography*, Vol. III, *Jacobean and Caroline* (Woodbridge, 1998), pp. 127–58

Sutton, Denys, 'London as an art centre II', *Apollo*, 114 (1981), pp. 298–313

Taylor, Francis Henry, *The Taste of Angels: A History of Art Collecting from Rameses to Napoleon* (Boston, 1948)

Thomson, W. G., *A History of Tapestry* (London, 1906)

Thurley, Simon, *Whitehall Palace: An Architectural History of the Royal Apartments, 1240–1690* (New Haven, 1999)

Trapier, Elizabeth du Gue, 'Sir Arthur Hopton and the interchange of paintings between Spain and England in the seventeenth century: part 1', *Connoisseur*, 164 (1967), pp. 239–43

The True Picture and Relation of Prince Henry, by W.H. (Leiden, 1634)

Underdown, David, *Pride's Purge: Politics in the Puritan Revolution* (Oxford, 1971)

Veevers, Erica, *Images of Love and Religion: Queen Henrietta Maria and Court Entertainments* (Cambridge, 1989)

Vergara, W. Alexander, 'The Count of Fuensaldaña and David Teniers: their purchases in London after the civil war', *Burlington Magazine*, 131 (1989), pp. 127–32

Vlieghe, Hans (ed.), *Van Dyck 1599–1999: Conjectures and Refutations* (Turnhout, 2001)

Vodret, Rossella, and Strinati, Claudio, 'Painted music: "A new and affecting manner"', in Beverly Louise Brown (ed.), *The Genius of Rome 1592–1623* (London, 2001), pp. 90–115

Walpole, Horace, *Anecdotes of Painting in England*, 4 vols (London, 1762)

Waterhouse, Ellis, *Painting in Britain 1530–1700* (New Haven, 1953; 5th edition, 1994)

Watson, Katharine, and Avery, Charles, 'Medici and Stuart: a grand ducal gift of "Giovanni Bologna" bronzes for Henry Prince of Wales (1612)', *Burlington Magazine*, 115 (1973), pp. 493–507

Webster, John, *A Monumental Column erected to the living memory of the ever-glorious Henry, late Prince of Wales* (London, 1613)

Weinstein, Rosemary, 'London at the outbreak of the civil war', in Stephen Porter (ed.), *London and the Civil War* (London, 1996), pp. 31–44

Wenzel, Michael, 'The *Windsor Beauties* by Sir Peter Lely and the collection of paintings at St. James's Palace, 1674', *Journal of the History of Collections*, 14, 2 (2002), pp. 205–13

Werstine, Paul, 'New Market Fayre', *Analytical and Enumerative Bibliography*, 6, 2 (1982), pp. 71–101

Wethey, Harold, *The Paintings of Titian*, 3 vols (London, 1975)

Whalley, J. Irene, 'Italian art and English taste: an early seventeenth-century letter', *Apollo*, 94 (1971), pp. 184–91

Wheelock, Arthur, 'The queen, the dwarf and the court: Van Dyck and the ideals of the English monarchy', in Hans Vlieghe (ed.), *Van Dyck 1599–1999: Conjectures and Refutations* (Turnhout, 2001), pp. 151–66

Whitaker, Lucy, 'L'accoglienza della collezione Gonzaga in Inghilterra', in Raffaella Morselli (ed.), *Gonzaga: La Celeste Galeria* (Milan, 2002), pp. 233–49

White, Christopher, *The Dutch Pictures in the Collection of Her Majesty the Queen* (Cambridge, 1982)

——— *Peter Paul Rubens* (New Haven, 1987)

Wilks, Timothy, 'The Court Culture of Henry, Prince of Wales, 1603–1613', D.Phil. thesis (Oxford, 1987)

——— 'The picture collection of Robert Carr, Earl of Somerset (*c.* 1587–1645), reconsidered', *Journal of the History of Collections*, 1, 2 (1989), pp. 167–77

——— 'Art collecting at the English Court from the death of Henry, Prince of Wales to the death of Anne of Denmark', *Journal of the History of Collections*, 9, 1 (1997), pp. 31–48

Williams, Richard, 'Collecting and religion in late sixteenth-century England', in Edward Chaney (ed.), *The Evolution of English Collecting: The Reception of Italian Art in the Tudor and Stuart Periods* (New Haven, 2003), pp. 159–200

Wilson, Arthur, *The History of Great Britain, Being the Life and Reign of King James the First* (London, 1653)

Wilson, Charles, *Profit and Power: A Study of England and the Dutch Wars* (London, 1957)

Wilson, Michael, *Nicholas Lanier: Master of the King's Musick* (Aldershot, 1994)

Winwood, Ralph, *Memorials of Affairs of State in the Reign of Queen Elizabeth and King James I* (London, 1725)

Wittkower, R., 'Inigo Jones – "Puritanissimo Fiero"', *Burlington Magazine*, 90 (1948), pp. 50–51.

Wood, Jeremy, 'Van Dyck and the Earl of Northumberland: taste and collecting in Stuart England', in Susan Barnes and Arthur Wheelock Jr (eds), *Van Dyck 350: Studies in the History of Art 46* (Washington, 1994), pp. 281–324

——— 'Taste and connoisseurship at the court of Charles I: Inigo Jones and the work Giulio Romano', in Eveline Cruickshanks (ed.), *The Stuart Courts* (Stroud, 2000), pp. 118–40

————— 'Van Dyck: a Catholic artist in Protestant England, and the notes on painting compiled by Francis Russell, 4th Earl of Bedford', in Hans Vlieghe (ed.), *Van Dyck 1599–1999: Conjectures and Refutations* (Turnhout, 2001), pp. 167–98

————— 'Van Dyck's "Cabinet de Titien": the contents and dispersal of his collection', *Burlington Magazine*, 132 (1990), pp. 680–96

————— 'Orazio Gentileschi and some Netherlandish artists in London: the patronage of the Duke of Buckingham, Charles I and Henrietta Maria', *Simiolus*, 28, 3 (2000–2001), pp. 103–28

Woolrych, Austin, *Britain in Revolution 1625–1660* (Oxford, 2002)

Worden, Blair, *The Rump Parliament 1648–1653* (Cambridge, 1974)

Index

extracts reading groups
competitions books new
discounts extracts extracts
competitions extracts discounts events
books new events reading groups
events books extracts discounts
extracts new reading groups
interviews events
events extracts discounts new books
discounts new books events
events new
discounts extracts discounts
www.panmacmillan.com
extracts events reading groups
competitions books extracts new